Innovation and Development of Knowledge Societies

This book examines the role that intellectual property plays in fostering innovation within knowledge societies, with a particular focus on the role of emerging technologies such as Artificial Intelligence tools.

Creativity and the generation of new knowledge across the broad spectrum of intellectual property are essential sources of growth for knowledge societies. This includes the major areas of copyright, inventions and patents, trademarks and geographical indications. This book acknowledges the societal and cultural character of knowledge societies, discussing how Intellectual Property (IP) Law plays a pivotal role in safeguarding innovation, thereby fostering evolution. As emerging technologies and artificial intelligence redefine the landscape, the book identifies both new challenges and opportunities in enhancing innovation prowess and nurturing knowledge societies. Suggesting regulations which prioritise copyright, trademarks and patents as fundamental instruments in international commerce, the book presents a framework for IP Law through which knowledge societies can thrive.

The book will appeal to researchers in the field of Intellectual Property Law, international law, business law and emerging technologies such as AI.

Nadia Naim is an Associate Dean International Law and Social Sciences, and is a Senior Lecturer in Law at Aston University. She is a qualified Barrister and Fellow of the HEA. She has published many scholarly articles in the areas of international intellectual property law, intangible asset financing and development, comparative law, and international law. She has authored books on contemporary intellectual property innovation and specialises in emerging areas of international development.

Alhanoof AlDebasi is Executive Director of Copyrights and Designs at the Saudi Authority for Intellectual Property (SAIP), and is a leading expert in Intellectual Property (IP) in Saudi Arabia. With degrees from the University of Pittsburgh and American University College of Law in the U.S., she has made significant contributions to IP law and policy. Her experience spans academia, government, and international collaborations, fostering innovation and protecting creative works.

David Price is Emeritus Professor International Law at Charles Darwin University, Australia. He holds degrees in law as well as international relations, industrial history, and Chinese. His primary research work has encompassed the strategic dynamics of the intersection of public international law, intellectual property law, and international trade agreements focussing on the Middle East. He has also researched and published Investor-State Dispute Settlement (ISDS) claims involving the GCC member states, Indonesia and Australia. Professor Price has held visiting professorships at universities in Indonesia and China and is on the journal editorial boards of institutions in Indonesia, Oman and Australia.

Routledge Research in Intellectual Property

Available:

Towards an Ecological Intellectual Property
Reconfiguring Relationships Between People and Plants in Ecuador
David Jefferson

The Transformation of EU Geographical Indications Law
the Present, Past and Future of the Origin Link
Andrea Zappalaglio

Copyright Law and Translation
Access to Knowledge in Developing Economies
Chamila S. Talagala

Patent Law, Green Technology and Innovation
Ankit Singh and Yogendra Kumar Srivastava

Intellectual Property and Development
Geographical Indications in Practice
Barbara Pick

Collective Management of Music Copyright
A Comparative Analysis of China, the United States and Australia
Qinqing Xu

Intellectual Property Rights and Competition Law in India
Edited by Rajni Malhotra Dhingra and Nisha Dhanraj Dewani

Digitization, Copyright and the Law
Copyleft and the Future of Intellectual Property
Ettore M. Lombardi

Intellectual Property and Emerging Technologies
Generated Global IP Issues and Challenges
Tshimanga Kongolo

Innovation and Development of Knowledge Societies
Artificial Intelligence and Knowledge-Based Socioeconomic Growth
Nadia Naim, Alhanoof AlDebasi and David Price

For more information about this series, please visit https://www.routledge.com/Routledge-Research-in-Intellectual-Property/book-series/INTELLPROP

Innovation and Development of Knowledge Societies

Artificial Intelligence and Knowledge-Based Socioeconomic Growth

Edited by Nadia Naim, Alhanoof AlDebasi and David Price

Routledge
Taylor & Francis Group
LONDON AND NEW YORK

First published 2025
by Routledge
4 Park Square, Milton Park, Abingdon, Oxon OX14 4RN

and by Routledge
605 Third Avenue, New York, NY 10158

Routledge is an imprint of the Taylor & Francis Group, an informa business

Papers presented at the thirteenth Gulf Research Meeting (GRM), Cambridge, July 11-13, 2023, organised by the Gulf Research Centre Cambridge.

British Library Cataloguing-in-Publication Data
A catalogue record for this book is available from the British Library

ISBN: 978-1-032-85925-5 (hbk)
ISBN: 978-1-032-86659-8 (pbk)
ISBN: 978-1-003-52851-7 (ebk)

DOI: 10.4324/9781003528517

Typeset in Times New Roman
by Deanta Global Publishing Services, Chennai, India

Contents

List of Contributors

Alhanoof AlDebasi
Saudi Authority for Intellectual Property

Noura Almutairi
Kuwait University, Kuwait

Rawan Alshammari
Information Technology & Services NEOM, Saudi Arabia

Sarah Alsudairy
King Saud University, Saudi Arabia

Mark Brady
Charles Darwin University, Australia

Amelia Hallam
Charles Darwin University, Australia

Nadia Naim
Aston University

Stefan Papastefanou
Bucerius Law School, Germany and White and Case LLP

David Price
Charles Darwin University

Jia Wang
Durham University, UK

Foreword

The Gulf Cooperation Council (GCC) nations stand at a crossroads, both confronted with unprecedented challenges and presented with extraordinary opportunities. The rapid acceleration of technological advancement, particularly in the realm of Artificial Intelligence (AI), is reshaping economies, societies, and the very fabric of our world. As the GCC strives to diversify its economies, foster innovation, and enhance the quality of life for its citizens, AI emerges as a critical catalyst for achieving these ambitions.

As we embark on this journey towards a knowledge-based future, it is imperative that we approach AI with a holistic perspective. While the technological advancements are awe-inspiring, it is equally important to consider the ethical, legal, and social implications of AI deployment.

This book, *Innovation and Development of Knowledge Societies: Artificial Intelligence and Knowledge-based Socioeconomic Growth*, is a timely and comprehensive exploration of the complex interplay between AI, intellectual property and the GCC's development. It is a product of the rigorous research and insightful discussions that were conducted during the Gulf Research Center Meetings.

The book serves as an invaluable resource for policymakers, business leaders, researchers, and all interested in the future of the GCC. It provides a solid foundation for understanding the opportunities and challenges associated with technology, intellectual property, and AI. The editors and contributors, a distinguished group of experts, offer a wealth of knowledge and experience, with analyses that are both rigorous and thought-provoking.

As the Chairman of the Gulf Research Center, I am proud to present this book as a contribution to the ongoing discourse on the future of the region. By fostering knowledge sharing and critical thinking, we can collectively shape a future where AI serves as a force for good, driving sustainable development and enhancing the well-being of our communities.

Dr. Abdulaziz Sager
Founder and Chairman of the Gulf Research Center
Riyadh, Saudi Arabia

Acknowledgements

Papers presented at the thirteenth Gulf Research Meeting (GRM), Cambridge, July 11–13, 2023, organised by the Gulf Research Centre Cambridge.

1 Innovation and Development of Knowledge Societies in the Gulf Cooperation Council Member States

An Introduction

David Price

Introduction

The contributions presented in this volume have been selected from papers delivered at a Workshop held under the auspices of the Gulf Research Council's 13th International Meeting at the University of Cambridge in July 2023. The theme of the Workshop as enshrined in its title was the *Innovation and Development of Knowledge Societies – Transformational Impact of IP on knowledge-based economic growth with focus on Frontier Technologies, Artificial Intelligence and IP Financing.*

The Workshop examined the complex area and understanding of innovation and knowledge societies as they particularly apply to the Gulf Cooperation Council member states, namely Bahrain, Kuwait, Oman, Qatar, Saudi Arabia and the United Arab Emirates, and their broad range of communities. Key to this examination was the role that intellectual property – through its promotion and protection – and the consequential technological development can play in fostering both innovation and the knowledge society and economy. In brief, innovation, knowledge, society, emerging technology, intellectual property and economic growth are intertwined and inseparable.

Included in the Workshop programme was an examination of issues relating to the emergence of artificial intelligence and its impact upon and relationship with intellectual property specifically and society generally. A common guiding reference in this regard were both the positive and not-so-positive messages within the context of the so-called "fourth industrial revolution" as originally espoused almost a decade ago by Klaus Schwab and the World Economic Forum, but which has since taken on its own momentum. A central characteristic and driver of the fourth industrial revolution is global and rapid technological advancements which impact economies and societies, including Gulf states. Society in this context is both institutional and individual, state and non-state, international and domestic, urban and rural.

Emerging from the Workshop was a consensus that creativity and the generation of new knowledges across the broad spectrum of technological development and associated intellectual property, are essential sources of nourishment if the GCC member states and their respective economies societies are to flourish. However,

DOI: 10.4324/9781003528517-1

creation of intellectual property also needs nourishment in the form of investment, recognition of risk and opportunity for reward, and appropriate institutional contexts and management.

Aims and Objectives of the Book and the Contributions

The editors and authors in this book offer the presentations herein as contributions to the further nourishment of a global network for innovation and more inclusive knowledge-based societies in the GCC and internationally by establishing foundations. It seeks to build capacity in innovation and digital intellectual property solutions through considering the international regulation of intellectual property law.

The contributions encourage innovation through addressing contemporary challenges in intellectual property development and contributing to a creative economy through key areas of technology, innovation, economic development, intellectual property law, Islamic law, education and ethics and sustainability. This will create new connections and resources to spearhead new developments in this area. It is hoped that the research themes discussed in the book will generate platforms for groundbreaking research on the future of intellectual property law in the GCC and the leading role the GCC can play on the development of knowledge-based societies in a global context. The themes consider the novel areas of religion and cultural norms, and opportunities to create new areas of intellectual property law that are inclusive, ethical, sustainable and with application both in the GCC and globally.

The editors and contributors represent a community of international researchers, academics and practitioners, with linkages to industry and to government and their intellectual property offices.

Engaging directly with experts from the fields of interest across several countries dissolves geographical boundaries between researchers and teaches valuable knowledge sharing exchanges for the growth of inclusive knowledge-based societies. The research is accessible and provides practical engagement with shared problems, strategies and methodologies. It may also help to establish a permanent consortium involving a wider network of scholars, educators and professionals.

The aim of the book is to contribute to the broader academic and professional discourse on the building of knowledge and capacity in the application of intellectual property law in the current digital revolution with emerging technologies. A further aim is to support innovative cross-disciplinary projects and pioneer new approaches to large scale global engagement. The research offers a new opportunity for interaction between different countries across the world on a novel area of research that is understudied and has the potential to lead to a new area of innovation.

Background: The Broader Gulf Context

The GCC member states are currently experiencing a period of diametrical change of direction as they embark on sweeping reforms to move away from being largely energy resource-based economies towards broader-based economies through diversification. The policy objectives as espoused in their recently developed and widely promoted "national vision" statements herald the pursuit of knowledge-based economic diversification and consolidation and, in varying degrees, social advancement. Within the various statements the term "knowledge-based economy" often appears. In a similar vein, declarations along the lines of "ensuring a balance between the legacy of the [nation's] civilisation and identity on the one hand, and the optimal exploitation of technical developments on the other hand to nurture pride within the society" are also present.[1] The sweeping reforms include nurturing, developing and benefiting from the talents of their people, particularly the younger generations.

The national vision statements also refer to the supremacy of Islam. There is by clear inference, where not otherwise stated, that any pursuit of knowledge, utilisation of frontier technologies and adoption of certain forms of artificial intelligence adoption must be in accordance with the Sharia. The Saudi vision statement, for example, concludes with the declaration "May Allah Bless Us and Guide Us to the Right Path".[2]

The societal and cultural character of the Gulf and its member communities are currently confronting these challenging questions relating to the application of frontier and emerging technologies. They include the broader issues of understanding, grasping and utilising artificial intelligence in its various and seemingly ever-increasing forms. But it also includes specific subjects, such as fundamentally rethinking the very understanding of the conventional nature of intellectual property, exploiting the new methods of IP financing, commercial transactions, blockchain, NFTs, risk sharing and equitable reward.

With frontier and emerging technologies and artificial intelligence come new challenges and opportunities for the GCC to expand its innovation capabilities and develop knowledge-based societies. Some of these challenges encompass:

- awareness (or lack thereof) of the potential that innovation and technological development can deliver to both economy and society across the Gulf region;
- appreciation by creator and user alike of the actual and potential contribution of intellectual property legislative regimes to growing the creative economy, fostering new frontier technologies and innovation;
- the capacity or incapacity of the current legislative and supporting strategic and policy regimes of the GCC member states to legally recognise, allow, forbid where necessary, manage, encourage and protect the emerging and frontier technologies and their transformational impact on their economies and societies;
- specifically, legislative and regulatory regimes with potential impact on inventions, technology and sciences, including but not limited to intellectual

1 Sultanate of Oman, 'Moving Forward with Confidence: Oman Vision 2040' (2020), p. 24, 2020 Oman Vision 2040 (2).pdf.

2 Kingdom of Saudi Arabia, *Vision 2030* (25 April 2016), 84, https://www.vision2030.gov.sa/.

property and artificial intelligence in both simple and sophisticated complexity and operation roles;
- the practicability or even possibility of the unification of relevant laws and policies and the introduction of regional frameworks in respect of frontier technologies across the GCC member states;
- broadening the domestic and regional commitment to the advancement of innovation to the international arenas through current and future trade and other agreements.

Declarations of commitment to innovation and technological development and protection of these advances are easy to make and often made. However, generation and maintenance of appropriate infrastructure, meaningful budgetary provisions from both public and private investment sources, and expertise for sustained long-term implementation of those declarations is either rather scarce or sometimes almost non-existent. Adequate and professional infrastructure and the availability of financing models to emerging fields of technological development, intellectual property and artificial intelligence will have an enormous impact on regional and local economies, technology and its transfer, and creativity. A key factor will be development and enforcement of necessary, enabling and effective laws in each country. Furthermore, the GCC member states must endeavour to work in harmony in regard to both regional relationships and regional and international commerce.

The Road Map of the Present Contributions

While the chapters offered in this book generally examine the application of their respective principles and perspectives within a GCC context, they also have differing degrees of application in the greater Muslim world and in a global context. The frontier technology elements of growth in the regional economies and their societies are gaining increasing attention, and there are important lessons to be learnt from, and by, both Muslim and non-Muslim economies and societies.

While the offerings presented in this volume might appear at first glance to be somewhat disparate, they nevertheless can be loosely grouped into three related perspectives in what might perceived as a journey along paths of innovation and development in a GCC context. That first perspective encompasses chapters on current national subject matter in general, the second perspective then focuses on specific subject matter or niche strategies for commercialisation and the third perspective includes chapters which raise issues with a future focus that require a broader GCC and regional consideration.

Some of the chapters have foci that spread across more than one perspective. They give attention to an intriguing area of increasing global interest accompanied by a certain degree of uncertainty generated in part by the absence of statutory control and the commercial imperative oversight extant in the established and conventional intellectual property industry. Hence, they consider emerging alternatives for funding intellectual property development and commercialisation avenues, still with either an Islamic flavour, potential application, or at least relevance. The chapters also bring forth the opportunity to speculate onto the nature of intellectual property and its creators in the future as well as the nature of potential interaction or conflict between intellectual property and artificial intelligence. They ponder on how legislative and regulatory systems and institutional authorities may consider and deal with those creators and the nature of protection, if any, that may be afforded. However, they also impress the message that, irrespective of the nature of intellectual property development and funding strategies for its exploitation, national command and control, however subtle, is still essential.

The final contributions continue with future scenarios on the intellectual property and artificial intelligence relationship but at the same revert back to both an Islamic context and a fundamental precept of Sharia as the foundational core of the Gulf economies and societies.

Perspective 1: Current National Subject Matter in General

The following four chapters offered within this perspective collectively explore economic and social development in the GCC member states from national perspectives, exploring the introduction of new technologies and autonomous systems, the imperative of proper legislative frameworks, the crucial significance of national development strategies and national economic diversification as a foundation for growth.

In the chapter, titled *Ensuring Sovereignty, Capability and Capacity of the Gulf States in the Technological Revolution*, Mark Brady examines the trajectory of the GCC member states towards becoming highly technological knowledge-based societies and economies. As the states seek to strengthen their economic stability through diversification, there is a corresponding increase in reliance upon new and innovative technologies and the benefits brought by technological innovation and knowledge transfer. Brady explores the issues of increasing automation in everyday systems and technology management and data and information security and associated risks.

Brady also argues that, as artificial intelligence becomes increasingly integrated into everyday life, and thus becomes intimately involved in the generation of new knowledge and information processing, it also brings with it a range of hitherto unforeseen concerns and uncertainties. Principal among these are facilitating the integration of new technologies into the Gulf and ensure security of intellectual property. Another concern relates to the way autonomous systems process information and create new knowledge without human input. When coupled with artificial intelligence capable of deep learning, the ability to operate autonomously and to generate new knowledge out of large data sets, is now unparalleled. As the GCC member states embrace a technologically mediated future characterised by highly autonomous systems, it becomes necessary to carefully balance the need for accessibility and transparency in certain areas while ensuring the security and confidentiality of others. With autonomous systems being deployed in industry, manufacturing, transport, finance, data collection, surveillance, and border protection, some important considerations arise. These include the effective use of technology, free from interference with data, while safeguarding intellectual property of local and international partners and protecting information generated by autonomous or other surveillance systems, and how they impact the user and those affected by them.

Brady posits that achieving substantial progress towards technological sovereignty requires effective data management and an understanding of the potential impacts of highly autonomous technologies on internal sovereignty and international expectations. Interpretation of extremely large data sets generated by autonomous systems mass data will be an area of growth for the states and has the potential to ensure continued development and security over the next several decades.

Brady suggests that an early introduction of legislative provisions to enable development of certain technologies and to restrict others may provide a more effective result for the GCC member states. One way that this could be managed is through proactive legislation allowing development of autonomous technology while making sure that the technological developments, and the benefits associated with them, always remain within control of the sovereign Gulf communities. The role of increasingly autonomous artificial intelligence driven systems in the states will have a significant and ongoing impact to the creation and maintenance of knowledge and as a corollary of that, intellectual property, and the sovereign capability and security of the Gulf region.

Rawan Alshammari, with *Building a Unified Legislative Framework for the Development and Registration of Emerging Technologies in the GCC*, examines existing and forthcoming agreements among GCC member states to recommend improvements in intellectual property laws that can drive the creative economy and technological advancements. She proposes that there is huge growth in supporting and accelerating innovation in the Gulf region, and significant legislative change to support such growth. She explores the potential for a unified legislative framework to regulate emerging technologies such as artificial intelligence, NFTs, and blockchain – within the GCC member states. The goal is to facilitate the GCC's transition from a petrochemical-dependent economy to one that is diversified and sustainable, with a strong emphasis on R&D, technology, knowledge and innovation. Effective regulation of the technology sector is crucial for fostering digital innovation and economic growth.

Alshammari argues that the lack of a legislative framework for the development and deployment of emerging technologies in GCC member states poses a significant challenge for regulating and effectively managing these technologies. These challenges lead to the need for a unified legislative framework for the registration, regulation, and commercialisation of these technologies in the GCC region. She proceeds to define the need for a legislative framework to regulate emerging technologies, the gaps in the current GCC member states' intellectual property regulations, and to determine if there is capacity to create a legislative framework in order to facilitate the transformation of the states' economies from a dependence on petrochemicals to more diversification and sustainability with important components based on research and development (R&D), technology, knowledge and innovation.

Alshammari examines the current legal landscape in GCC member states and analyses existing data, literature and resources related to the development of legislative frameworks and regulations using an analytical research methodology that aims to identify the gaps and challenges in the existing legal framework and to address the role of a unified legislative framework in mitigating the legal, economic and social risks that may impact the utilisation of emerging technologies. This approach focuses on synthesising information, drawing connections and evaluating the level of regulatory maturity of emerging technologies.

Focusing on the United Arab Emirates (UAE) and the Kingdom of Saudi Arabia as the leading economies in the region, Alshammari highlights the advanced technology legislation and their impact. She concludes that the current legislative frameworks in GCC member states is sufficient and effective for potential unification. However, practical steps are still recommended to develop a unified regulatory framework, leveraging the UAE and Saudi Arabia experiences to enhance regional attractiveness for innovation and reduce dependency on oil and gas.

In closing, Alshammari highlights the key benefits and recommendations of developing unified laws and regulations for emerging technologies in the GCC member states' countries. However, she also cautions that there are potential drawbacks and challenges associated with a unified legislative framework for developing and registering emerging technologies in the GCC region because of each State's unique economic, social and cultural contexts and the differences in their respective rates of technological advancement. But overall, a unified legislative framework would provide regulatory clarity, promote innovation, and ensure safe and responsible deployment of emerging technologies in the GCC region.

Alhanoof AlDebasi offers a critical analysis of the performance of the GCC member states in developing and implementing national intellectual plans in *Enablers of Knowledge-based Economies: GCC National Intellectual Property Strategies*. Her chapter explores these strategies as tools to maximise the value of the intellectual property wealth and potential of a country in order to transform it into a knowledge-based economy through stimulating investment and technology, advancing in research and development, creating high-quality jobs, and contributing to an ongoing increasing the national gross domestic product.

AlDebasi commences by introducing the concept of a national intellectual property strategy, its strategic importance and the challenges that a national government, an economy and a society may face in ensuring its successful implementation. She then highlights the role of the World Intellectual Property Organization in assisting countries in developing and implementing an effective national IP strategy that can achieve objectives.

She then explores how a well-crafted intellectual property strategy can stimulate investment, foster research and development, generate high-quality employment opportunities and ultimately boost a nation's gross domestic product. She suggests that such strategies also contribute to newly established business ventures as well as employment rates. They directly impact growth of startups that use intellectual property rights as an integral part of their corporate structure and indirectly influence employment rates – all of which play a crucial part in the innovation environment. When a country focuses first on raising awareness on the importance of the intangible assets such as intellectual property, it enhances the asset's registration and ongoing administration and enables IP grants and protection to take effect and positively impact in a timely matter. All of which will positively contribute to the economic advancement of a country.

AlDebasi gives particular attention as an exemplar to Saudi Arabia's development of its national IP strategy, its contribution to the Kingdom's current national development plan, *Vision 2030,* and the role of its national organisation for the management of intellectual property, the Saudi Authority for Intellectual Property (SAIP). With a particular focus on Saudi Arabia, she analyses the efforts of SAIP in aligning its IP strategy with the ambitious *Vision 2030* national development plan by examining the initiatives undertaken by SAIP to cultivate a robust IP ecosystem, and understand the practical steps involved in transforming IP potential into economic reality.

AlDebasi concludes with summary of both suggestions and steps for countries desiring to develop their national intellectual property strategies to ensure successful outcomes. While artificial intelligence presents both opportunities for and challenges to intellectual property rights, proactive efforts in legal, ethical and regulatory domains can help harness the benefits of artificial intelligence while minimising potential threats. Striking a balance between innovation and the protection of intellectual property rights is crucial in navigating the evolving landscape shaped by artificial intelligence technologies. However, a successful strategy is not merely a theoretical construct but a reflection of a country's unique political, economic and institutional landscape.

Amelia Hallam's contribution to the volume with *The Impact of Economic Diversification in the GCC in the Arabian Gulf,* adopts a more economic perspective that the preceding chapters. She argues that the GCC member states have embarked on sweeping reforms designed to build societies of the future. They stand to gain from both a social and economic perspective from investing in knowledge creation and technological development, particularly if they focus on their comparative strengths. Foreign direct investment is a means by which to access new information and fund investment in locally developed knowledge. However, it needs to be harnessed in a way that enhances local learning, knowledge sharing and commercial application.

Hallam maintains that there is also a need for policy makers to address the widening gap between novel technology and regulation. Knowledge is both a capital-building public good and private good requiring protection and promotion. GCC regulators must strike a delicate balance in this regard, particularly in acutely impacted areas including dispute settlement processes such as mediation, conciliation and arbitration. Policy makers also need to invest in knowledge as a means of income generation into the future. They also need to ensure that the distribution of these gains is equitable and reflects inputs in order to optimise economic performance and promote intergenerational wealth and future knowledge creation.

Hallam suggests that while the GCC member states have published visions for the future with a focus on developing their economies, and with emphasis in some on knowledge-based economies, there is not always consensus among them on what might constitute knowledge-societies. Notwithstanding these gaps, leading commentators have argued that economic development, and therefore social welfare, is dependent on nations learning how to learn, fostering further knowledge development internally and focusing on areas of comparative advantage.

The absence of clear definition of a knowledge-society or economy means that it may be a difficult objective to achieve in practice and, even if it was achieved, a difficult concept to measure. Economic principles such as total factor productivity may not be precise enough to measure the economic consequence of locally developed new-knowledge, but rather measure a residual non-capital related figure. Knowledge and technological development are intrinsic to economic performance in the context of the digital global economy. Yet, data and information are so ubiquitous that access to knowledge, including its importation, without critical assessment of its quality and local application and development is not enough to sustain and improve economic development and enhance social welfare.

Hallam concludes with the suggestion that the question for policy makers is how they address these gaps and how the pursuit of knowledge will benefit society, not just in the trade and commercial fields, but in all facets of society. There is a need to balance corporate privacy (including for example, commercial-in-confidence information) and knowledge promotion and transfer. However, this is a difficult balance to strike in practice, requiring careful management within the legal framework at the domestic, regional and international levels. Policy makers are also faced with the challenge of determining how best, and to what level, traditional knowledge and cultural heritage must be preserved and fostered. The degree to which this is achieved requires further consideration.

Perspective 2: Specific Subject Matter or Niche Strategies for Commercialisation

The following four chapters offered within this perspective collectively explore a range of specific subject matter and/or niche strategies for commercialisation, including the nature of the artificial intelligence/intellectual property protection conundrum in respect of both patentability and creativity, and safe harbour provisions and the potential for blockchain technology in a commerce context.

Noura Almutairi, in her contribution titled, *Artificial Intelligence and the Future of Patent Law in the GCC Nations*, examines the challenging issue of the patentability of artificial intelligence-generated inventions under current intellectual property statutory regimes. She does so firstly by analysing the proceedings and outcomes of judicial proceedings across a number of jurisdictions globally over two inventions generated by the DABUS artificial intelligence system. She discusses the nature of the generally negative outcomes across the various jurisdictions.

Almutairi then examines the extent to which the patent regulations of the GCC (PRGCC) can accommodate the inventions generated by AI systems such as DABUS. If it cannot so accommodate, she considers the extent to which adjustments are deemed necessary, and how the patent legal system in the GCC countries can be revamped to keep up with the advance of artificial intelligence systems. This examination highlights the Saudi Authority for Intellectual Property's recent determination to also reject the DABUS patent applications because of their non-alignment with Saudi Arabia's patent law provisions, spirit and wording which require the inventor to be a natural person and to be named on the patent application.

She reports that neither the PRGCC's provisions nor the Saudi Patent Law's provisions accommodate AI-generated inventions and cannot face the challenges they pose. To be granted the patents sought, DABUS's inventions must meet the patentability criteria of inventions. However, assessing whether an invention meets the inventive step criterion or is non-obviousness to a person skilled in the art is difficult and complex, especially in the era of artificial intelligence.

After examining the insufficiency of facing the challenges of AI-generated inventions to the patent system, Almutairi emphasises the need for the PRGCC to be updated within the GCC states to keep pace with patent inventions created by advanced systems, as these inventions will continue to grow. This raises the need to protect innovation to flourish the GCC states' economies, which will enable the states to reach their goals of economic diversification with cutting-edge digital technologies driving growth. However, she suggests that issuance of a new law may not be necessary, since the PRGCC can be amended. She thus proposes recommendations for policymakers in the GCC states to address the challenges of patenting AI-generated inventions. These recommendations include policymakers stipulating AI usage in patent offices to assess whether an application meets the patentability requirement, especially non-obvious ones. However, this way of assessing the non-obvious requirement raises the bar for patentability and may affect innovation. It could hinder granting a patent for inventions created by AI or humans.

Almutairi suggests that another challenge for policymakers to address is that of the capability of artificial intelligence to enjoy status as a legal personality in order to be recognised as an inventor under the PRGCC. This inventorship issue currently precludes the AI-generated inventions from being patentable and legally protected even without any examination of patentability on their merits. She recommends expanding and defining the term 'inventor' within the PRGCC to include the machine-generation to address these issues and to enable protection for the inventions that AI generates.

Continuing the theme of this section of subject-specific issues in respect of emerging technologies, Stefan Papastefanou proposes that assessment of any AI-related technology necessitates at least a fundamental understanding of the underlying technology. In *AI-Generated Content in Copyright Law – A Roadmap for Updating GCC Copyright Law* he considers the proposition of establishing a progressive legal framework for the copyright protection of AI-generated images to realise the full potential of artificial intelligence promotion in the public and private sector. Accordingly, he takes an in-depth technical approach to the specific technology of Text-to-Image Diffusion Models (TIDM) using the example of the DALL·E 2 model to analyse the most recent issues in copyright law and who may be considered an author. He draws insights from the most important legislations when it comes to AI systems and copyright, especially those of the European Union and the United States and their respective approach to the protection of AI-generated images.

Papastefanou first scrutinises the technical functioning of DALL·E 2 in order to identify the essential elements of TIDM relevant to copyright. He then analyses whether, according to current European copyright law, the images generated constitute a work in the sense of a personal intellectual creation and the actors involved who may be entitled to rights in this respect. He aims at establishing differences and similarities between the protection requirements under German and US Law and the possible future copyright laws of the GCC member states. Finally, he discusses how Kuwait and the other states can utilise these challenges to adjust and modernise their current copyright regime for the purposes of attracting innovation. He also draws insights from other prominent legislative frameworks to endeavour to determine if and how they could serve as a role model or negative example for possible copyright protection in the states This is done from two perspectives, namely, whether there a need for copyright protection extension in the DALL·E 2 context, and whether these products possibly lead to new challenges for the protection of classical works that cannot be met by existing copyright law.

Papastefanou draws two main results can be drawn from the analysis. Firstly, very mature *text-to-image* model DALL·E 2 and other TIDM products do not legally enjoy copyright protection, but there is no need to extend copyright protection for economic incentive reasons. In principle, it is advisable to legally reorganise the evidentiary questions on the character of the work to maintain the existing level of protection and to counteract a threatening de facto devaluation through impossible evidentiary requirements. He suggests that TIDM require a rethinking on several levels – factual, legal and possibly even artistic.

Broadening the possibilities of creative use of AI systems can provide AI-focused creators with a modern and unambiguous legal framework to protect and exploit their creations. Ultimately, providing a clear solution to these legal challenges and finding a balance between the artist's copyright and the enabling of AI usage will determine the success of Kuwait's and other GCC member states' economic transformation.

Sarah Alsudairy's chapter, titled *How Can Safe Harbour Provisions Support Technology Development and Online Business in Saudi Arabia*, focuses on the rising importance of adopting safe harbour provisions within the current Saudi Copyright Law after economic reforms proposed by its national development strategy, *Vision 2030*. Alsudairy suggests that these provisions will provide the law with balance and certainty, which will consequently encourage information technology and online businesses to develop within and invest in Saudi Arabia.

Alsudairy contends that the problem with the current Saudi Copyright Law is its ambiguity insofar as it does not include any article that specifically regulates internet service providers' (ISPs) liability for third party infringing content. Nor does it impose any specific obligations upon them or provide them with exceptions from liability. Hence, the Saudi Authority for Intellectual Property (SAIP) has raised the implementation of the law to support copyright industries after *Vision 2030* without legal clarification of the rights and obligations of ISPs including all new emerging technologies. Adopting safe harbour provisions is important in this critical stage to guarantee a balance between right holders' rights and all types of ISPs.

Accordingly, Alsudairy debates how safe harbour provisions should be adopted within the Copyright law in a way that is compatible with the Saudi legal and judicial system. She examines safe harbour provisions regulating three types of online activities, namely ISPs acting as mere conduits, as providers of caching capacities and acting as hosts. She draws upon the experience of the UK in regulating safe harbour provisions with its legal frameworks legislation to explain how the provisions should be adopted within the law and considers whether they are capable of adoption in current form or to what extent they need to be modified before adoption in Saudi Arabia.

Alsudairy suggests that it is possible to adopt defences against secondary liability, similar to the UK's safe harbour provisions. However, suggesting the adoption of an immunity framework does not represent an attempt to copy the UK legal framework literally but reflects an essential need to benefit from their experience and build a framework that balances different rights in way that does not contradict with legal or judicial system in Saudi Arabia.

Alsudairy concludes with the assertion that the Saudi government should be encouraged to adopt a legal framework that exempts ISPs from liability since safe harbour provisions can provide the Copyright Law with the needed clarity to overcome its ambiguity regarding ISP liability and would set the boundaries of any possible obligation imposed on them. It would also help in developing rapid and reliable procedures for removing and disabling access to infringing content. In fact, giving ISPs such a role might help reduce SAIP's authority in monitoring and taking down content, which would reduce the government expenditure on filtration and give SAIP a legal supervisory role only. Furthermore, an important economic imperative exists to provide exceptions from secondary liability. Safe harbours are a way to support online business and e-commerce in general which the Saudi government can target to develop.

Changing direction and focus, Jia Wang provides a probing perspective on a global issue of contention with a specific application. In *Trading Artwork on the Blockchain – An* Opportunity *for the Gulf States to Shift to a Digital Economy*, Wang argues that the advancing blockchain infrastructure in many Gulf states opens up multiple new possibilities for businesses and individuals in trading artworks with tokenisation on blockchain. Non-fungible tokens (NFTs) are widely adopted by the token owner in the form of a record and hash codes that show ownership of the unique token associated with a particular digital asset. Wang's stated objectives are to contextualise the discussion against the background of the trade in a blockchain environment and to examine the most recent legislation and court decisions concerning NFTs and cryptocurrency.

The chapter first introduces the shift to a digital economy taking place in the Gulf states. It then scrutinises the types of blockchain and NFTs as an application of blockchain technologies, particularly the tokenisation of artwork, and examines how artworks are traded in the mortar-and-brick era and the digital era. It scrutinises the common law and civil law approaches towards NFTs and the NFT'd artwork. The chapter then discusses the Gulf approach towards NFTs and crypto-currencies and finally offers a comparative analysis of the different approaches.

Wang provides a comparative study between the selected common law and civil law systems of their concept of assets and property in relation to NFTs. Based on the comparison, she provides recommendations for the Gulf states to adopt block-chains to facilitate the trade of NFT'd artwork with the caveats learnt from the study.

Wang investigates the relevant laws in the Anglo-American countries, then turns to Europe, China and GCC countries as civil law jurisdictions to offer insight into whether the convergence of law applies to legal issues of global relevance in a digital environment. Her investigation includes a study of the most recent court decisions concerning property and intellectual property issues. As the legislation lags behind the speedy advancement of technologies, court decisions offer a time-lier reflection of the judiciary's attitude to NFTs.

Wang recommends that the Gulf states consider lessons from jurisdictions such as the United Kingdom, Singapore, Europe and China and develop their legal framework to potentially align with international practice to facilitate cross-border trade of artwork and digital assets. She also suggests that, if the Gulf states are to develop their legal and regulatory frameworks further to facilitate the trade of NFT'd artwork on blockchains, the primary aim that needs to be kept in mind is the adjustment of the legal frameworks around digital assets with the Sharia Law. Sharia Law is not jurisprudentially formalistic, and thereby, if the digital assets law can be made Sharia compliant, the current rulings by gulf countries like Iraq, Egypt, Bahrain and others may change.

Wang concludes that NFTs, recognised as incorporeal assets conferring quasi-property rights, necessitate a recalibration of traditional property concepts. This adaptation should shift from exclusive control to the use and social utility of digital assets, ensuring a legally and ethically robust framework for NFT'd artwork in the Gulf states.

Perspective 3: Future Focus and Broader Application

The following two chapters offered within this perspective explore core aspects or perhaps consequences of innovation and emerging technologies upon their respec-tive environments – both economic and social. The first chapter, in positive mode, promotes an Islamic finance–compliant intellectual property funding model, with significant opportunity for both Muslim and non-Muslim environments. The sec-ond and concluding chapter, by contrast in a cautionary mode, stresses the impera-tive for appropriate national involvement and frameworks in respect of innovations and emerging technologies for the benefit of their economies and societies.

In her chapter titled *An Examination of the Tangible Value of IP Financing*, Nadia Naim asserts that there is a need for a new industry and new frameworks for a value-based intellectual property model that is Islamic finance compliant. She examines opportunities to address the challenges and barriers to intellectual property growth, to emerging technologies, and to developing new strategies and methodologies for encouraging innovation in the GCC member states on harmonising intellectual property and Islamic finance laws. She proposes establishing a common framework for linking data about the hesitancy towards intellectual property and emerging technology development in the GCC to improve the understanding of their positive impacts. She also proposes the development of novel legal framework models for enterprises and investors to extract the value of their intangible and digital assets.

Naim suggests that there is opportunity to create new areas of intellectual property law that are inclusive, ethical and sustainable with application both in the GCC and beyond. Researching the IP and Islamic finance sector will facilitate the creation of legal conditions and benchmarks from which new industries can be developed. For the GCC, it will create the legal maxims for Islamic finance–compliant intellectual property frameworks and increase economic growth in the intellectual property ecosystem.

Naim reports that the research on value–based intellectual property and emerging technology model that is Islamic finance–compliant has three clear vision areas; firstly, to provide a detailed need for frameworks and toolkits for intellectual property practices and their relationship to business productivity, with a focus on enterprises without alternatives to current intellectual property valuation methods. Secondly, to ensure that the intellectual property system is responsive to the current need of digital innovation in the intellectual property and Islamic finance fields by virtue of a new valuation system that delivers measurable solutions. Thirdly, to solve problems in categorising and managing intellectual property assets that are Islamic finance–compliant and amplified by artificial intelligence and evolving technology. Naim offers the unique context of the UK in this regard, as being the only Global Innovation Index Top 10 country with an established and successful Islamic finance sector, and which can provide the necessary regulatory, capacity–building and human resource management expertise to support the creation of an Islamic intellectual property finance model appropriate for the GCC countries and more widely in the region.

Naim addresses the challenges to an Islamic IP finance model and deals with the core hesitancies of the Islamic finance sector towards IP. She contends that the hesitation stems from Islamic finance institutions and banks and how to leverage IP assets for lending, securitisation, equity funding or collateral. Despite official resolutions, Islamic banks and Islamic financial institutions lack a valuation model for intellectual property assets to meet Islamic finance lending requirements. The main concerns have been that IP assets cannot generate regular revenue. Naim contends that the GCC countries have made clear their vision to grow as knowledge-based societies, and the timeliness of the research aligns with the GCC national visions as being relevant to the communities at large in the region, adheres to religious beliefs and supports economic growth.

The final chapter in this volume, namely *Intellectual Property, Artificial and the Global "Fourth Industrial Revolution" in Progress – Implications for the Gulf States and the GCC* by David Price, continues the theme of change, future directions and the imperative of considered national regulatory management or control by the GCC and its member states of innovation and these emerging technologies. He explores their potential for impact, both positive and uncertain, upon the states' economies and societies. In brief, innovation and emerging technologies, economic growth, intellectual property rights and their communities in which they develop are intertwined and inseparable, and with the new opportunities come new challenges. This hopefully brings broad harmony across society in its broadest sense – but equally it may also have the potential sow seeds of disharmony.

Price opens the debate on innovation and emerging technologies by considering the breakneck speed of developments in the field of artificial intelligence – from performing specific tasks driven directly by user input to super-intelligent machines with sentient capacity or which can combine both technological and human genetic material, and offers examples of selected sources that praise or express caution. He then reviews the current national development plans of the GCC member states and discusses their initiatives to plan for their futures and embrace these emerging technologies through their respective plans. He notes the differing priorities displayed in these plans, ranging from economic utilitarianism to societal prominence. Since Saudi Arabia is the largest GCC member state in terms of population, GDP and global influence, the state's national development plan, *Vision 2030*, enjoys particular attention.

Price also adds to the contentious global academic debate over notion of some form of 'rights', such as intellectual property rights, or even limited 'citizenship' for sentient machines/robots, using the exemplar of 'Sophia the Robot'. He takes note of the societal and cultural character of the Gulf and its member communities and how they might need to confront the challenging question of the application of these frontier technology outcomes.

Price draws upon the numerous references by earlier contributors to the fourth Industrial Revolution and its impact upon the GCC member states in their push for economic diversification and development through the adoption and exploitation of frontier technologies such as artificial intelligence. Relying on the Klaus Schwab thesis on the fourth industrial revolution, he considers both exultations and warnings in respect to the unbounded development and exploitation of artificial intelligence. The fourth industrial revolution fundamentally changes the way that members of society at all levels live, work and relate to each other. 'Society' in this context is both institutional and individual, state and non-state, international and domestic, urban and rural.

Price concludes both chapter and book by contending that emerging technologies and artificial intelligence represent or accompany new opportunities as well as challenges for the GCC to expand its innovation capabilities and develop knowledge-based economies and societies. He endorses the warning by Schwab that the challenges or limitations are real and are ignored at society's peril. However, they are more legal, regulatory and ethical than technical.

2 Ensuring Sovereignty, Capability and Capacity of the GCC Member States in the Technological Revolution

Mark Brady

Introduction

While the modern Gulf Cooperation Council (GCC) member states have generally been known for the massive wealth arising out of oil production, recently there have been moves to achieve non-reliance upon fossil fuel for income. This involves significant investment, both internally and abroad, including in manufacturing, aviation, and other commodity transactions, as the GCC states seek to strengthen their economic stability through diversified economies in sectors such as finance, trade, and tourism, through the application of highly advanced technology.[1] Accordingly, there is a corresponding increase in reliance upon new and innovative technologies, and the benefits brought by technological innovation and knowledge transfer. This takes the form of technologically enhanced manufacturing, industrialisation, and integration into increasingly techno-centric realities. Being able to build stable international partnerships between the States and external partners is therefore crucial to ensuring the ongoing capacity and capability of the region.[2]

As artificial intelligence (AI) becomes increasingly integrated into everyday life and involved in the generation of new knowledge, and information processing, it also brings with it a range of hitherto unforeseen concerns. Principal among these are how to facilitate integration of new technology into the Gulf and ensure security of intellectual property. Another concern is around the way autonomous systems process information and create new knowledge without human input. When coupled with AI capable of deep learning, the ability, to operate autonomously and to generate new knowledge out of large data sets, is now unparalleled. As the GCC member states embrace a technologically mediated future characterised by highly autonomous systems, it becomes necessary to carefully balance the need for accessibility and transparency in certain areas while ensuring the security and confidentiality of others. With autonomous systems being deployed in industry,

1 J. E. Peterson, 'Life after Oil: Economic Alternatives for the Arab Gulf States' (2009) 20(3) *Mediterranean Quarterly* 1–18, muse.jhu.edu/article/317557.

2 David P. Hajjar, George W. Moran, Afreen Siddiqi, Joshua E. Richardson, Laura D. Anadon, and Venkatesh Narayanamurti, 'Prospects for Policy Advances in Science and Technology in the Gulf Arab States: The Role for International Partnerships' (2014) 3(3) *International Journal of Higher Education* 45–57.

DOI: 10.4324/9781003528517-2

manufacturing, transport, finance, data collection, surveillance, and border protection, some important considerations arise. These include the effective use of technology, free from interference with data, while safeguarding intellectual property of local and international partners and protecting information generated by autonomous or other surveillant systems, and how they impact the user and those affected by them.

To achieve substantial progress towards technological sovereignty requires effective data management, and understanding the potential impacts of highly autonomous technologies on internal sovereignty and international expectations.[3] The extremely large data sets generated by autonomous systems and the vast sample sizes require autonomous systems to sift and recognise patterns in data that may have significant impact to the GCC member states.[4] Interpretation of mass data will be an area of growth for the States and has the potential to ensure continued development and security over the next several decades. Additionally, the expansion of autonomous systems raises questions as to how they can be accredited as trustworthy in future and how their control and management can be ensured.[5] With some artificial intelligence systems there are concerns that once the AI 'genie is out of the bottle' it will be impossible to put back. This chapter seeks to clarify areas of opportunity, and risk to the States as they adopt increasing automation in many facets of society and security.[6] Managing intellectual property associated with autonomous systems in increasingly technologically mediated knowledge societies also needs to be addressed at the planning stage to best take advantage and allow exploitation of the knowledge generated.[7]

Where legislative provisions are introduced early, to enable development of certain technologies and to restrict others, a more effective result may be had for GCC member states.[8] The States, being mindful of the benefits of autonomous technology and how it can be effectively legislated, provides a unique opportunity where

3 See generally, Jakob Edler, Knut Blind, Henning Kroll, and Torben Schubert, 'Technology Sovereignty as an Emerging Frame for Innovation Policy. Defining Rationales, Ends and Means' (2023) 52(6) *Research Policy* 104765, https://doi.org/10.1016/j.respol.2023.104765.

4 See, Yue-ting Zhuang and others, 'Challenges and Opportunities: From Big Data to Knowledge in AI 2.0' (2017) 18 *Frontiers of Information Technology & Amp; Electronic Engineering* 3, https://doi.org/10.1631/FITEE.1601883 .

5 See generally, Pekka Ala-Pietilä, Yann Bonnet, Urs Bergmann, Maria Bielikova, Cecilia Bonefeld-Dahl, Wilhelm Bauer, Loubna Bouarfa et al., *The Assessment List for Trustworthy Artificial Intelligence (ALTAI)* (European Commission, Brussels, Belgium, 2020); Nathalie A. Smuha, 'The EU Approach to Ethics Guidelines for Trustworthy Artificial Intelligence' (2019) 20(4) *Computer Law Review International* 97–106, https://doi.org/10.9785/cri-2019-200402.

6 Hisham O. Khogali and Samir Mekid, 'The Blended Future of Automation and AI: Examining Some Long-term Societal and Ethical Impact Features' (2023) 73 *Technology in Society* 102232, https://doi.org/10.1016/j.techsoc.2023.102232 .

7 For an overview of IP management in corporations, see, C. F. Cheung, W. M. Wang, Y. L. Tse and Ricky Ma, 'Knowledge-based Intellectual Property Management for Technology Development Industry' (2013) 14(2) Pages 1–12, *Journal of Knowledge Management Practice*.

8 See, Lyria Bennett Moses, 'Adapting the Law to Technological Change: A Comparison of Common Law and Legislation' (2003) 26(2) Pages 394–417, *UNSW Law Journal*.

the development of technology-based international trade can be encouraged while allowing integration into future Gulf communities. One possible way that this can be managed is through proactive legislation allowing development of autonomous technology while making sure that the technological developments, and the benefits associated with them, always remain within control of the sovereign Gulf communities.[9] Accordingly, the role of increasingly autonomous artificial intelligence driven systems in the States will have a significant and ongoing impact to the creation and maintenance of knowledge and as a corollary of that, intellectual property, and the sovereign capability and security of the Gulf region. Careful curation and development of system-generated intellectual property is therefore necessary to best achieve desirable outcomes for the States. This chapter examines the growth of the GCC and the increasing integration of the States into highly technologically mediated societies. It considers how the States may best manage technology while protecting their data and IP security. It explores increasing automation in everyday systems such as transport, communications, drones, surveillant systems, and security. It identifies potential risks and considers how to best implement control over autonomous technology for the benefit of the Gulf societies while mindful of their individual priorities, international relationships, and international trade obligations.

The Growth of the GCC

The Gulf Cooperation Council is both a collective term and a regional organisation referring to Bahrain, Kuwait, Oman, Qatar, Saudi Arabia, and the United Arab Emirates (UAE) – states that occupy the geographical proximity to the Persian Gulf.[10] In a historical context, the rapid development of the modern Gulf State has occurred in roughly the space of just two generations.[11] In that time, through the exploitation of oil reserves, the States have moved from fairly humble beginnings to among the highest standards of living in the world. The States have had a complex interrelationship throughout history.[12] The various monarchies that make up the States have different political, structural, or economic approaches, and ideological standpoints.[13] However, all the States are ideologically aligned to different extents and have a relationship to Islam and the tenets of the Holy Q'uran.

9 See, Lyria Bennett Moses, 'Adapting the Law to Technological Change: A Comparison of Common Law and Legislation' (2003) 26(2) *UNSW Law Journal.*

10 See generally David Commins, *The Gulf States: A Modern History* (Bloomsbury Publishing, London, 2012).

11 John Peterson 2016, *The Emergence of the Gulf States: Studies in Modern History* (Bloomsbury Academic, New York, 18 May 2023), https://search.ebscohost.com/login.aspx?direct=true&AuthType=shib&db=e000xww&AN=1240424&site=ehost-live.

12 John Peterson 2016, *The Emergence of the Gulf States: Studies in Modern History* (Bloomsbury Academic, New York, 18 May 2023), https://search.ebscohost.com/login.aspx?direct=true&AuthType=shib&db=e000xww&AN=1240424&site=ehost-live.

13 Adam Hanieh, *Money, Markets, and Monarchies: The Gulf Cooperation Council and the Political Economy of the Contemporary Middle East* (Cambridge University Press, Cambridge, 2018).

This ideological orientation is sometimes in tension with the more Western values around international trade, intellectual property laws and business transactions.[14]

The period leading up to the formation of the GCC was marked by regional tensions and growing concerns about security and stability in the Persian Gulf region. One of the major events during this period was the Iran-Iraq War, which lasted from 1980 to 1988. The conflict had a significant impact on the region, with neighbouring Gulf countries facing security concerns and economic disruptions due to the proximity of the conflict. The Iranian Revolution also had a significant impact on the geopolitical tensions in the Persian Gulf region, fuelling concerns about the spread of revolutionary ideologies and the potential for political destabilisation in the region.[15] Accordingly, the region witnessed heightened security challenges during this period, including border disputes, territorial claims, and occasional skirmishes between neighbouring countries. These tensions underscored the need for greater regional cooperation and collaboration to address shared security concerns.

The geopolitical dynamics in the region were also influenced by several external factors.[16] The Soviet invasion of Afghanistan in 1979 and its subsequent impact on regional stability, as well as the ongoing Cold War tensions between the United States and the Soviet Union, shaped the security environment and growing tensions.[17] Despite regional tensions, there were some shared interests and common objectives among the Gulf countries.[18] Economic considerations played a significant role in the formation of the GCC. The GCC member states recognised the potential benefits of increased economic integration and cooperation in the face of fluctuating oil prices, and uncertain regional dynamics, as well as the desire to diversify their economies beyond oil.[19] These shared interests included the desire to promote stability, security, economic development, and closer cooperation in various areas to address common challenges and enhance the international standing of the Gulf region. The formation of the GCC therefore, aimed to address these concerns and foster greater cooperation and integration among the States.

In 1981 the GCC was formed, and its respective member states agreed to work together to further the prosperity of the Gulf nations.[20] Since the advent of the GCC, a new path has been set in motion for the States towards increasing intra-state

14 John Carroll, 'Intellectual Property Rights in the Middle East: A Cultural Perspective' (2001) 11 *Fordham Intellectual Property Media & Entertainment Law Journal* 555, 556.

15 See generally, David Commins (n 10).

16 M. Hafner, P. P. Raimondi, and B. Bonometti, 'Geopolitics of Oil and Gas in the MENA Region' in *The Energy Sector and Energy Geopolitics in the MENA Region at a Crossroad. Perspectives on Development in the Middle East and North Africa (MENA) Region* (Springer, Cham, 2023), https://doi.org/10.1007/978-3-031-30705-8 _5

17 Ofer Israeli, 'The Roundabout Outcomes of the Soviet-Afghan War' (2022) 46(1) *Asian Perspective* 1–20, https://doi.org/10.1353/apr.2022.0000.

18 Ofer Israeli, 'The Roundabout Outcomes of the Soviet-Afghan War' (2022) 46(1) *Asian Perspective* 1–20, https://doi.org/10.1353/apr.2022.0000.

19 See generally David Commins (n 10).

20 Gulf Cooperation Council, *Charter of the Gulf Cooperation Council (GCC)* (Riyadh, Saudi Arabia, 1981), https://www.files.ethz.ch/isn/125347/1426_GCC.pdf.

cooperation and sharing of information and knowledge.[21] By working together, the GCC hoped to enhance regional stability, boost economic cooperation, and address common security challenges in the Persian Gulf region.[22] The ongoing cooperative focus of the GCC has been in working towards the creation of new knowledge societies in the Gulf region, and amongst the GCC member states themselves. One of the GCC stated objectives is:

> To stimulate scientific and technological progress in the fields of industry, mining, agriculture, water, and animal resources; to establish scientific research; to establish joint ventures and encourage cooperation by the private sector for the good of their peoples.[23]

This statement arguably suggests tacit recognition by the GCC of the importance of intellectual property, as it emphasises stimulating scientific and technological progress in various fields, the establishment of scientific research, the encouragement of joint ventures and private sector cooperation. This implies acknowledgement by the GCC of the inherent role of intellectual property in facilitating such collaborations, protecting knowledge transfer, and driving economic growth and scientific development in the region. This is clearly a work in progress for the GCC member states as there have been some difficulties along the way to harmonisation of intellectual property laws. In respect of harmonisation and integration of specific areas of intellectual property matters, the GCC took many years to be able to achieve a degree of success in respect of a regional trademark law and a patent law but has not yet been successful in respect of a uniform copyright law even after many years of trying. Saudi Arabia have specifically prioritised attracting foreign investment in their *Vision 2030* with their intention to 'apply international legal and commercial regulations strictly and create a business environment conducive to long-term investment'.[24]

Harmonisation and Integration between the GCC Member States

It is important to also note that the progress towards alignment between the GCC member states has not always been harmonious and there have been ongoing tensions between States. During the period between 2006 and 2009, when Bahrain[25] and Oman[26] entered into Free Trade Agreements (FTAs) with the United States, there was an increasing degree of acrimony among some States. This disharmony

21 David Price and Alhanoof AlDebasi, *Protecting Intellectual Property in the Arabian Peninsula: The GCC States, Jordan and Yemen* (Routledge, Cavendish, 2018).

22 See generally David Commins (n 10).

23 GCC Charter (n 20), Article 4.

24 Kingdom of Saudi Arabia, *Vision 2030* (25 April 2016), 50, https://www.vision2030.gov.sa/ .

25 United States - Bahrain Free Trade Agreement, https://ustr.gov/trade-agreements/free-trade-agreements/bahrain-fta .

26 United States – Oman Free Trade Agreement, https://ustr.gov/trade-agreements/free-trade-agreements/oman-fta .

stemmed from various factors, including concerns over the perceived influence of foreign powers, the potential impact on domestic industries, and the implications for local economies and labour markets. Additionally, there were debates surrounding the compatibility of the FTAs with national laws, cultural values, and State sovereignty.[27] Saudi Arabia argued the FTAs violated the GCC agreement where 'no member state may grant to a non-member state any preferential treatment exceeding that granted herein to member states, nor conclude any agreement that violates provisions of this agreement'.[28] These issues sparked discussions and debates within the States, reflecting differing perspectives and interests regarding the decision to forge closer economic ties with the United States.

The recent serious diplomatic crisis between Qatar and Saudi Arabia, the UAE, and Bahrain highlighted significant difficulties that still exist within the GCC member states.[29] This crisis, which began in 2017, involved the severing of diplomatic ties, trade embargoes, and airspace restrictions imposed on Qatar by its neighbouring countries. The rift exposed deep-rooted disagreements and grievances among the States, including differing approaches to regional issues, political alliances, and accusations related to support for terrorism and meddling in internal affairs.[30] The crisis underscored the challenges in maintaining unity and consensus within the GCC, and revealed fractures in relationships between members, and the complexities of reconciling their divergent interests and priorities within the States.

Despite the ongoing challenges, in recent years the GCC member states have embraced the adoption of increasingly advanced technologies, which hold significant potential for transformative impact across the region. From the cooperation started in the GCC there is now an ongoing push towards creating an increasingly technological society amongst its member states.[31] The commitment by the States towards creating a technologically progressive society is evident in initiatives aimed at enhancing digital infrastructure, promoting digital literacy, and encouraging the adoption of autonomous technologies in industries such as manufacturing, energy, finance, and advanced telecommunications. The emphasis on technology revolves around the development of knowledge societies centred around advanced artificial intelligence, autonomous systems, and generative AI technologies.

By leveraging their collective strengths and resources, the GCC member states are working towards realising a future that employs technology as a catalyst for

27 See, Price and AlDebasi (n 21).

28 Unified Economic Agreement Between the Countries of the Gulf Cooperation Council, art. 31, http://www.gcc-sg.org/ar-sa/CognitiveSources/DigitalLibrary/Lists/DigitalLibrary/الاتفاقيات/1111318748548.pdf.

29 See A. Baabood, 'The Future of the GCC Amid the Gulf Divide' in A. Krieg (ed) *Divided Gulf: Contemporary Gulf Studies* (Palgrave Macmillan, Singapore), https://doi.org/10.1007/978-981-13-6314-6_10.

30 See A. Krieg, 'The Gulf Rift—A War Over Two Irreconcilable Narratives', *Defense in Depth* (27 June 2017), https://defenceindepth.co/2017/06/26/the-gulf-rift-a-war-over-two-irreconcilable-narratives/.

31 David Hajjar et al. (n 2).

economic growth, social development, and enhanced quality of life for their respective populations. Accordingly, the States are unequivocally looking to the future. Qatar, for example, has the *National Vision 2030* which sees the State working towards:

> A knowledge-based economy characterised by innovation; entrepreneurship; excellence in education; a world class infrastructural backbone; the efficient delivery of public services; and transparent and accountable government.[32]

The 2022 GCC *Engineering Net Zero Report* notes an urgent need to drive change that 'capitalises on new technologies and skills as a long-term plan to replace oil & gas revenues'.[33] The *Economist Intelligence Unit, Innovating through Tech in the GCC, Report for the Economic Development Board of Bahrain (EIU Report)* highlights the strengthening of digital infrastructure along with increasing reliance on advanced digital technologies in future.[34] Saudi Arabia has developed its *Vision 2030,* which sets out the aspirations of the State moving forward.[35] As the Gulf moves away from reliance on fossil fuel production, advanced technology will become critical to its future success.[36] The UAE has the Fourth Industrial Revolution (4IR) Strategy, which aims to position the UAE as 'a leading global hub and an open lab for the Fourth Industrial Revolution's applications'.[37] The UAE vision includes augmented learning, personalised medicine, robo-care, augmented healthcare, advanced defence manufacturing, intelligent cities, next-gen. mobility, intelligent grids, 3D printed construction, intelligent supply chains, cognitive human enhancement, integrated cyber-secured data environment, and the preparation of a national talent pool.[38] Oman also has a comprehensive plan that aims to transform the nation into a competitive, knowledge-based economy, that leverages technology where:

> The new economy will capture global trends in technology, innovation and industrial revolutions in order to keep up with and incorporate such trends in the national plans and programs in a safe knowledge and technology-based environment that ensures transformation to technology, knowledge and innovation-based economy.[39]

32 Qatar *National Vision 2030.*

33 Gulf Cooperation Council Report, *Engineering Net Zero* (SNC Lavalin, June 2022) 5.

34 The Economist Intelligence Unit, *Innovating through Tech in the GCC*, Report for the Economic Development Board of Bahrain (EIU 2020) (*EIU Report*) Dubai 10–14.

35 Kingdom of Saudi Arabia. *Vision 2030*, www.vision2030.gov.sa.

36 EIU Report (n 34) 5.

37 The UAE's Fourth Industrial Revolution (4IR) Strategy, https://u.ae/en/about-the-uae/strategies-initiatives-and-awards/strategies-plans-and-visions/government-services-and-digital-transformation/the-uae-strategy-for-the-fourth-industrial-revolution.

38 The UAE's Fourth Industrial Revolution (4IR) Strategy, https://u.ae/en/about-the-uae/strategies-initiatives-and-awards/strategies-plans-and-visions/government-services-and-digital-transformation/the-uae-strategy-for-the-fourth-industrial-revolution.

39 Sultanate of Oman, *Vision Oman 2040* (11 September 2019) 30.

Oman has clearly stated this in their *Vision 2040* under the priority of 'Economic Diversification and Fiscal Sustainability' as a strategic objective of a 'diversified and sustainable economy that is based on technology, knowledge and innovation, operates within integrated frameworks, ensures competitiveness, embraces industrial revolutions and achieves fiscal sustainability'.[40] However, this move towards a highly technological society has not been completely by choice. Oman has the most limited oil reserves of the GCC member states, and is consequently being forced to realise its goal of becoming a purely market economy, as Fromson and Simon note:

> Oman offers insight into the challenges of reforming other Middle Eastern rentier states. It will be the first major oil-dependent economy in the region forced to transition back to non-rentier modes of production, and the difficulties it has faced may have broad implications for policymakers and academics thinking about other GCC states.[41]

Additionally, as Sachs and Warner suggest, research has shown 'evidence of a "curse of natural resources" – countries with great natural resource wealth tend nevertheless to grow more slowly than resource-poor countries...Resource-abundant countries tended to be high-price economies and, perhaps as a consequence, these countries tended to miss-out on export-led growth'.[42] This tends to dampen economic diversification in the Gulf region.

The withdrawal of the United States as a strategic partner in the Gulf area puts additional pressure on the Gulf nations to manage their own strategic partnerships.[43] Saudi Arabia, likely in response from the withdrawal of the United States from the area, has a stated objective of creating localised defence industries to 'transfer knowledge and technology, and build national expertise in the fields of manufacturing, maintenance, repair, research and development'.[44] Additionally, the strategic vacuum created by the withdrawal of the United States provides opportunities for rise of other strategic partnerships to develop in the Gulf region. China's investments in the region,[45] particularly in energy, transportation, and trade, offer potential benefits to the GCC, but also raise concerns about geopolitical influence and debt sustainability. According to Price and AlDebasi, 'The nature and significance of a China-GCC should not be under-estimated. China has overtaken the United States as the largest exporter to the GCC'.[46] China's Belt and Road Initiative (BRI)

40 Sultanate of Oman, *Vision Oman 2040* (11 September 2019) 30.

41 James Fromson and Steven Simon, 'Visions of Omani Reform' (2019) 61(4) *Survival* 99–116, https://doi.org/10.1080/00396338.2019.1637117.

42 Jeffrey Sachs and Andrew Warner, 'Natural Resources and Economic Development: The Curse of Natural Resources' (2001) 45 *European Economic Review* 827.

43 Price and AlDebasi (n 21).

44 Kingdom of Saudi Arabia (n 35) 48.

45 See, Karen Young, 'The Gulf's Eastward Turn: The Logic of Gulf–China Economic Ties' (2020) 9(2) *Journal of Arabian Studies* 236–252, https://doi.org/10.1080/21534764.2019.1768655.

46 Price and AlDebasi (n 21) 277.

is seen as an opportunity to increase infrastructure development and economic cooperation.[47] China is not alone in the push to secure partnerships with the GCC.[48] Russia has also intensified its engagement with the GCC member states through increased investments and trade partnerships.

Russian energy companies have sought to expand their presence in the Gulf region, while defence cooperation and joint military exercises have further deepened the bilateral ties between Russia and a number of Gulf countries including Saudi Arabia, the UAE, Qatar, Kuwait, and Oman. However, as Bianco argues, 'despite signing strategic agreements with Saudi Arabia and the UAE, Russia is not in a position to replace the United States as a regional security guarantor or a strategic defence partner'.[49] Accordingly, as the Gulf nations navigate these evolving dynamics, they face the complex task of balancing their strategic partnerships, diversifying alliances, and ensuring their long-term economic growth and security amidst the changing geopolitical landscape which has witnessed significant growth and diversification across various domains. Technology is therefore becoming increasingly necessary to enable states to amplify capacity and capability and boost strategic and economic stability. However, cooperation is required when dealing with technological advancements and the resulting competitive pressures that arise from escalations in the global uptake of technology.[50] Along with the adoption of increasingly advanced technologies come concerns around intellectual property and how technology transfer might be affected by the GCC member states' intellectual property regimes. Accordingly, how the technologies are integrated, and the intellectual property managed, will set the stage for the next 50 years of Gulf State prosperity.

Intellectual Property and Technology Transfer in the Gulf Region

Recent movement among the GCC member states has been towards creating 'knowledge-based societies with less reliance on natural resources'.[51] As a result, autonomous systems and the generation of new knowledge have now begun an exponential growth trajectory among the States. This trajectory has seen artificial intelligence driven systems increasingly integrated into global communities, and throughout the States. According to the Business Software Alliance, 'Artificial

47 Charles W. Dunne, *China's Belt and Road Initiative and US Middle East Policy* (Arab Centre, Washington, DC, 2023), https://arabcenterdc.org/resource/chinas-belt-and-road-initiative-and-us-middle-east-policy/ .

48 See generally, R. Bailey, 'Is China Set to Become the GCC's Most Important Economic Partner by 2020? And What Does This Mean for the Region?' *Gulf Business* (16 April 2013), http://gulfbusiness.com/china-and-gcc-growing-ties/#.ViEQUi6gyoM .

49 Cinzia Sidlo, 'Balance of Power: Gulf States, Russia, and European Energy Security' *European Council on Foreign Relations* (16 March 2022), https://ecfr.eu/article/balance-of-power-gulf-states-russia-and-european-energy-security/.

50 See, T. K. Das and Bing-Sheng Teng, 'Between Trust and Control: Developing Confidence in Partner Cooperation in Alliances' (1998) 23(3) *The Academy of Management Review* 491.

51 G. Donn and Y. Al Manthri (eds), *Education in the Broader Middle East: Borrowing a Baroque Arsenal* (Symposium Books, Oxford, England, 2013).

intelligence (AI) fuels digital transformation in every sector of the economy'.[52] Until very recently, autonomous systems were largely process driven and engaged to undertake repetitive tasks.[53] Understanding this seismic shift requires consideration of the various technological developments that may affect existing legislative, social, and technological frameworks in the Gulf. The Gulf communities are rapidly reaching a crossroads where technology itself will be a generator of both new knowledge and new realities.

The increasing adoption and integration of technology in various sectors within the GCC member states, such as e-commerce, telecommunications, digital media, and innovation-driven industries are having a transformative impact on societal, economic, and cultural aspects in the region. For example, the *EIU Report* notes business leaders and entrepreneurs in the GCC are enhancing product and service offerings by incorporating 'technologies such as the Internet of Things (IoT), artificial intelligence (AI), augmented and virtual reality (AR/VR), and blockchain'.[54] As these advanced technologies proliferate it will likely be considered necessary to carefully curate and manage the way they are integrated into the States to best manage the future society it will create in accordance with GCC cultural and ideological norms. This ongoing transfer of technology is necessary in order to adequately prepare to compete in world markets and to maintain existing competitive advantage. However, the creation of knowledge societies is sometimes hampered by the fortunate position some states find themselves in. For example, in Kuwait, the UAE, and Qatar the 'reservation wage' set for the public service for citizens is so lucrative that it operates as a disincentive to private sector involvement.[55] Arman and Immarino see this as a barrier to knowledge transfer where:

> It is not surprising that the business sector has little incentive to employ citizens; this is especially true for those with fewer skills. Expatriate wages in the private sector, for all but the most skilled labour, are well below the level paid to citizens in the public sector. These labour market features provide no incentives for organisations to invest in transferring knowledge to nationals and hamper risk-taking private ventures such as entrepreneurship that generate value added.[56]

52 Business Software Alliance, US position Paper 2023, *AI Developers and Deployers: An Important Distinction* (BSA, 16 March 2023), https://www.bsa.org/policy-filings/ai-developers-and-deployers-an-important-distinction.

53 See generally, Mohammed Kamal, M. D. Dahlan, Natrah Abdullah, and Ahmad Iqbal Hakim Suhaimi, 'Industrial Revolution Reshaping Repetitive Task in Digital Workplace' (2019) 8(1.6) *International Journal of Advanced Trends in Computer Science and Engineering* 347.

54 EIU Report (n 34) 5.

55 Husam Arman, Simona Iammarino, J. Eduardo Ibarra-Olivo, and Neil Lee, 'Breaking Out of the Innovation Trap? Towards Promoting Private R&D Investment in Kuwait' *LSE Middle East Centre*, Kuwait Programme Paper Series. London School of Economics and Political Science (9 March 2021) 11.

56 Husam Arman, Simona Iammarino, J. Eduardo Ibarra-Olivo and Neil Lee, 'Breaking Out of the Innovation Trap? Towards Promoting Private R&D Investment in Kuwait' *LSE Middle East Centre*,

An important corollary of technological advancement is that to remain competitive on the world stage the States must keep abreast of technological developments. Anything which impedes the transfer of technology, or the creation of knowledge societies is therefore to be avoided. As the States move away from reliance on fossil fuels, technology is clearly going to play an increasing role in building the knowledge capacity, capability, and sovereignty of the States as they understand the growing importance of technological advancements, knowledge societies, and digital infrastructure in driving their future economic growth.

As a driver of economic growth, the transfer of increasingly innovative technology is becoming necessary to compete on the global stage.[57] Technology transfer is already on the agenda for some GCC member states. For example, Oman has a stated objective of creating an 'effective national system that nurtures scientific research, innovation, and creativity to build a knowledge-based economy and society'.[58] According to Ricken and Malcotsis, 'technology impacts the economic growth and competitive advantage of regions and nations'.[59] Technology transfer is defined as 'mechanisms for shifting information across borders and its effective diffusion into recipient or host economies'.[60] However, technology and the benefits of technological transfer are usually not provided without some *quid pro quo*, or contractual relationship between parties holding the intellectual property in new knowledge or technology. This technology transfer is usually found in some form of business relationship or investment arrangement. Accordingly, the most direct way for a region to assimilate technology in the States is often through foreign direct investment, which is usually by way of multinational corporations.[61] Intellectual property laws therefore play a crucial role in promoting continued technology transfer to the States, by facilitating innovation, fostering economic growth, and attracting foreign investment. The adoption and enforcement of robust intellectual property protection measures, in line with international benchmarks, are therefore instrumental in creating a favourable environment for knowledge-based industries, multinational corporations, and technology-driven economies to engage with the States.

Kuwait Programme Paper Series. London School of Economics and Political Science (9 March 2021) 11.

57 Boris Ricken and George Malcotsis, *The Competitive Advantage of Regions and Nations: Technology Transfer Through Foreign Direct Investment* (Taylor & Francis Group, Farnham, 2011).

58 Oman (n 39) 20.

59 Ricken and Malcotsis (n 57) 31.

60 E. Dinopoulos and P. Segerstrom, 'Intellectual Property Rights, Multinational Firms and Economic Growth' (2010) 92(1) *Journal of Development Economics* 13–27.

61 D. S. Elmuti and A. S. Abou-Zaid, 'Patterns of Technology Transfer among the Arab Gulf States: Opportunities and Challenges' (2013) 23(4) *International Journal of Commerce and Management* 339–353, https://doi.org/10.1108/IJCoMA-02-2012-0012.

International Benchmarks on Intellectual Property Protection and Management

International benchmarks on intellectual property protection and management, such as those established by organisations like the World Intellectual Property Organization (WIPO), provide guidance and best practices for participating countries to develop comprehensive legal frameworks. As Price argues, an important starting point 'is the benchmark represented by the World Trade Organization's (WTO) Agreement on Trade-Related Aspects of Intellectual Property Rights (TRIPS), and the states' response to their obligations to meet TRIPS requirements'.[62] Adhering to these benchmarks enhances the credibility and attractiveness of the GCC member states to foreign technology providers, as it ensures the safeguarding of their intellectual property while encouraging beneficial technology transfer agreements. Another important benchmark is the United States Trade Representative's (USTR) annual *Special 301 Report.* The USTR *Special 301 Report* evaluates global intellectual property protection and enforcement efforts. A favourable assessment in this report signifies a state commitment to strong intellectual property protection and management, which can bolster the Gulf States' image as suitable destinations for increased technology transfer and foreign investment. The 2022 USTR *Special 301 Report* noted:

> Saudi Arabia is removed from the Priority Watch List this year due to steps taken by SAIP to publish its IP enforcement procedures; increase enforcement against counterfeit and pirated goods and online pirated content; create specialized IP enforcement courts with trained judges and expedited timelines; conduct strong IP awareness, outreach, training, and support; set up a centralized committee to coordinate IP enforcement actions across multiple authorities; and train IP specialists in 76 different authorities to increase government compliance with IP laws.[63]

Kuwait was similarly removed from the USTR watch list 'for making continued and significant progress on concerns that stakeholders identified with intellectual property (IP) enforcement and transparency'.[64] The removal of Kuwait and Saudi Arabia from the USTR watch list are significant as the report publicly recognises their efforts in addressing intellectual property concerns and promoting an environment conducive to innovation and investment. This can significantly enhance their global reputation, attract foreign investment, and contribute to the economic growth, knowledge transfer, and overall development of both countries.

62 David Price, 'The GCC Intellectual Property Regimes: Global Harmonization or Regional Integration?' in M. Ramady (ed) *The GCC Economies* (Springer, New York, 2012) 1.

63 Office of the United States Trade Representative, *Special 301 Report* 2022 (United States Government Publishing Office, Washington, DC, 2022) 10.

64 Office of the United States Trade Representative, *Special 301 Report* 2022 (United States Government Publishing Office, Washington, DC, 2022) 10.

Another international benchmark found in the Business Software Alliance (BSA) *Piracy Report*, which provides insights into software piracy rates, is also relevant to Gulf State technology transfer endeavours. A lower piracy rate indicates a stronger intellectual property protection regime, which in turn encourages technology companies to invest in the region, with the understanding that their intellectual property rights will be respected, and their confidentiality maintained. Furthermore, collaboration with international organisations like WIPO and the United Nations Office on Drugs and Crime (UNODC) in the Middle East can assist the GCC member states in capacity building, raising awareness, and implementing effective measures to combat intellectual property infringement.

This collaboration can contribute to the development of a robust intellectual property ecosystem that supports technology transfer and encourages the creation and dissemination of knowledge-based industries. Accordingly, robust intellectual property laws aligned with international benchmarks, are essential for the GCC member states to promote increasing technology transfer. Compliance with these standards, as assessed by reports like the USTR *Special 301 Report* and the *BSA Piracy Report*, enhance the attractiveness of the Gulf region to technology providers and foreign investors. Collaborations with organisations like WIPO and UNODC can further strengthen the intellectual property protection regime, and thereby foster a conducive environment for innovation, economic growth, and technology transfer to the States. The *EIU Report* observed that 'reform of the business environment has been on a steady rise across the GCC economies in recent years, as the World Bank notes in its "Doing Business 2020" report'.[65] However, there are some fundamental philosophical and ideological challenges to overcome when undertaking technology transfer with the States.

Gulf State Priorities, International Relationships, and Trade Obligations

The GCC member states often have fundamentally different priorities to those of their Western counterparts, particularly with respect to the structure and organisation of society, religion, investment, and trade. These differences indirectly impact the way knowledge is transferred between countries and how this affects intellectual properly generated within the States and transfer between trading partners. According to Price, 'intellectual property as an intangible object being the product of one's mental labours is a recent concept not expressly mentioned in either the holy Quran, the Sunnah or the early Islamic jurisprudence'.[66] This leads to some confusion around the ownership and protection of intellectual property in the States where everything happens *Insha'Allah*. This translates to 'if Allah wills' or 'God willing' in English and is a commonly used expression in the Islamic faith, often

65 EIU Report (n 34); World Bank Group, *Doing Business 2020: Comparing Business Regulation in 190 Economies, Report*, 8–9.

66 Price and AlDebasi (n 21) 26–27.

used to express the belief that the outcome of a future event is ultimately in the hands of God and subject to His divine will.

The absence of explicit mention of intellectual property in religious texts or early Islamic jurisprudence does not diminish the importance of addressing its ownership and protection in the GCC member states. In a rapidly evolving global economy driven by innovation and knowledge-based industries, intellectual property rights have become a crucial aspect of economic development and international trade. Recognising the significance of intellectual property as a catalyst for innovation, many countries have developed legal frameworks and international agreements to safeguard creators' rights and promote technological advancements. The States, in their pursuit of progress and economic diversification, can thus benefit from adopting comprehensive intellectual property laws – that balance cultural sensitivities with global standards – fostering an environment conducive to creativity, innovation, and technological advancement.

Harmonising intellectual property practices within the GCC member states and aligning them with international norms would enhance regional collaboration, attract foreign investment, and promote technology transfer. By providing clear guidelines for intellectual property protection and enforcement, the States can create an environment that encourages creativity and rewards innovation, benefiting both local and international stakeholders. In line with the need for protection of intellectual property to stimulate knowledge transfer into the States, 'all states have established comprehensive legislative regimes for the protection of intellectual property'. With respect to the GCC, 'most, but by no means all, of their intellectual property laws generally reveal a willingness to comply with the international standards as enshrined in both TRIPS and the TRIPS plus conventions, even if at times some still fall a little short in respect of the detail and practise'.[67] Additionally, the emerging intellectual property frameworks in line with the WIPO guidelines can facilitate faster knowledge exchange, attract research and development investment, and nurture a culture of entrepreneurship, contributing to long-term economic growth and global competitiveness in the region. Understanding the fundamental difference in Gulf State priorities with respect to their international relationships and trade obligations is therefore crucial to developing ongoing trade relationships and technology transfer between Western countries and the States.

GCC Member State Challenges in the Technological Revolution

The GCC member states face a major challenge centred around the introduction of new technologies, in particular telecommunications and their intrusion into the public/private space. Balancing this public/private divide will be crucial to ensure continued success for Gulf societies. As the Gulf moves towards a highly autonomous future some consideration is required with respect to increasing the transparency of certain surveillant systems while maintaining the security and opacity of

67 Price and AlDebasi (n 21) 324.

others. With the use of autonomous systems for data collection, and border protection, a problem may arise around the growth of surveillant societies within the States. Some States have been traditionally hesitant towards allowing unfettered access to information by their population, and new technologies are often seen as encroaching upon the sovereignty of the particular State. A corollary of this is that the rapid increase in technological advancement also brings with it the potential for an increasingly surveillant society. As Demmelhuber et al argue, it provides 'a window of opportunity for Middle Eastern autocrats to further fine-tune their modes of digital surveillance and repression'.[68]

A surveillant society uses technology to increasingly focus on the behaviour and movements of the population. Surveillant practices in GCC member states, as in Western countries, involve various methods centred around gathering information and monitoring populations. This may include interception and monitoring of electronic communications, including phone calls, emails, text messages, and social media interactions. Internet monitoring is another common surveillance method used in the States.[69] Governments are able to monitor internet usage, including browsing history, online activities, and social media interactions, to monitor individual online behaviour, identify potential risks, or gather intelligence related to security or enforcing public order. Closed-circuit television systems (CCTV) are often deployed in public spaces to monitor activities and maintain state scrutiny. CCTV cameras and facial recognition technology are also widely used in the States. Facial recognition technology allows the state to identify individuals and track their movements, contributing to surveillant societies, and digitally enhanced repressive capability. As Martin argues, 'The constant possibility of being surveilled electronically reinforces the notion that the Internet has indeed become Foucault's virtual Panopticon'.[70] The state can now have an all-seeing artificially intelligent eye on the actions of the population.

However, this increase in surveillance capability can work both ways and operate as a virtual double-edged sword against the regime elites. With the proliferation of mobile devices in the hands of an increasingly technologically savvy population, and with each device having photographic and video capability, there exists the potential for a population driven reverse panopticon.[71] This, described by Foucault with respect to surveillance within the panopticon, 'visibility is a trap',[72] when

68 Thomas Demmelhuber, Julia Gurol, and Tobias Zumbrägel, 'The COVID-19 Temptation?: Sino–Gulf Relations and Autocratic Linkages in Times of a Global Pandemic' in Zeina Hobaika, Lena-Maria Möller, and Jan Claudius Völkel (eds) *The MENA Region and COVID-19: Impact, Implications and Prospects* (Routledge, London, 2022) 19–35.

69 See generally, Adrian Shahbaz, *Freedom on the Net 2018: The Rise of Digital Authoritarianism* (Freedom House, New York, 2018), https://freedomhouse.org/report/freedom-net/2018/rise-digital-authoritarianism.

70 C. Dianne Martin, 'The Internet as a Reverse Panopticon' *Computers and Society* (10 March 2022).

71 C. Dianne Martin, 'The Internet as a Reverse Panopticon' *Computers and Society* (10 March 2022).

72 Michel Foucault, 'Panopticism' in A. Sheridan (ed) *Discipline & Punish: The Birth of the Prison* (Vintage Books, 1995) New York 195–228.

coupled with new mobile technologies enables reverse surveillance by the population on the actions of government entities and actors. Where there may be some infringement of human rights the population are able to instantly record and disseminate this information globally. This then brings the hitherto opaque operation of government departments into the public domain wherever there are mobile devices and people willing to record the events. Accordingly, as the technological capability of creating a highly surveillant society exists, so does the potential for exposure on the world stage of any human rights breaches or other controversial activity undertaken by the ruling elites. With paradoxical effect, 'a state of conscious and permanent visibility that assures the automatic functioning of power'[73] that now challenges the sovereignty of the ruling power structures by making their actions visible to the world at large.

The collection of biometric data is another aspect of surveillance in the Gulf region. Governments collect and utilise biometric information such as fingerprints, iris scans, or facial recognition data to establish identification systems or enhance their surveillance capabilities. Along with this, data retention and analysis plays a significant role in surveillant practices. Governments in the GCC member states may retain and analyse large amounts of data, including metadata, browsing history, and communication records. This allows governments to gather intelligence, track individuals or groups of interest, and potentially identify threats to religious order, national security, social stability or state sovereignty. Arguably some of the inherent isolationist and authoritarian tendencies have been facilitated through the Chinese Belt and Road initiative whereby authoritarian practise has been transferred to the States, or at least encouraged. According to Demmelhuber et al, 'an evolving density of ties and established political and entrepreneurial networks of collaboration facilitated cooperation schemes that allowed the exchange and diffusion of autocratic ideas, norms and digital techniques from China to the Gulf'.[74] By appealing to the inherent isolationist tendencies of some of the States, China has been able to transfer surveillant technology to enable partnerships built upon authoritarian rule to be fostered and encouraged. Technology in these circumstances is polyvalent and caution must be exercised when comparing GCC member state priorities, against traditional Western norms and assumptions, as they are fundamentally different sovereign ideologies.

Future Technologies and the Gulf States

The Gulf States are in a unique position to facilitate the proliferation and integration of new technologies. As the Gulf States have the ability to initiate new legislation relatively quickly, they are better positioned pave the way for the

73 Michel Foucault, 'Panopticism' in A. Sheridan (ed) *Discipline & Punish: The Birth of the Prison* (Vintage Books, 1995) 195–228.

74 Demmelhuber et al. (n 68) 30.

integration of new technological solutions into Gulf State societies. In the area of drones for example, Western countries often have multiple overlapping layers of slow-to-change legislation and regulation around Civil Aviation and therapeutic goods permissions within the operational domain of unmanned aerial vehicles. For example, in Australia, the Civil Aviation Authority requires complex planning and permissions before drones are allowed to operate within the airspace provided to them. This can often mean delays of weeks before successful drone flights can take place, even if they are operating only over short distances and within visual line of sight (VLOS). Moreover, the Therapeutic Goods Administration also have strict regulations around the chain of custody of schedule drugs. This somewhat onerous bureaucratic layering of legislation operates to hamper the development of drones for the delivery of things such as medicine within Australia. However, compliance with the various General Civil Aviation Authority and other Civil Aviation Regulations, is not as onerous in the Gulf States. The UAE, under their Fourth Industrial Revolution (4IR) strategy have a commitment to 'develop conducive and innovative policies and regulations that cover the Fourth Industrial Revolution's themes and applications to ensure maintaining the privacy and well-being of citizens'.[75] Dubai, for example, already allows cutting edge medical supply delivery to be developed and deployed using drones. The Fakheeh University Hospital recently flew a delivery of medical supplies to an urban residence within a 10 km radius of the hospital.[76] According to the researchers, this beyond visual line of sight (BVLOS) delivery followed 'a series of trials that were conducted for a year at DSO, a special economic zone for knowledge and innovation and a member of the Dubai Integrated Economic Zones Authority (DIEZ)'.[77] Abu Dhabi also launched its own drone delivery of medical supplies under the UAE Fourth Industrial Revolution (4IR) Strategy, which seeks to 'strengthen the UAE's position as a global hub for the Fourth Industrial Revolution and to increase its contribution to the national economy by means of advancing innovation and future technologies'.[78] The ongoing commitment shown by some of the GCC member states, and the agility with which technology is deployed, is evidence of the ability for the Gulf to move forward at the cutting edge of technology and become a world leader in many areas of autonomous systems and deployment within their respective societies.

75 The UAE's Fourth Industrial Revolution (4IR) Strategy (n 37).

76 Khaleej Times, 'Dubai Hospital's Drone Delivers Medicines to Patient's House in First Successful Trial' *ZAWYA* (31 May 2023), https://www.zawya.com/en/business/healthcare/dubai-hospitals-drone-delivers-medicines-to-patients-house-in-first-successful-trial-eo5wbd6q.

77 Khaleej Times, 'Dubai Hospital's Drone Delivers Medicines to Patient's House in First Successful Trial' *ZAWYA* (31 May 2023), https://www.zawya.com/en/business/healthcare/dubai-hospitals-drone-delivers-medicines-to-patients-house-in-first-successful-trial-eo5wbd6q.

78 The UAE's Fourth Industrial Revolution (4IR) Strategy (n 37).

Concluding Remarks

The GCC member states are now approaching a crossroads where their ongoing future prosperity and sovereignty will be determined by their actions over the next few years. Despite the humble beginnings, rapid development, and ongoing tensions between the States, the modern Gulf community is notable for its high standard of living and increasing adoption of new ideas. As the States seek to move away from reliance on fossil fuels as their primary source of income, they are embracing increasingly sophisticated technological solutions to boost capacity and capability in all sectors of society. Amidst this changing geopolitical dynamic, the States are now moving away from waning Western influence towards China and Eastern Europe as increasingly influential trading partners. This seismic shift in alliances has potentially serious ramifications for the States and provides new vectors of influence across the Gulf. Ensuring the States' stability and sovereignty involves the fostering and development of new knowledge societies and the building of new knowledge capability and capacity within the GCC. To do this requires substantial foreign direct investment, and along with that investment comes strategic technology partnerships with multinational corporations, institutions, and research centres. In order to facilitate these arrangements, it is therefore necessary to ensure compliance with protections afforded under international intellectual property protection regimes. While the States have not always been entirely successful in their endeavours to comply with world intellectual property regimes, they are making significant progress towards achieving compliance across member states and improving the ability to attract technology partnerships and foreign direct investment. As the States move towards an uncertain and exciting post-fossil fuel future, their ability to integrate and capitalise on the benefits offered by increasingly automated technologies will be crucial to their ongoing survival and continued sovereignty.

Bibliography

Ala-Pietilä, Pekka, Yann Bonnet, Urs Bergmann, Maria Bielikova, Cecilia Bonefeld-Dahl, Wilhelm Bauer, and Loubna Bouarfa, *The Assessment List for Trustworthy Artificial Intelligence (ALTAI)*. European Commission (2020).

Arman, Husam, Simona Iammarino, J. Eduardo Ibarra-Olivo, and Neil Lee, 'Breaking Out of the Innovation Trap? Towards Promoting Private R&D Investment in Kuwait', LSE Middle East Centre, Kuwait Programme Paper Series (9 March 2021).

Baabood, A., 'The Future of the GCC Amid the Gulf Divide', in A. Krieg (ed.) *Divided Gulf. Contemporary Gulf Studies* (Singapore: Palgrave Macmillan, 2019), https://doi.org/10.1007/978-981-13-6314-6_10

Bailey, R., 'Is China Set to Become the GCC's Most Important Economic Partner by 2020? And What Does This Mean for the Region?', *Gulf Business* (2013), http://gulfbusiness.com/china-and-gcc-growing-ties/#.ViEQUi6gyoM

Bennett Moses, Lyria, 'Adapting the Law to Technological Change: A Comparison of Common Law and Legislation', (2003) 26(2) *UNSW Law Journal* 394–417 .

Business Software Alliance, US Position Paper 2023, 'AI Developers and Deployers: An Important Distinction', BSA (16 March 2023), https://www.bsa.org/policy-filings/ai-developers-and-deployers-an-important-distinction

Carroll, John, 'Intellectual Property Rights in the Middle East: A Cultural Perspective', (2001) 11 *Fordham Intellectual Property Media & Entertainment Law Journal* 555.

Cheung, C. F., W. M. Wang, Y. L. Tse and Ricky Ma, 'Knowledge-Based Intellectual Property Management for Technology Development Industry', (2013) 14(2) *Journal of Knowledge Management Practice* 1–12.

Commins, David, *The Gulf States: A Modern History* (London: Bloomsbury Publishing, 2012).

Das, T. K. and Bing-Sheng Teng, 'Between Trust and Control: Developing Confidence in Partner Cooperation in Alliances', (1998) 23(3) *The Academy of Management Review* 491–512.

Demmelhuber, Thomas, Julia Gurol and Tobias Zumbrägel, 'The COVID-19 Temptation?: Sino–Gulf Relations and Autocratic Linkages in Times of a Global Pandemic', in Zeina Hobaika, Lena-Maria Möller and Jan Claudius Völkel (eds.) *The MENA Region and COVID-19: Impact, Implications and Prospects* (London: Routledge, 2022), 19–35.

Dinopoulos, E. and P. Segerstrom, 'Intellectual Property Rights, Multinational Firms and Economic Growth', (2010) 92(1) *Journal of Development Economics* 13–27.

Donn, G. and Y. Al Manthri (eds.), *Education in the Broader Middle East: Borrowing a Baroque Arsenal* (Oxford: Symposium Books, 2013).

Dunne, Charles W., 'China's Belt and Road Initiative and US Middle East Policy', Arab Centre, Washington, DC, (2023), https://arabcenterdc.org/resource/chinas-belt-and-road-initiative-and-us-middle-east-policy/

Edler, Jacob, Knut Blind, Henning Kroll and Torben Schubert, 'Technology Sovereignty as an Emerging Frame for Innovation Policy. Defining Rationales, Ends and Means', (2023) 52(6) *Research Policy* 104765, https://doi.org/10.1016/j.respol.2023.104765

Elmuti, D. S. and A. S. Abou-Zaid, 'Patterns of Technology Transfer Among the Arab Gulf States: Opportunities and Challenges', (2013) 23(4) *International Journal of Commerce and Management* 339–353, https://doi.org/10.1108/IJCoMA-02-2012-0012

Foucault, Michel, *Discipline & Punish: The Birth of the Prison*, translated by A. Sheridan (New York: Vintage Books, 1995), 195–228.

Fromson, James and Steven Simon, 'Visions of Omani Reform', (2019) 61(4) *Survival* 99–116, https://doi.org/10.1080/00396338.2019.1637117

Gulf Cooperation Council, *Charter of the Gulf Cooperation Council* (GCC) (Riyadh, 2013), https://www.files.ethz.ch/isn/125347/1426_GCC.pdf

Gulf Cooperation Council Report, 'Engineering Net Zero', SNC Lavalin (June 2022).

Hafner, M., P. P. Raimondi and B. Bonometti, 'Geopolitics of Oil and Gas in the MENA Region', in *The Energy Sector and Energy Geopolitics in the MENA Region at a Crossroad. Perspectives on Development in the Middle East and North Africa (MENA) Region* (Cham: Springer, 2023), 265–339, https://doi.org/10.1007/978-3-031-30705-8_5

Hajjar, David P., George W. Moran, Afreen Siddiqi, Joshua E. Richardson, Laura D. Anadon and Venkatesh Narayanamurti, 'Prospects for Policy Advances in Science and Technology in the Gulf Arab States: The Role for International Partnerships', (2014) 3(3) *International Journal of Higher Education* 45–57.

Hanieh, Adam, *Money, Markets, and Monarchies: The Gulf Cooperation Council and the Political Economy of the Contemporary Middle East* (Cambridge: Cambridge University Press, 2018).

Israeli, Ofer, 'The Roundabout Outcomes of the Soviet-Afghan War', (2022) 46(1) *Asian Perspective* 1–20, https://doi.org/10.1353/apr.2022.0000

Kamal, Mohammed, Dahlan, Natrah Abdullah and Ahmad Iqbal Hakim Suhaimi, 'Industrial Revolution Reshaping Repetitive Task in Digital Workplace', (2019) 8(1.6) *International Journal of Advanced Trends in Computer Science and Engineering* 347–354.

Khaleej Times, 'Dubai Hospital's Drone Delivers Medicines to Patient's House in First Successful Trial', *ZAWYA* (31 May 2023), https://www.zawya.com/en/business/healthcare/dubai-hospitals-drone-delivers-medicines-to-patients-house-in-first-successful-trial-eo5wbd6q

Khogali, Hisham O. and Samir Mekid, 'The Blended Future of Automation and AI: Examining Some Long-Term Societal and Ethical Impact Features', (2023) 73 *Technology in Society* 102232, https://doi.org/10.1016/j.techsoc.2023.102232

Kingdom of Saudi Arabia, 'Vision 2030' (25 April 2016), 50, https://www.vision2030.gov.sa/

Krieg, A., 'The Gulf Rift—A War Over Two Irreconcilable Narratives', *Defense in Depth* (27 June 2017), https://defenceindepth.co/2017/06/26/the-gulf-rift-a-war-over-two-irreconcilable-narratives/

Martin, C. Dianne, 'The Internet as a Reverse Panopticon', *Computers and Society* (10 March 2022).

Office of the United States Trade Representative, *Special 301 Report* (Washington, DC: United States Government Publishing Office, 2022).

Office of the United States Trade Representative, *United States – Kingdom of Bahrain Free Trade Agreement*, https://ustr.gov/trade-agreements/free-trade-agreements/bahrain-fta.

Office of the United States Trade Representative, *United States – Sultanate of Oman Free Trade Agreement,* https://ustr.gov/trade-agreements/free-trade-agreements/oman-fta.

Peterson, John, 'Life after Oil: Economic Alternatives for the Arab Gulf States', (2009) 20(3) *Mediterranean Quarterly* 1–18.

———, *The Emergence of the Gulf States: Studies in Modern History* (New York: Bloomsbury Academic, 2016), https://search.ebscohost.com/login.aspx?direct=true&AuthType=shib&db=e000xww&AN=1240424&site=ehost-live

Price, David, 'The GCC Intellectual Property Regimes: Global Harmonization or Regional Integration?', in M. Ramady (ed.) *The GCC Economies* (New York: Springer, 2012), https://doi.org/10.1007/978-1-4614-1611-1_11

Price, David and Alhanoof AlDebasi, *Protecting Intellectual property in the Arabian Peninsula: The GCC States, Jordan and Yemen* (London: Routledge, 2018).

Ricken, Boris and George Malcotsis, *The Competitive Advantage of Regions and Nations: Technology Transfer Through Foreign Direct Investment* (Farnham: Taylor & Francis Group, 2011).

State of Qatar, *National Vision 2030.*

Shahbaz, Adrian, *Freedom on the Net 2018: The Rise of Digital Authoritarianism* (New York: Freedom House, 2018), https://freedomhouse.org/report/freedom-net/2018/rise-digital-authoritarianism

Smuha, Nathalie A., 'The EU Approach to Ethics Guidelines for Trustworthy Artificial Intelligence', (2019) 20(4) *Computer Law Review International* 97–106, https://doi.org/10.9785/cri-2019-200402

Sultanate of Oman, *Vision Oman 2040* (11 September 2019).

The Economist Intelligence Unit, *Innovating through Tech in the GCC*, Report for the Economic Development Board of Bahrain (EIU 2020) 10–14.

World Bank Group, *Doing Business 2020: Comparing Business Regulation in 190 Economies*, Report, 8–9.

Young, Karen E., 'The Gulf 's Eastward Turn: The Logic of Gulf–China Economic Ties', (2020) 9(2) *Journal of Arabian Studies* 236–252, https://doi.org/10.1080/21534764.2019.1768655

Zhuang, Y. and others, 'Challenges and Opportunities: From Big Data to Knowledge in AI 2.0', (2017) 18 *Frontiers of Information Technology & Electronic Engineering* 3, 3–14.

3 Building a Unified Legislative Framework for the Development and Registration for the Emerging Technologies in the GCC

Rawan Alshammari

Introduction

The GCC member states, which comprise Bahrain, Kuwait, Oman, Qatar, Saudi Arabia, and the United Arab Emirates (UAE), have made significant strides in establishing legal frameworks to protect intellectual property rights over the past few decades. These efforts are driven by the need to create a conducive environment for innovation and creativity in the region to support economic growth. In recent years, emerging technologies, such as artificial intelligence (AI), non-fungible token (NFT's) and blockchain, have become an integral part of the modern economy, contributing to economic growth, innovation, and improved quality of life. Accordingly, GCC member states have witnessed significant evolution in the adoption of emerging technologies. The rapid pace of technological advancements has led to the development of new products and services that have the potential to transform various sectors in their economies. However, the lack of a legislative framework for the development and deployment of emerging technologies in GCC member states poses a significant challenge for regulating and effectively managing these technologies. These challenges led to the need for a unified legislative framework for the registration, regulation, and commercialization of these technologies in the GCC region. This chapter aims to define the need for a legislative framework to regulate emerging technologies, the gaps in the current GCC member states' intellectual property regulations, and determine if we can create a legislative framework to regulate the emerging technologies in GCC member states in order to facilitate the transformation of their economies from an economy dependent on petrochemicals to more diversified and sustainable economies with an important component based on R&D, technology, knowledge, and innovation. The chapter examines the current legal landscape in GCC member states and analyses existing data, literature, and resources related to the development of legislative frameworks and regulations using an analytical research methodology that aims to identify the gaps and challenges in the existing legal framework and address the role of a unified legislative framework in mitigating the legal, economic, and social risks that may impact the utilization of emerging technologies. This approach focuses on synthesizing information, drawing connections, and evaluating the level of regulatory maturity of emerging technologies.

Unifying the legal framework should consider the unique characteristics of each technology and provide a comprehensive legal framework that balances the

DOI: 10.4324/9781003528517-3

interests of all stakeholders including developers, investors, users, and regulators. One of the most prominent successful experiences of GCC member states in this regard is the establishment of the GCC Patent Office, which grants patents enforceable in all member states. The office also provides a unified platform for patent filing and examination, which reduces the time and costs associated with the patent application process. In addition to patents, GCC member states have enacted laws to protect trademarks, copyrights, and trade secrets. These laws provide legal recourse to owners of intellectual property rights and serve as deterrents to infringement and piracy. Overall, this study aims to contribute to the development of a robust and comprehensive legal framework for emerging technologies in GCC member states, which would encourage innovation, protect public safety, and promote economic growth. In conclusion, this study provides insights into the need for a unified legislative framework for the development and registration of emerging technologies in the GCC member states.

Background and Context

The Gulf Cooperation Council (GCC) Member States

The Gulf Cooperation Council (GCC) member states are an economic and political alliance comprising Bahrain, Kuwait, Oman, Qatar, Saudi Arabia, and the United Arab Emirates (UAE). The GCC was formed in 1981 with the aim of promoting economic cooperation and integration between its member states. Over the years, the GCC has undertaken several initiatives to promote regional economic growth and development.[1]

One of the key areas of focus for the GCC is the development of a unified legal framework to govern various aspects of economic activity in the region. GCC member states have recognized the importance of a harmonized legal system to promote economic integration, facilitate cross-border trade, and attract foreign investment.

The GCC has made significant progress in developing a unified legal framework in several areas including trade, customs, and investment. For instance, the GCC has implemented a unified customs law that regulates the movement of goods within a region and facilitates cross-border trade.[2] Similarly, the GCC developed a unified investment law that provides a legal framework for foreign investment in the region.[3]

1 Gulf Cooperation Council, https://www.gcc-sg.org/en-us/GCC/Pages/default.aspx
2 Gulf Cooperation Council, 'Customs Union', https://www.gcc-sg.org/ar-sa/CooperationAndAchievements/Achievements/EconomicCooperation/TheCustomsUnion/Achievements/Pages/IITheGCCCustomsUnionJanuary200.aspx
3 International Monetary Fund, 'GCC Trade and Foreign Investment', *IMF Policy Papers* (4 December 2018), https://www.imf.org/en/Publications/Policy-Papers/Issues/2018/12/04/pp120618gcc-trade-and-foreign-investment.

However, the development of a unified legal framework for emerging technologies remains in its early stages. The rapid pace of technological advancement has created a fragmented and inconsistent legal landscape that can impede innovation and hinder the growth of emerging technology sectors. This has prompted calls for the development of a unified legal framework that can facilitate the development and registration of emerging technologies in the region and provide clarity and certainty to businesses and investors operating in the region.

In recent years, several initiatives have been undertaken to develop a unified legal framework for emerging technologies in the GCC member states. For instance, the UAE takes a soft approach to regulate AI products, mostly in the form of non-binding guidelines in various sectors of the economy, including healthcare and transportation.[4]

Despite these initiatives, a comprehensive and unified legal framework for emerging technologies in GCC member states have yet to be developed.

Regulatory Challenges and Opportunities for Emerging Technologies in GCC Member States

Emerging technologies, such as Artificial Intelligence (AI), blockchain, and the Internet of Things (IoT), have the potential to transform various sectors of the economy, including healthcare, finance, transportation, and energy. Although these technologies offer considerable opportunities for economic growth and social welfare, they also pose significant challenges for regulators. The emergence of new technologies has created the need for a comprehensive framework to ensure safe and responsible development and deployment. GCC member states, like many other nations, have recognized the importance of emerging technologies for their economic growth and have taken various steps to promote their development. However, the absence of a unified legislative framework has created regulatory gaps, resulting in uncertainty and hindering the growth of emerging technological industries.

Several studies have been conducted on the regulatory challenges and opportunities for emerging technologies, with a focus on developing member states such as the majority of GCC member states. Similarly, Shkvarya et al. analyzed the development of the high-tech segment in the GCC, focusing on the aviation component of Bahrain. Specific to the aviation sector, this study sheds light on the efforts and challenges of developing a high-tech industry in the GCC. These findings contribute to understanding the broader context in which a unified legislative framework for emerging technologies can be implemented.[5] By contrast, some studies have focused on regulatory frameworks for emerging technologies in developed

4 Digital Dubai, 'Artificial Intelligence Principles & Ethics', *Version 1.6* (30 December 2018), https://www.digitaldubai.ae/initiatives/ai-principles-ethics

5 L. V. Shkvarya, Irina A. Aidrous, Elizaveta I. Ruzina, A. V. Savinsky and Sergey I. Rodin, 'Development of High-Tech Segment in the GCC Region on the Example of the Aviation Component of the Kingdom of Bahrain', *IOP Conference Series: Materials Science and Engineering* 476 (2019): 1–7.

member states. Floridi and Cowls examined the ethical and regulatory challenges in the deployment of artificial intelligence in the European Union, emphasizing the need for a human-centric approach.[6] Furthermore, Floridi's work delves into the concept of the "infosphere" and its impact on human reality. Although not specifically focused on the GCC, Florida's research provides a theoretical understanding of how emerging technologies are reshaping society and highlights the need for legal frameworks to adapt to these transformative changes.[7]

In the context of IoT, Fabiano examined the legal issues related to data protection laws and the Internet of Things (IoT), with a focus on the European General Data Protection Regulation (GDPR). Although not specific to the GCC region, Fabiano study provides insights into the legal considerations and challenges associated with the IoT, which are relevant to the development of a unified legislative framework.[8]

Other scholars have emphasized the need for a unified legal framework for emerging technologies in the GCC region. For instance, Zulu[9] explored the development of an emerging information and communication technology policy framework for Africa. Although not directly related to the GCC region, Zulu's study provides insights into policy considerations and approaches to emerging technologies in a regional context. These findings contribute to the broader discourse on building effective legislative frameworks for emerging technologies, which can inform the development of a unified legislative framework in the GCC.[10]

On the other hand, several studies point to the growing gap between emerging technologies and law. For instance, Marchant's[11] study examined the growing gap between emerging technologies and existing legal frameworks. Marchant's study highlights the challenges faced by regulators in keeping pace with rapidly advancing technologies and suggests the need for adaptable and flexible legal frameworks. The insights from this study are applicable to the GCC context and provide a foundation for developing a unified legislative framework that can accommodate emerging technologies. In addition, Ludlow et al. explored the limitations of traditional regulatory approaches and the regulatory challenges associated with

6 L. Floridi and Josh Cowls, 'A Unified Framework of Five Principles for AI in Society', *Harvard Data Science Review* 1 (2019): 2–15.

7 L. Floridi, *The Fourth Revolution: How the Infosphere Is Reshaping Human Reality* (Oxford: Oxford Unversity Press, 2014).

8 Nicola Fabiano, 'Internet of Things and the Legal Issues Related to the Data Protection Law According to the New European General Data Protection Regulation', *Athens Journal of Law* 3 (2017): 201–214.

Karinne Ludlow, Diana Meagan Bowman, Jake Gatof and Michael G. Bennett. 'Regulating Emerging and Future Technologies in the Present', *NanoEthics* 9 (2015): 151–163.

9 Saul F. C. Zulu, 'Emerging Information and Communication Technology Policy Framework for Africa', *The International Journal of ICT Research and Development in Africa* 1 (2010): 46–64.

10 Saul F. C. Zulu, 'Emerging Information and Communication Technology Policy Framework for Africa', *The International Journal of ICT Research and Development in Africa* 1 (2010): 46–64.

11 Gary E. Marchant, *The Growing Gap Between Emerging Technologies and the Law* (Berlin: Springer, 2011).

emerging and future technologies, while emphasizing the need for proactive and anticipatory governance frameworks.[12] The insights from the Ludlow et al. study are relevant for building a unified legislative framework in the GCC that promotes innovation while addressing potential risks and ethical concerns. Finally, to define the general framework for Gulf Cooperation Council (GCC) member states, Alhaiyaf critically analyzed the legal role and functions of GCC member states. While not specifically focused on emerging technologies, Alhaiyaf's study provides valuable insights into the legal framework and governance structures of the GCC. Understanding the legal context and role of the GCC is crucial for building a unified legislative framework for emerging technologies in the region.[13]

In conclusion, the reviewed papers highlight the importance of developing a unified legislative framework for emerging technologies in GCC. These studies emphasize the transformative potential of technologies such as blockchain, IoT, and nanotechnology, while discussing the legal considerations, challenges, and opportunities associated with their adoption. The insights provided contribute to the understanding of the complexities surrounding the development of a unified legislative framework in GCC, emphasizing the importance of adaptable and forward-thinking governance approaches. Further research should focus on addressing the specific legal challenges within the GCC context and provide practical recommendations for policymakers and stakeholders to build an effective and harmonized regulatory framework.

Gaps in the GCC Countries' Legal Systems Related to the Implementation of Emerging Technologies

GCC member states have recognized the importance of emerging technologies for their economic growth and have taken various steps to promote their development. However, the absence of a unified legislative framework has created regulatory gaps, resulting in uncertainty and hindering the growth of emerging technology industries.

In the area of AI, GCC member states have shown an interest in promoting AI innovation and have established several initiatives and strategies to foster its development. For instance, the UAE launched its AI strategy in 2017, which aims to position it as a global leader in AI by 2031. The strategy includes several initiatives, such as the establishment of the UAE Artificial Intelligence Office and development of a national Artificial Intelligence Strategy. Similarly, Saudi Arabia has launched its National Strategy for Data and Artificial Intelligence (NSDAI), which aims to position it as a global hub for data and AI by 2030.[14]

12 Karinne Ludlow et al. (n 8).

13 Khalid Nasser Ali Alhaiyaf, 'A Critical Analysis of the Legal Role and Functions of the Gulf Cooperation Council (GCC)', Thesis, University of Sussex, 2014.

14 Government of UAE, 'UAE National Strategy for Artificial Intelligence 2031', https://ai.gov.ae/wp-content/uploads/2021/07/UAE-National-Strategy-for-Artificial-Intelligence-2031.pdf.

In the area of blockchain, the GCC member states have also shown interest in promoting blockchain innovation. For instance, the UAE launched its Blockchain Strategy 2021,[15] which aims to position it as a global leader in blockchain technology by 2021. The strategy includes several initiatives, such as the establishment of the Emirates Blockchain Strategy and the development of a Blockchain Regulatory Framework. Similarly, Bahrain[16] established the region's first regulatory sandbox for fintech and blockchain startups, allowing companies to test their products and services in a controlled environment.

In the area of the IoT, GCC member states have recognized the importance of data protection and privacy in the context of IoT and have taken several measures to promote data protection and privacy. For instance, the UAE has established the Emirates Data Protection Authority (EDPA), which is responsible for enforcing data protection and privacy regulations. Similarly, Saudi Arabia has enacted the Personal Data Protection Law, which aims to protect the privacy of personal data.[17]

Despite these initiatives, the absence of a unified legislative framework for the development and registration of emerging technologies has created regulatory gaps, resulting in uncertainty and hindering the growth of these industries. A unified legislative framework would provide regulatory clarity, promote innovation, and ensure safe and responsible deployment of emerging technologies in the GCC region.

The framework should address the legal and regulatory challenges of emerging technologies, while considering their unique economic, social, and cultural contexts. Furthermore, it should foster collaboration among governments, industries, and civil society to promote innovation, investment, and social welfare.

GCC member states have shown keen interest in promoting emerging technologies – including AI, blockchain, and IoT – and have established several initiatives and strategies to foster their development. In this section, I discuss the development of legislative frameworks and regulations in each of the GCC member states separately to determine the level of regulatory maturity in relation to emerging technologies.

Saudi Arabia

In recent years, Saudi Arabia has taken significant steps to promote the development of emerging technologies and create a regulatory environment that supports innovation while safeguarding the public interest. One notable initiative was the

15 Government of UAE. 'UAE Blockchain Strategy 2021 Sets Ambitious Goals to Make the Country a World Leader in the Field', https://u.ae/en/about-the-uae/strategies-initiatives-and-awards/strategies-plans-and-visions/strategies-plans-and-visions-untill-2021/emirates-blockchain-strategy-2021.

16 Kingdom of Bahrain, 'Fintech and Blockchain', https://www.cbb.gov.bh/fintech/.

17 Kingdom of Saudi Arabia, 'Personal Data Protection Law', https://www.my.gov.sa/wps/portal/snp/content/dataprotection/?lang=en

NSDAI, launched in 2019. The strategy aims to position Saudi Arabia as a global hub for data and AI innovation, and set ambitious targets for the development and adoption of these technologies.[18] To achieve these goals, the strategy includes a comprehensive framework that covers various aspects of the data and AI ecosystem including governance, infrastructure, talent development, and regulatory and legal frameworks. This framework is designed to provide clarity and certainty for investors and entrepreneurs, foster innovation and creativity, and ensure the development and deployment of emerging technologies in a responsible and ethical manner.

In addition to the NSDAI, Saudi Arabia has established several regulatory bodies to monitor the development and deployment of emerging technologies. For example, the Saudi Data and Artificial Intelligence Authority (SDAIA) is responsible for driving the implementation of the NSDAI and overseeing the development of the data and AI ecosystems in the country. The authority has been given broad powers to regulate the collection, processing, and sharing of data as well as the development and deployment of AI technologies.[19]

Moreover, Saudi Arabia has introduced several regulations to facilitate the development of emerging technologies, such as the Cloud Computing Regulatory Framework which came into force from 18/4/1442H, corresponding to 3/12/2020,[20] to set out the requirements for cloud service providers operating in the country. The framework includes provisions on data security, privacy, and cross-border data flows, and is designed to provide a secure and enabling environment for cloud computing services. Furthermore, Saudi Arabia has been active in promoting blockchain technology, with several government initiatives and partnerships aimed at developing blockchain solutions for various sectors such as finance, logistics, and healthcare. Overall, Saudi Arabia's regulatory framework for emerging technologies is evolving rapidly with significant investments and initiatives aimed at promoting innovation and providing a supportive environment for entrepreneurs and investors. While challenges remain, such as the need to ensure the privacy, security, and ethical use of emerging technologies, Saudi Arabia's regulatory landscape is moving in a positive direction, with a clear focus on creating a conducive environment for innovation and growth.

United Arab Emirates

The UAE is one of the leading member states in the GCC region in terms of its regulatory framework for emerging technologies. The UAE government has taken

18 Saudi Data and Artificial Intelligence Authority, 'National Strategy for Data and Artificial Intelligence', https://ai.sa/.

19 Saudi Data and Artificial Intelligence Authority, 'SDAIA Regulatory Arrangements', https://sdaia.gov.sa/ar/SDAIA/about/Pages/RegulationsAndPolicies.aspx.

20 'Saudi Cloud Computing Regulatory Framework', The Communications, Space & Technology Commission, https://www.cst.gov.sa/en/RulesandSystems/RegulatoryDocuments/Pages/CCRF.aspx.

a proactive approach to promote innovation and has established various initiatives to support the development and deployment of emerging technologies, such as AI, blockchain, and IoT.

In 2017, the UAE government launched the UAE Strategy for Artificial Intelligence[21], which aimed to position the country as a leader in AI research and development. The strategy includes initiatives such as the establishment of the National Program for AI, creation of a regulatory framework for AI, and promotion of AI education and training programs. The UAE has also launched various initiatives to promote the development of blockchain technology, including the Emirates Blockchain Strategy[22] and Dubai Blockchain Strategy, both of which aim to make the Emirates the first blockchain-powered government.[23]

The UAE government has implemented various regulations to ensure safe and responsible deployment of emerging technologies. For instance, in 2019, the UAE government enacted the UAE Cybersecurity Laws and regulations, which includes provisions related to the protection of critical information infrastructure and the prevention of cybercrime. The law also mandates that all organizations in the UAE comply with certain cybersecurity standards and adopt appropriate measures to protect their networks and systems.[24]

In the area of the Internet of Things (IoT), Ghandour and Woodford study on "Regulating Internet of Things: The Case of the United Arab Emirates" highlights several key points. Ghandour and Woodford's study emphasizes that individuals and businesses in the UAE have the right to information, including data generated by the Internet of Things (IoT). However, alongside this right, there is an ethical obligation to use information responsibly and ethically. The study also emphasizes the importance of accountability and control in IoT systems to prevent potential crimes and ensure a well-managed environment.[25]

The UAE recognized the potential risks and issues associated with the widespread adoption of IoT technology and implemented IoT policies and procedures as early as 2019. These policies and procedures aim to govern the effective and efficient use of IoT technology, considering the five moral dimensions that serve as a basis for governing IoT usage. These dimensions are likely to refer to ethical considerations related to privacy, security, data ownership, transparency, and consent.

21 Government of UAE, 'Emirates Strategy for Artificial Intelligence' (2017), https://u.ae/en/about-the-uae/strategies-initiatives-and-awards/strategies-plans-and-visions/government-services-and-digital-transformation/uae-strategy-for-artificial-intelligence

22 Government of UAE, 'Emirates Blockchain Strategy' (2018), https://u.ae/en/about-the-uae/strategies-initiatives-and-awards/strategies-plans-and-visions/strategies-plans-and-visions-untill-2021/emirates-blockchain-strategy-2021

23 Government of Dubai, 'Dubai Blockchain Strategy', https://www.digitaldubai.ae/initiatives/blockchain

24 Government of UAE, 'UAE Cybersecurity Law' (2021), https://u.ae/en/resources/laws

25 Ghandour, Ahmad and Brendon J. Woodford, 'Regulating Internet of Things: The Case of the United Arab Emirates', *TEM Journal* (2021), https://doi.org/10.18421/TEM103-04

While acknowledging the weaknesses, risks, and challenges associated with IoT, the Ghandour and Woodford study argues that the significant benefits of IoT outweigh its disadvantages, particularly in the context of today's strong internet connectivity.[26] Overall, the UAE's regulatory framework for emerging technologies is comprehensive and proactive, reflecting its commitment to promoting innovation and ensuring the safe and responsible deployment of emerging technologies. However, as with any regulatory framework, challenges and opportunities for improvement still exist. For instance, it is necessary to ensure that the regulatory framework remains flexible and adaptive to new and emerging technologies and that it balances the interests of all stakeholders, including consumers, businesses, and government agencies.

Bahrain

Bahrain has also actively promoted emerging technologies, particularly in the financial sector. The Central Bank of Bahrain has been a pioneer in developing regulatory sandboxes, which allow fintech firms to test and experiment with new technologies in a controlled environment before going to market.[27] Bahrain has also established a FinTech Bay, a co-working space and incubator for fintech start-ups, and launched a regulatory sandbox for open banking in 2019.[28]

In terms of AI, Bahrain has also been active in developing policies and strategies for its safe and responsible deployment. In 2018, the government launched its National Artificial Intelligence Strategy,[29] which aimed to establish Bahrain as a regional hub for AI development and deployment. This strategy includes initiatives to promote AI research and development, build AI infrastructure, and establish a legal and regulatory framework for AI.

Bahrain has taken steps to promote the development of blockchain technology, particularly in the financial sector. In 2019, the Central Bank of Bahrain issued regulations for crypto-asset services, which established a regulatory framework for crypto-assets and related activities, such as trading, custody, and transfer. These regulations also require companies engaged in crypto-asset services to comply with anti-money laundering and counterterrorism financing measures.[30]

Overall, Bahrain's regulatory framework for emerging technologies is characterized by a focus on innovation, experimentation, and collaboration between the

26 Ghandour, Ahmad and Brendon J. Woodford, 'Regulating Internet of Things: The Case of the United Arab Emirates', *TEM Journal* (2021), https://doi.org/10.18421/TEM103-04

27 Central Bank of Bahrain, 'Central Bank of Bahrain Enhances Fintech Regulatory Sandbox to Boost Innovation', https://www.cbb.gov.bh/media-center/central-bank-of-bahrain-enhances-fintech-regulatory-sandbox-to-boost-innovation/

28 Central Bank of Bahrain, 'Regulatory Sandbox Framework', https://www.cbb.gov.bh/fintech/.

29 H. Al-Ammal and M. Aljawder, 'Strategy for Artificial Intelligence in Bahrain: Challenges and Opportunities', In Azar, E., Haddad, A.N. (Eds.) *Artificial Intelligence in the Gulf* (Palgrave Macmillan, Singapore, 2021), 47–67.

30 Central Bank of Bahrain, 'Crypto-Asset Platform Operators' (2019), https://www.cbb.gov.bh/wp-content/uploads/2018/12/Crypto-Currency-Regulation-Version-7.pdf

public and private sectors. The country's regulatory sandboxes and fintech initiatives have helped to create a supportive environment for the development of emerging technologies, particularly in the financial sector. Simultaneously, Bahrain recognized the importance of establishing a legal and regulatory framework for emerging technologies to ensure their safe and responsible deployment, as demonstrated by its initiatives in the areas of artificial intelligence and blockchain.

Kuwait

Kuwait has also taken steps to promote the development and adoption of emerging technologies, particularly in the areas of AI and IoT. In 2019, the government launched the Kuwait Vision 2035 initiative,[31] which aimed to transform the country into a hub for innovation and technology. As part of this initiative, the government established several programs and initiatives to support the development of emerging technologies. One such initiative is the Kuwait Foundation for the Advancement of Sciences (KFAS), which launched several initiatives to support the development of emerging technologies, including the KFAS Innovation Challenge, which provides funding and mentorship to innovative start-ups and small to medium size enterprises (SMEs). The KFAS has also established several research centers and institutes in collaboration with local and international partners to advance research and development in various fields, including AI and robotics.[32]

Despite these efforts, the regulatory framework for emerging technologies in Kuwait is still in its early stages and there is a need for a comprehensive legal framework to ensure their safe and responsible development and deployment.

Overall, Kuwait is taking steps to promote the development and adoption of emerging technologies; however, there is still a need for a comprehensive legal and regulatory framework to ensure their safe and responsible deployment. The initiatives and programs launched by the government and organizations include Kuwait National Industrial Projects (KNIP) to provide a strong foundation for the development of emerging technologies in Kuwait, which should be further supported by a comprehensive legal framework that balances innovation and regulation.

Oman

Oman is taking steps to promote the development and adoption of emerging technologies, particularly in the areas of AI and blockchain. The Omani government has recognized the potential of emerging technologies to transform the country's economy and society and has launched several initiatives to support its development.

One of the key initiatives in this regard is Oman Vision 2040, which was launched in 2020 with the aim of transforming Oman into a knowledge-based

31 State of Kuwait, 'Kuwait Vision 2035 "New Kuwait"', Ministry of Foreign Affairs, https://www.mofa.gov.kw/en/kuwait-state/kuwait-vision-2035/

32 Kuwait Foundation for the Advancement of Sciences, 'Innovation', https://www.kfas.org/

society and diversified economy. As part of this vision, the government has identified emerging technologies, such as AI, blockchain, and IoT, as key enablers and has outlined several initiatives to support their development and adoption.[33] For instance, the government launched the Oman Digital Strategy, which aims to provide a comprehensive roadmap for the development of the digital economy in Oman. This strategy includes initiatives to promote the development of emerging technologies, such as AI and blockchain, and to create an enabling environment for their adoption by businesses and government agencies.[34]

In addition, the government has established several initiatives to support the development of emerging technologies, including the Oman Technology Fund, which provides funding and support to startups and SMEs in the technology sector. The fund focuses on supporting companies that are working on emerging technologies, such as AI, blockchain, and IoT, and has established several incubators and accelerators to support their development.[35]

Despite these initiatives, the regulatory framework for emerging technologies in Oman is still in its early stages and there is a need for a comprehensive legal framework to ensure their safe and responsible development and deployment. The Omani government has recognized this need and taken steps to establish a legal and regulatory framework for emerging technologies as part of Oman Vision 2040.

For instance, in 2019, the Omani government issued a Royal Decree on the Protection of Personal Data,[36] which aimed to regulate the collection, processing, and storage of personal data in Oman. The decree includes provisions related to emerging technologies such as AI and blockchain, and is expected to create a legal framework for their safe and responsible deployment.

Overall, Oman is taking steps to promote the development and adoption of emerging technologies, particularly AI and blockchain. The initiatives launched by the government, such as Oman Vision 2040 and Oman Digital Strategy, provide a strong foundation for the development of emerging technologies in Oman. However, there remains a need for a comprehensive legal and regulatory framework to ensure safe and responsible deployment.

Qatar

Qatar has taken steps to promote the development and adoption of emerging technologies, particularly in the areas of AI and blockchain. The Qatari government has recognized the potential of emerging technologies to transform the

33 Sultanate of Oman, Ministry of Commerce, 'Industry and Investment Promotion', *Oman Vision 2040* (2020), https://www.oman2040.om/programs?lang=en

34 Oman, Ministry of Transport, Communications and Information Technology, 'Oman Digital Strategy' (2020), https://www.ita.gov.om/itaportal/mediacenter/Document_detail.aspx?NID=55

35 Oman Technology Fund, https://www.otf.om/

36 Oman, *Royal Decree 6/2022 Promulgating the Personal Data Protection Law of the Sultanate of Oman.*

country's economy and society and has launched several initiatives to support its development.[37]

One of the key initiatives in this regard is Qatar National Vision 2030, which was launched in 2008 with the aim of transforming Qatar into an advanced society capable of achieving sustainable development. As part of this vision, the government has identified emerging technologies such as AI, blockchain, and IoT as key enablers and has outlined several initiatives to support their development and adoption. For instance, the government launched the Digital Qatar strategy, which aims to provide a comprehensive roadmap for the development of the digital economy in Qatar. The strategy includes initiatives to promote the development of emerging technologies, such as AI and blockchain, and to create an enabling environment for their adoption by businesses and government agencies.[38]

In addition, the government has established several initiatives to support the development of emerging technologies, including Qatar Science and Technology Park, which provides funding and support to start-ups and SMEs in the technology sector. The park focuses on supporting companies that are working on emerging technologies, such as AI, blockchain, and IoT, and has established several incubators and accelerators to support their development.[39] Despite these initiatives, the regulatory framework for emerging technologies in Qatar is still in its early stages and there is a need for a comprehensive legal framework to ensure their safe and responsible development and deployment. The Qatari government has recognized this need and taken steps to establish a legal and regulatory framework for emerging technologies. For instance, in 2020, the Qatari government issued a Data Privacy Law that aimed to regulate the collection, processing, and storage of personal data in Qatar. The law includes provisions related to emerging technologies such as AI and blockchain, and is expected to create a legal framework for their safe and responsible deployment.[40]

Overall, Qatar is taking steps to promote the development and adoption of emerging technologies, particularly in AI and blockchain. The initiatives launched by the government, such as the Qatar National Vision 2030 and the Digital Qatar strategy, provide a strong foundation for the development of emerging technologies in Qatar. However, there is still a need for a comprehensive legal and regulatory framework to ensure their safe and responsible deployment.

37 State of Qatar, 'Qatar National Vision 2030', Ministry of Foreign Affairs of Qatar, Qatar National Vision 2030 - Government Communications Office (gco.gov.qa)

38 'Digital Qatar', Ministry of Transport and Communications, https://www.mcit.gov.qa/en/qatar-digital-government .

39 'Qatar Science & Technology Park', *Qatar Foundation*, https://qstp.org.qa/

40 'Data Privacy Law', Ministry of Transport and Communications, https://hukoomi.gov.qa/en/news/motc-releases-guidelines-on-personal-data-privacy-protection-law

Recommendations to Develop the GCC Countries' Laws and Regulations in the Area of the Emerging Technologies

The GCC member states are in a unique position to take advantage of the opportunities presented by emerging technologies. The region has a young and growing population, strong economy, and commitment to innovation. With the right regulatory framework in place, GCC member states can become leading hubs for the development and deployment of emerging technologies. As evidenced by the analysis of the current regulations and future initiatives in the GCC member states with regard to emerging technology laws and regulations, there is a huge gap between the GCC member states; some are very advanced and pay great attention to supporting the growth of emerging technologies legislatively, while others are still suffering in terms of developing the legislative environment to comply with the growth of emerging technologies. Accordingly, the absence of a unified legislative framework has created challenges in the development, registration, and deployment of these technologies. A unified legal framework would provide regulatory clarity, promote innovation, and ensure safe and responsible deployment of emerging technologies in the GCC region.

Developing Unified Laws and Regulations in Emerging Technologies for GCC Member States' Key Benefits

Developing unified laws and regulations in the area of emerging technologies for GCC member states offers several benefits:

- Harmonization and consistency: By establishing unified laws and regulations, GCC member states can ensure consistency and coherence in their approaches to regulating emerging technologies. This eliminates discrepancies and contradictions that may arise from separate and fragmented regulatory frameworks, creating a more predictable and favorable environment for businesses and investors operating across the GCC region.
- Facilitating cross-border collaboration: Emerging technologies often transcend national boundaries and require seamless collaboration and interoperability between member states. Unified laws and regulations enable smoother cross-border transactions, data sharing, and technology adoption which facilitates innovation, research, and development across the GCC member states.
- Attracting foreign investments and talent: A unified regulatory framework signals a cohesive and progressive approach to emerging technologies, making the GCC region an attractive destination for foreign investors and talented individuals. It provides a clear and stable regulatory environment, reduces barriers to entry, and fosters innovation-driven economic growth.
- Sharing best practices and knowledge: Developing unified laws and regulations encourages knowledge sharing and the exchange of best practices among the GCC member states. This enables them to leverage each other's experiences and expertise, avoid duplication of efforts, and benefit from collective wisdom to shape effective regulatory frameworks for emerging technologies.

- Enhancing regional competitiveness: A unified regulatory framework in the area of emerging technologies allows GCC member states to position themselves as unified blocs, presenting a stronger and more competitive front in the global landscape. This cohesive approach enhances the region's attractiveness as a hub for emerging technology research, development, and deployment which fosters collaboration and creates a critical mass of expertise and resources.
- Addressing transnational challenges: Many emerging technologies pose transnational challenges that require a coordinated response. Issues such as data protection, cybersecurity, and cross-border data flows can be addressed more effectively through unified regulations that ensure a consistent and cohesive approach across GCC member states.
- Streamlining compliance and enforcement: Unified laws and regulations simplify the compliance and enforcement processes for businesses operating within the GCC region. This reduces the burden of navigating multiple regulatory regimes, making it easier for companies to understand and comply with the rules, resulting in improved efficiency and reduced costs.

Overall, developing unified laws and regulations in the area of emerging technologies for GCC member states has numerous advantages, including harmonization, collaboration, attractiveness to foreign investment, enhanced competitiveness, and streamlined compliance. It sets the stage for a unified and forward-looking approach to regulating emerging technologies, enabling the GCC region to unlock the full potential of these technologies for economic growth and societal development.

Recommendations for Developing Unified Laws and Regulations in the Area of Emerging Technologies in the GCC Member States

The development of a unified regulatory framework for emerging technologies is complex and challenging. However, the GCC member states have the potential to become leaders in this area. They can create a supportive environment for innovation and economic growth by developing a comprehensive and flexible framework that balances the interests of all stakeholders.

- The framework should be sufficiently comprehensive and flexible to accommodate the rapid pace of technological change.
- The framework should balance the interests of all stakeholders including governments, businesses, and consumers.
- The framework should be transparent and accessible to all stakeholders.
- The framework should be enforced effectively in all the GCC member states.

In conclusion, this chapter has highlighted the key benefits and recommendations of developing unified laws and regulations for emerging technologies in GCC member states based on the analyses of the current situation in GCC member states; however, it is worth noting that there are potential drawbacks and challenges associated with building a unified legislative framework for the development and registration of emerging technologies in the region. There is a unique difference in the economic, social, and cultural contexts of each GCC country. Moreover, some member states may be more advanced in certain areas of emerging technologies than others. Implementing a unified legislative framework may hinder the progress of member states that are more advanced as they may need to align their regulations with less technologically advanced member states. Conversely, less advanced member states may struggle to comply with the regulatory requirements imposed by more advanced member states. Any unified regulatory approach should carefully consider these factors to ensure safe and responsible development and deployment of emerging technologies in the GCC region. Moreover, a unified legislative framework would provide regulatory clarity, promote innovation, and ensure safe and responsible deployment of emerging technologies in the region.

Further research and analysis are required to address specific legal challenges and to provide recommendations for building a comprehensive and adaptable regulatory framework that fosters the growth of emerging technologies in GCC member states.

Bibliography

Al-Ammal, H. and M. Aljawder, 'Strategy for Artificial Intelligence in Bahrain: Challenges and Opportunities', In Azar, E., Haddad, A.N. (Eds), *Artificial Intelligence in the Gulf* (Palgrave Macmillan, Singapore, 2021), 47–67.

Alhaiyaf, Khalid Nasser Ali, 'A Critical Analysis of the Legal Role and Functions of the Gulf Cooperation Council (GCC)', (2014). Thesis. https://hdl.handle.net/10779/uos.23402909.v1

Ashton, Kevin, 'That 'Internet of Things' Thing', *RFiD Journal* 22, no. 7 (2009): 97–114.

Central Bank of Bahrain, 'Central Bank of Bahrain Enhances Fintech Regulatory Sandbox to Boost Innovation', https://www.cbb.gov.bh/media-center/central-bank-of-bahrain-enhances-fintech-regulatory-sandbox-to-boost-innovation/

Central Bank of Bahrain, 'Crypto-Asset Platform Operators' (2019), https://www.cbb.gov.bh/wp-content/uploads/2018/12/Crypto-Currency-Regulation-Version-7.pdf

Central Bank of Bahrain, 'Regulatory Sandbox Framework', https://www.cbb.gov.bh/fintech/

Data Privacy Law, 'Ministry of Transport and Communication'.

Digital Dubai, 'Artificial Intelligence Principles & Ethics', Version 1.6, Issued on 30/12/2018, https://www.digitaldubai.ae/initiatives/ai-principles-ethics

Digital Qatar, 'Ministry of Transport and Communications', https://www.mcit.gov.qa/en/qatar-digital-government

Fabiano, Nicola, 'Internet of Things and the Legal Issues Related to the Data Protection Law According to the New European General Data Protection Regulation', (2017).

Floridi, L., 'The Fourth Revolution: How the Infosphere is Reshaping Human Reality' Oxford University Press (2014).

Floridi, L. and Josh Cowls, 'A Unified Framework of Five Principles for AI in Society, Harvard Data Science Review 1–14', *1*(1) (2019).

Ghandour, Ahmad and Brendon J. Woodford, 'Regulating Internet of Things: The Case of the United Arab Emirates', 1031–1038, *TEM Journal* (2021).

Government of Bahrain, 'Fintech and Blockchain', https://www.cbb.gov.bh/fintech/

Government of Dubai, 'Dubai Blockchain Strategy', https://www.digitaldubai.ae/initiatives/blockchain

Government of Saudi Arabia, 'Personal Data Protection Law', https://www.my.gov.sa/wps/portal/snp/content/dataprotection/?lang=en

Government of UAE, 'Emirates Blockchain Strategy' (2018), https://u.ae/en/about-the-uae/strategies-initiatives-and-awards/strategies-plans-and-visions/strategies-plans-and-visions-untill-2021/emirates-blockchain-strategy-2021

Government of UAE, 'Emirates Strategy for Artificial Intelligence' (2017), https://u.ae/en/about-the-uae/strategies-initiatives-and-awards/strategies-plans-and-visions/government-services-and-digital-transformation/uae-strategy-for-artificial-intelligence

Government of UAE, 'UAE Blockchain Strategy 2021 Sets Ambitious Goals to Make the Country a World Leader in the Field', https://u.ae/en/about-the-uae/strategies-initiatives-and-awards/strategies-plans-and-visions/strategies-plans-and-visions-untill-2021/emirates-blockchain-strategy-2021

Government of UAE, 'UAE Cybersecurity Laws' (2021), https://u.ae/en/resources/laws

Government of UAE, 'UAE National Strategy for Artificial Intelligence 2031', https://ai.gov.ae/wp-content/uploads/2021/07/UAE-National-Strategy-for-Artificial-Intelligence-2031.pdf

Gulf Cooperation Council, 'Customs Union', https://www.gcc-sg.org/ar-sa/CooperationAndAchievements/Achievements/EconomicCooperation/TheCustomsUnion/Achievements/Pages/IITheGCCCustomsUnionJanuary200.aspx

Gulf Cooperation Council, https://www.gcc-sg.org/en-us/GCC/Pages/default.aspx

International Monetary Fund, 'GCC Trade and Foreign Investment', IMF Policy Papers (4 December 2018), https://www.imf.org/en/Publications/Policy-Papers/Issues/2018/12/04/pp120618gcc-trade-and-foreign-investment

Kuwait Foundation for the Advancement of Sciences, 'Innovation', https://www.kfas.org/

'Kuwait Vision 2035 "New Kuwait"', Kuwait Government, Ministry of Foreign Affairs, https://www.mofa.gov.kw/en/kuwait-state/kuwait-vision-2035/

Ludlow, Karinne, Diana Meagan Bowman, Jake Gatof and Michael G. Bennett, 'Regulating Emerging and Future Technologies in the Present, 151-163', *NanoEthics* 9 (2015).

Marchant, Gary E., 'The Growing Gap Between Emerging Technologies and the Legal-Ethical Oversight, The Pacing Problem, Springer' (2011).

Ministry of Commerce, 'Industry and Investment Promotion', Oman Vision 2040 (2020), https://www.oman2040.om/programs?lang=en

Ministry of Transport, Communications and Information Technology, 'Oman Digital Strategy' (2020), https://www.ita.gov.om/itaportal/mediacenter/Document_detail.aspx?NID=55

Nakamoto, S., 'Bitcoin: A Peer-to-Peer Electronic Cash System' Satoshi Nakomoto Institute, Texas, US (2008).

Oman Technology Fund, https://www.otf.om/

'Qatar National Vision 2030', Ministry of Foreign Affairs of Qatar, Government Communications Office, gco.gov.qa.

Qatar Science & Technology Park, 'Qatar Foundation', https://qstp.org.qa/

Rotolo, Daniele, Diana Hicks, and Ben R. Martin, 'What is an Emerging Technology?', *Research Policy* 44, no. 10 (2015): 1827–1843.

Royal Decree 6/2022 Promulgating the Personal Data Protection Law of the Sultanate of Oman.

'Saudi Cloud Computing Regulatory Framework', The Communications, Space & Technology Commission, https://www.cst.gov.sa/en/RulesandSystems/RegulatoryDocuments/Pages/CCRF.aspx

Saudi Data and Artificial Intelligence Authority, 'National Strategy for Data and Artificial Intelligence', https://ai.sa/

Saudi Data and Artificial Intelligence Authority, 'SDAIA Regulatory Arrangements', https://sdaia.gov.sa/ar/SDAIA/about/Pages/RegulationsAndPolicies.aspx

Shkvarya, L. V., Irina A. Aidrous, Elizaveta I. Ruzina, A. V. Savinsky and Sergey I. Rodin, 'Development of High-Tech Segment in the GCC Region on the Example of the Aviation Component of the Kingdom of Bahrain 1–7', *IOP Conference Series: Materials Science and Engineering, Moscow, Russia* 476 (2019).

Turing, A. M., 'Computing Machinery and Intelligence', *Mind, Oxford University Press* 59, no. 236 (1950): 433–460.

Zulu, Saul F. C., 'Emerging Information and Communication Technology Policy Framework for Africa', *International Journal of ICT Research and Development in Africa* 1 (2010): 46–64.

4 Enablers of Knowledge-Based Economies

National Intellectual Property Strategies

Alhanoof AlDebasi

Introduction

Intellectual property (IP) has emerged as a critical asset in the global economy, driving innovation, investment, and economic growth. Recognizing its potential to transform nations into knowledge-based powerhouses, many countries have adopted national IP strategies. This chapter examines the significance of these strategies in maximizing a country's intellectual wealth and contributing to its overall development.

The chapter explores how a well-crafted IP strategy can stimulate investment, foster research and development, generate high-quality employment opportunities, and ultimately boost a nation's GDP. It will also highlight the challenges governments face in implementing such strategies and the crucial role of IP offices, including the World Intellectual Property Organization (WIPO) in providing support.

With a particular focus on Saudi Arabia, it analyzes the efforts of the Saudi Authority for Intellectual Property (SAIP) in aligning its IP strategy with the ambitious *Vision 2030* by examining the initiatives undertaken by SAIP to cultivate a robust IP ecosystem, and understand the practical steps involved in transforming IP potential into economic reality.

Ultimately, this chapter underscores the importance of tailoring IP strategies to specific national contexts. As the concluding quote suggests, a successful strategy is not merely a theoretical construct but a reflection of a country's unique political, economic, and institutional landscape.

Intellectual Property and National Strategies:

Defining a National Intellectual Property Strategy (NIPS) requires an understanding of the nature of intellectual property (IP) and its application. IP refers to the creations of the human mind, namely innovations and creative work such as the arts, music, movies, and literary works.[1] There are many types of IP depending on the work that is created, invented or developed. They include:[2]

1 'What Is Intellectual Property?' *WIPO,* at https://www.wipo.int/about-ip/en/#:~:text=Intellectual%20property%20(IP)%20refers%20to,and%20images%20used%20in%20commerce.

2 David Price & Alhanoof AlDebasi, *Protecting Intellectual Property in the Arabian Peninsula: The GCC States, Jordan and Yemen* (Routledge: Cavendish, 2018).

DOI: 10.4324/9781003528517-4

- Trademarks as applied to signs and logos used in the course of trade for distinguishing goods or services of one entity from another;
- Patents as rights granted for an innovation, whether a product or a process, that provides a new way of doing something, or offers a new technical solution to a problem;
- Industrial designs for the external design of the products, that consist of three-dimensional features, such as the shape of an article, or two-dimensional features, such as patterns, lines or color;
- Geographical indications as indications used on goods that have quality, reputation or characteristics attributed to a specific geographical area;
- Trade secrets as confidential information that has a commercial value if it is sold or leaked, is known only to a limited group of persons, and the rightful holder has taken reasonable steps to keep it secret;
- Copyrights as a bundle of rights that creators hold on their creative works ranging from databases, books, articles, paintings, maps, and advertisements, also software systems and related rights of a creative work not connected with the work's actual author; and
- Plant varieties as the rights of plant breeders to cultivate a specific plant that meets certain criteria.[3]

Similar to real estate ownership, IP rights grant ownership on creativity and innovation created as well as the applicability of legal actions due to such ownership. The difference to real estate is that IP applies to intangible asset by establishing rights on the work that is created or produced. Much like any other industry, IP contributes to a national economy by the copyrighted works that are produced and published or otherwise commercially exploited, the number and value of commercially utilized patents and industrial designs, the value of trademarks in terms of the goods in traded which they identify, and the widespread protection of goods with geographical indications.

A national strategy is a set of policy measures formulated and implemented by a country to improve a specific ecosystem, whether a strategy on artificial intelligence, energy, investment or any other area that a country needs to develop a national strategy for. When it comes to IP, developing a NIPS means developing and implementing a framework in order to enhance, through careful management and exploitation, the value of the IP and innovation environment in light of the social, cultural and economic development goals.[4]

To formulate and develop a national IP strategy, a country must take into consideration many sectors that are directly and indirectly influenced by IP. Due to the fact that IP is a cross-cutting issue that is relevant to all types of industries and services,[5]

3 David Price & Alhanoof AlDebasi, *Protecting Intellectual Property in the Arabian Peninsula: The GCC States, Jordan and Yemen* (Routledge: Cavendish, 2018).
4 'National Intellectual Property Strategies', *WIPO,* at https://www.wipo.int/ipstrategies/en/
5 'National Intellectual Property Strategies', *WIPO,* at https://www.wipo.int/ipstrategies/en/

NIPS requires the participation and coordination of many sectors such as culture, energy, health, science and technology, trade and services, customs, justice, education, and finance, all of which play a critical role in the IP environment and contribute to the innovation and creativity in a country.[6]

With a national IP strategy, IP offices usually lead or play a significant role in the development of that strategy. With the knowledge and expertise in the field, IP offices can significantly contribute to the development of the national strategy as they can identify the areas for improvements, challenges and opportunities, and strengths. IP offices are also reliable source of IP-related data. Naturally, IP offices are actively involved in all aspects of a national IP strategy from developing action plans to implementation, monitoring and evaluation.[7]

The Role of The World Intellectual Property Organization (WIPO)

The World Intellectual Property Organization (WIPO) is a designated IP agency of the United Nations which was established in 1967 by the WIPO Convention. It consists of 193 member states.[8] WIPO's mission is to lead the development of a balanced and effective international IP system that enables innovation and creativity for the benefit of all.[9]

WIPO provides a bundle of services, policies and tools that help shapes international IP rules and procedures as well as assisting in the technical infrastructure of member states to enable IP systems and to enhance share IP knowledge. WIPO also focuses on cooperation and capacity-building programs to enable all countries to use IP for economic, social, and cultural development. WIPO is considered "a world reference source for IP information and reliable global database."[10] Not only does WIPO support and assist member states, particularly developing and least developed country members, it also administers more than 26 intellectual-property treaties.[11] WIPO also manages the World Trade Organization's (WTO) Agreement

6 Guidance for the Development of an Intellectual Property (IP) Strategy in Countries in Transition Version Two Prepared by the Division for Certain Countries in Europe and Asia)

7 'Models of Intellectual Property Governance and Administration' (2024), *WIPO*, 17 at https://www.wipo.int/publications/en/details.jsp?id=4751&plang=EN

8 'About WIPO', *WIPO*, at https://www.wipo.int/about-wipo/en/

9 'About WIPO', *WIPO*, at https://www.wipo.int/about-wipo/en/

10 'About WIPO', *WIPO*, at https://www.wipo.int/about-wipo/en/

11 Treaties administrated by WIPO are: Beijing Treaty on Audiovisual Performances (2012); Berne Convention for the Protection of Literary and Artistic Works (1886); Brussels Convention Relating to the Distribution of Programme-Carrying Signals Transmitted by Satellite (1974); Madrid Agreement for the Repression of False or Deceptive Indications of Source on Goods (1891, revised Washington (1911) The Hague (1925) London (1934) Lisbon (1958) and Stockholm (1967); Marrakesh Treaty to Facilitate Access to Published Works for Persons Who Are Blind, Visually Impaired or Otherwise Print Disabled (2013); Nairobi Treaty on the Protection of the Olympic Symbol (1981); Paris Convention for the Protection of Industrial Property (1883); Patent Law Treaty (2000); Convention for the Protection of Producers of Phonograms Against Unauthorized Duplication of Their Phonograms (1971); Rome Convention for the Protection of Performers, Producers of Phonograms and Broadcasting Organizations (1961); Singapore Treaty on the Law of Trademarks (2006); Trade-

on Trade-Related Aspects of Intellectual Property Rights (TRIPs Agreement), being the global minimum standards benchmark on IP rights and protection on behalf of the WTO.

WIPO assists developing countries and least developed countries (LDCs) in formulating NIPS that positively impact their economic development, innovative and creative capacity, and the vitality of enterprises. It provides specialized assistance to countries that wish to develop NIPS and works with them to closely formulate their IP goals, needs, and importance to the countries. To initiate such a process, WIPO first develops a baseline questionnaire that is designed to determine the current status address of a country's IP system so that the strengths, and particularly, the shortcomings of the current national system, if any, can be identified and assessed. The questionnaire examines the following seven cluster areas of business:

- Administration and management of IP;
- Generation of IP by universities, research organizations, businesses, industries, small and medium enterprises (SMEs) and individuals;
- Commercialization of IP and technology transfer by universities, research organizations, businesses, industries, SMEs and individuals;
- Copyright and copyright industries;
- Plant variety rights and seed industries;
- Enforcement of IP rights; and
- IP and public policy.[12]

Therefore, many countries when planning to draft a NIPS, communicate with WIPO to seek provision of the necessary tools, knowledge, and framework that will enable them to best build a NIPS suitable for their needs, and their IP and innovation environment. IP strategies can come in different forms. Some countries do not have a dedicated strategy document at all but are nonetheless strategic in their approach to IP. According to WIPO, a growing number of developing countries

mark Law Treaty (1994); Washington Treaty on Intellectual Property in Respect of Integrated Circuits (1989); WIPO Copyright Treaty (1996); WIPO Performances and Phonograms Treaty (1996); Budapest Treaty on the International Recognition of the Deposit of Microorganisms for the Purposes of Patent Procedure (adopted 1977); Madrid Agreement Concerning the International Registration of Marks (1891); Protocol Relating to the Madrid Agreement Concerning the International Registration of Marks (1989); Hague Agreement Concerning the International Registration of Industrial Designs (1999 Act and 1960 Act); Lisbon Agreement for the Protection of Appellations of Origin and their International Registration (1958); Geneva Act of Lisbon Agreement for the Protection of Appellations of Origin and their International Registration (2015); Patent Cooperation Treaty (1970); Locarno Agreement Establishing an International Classification for Industrial Designs (1968); Nice Agreement Concerning the International Classification of Goods and Services for the Purposes of the Registration of Marks (1957); Strasbourg Agreement Concerning the International Patent Classification (1971); Vienna Agreement Establishing an International Classification of the Figurative Elements of Marks (1973), at https://www.wipo.int/treaties/en/

12 'Methodology for the Development of National Intellectual Property Strategies' (2016), *WIPO*, 9–10, at https://www.wipo.int/ipstrategies/en/.

are in the process of formulating and/or implementing IP strategies under a variety of denominations (IP strategy/IP policy/IP plan of action), for example, China, Egypt, India, Rwanda, and South Africa to name a few. Egypt, Austria, and Ireland are examples of countries that have recently been developing IP strategies driven from the policy level, rather than by a national IP office. Denmark has introduced IP statements into sectoral strategies, making IP issues more tangible and tailoring policy goals to specific needs in particular industries technologies. Egypt launched its five-year National Strategy for Intellectual Property (2022–2027) in 2022.

The Role of National IP Offices

The role of IP offices differs depending on IP governance in a country, which "ranges from the more traditional model, where IP is seen primarily as a legal and regulatory function, to a more modern approach, which recognizes IP as an enabling tool for broader innovation, creativity and economic development goals."[13]

The majority of countries are positioning the IP office to a ministry that reflects the government's view of IP and its priorities. Hence, some countries place the office with the ministry of commerce or industry, as occuring in Botswana and India. As a result, the office focuses on economic growth, trade and industrial development. Other countries, such as Germany, govern IP under the ministry of justice and legal affairs, whereas Chile places the IP office under the authority of the ministry of economy, which reflects the government interest of the economic value of IP.

Other countries separate the copyright office and industrial property office. With that, the copyright office will often be governed by the ministry of culture, arts or heritage.

However, a very few countries combine all IP matter under one authority and one overall ministerial level organization. Such structure helps IP to evolve and thrive. This can be evident in Saudi Arabia.

There is no right governance for an IP office. The right framework is the one that work best for the government and best serves its IP perspectives. Yet, every IP office plays an important role to the development and implementing of a NIPS as long as the strategy is well drafted and it reflects the country's IP future.

The Importance of a National Intellectual Property Strategy

A well-constructed NIPS enhances a country's ability to create, protect and commercialize economically valuable IP assets. It fosters an enabling environment to harness a country's innovative and creative potentials.[14] To demonstrate how NIPS

13 'Methodology for the Development of National Intellectual Property Strategies' (2016), *WIPO*, 9–10, at https://www.wipo.int/ipstrategies/en/.

14 'Methodology for the Development of National Intellectual Property Strategies' (2016), *WIPO*, 9–10, at https://www.wipo.int/ipstrategies/en/.

generates and commercializes valuable IP assets and contributes to the country's economic growth, Albert Hu and IPL Png conducted a study to investigate whether stronger patent rights regime led to faster economic growth in a sample of countries that spans a wide spectrum of level of economic development. The research was conducted on 58 countries between 1980 to 2003 proving a connection between the increase of patents and the increase of GDP.[15] The study reported that when the number of patents increased by 1%, the gross domestic product (GDP) increased by 0.65% per person.[16] The result of the study can be evident in South Korea, Japan, and the Group of Seven (G7) countries.[17] More recently, Turkey was case studied during the period 1990 to 2015. The research examined not only the impact of IP rights on economic growth, but also the effect of IP legislation, technology and IP sanctions on the advances of IP on innovation processes and economic growth, as one cannot processed without the other.[18] The results demonstrated that exports of advanced technologies and patents accelerate economic growth in both the short and long term.[19]

NIPS also contribute to newly established business ventures as well as employment rates. They directly impact growth of startups that use IP rights as an integral part of their company and indirectly influence employment rates which all play a crucial part in the innovation environment. When a country focuses first on raising awareness on the importance of the intangible assets, namely IP, it enhances the administration of IP, namely the registration process at the IP Office, and enables IP grants and protection to take effect and positively impact in a timely matter. All of which will positively contribute to the economic advancement of a country. Laurent Belsie demonstrated that startup companies with granted patents have a higher revenue of 51%, and 36% employment growth after five years than those companies without patents.[20] Similarly, delays in approving applications because of merely administrative factors can have an adverse effect on startup companies to the same extent as outright rejection of applications would have. Belsie's study found that every year of delay in reviewing an eventually successful application,

15 Albert Hu and IPL Png, 'Patent Rights and Economic Growth: Evidence from Cross-country Panels of Manufacturing Industries' (2013 July) *Oxford Economic Papers*, vol 65(3) Special Issue: Innovation And Intellectual Property, 675–698.

16 Albert Hu and IPL Png, 'Patent Rights and Economic Growth: Evidence from Cross-country Panels of Manufacturing Industries' (2013 July) *Oxford Economic Papers*, vol 65(3) Special Issue: Innovation And Intellectual Property, 675–698.

17 The Group of Seven (G7) is an informal grouping of seven of the world's advanced economies, namely, Canada, France, Germany, Italy, Japan, the United Kingdom, and the United States, as well as the European Union.

18 'The Long-run Relationships between Number of Patents and Economic Growth' (2020 June) *European Research Studies Journal* XXIII (3), 548–563

19 D. D. Dereli, 'The Relationship between High-technology Exports, Patent and Economic Growth in Turkey (1990–2015)' (2019) *Journal of Business, Economics and Finance*, vol. 8(3), 173–180.

20 Laurent Belsie, 'Prompt Patent Approval Spurs Startup Growth' (2016) *National Bureau of Economic Research*, vol. 3. 1–6

reduces rates of employment and revenues over a five-year period, which can cause the collapse of the startup.[21]

Market behavior has been changing since 1975, focusing more on intangible assets that have commercial value and can be traded in the market. A case study conducted in 2020 examined the market share and value from 1995 to 2020, which showed that the share of intangible asset market value increased from 68% to 90%.[22] Interestingly, the study found that the period of COVID-19 actually enhanced the trend of increasing intangible assets share, with intangible assets now commanding 90% of the Standard and Poor's 500 (S&P 500) market value.[23] A study by Ocean Tomo, an international management consultancy company on IP across the S&P 500 market in the United States, demonstrates the growth in the value of IP equity when evaluating the market capitalization of the S&P 500.[24]

The Challenges of a National Intellectual Property Strategy

With developing such an impressive plan to uplift the IP environment in a country, certain complications or obstacles may appear that can jeopardize the successful implementation of a NIPS. Firstly, improper implementation of a NIPS often occurs because there is no clear ownership in the implementation. An implementation strategy encompasses projects and initiatives that collectively deliver the NIPS goals. Each project must have an owner and contributors. The owner is responsible for implementing the project and aligning with contributors in order to ensure that the project's plan is on track and that the outcomes of the project is complete. If there is no clear definition of the person constituting the owner, the flow of the project or the initiative will be disturbed or disrupted, which will consequently negatively impact the NIPS implementation. Secondly, the absence of initiatives or projects to addresses NIPS components in order to achieve its goals results in the absence of an implementation plan for the intended project, and consequently the desired outcome or owner who can ensure a successful implementation. Consequently, the NIPS implementation will not be completed and the outcomes will not be achieved.

Another challenge is lack of a proper evaluation and indicator system to assess the progress of NIPS towards implementation. Even if there are projects and initiatives that will address certain parts of the NIPS, there is a need for a body or a committee to supervise its implementation as a whole, and to consistently evaluate the process of the implementation phase and address any issue that will affect progress. The committee will create an indicator system by which it will ensure that the projects are proceeding as planned and the owners are managing their projects in a

21 Laurent Belsie, 'Prompt Patent Approval Spurs Startup Growth' (2016) *National Bureau of Economic Research*, vol. 3.

22 'Intangible Asset Market Value Study' (2020) *Ocean Tomo*, at https://oceantomo.com/intangible-asset-market-value-study/t.

23 The Standard and Poor's 500 (S&P 500) is a stock market index tracking the stock performance of 500 of the largest companies listed on stock exchanges in the United States.

24 Ocean Tomo (n 22).

timely and effective matter. If there is no body or a committee to ensure a smooth plan of execution, the NIPS will most likely not produce all or some of its goals. It will solely depend on project owners in succeeding in their individual projects, without having a clear picture of the NIPS as a whole.

A further challenge is setting unrealistic or insufficiently selective goals. This challenge usually appears in the planning stage of the NIPS. It is crucial to have realistic, achievable, and efficient goals that address the current environment. When the NIPS goals are unrealistic or insufficiently selective, the implementation process will not be successful as the goals are unachievable from the beginning. In the process of addressing unrealistic goals, the NIPS committee needs to evaluate and modify the goals in order to produce outcomes that are actually achievable.

Kingdom of Saudi Arabia

The Saudi Authority for Intellectual Property (SAIP) is a governmental organization which reports to the Prime Minister.[25] It was established in 2018 to regulate, support, develop, sponsor, protect, and enforce IP rights in Saudi Arabia.

Before the establishment of SAIP, IP oversight was scattered between three different entities, each with different agendas and scope. First, the Ministry of Commerce was responsible for trademarks, specifically trademark law and regulation, registration, and international representation. Second, the Ministry of Media was responsible for enforcing copyrights and related rights. Lastly, the King Abdulaziz City for Science and Technology (KACST) administered the systems for registration of patents, industrial designs, layout designs for integrated circuits, and new plant varieties. Each entity worked independently and separately from the others, which resulted in variation in approaching IP – whether from a legal framework, registration or even enforcement.

The launching of SAIP was a turning point for IP management and protection in Saudi Arabia. Under SAIP, all types of IP, including trademark and geographical indication, copyrights and related rights, patents, industrial designs, layout designs for integrated circuits and new plants varieties, and trade secrets, are given the same interest, care, and space for the development of the national IP environment.

SAIP has a unique structure, rarely found in any other country, through which it combines and unifies both offices – copyright office and industrial property office – and an IP enforcement body. It can be best described as "SAIP serves as a one-stop shop."[26]

Since its establishment in 2018, SAIP has been operating, and will continue to do so, in accordance with three strategic developmental phases, namely:

25 Ministerial Resolution No. 410 dated 28/6/1438 AH.
26 'Saudi Arabia Gears Up on IP', *WIPO Magazine* (September 2020), at https://www.wipo.int/wipo_magazine/en/2020/03/article_0008.html

- Phase 1. Build and Operate strategy (years 2018–2022): Merging different entities, transferring jurisdiction, building the authority, controlling the institutional infrastructure, and starting to operate the authority's activities;
- Phase 2. Growth and Development strategy (years 2022–2025): Developing the Authority's activities and growing extensively in providing services, raising institutional quality, and starting to achieve the strategic benefit of the Authority's business; and
- Phase 3. Sustainability strategy (years 2025–2030): Reaching the stage of financial sustainability and achieving impact.

Since SAIP's establishment, IP has been going through major transformations in respect of the framework and the services provided. One of the obstacles any IP field can face is the provision to rightsholders of the correct advice, especially since IP has a special nature that differs from any other area. Thus, SAIP has launched IP Clinics to provide counseling and advice to individuals and companies on matters related to IP, such as eligibility, filing, registrations, and identifying protentional IP rights.[27] The counseling sessions are conducted privately and free of charge in order to raise awareness about IP, and to promote creators and inventors to protect their creations.

The SAIP Academy was established in 2021 to build human capabilities in IP by offering education, training, and skills-building in the IP environment. Since its establishment, the SAIP Academy has trained more than 39,600 people and offered more than 170 training courses.[28] It has also developed two specialized professional certifications, namely, the IP Enforcement Certificate and the IP Service Provider Certificate. The IP Enforcement Certificate is a professional certification credential in IP rights and their enforcement. Certification signifies that the person possesses knowledge in the areas of IP enforcement, laws and regulations, confiscation, investigation and professional ethics. The IP Service Provider Certificate is a required professional certification credential in the area of IP for service providers. The certification signifies that the person possesses knowledge in the areas of IP laws and regulations, IP services, and professional ethics. Cooperating with WIPO and Umm al-Qura University, SAIP has launched an executive master on IP, Entrepreneurship and Innovation (MIPEI), to be WIPO's first joint master's degree program in the Arab region.[29]

Saudi Arabia has been a strong advocate for the importance of the Arabic language in the international organizations. Although Arabic is one of the official languages of the UN, SAIP has been taking major efforts to ensure the inclusion

27 SAIP Annual Report, December 2023, 76 SAIP Annual Report 2023.

28 SAIP Academy Achievement 2022 Report, December 2022; SAIP Academy Achievement 2023 Report, January 2024.

29 'WIPO Director General Pledges WIPO's Support in Efforts to Strengthen Innovation Ecosystem in Saudi Arabia' (2023), *WIPO*, at WIPO Director General Pledges WIPO's Support in Efforts to Strengthen Innovation Ecosystem in Saudi Arabia.

of Arabic in the Hague system for the international design system, and the Madrid system for the international registration of marks, in efforts to advance the Arabic language in the international arena.[30]

In order to raise awareness on IP and to raise the young generation on respecting and protecting intellectual property, SAIP has integrated IP education in school curricula, in all levels and in varies subject matters such as science and math.[31] SAIP also offers discounted rates for students wanting to register their copyrights in an effort to raise awareness on the importance of copyrights registration and to support the young creatives who are still in school.

More recently, in its efforts to further support IP development projects, Saudi Arabia is establishing a trust fund of five million Swiss francs to implement projects and programs that serve national interest in the field of IP rights.[32]

Furthermore, it has been accredited as an international searching and preliminary examining authority under the Patent Cooperation Treaty during the WIPO PCT Assembly in 2023.[33] Pursuant to the approval of The Council of Ministers on joining the Hague system for the international design system and the Madrid system for the international registration of marks, Saudi Arabia has tremendously increased ratification to 15 treaties, 60% of which were ratified in the past four years.

The *Arab News* reported on 14 February 2024 that Saudi Arabia's Public Prosecution approved the establishment of the Intellectual Property Prosecution body.[34] The move is in line with the NIPS, which was launched by the Crown Prince and Prime Minister, His Royal Highness Prince Muhammad bin Salman and aims to create a superior framework for the provision, organization, and enhancement of judicial services regarding intellectual property matters.

The new body will be tasked with investigating and initiating criminal proceedings in cases related to IP rights infringements as outlined in the Kingdom's trademark law, copyright protection law, and law of patents, layout designs of integrated circuits, plant varieties, and industrial designs. SAIP will refer selected cases to the new body, emphasizing the achievement of the goals outlined in the country's *Vision 2030*.

30 Saudi Arabia General Statement, Assemblies of the Member States of WIPO Sixty-Third Series of Meetings - A 63 Day 1 Afternoon, 14 July 2022 (2022), *WIPO*, at WIPO Webcast - Assemblies of the Member States of WIPO Sixty-Third Series of Meetings - A 63 Day 1 Afternoon.

31 'WIPO Director General Pledges WIPO's Support in Efforts to Strengthen Innovation Ecosystem in Saudi Arabia (n 29); *See also* تقرير ادراج الملكية الفكرية في المناهج الدراسية في التعليم العام, *SAIP*, August 2023, Incorporating IP into the general education curriculum Report 2023.

32 Saudi Arabia General Statement, Assemblies of the Member States of WIPO Sixty Fifth Series of Meetings - A 65 Day 1 Morning, 09 July 2024, *WIPO*, at WIPO Webcast - Assemblies of the Member States of WIPO Sixty Fifth series of meetings - A 65 Day 1 Morning.

33 https://www.wipo.int/pct/en/newslett/2023/article_0001.html

34 'Saudi Public Prosecution Approves Establishment of Intellectual Property Body', *Arab News* (14 February 2024), at https://www.arabnews.com/node/2460186/saudi-arabia

The body will comprise a team of skilled public prosecutors, specifically trained and equipped with the necessary competencies to deal appropriately with IP rights violations. It hopes to achieve the Kingdom's *Vision 2030* goals, and highlight efforts to achieve speedy justice against IP violations.

It is one of the main possibilities for realizing the goals of the Kingdom's *Vision 2030* and to confirm the integration with the Public Prosecution in the governance of criminal work related to IP to achieve speedy justice.

In conclusion, it is worth noting that the United States Trade Representative (USTR) *Special 301 Report 2022*, which notes and lists perceived egregious conduct in respect of IP rights by trading partners of the United States, removed the Kingdom from its Priority Watch List in 2022 after many years of placement. The USTR did so because of action by SAIP to publish its IP enforcement procedures; increase enforcement against counterfeit and pirated goods, and online pirated content; create specialized IP enforcement courts with trained judges and expedited timelines; conduct strong IP awareness, outreach, training, and support; set up a centralized committee to coordinate IP enforcement actions across multiple authorities; and train IP specialists in 76 different authorities to increase government compliance with IP laws.[35]

And in its *Special 301 Report 2023*, the USTR commented favorably upon and used as an example of best practice, SAIP's initiative in creating the permanent National Committee for the Enforcement of Intellectual Property to coordinate IP enforcement, issue reports and case studies, and the development of IP legislation and regulations.[36]

The Kingdom's Vision 2030

Saudi Arabia's *Vision 2030* represents a transformative and deeply ambitious plan to unlock the Kingdom's vast potential by creating a diversified, innovative, and world-leading nation, for the benefit of future generations.

Vision 2030 is a grand visionary transformation of Saudi Arabia from an oil-based economy to a knowledge-based global economy. In this visionary plan for a prosperous, sustainable, and cohesive Saudi society, Saudi Crown Prince and Prime Minister, His Royal Highness Prince Muhammad bin Salman, judiciously dovetails the enhancement of human capital with the diversification of the economy to transform Saudi Arabia into a leading global economy.

Vision 2030 offers three themes around which the development plan is built, namely:

- a vibrant society;
- a thriving economy; and
- an ambitious nation.

35 Special 301 Report 2022, *United States Trade Representative*, 10.
36 Special 301 Report 2023, *United States Trade Representative*, 12.

The plan declares that "Islam and its teachings are our way of life. They are the basis of all our laws, decisions, actions and goals…Therefore, the principles of Islam will be the driving force for us to realize our Vision. The values of moderation, tolerance, excellence, discipline, equity, and transparency will be the bedrock of our success."[37]

Vision 2030 Pillar 2: Thriving Economy

The vision for Pillar 2, a thriving economy, will be reached by creating an environment that unlocks business opportunities, broadens the economic base, and creates jobs for all Saudis by leveraging Saudi Arabia's unique location and potential, attracting the best talent, and increasing global investment. The Thriving Economy objectives include:

- Raise the share of non-oil exports from 16% to 50%;
- Raise Saudi Arabia's global ranking in the logistics performance index from 40 to 25 and ensure the Kingdom is a regional leader;
- Increase the private sector's contribution to GDP from 40% to 65%;
- Increase foreign direct investment from 3.8% to the international level of 5.7% of GDP;
- Raise Saudi Arabia from its current position on the Global Competitiveness Index at number 25 to amongst the Index's Top 10 Countries;
- Increase the public investment fund's assets from SAR600 billion to SAR7 trillion;
- Improve Saudi Arabia's current standing as the 19th largest economy globally to the 15th largest economy globally;
- Increase the localization of oil and gas sectors from 40% to 75%;
- Increase women's participation in the workforce from 22% to 30%;
- Increase small and medium enterprise contribution to GDP from 20% to 35%; and
- Lower the rate of unemployment from 11% to 7%.[38]

The ultimate goal of *Vision 2030* is the development of the national economy and society. IP is one of the key pillars for achieving the Kingdom's vision objectives. where projections indicate that the growth of technology-based industries and the expansion of the intellectual property services industry will positively affect the stimulation of production and goods in various industries.

The Saudi Arabia National IP strategy

Saudi Arabia launched its own NIPS in 2022 aiming to develop a comprehensive well-balanced IP value chain that advances innovation and economic growth.

37 Special 301 Report 2023, *United States Trade Representative*, 16.
38 Kingdom of Saudi Arabia (2017), *Vision 2030,* 6, at https://www.vision2030.gov.sa/en/

The Saudi NIPS is a five-year plan with the intention to achieve its established goals by 2028. The NIPS corresponds with Saudi Arabia's national development plan *Vision 2030*, which in turn aims to transform the country from an oil-based economy to a knowledge-based economy and vibrant society.[39] In order to have a knowledge-based economy, it must have a cultivated IP environment that will advance the economy and will contribute to the achievement of the objectives of *Vision 2030*.

The Vision of the NIPS is to establish a comprehensive well-balanced IP value chain that promotes innovation, competitiveness and economic growth, with the objectives of developing creative individuals based on imagination and challenge, fostering enterprises based on IP, and achieving a society based on respect for creative effort.

On the occasion of the launch of the Strategy, the Crown Prince and Prime Minister, His Royal Highness Prince Mohammad bin Salman stressed both the strength of the national intellectual potential and the crucial importance of a national IP plan. He declared that:

> We have minds and energies passionate about innovation and creativity, and by enabling them, the Kingdom of Saudi Arabia will become a vibrant environment for knowledge economy based on an integrated Intellectual Property ecosystem that develops innovative technologies and industries and contributes to growth of enterprises. The National Intellectual Property Strategy (NIPS) will further enable stimulating investment, create high quality jobs, and raise awareness of creators and innovators rights.[40]

The NIPS document explains the current situation of IP in Saudi Arabia compared to some of the leading countries in the field. It contains the main data and statistics in the Kingdom. It also contains a deep analysis of the Kingdom's strengths and the challenges it faces in establishing a sustainable intellectual property environment. It consists of four main pillars, namely, generation of IP, management of IP, commercial investment of IP, and protection of IP. The document displays the most important aspects of developing the strategy, defining its vision and objectives, the implementation plan, the roles, and responsibilities of the national agencies to ensure the achievement of the set goals.

SAIP as the national IP Office is the driver behind the NIPS. It is also the main stakeholder ensuring the successful implementation of NIPS projects with the participation and cooperation of 37 entities. According to Dr Abdulaziz M Alswailem, the CEO of the Authority:

39 'Saudi Arabia Launches National Intellectual Property Strategy' (2022) *Saudi Gazette*, at https://saudigazette.com.sa/article/628250

40 Crown Prince and Prime Minister His Royal Highness Prince Muhammad bin Salman, National Intellectual Property Strategy (2022) *Saudi Authority for Intellectual Property*, (Introduction).

We seek [through NIPS] to enhance respecting and protecting the creators and innovators efforts, to thrive with them in the Kingdom and advance to a promising future full of human creativity and successful investments."[41]

National IP Strategy Pillars

The NIPS mission and objectives are supported by four strategic pillars, namely:

- IP Creation: which aims to generate a range of ideas from creative minds and young talents that can be transformed through research and development into innovative technologies or services which is the starting point of the IP environment;
- IP Administration: which aims to ensure effective management of creations and improve the value of IP by establishing a fast, high-quality system for registration;
- IP Commercialization: which aims to facilitate IP-based start-ups, financing and trading them to enhance their competitive market values, which ultimately builds an integrated cycle through which economic value can be created for IP and be reinvested back into research and development; and
- IP Protection: which aims to ensure adequate protection of IP-based products and services, thereby encouraging creative activities and strengthening the IP environment. It includes a number of projects that contribute to national needs by providing an integrated IP protection plan, to achieve benchmarks that contribute to improving the level of IP protection nationally and globally.

Saudi National IP Strategy Goals and Indicators

The NIPS implementation plan commenced operating in 2023 and aims to finalize and achieve its goals by 2028, with the participation and cooperation of 37 governmental stakeholders, such as the Ministry of Culture, the Ministry of Justice and the Ministry of Education. The implementation plan includes a comprehensive analysis of the IP environment in the Kingdom as well as its vision, objectives, Key Performance Indicators (KPIs), strategic initiatives, and projects.[42]

KPIs for the NIPS can be categorized into three primary domains, namely, individual, enterprise, and societal impact. Each domain is equipped with a specific set of KPIs, accompanied by baseline data (typically from 2018 or 2019) and corresponding targets established for the year 2028.

41 His Excellency CEO of the Saudi Authority for Intellectual Property Dr. Abdulaziz M. Alswailem, National Intellectual Property Strategy (2022) *Saudi Authority for Intellectual Property,* (Introduction).

42 'National Intellectual Property Strategy' (2022) *SAIP*, at Saudi NIPS Document.

First: Individual Domain:

- Number of Inventors (Creative Talents): The baseline established in 2018 reflects a figure of 1,176 inventors. The target for 2028 signifies a significant increase, aiming to reach 13,200 inventors;
- IP Applications per one million People: Baseline data (2018) for IP applications per million people indicates 30 industrial designs, 998 trademarks, and 95 patents. Ambitious targets for 2028 are set at 60 industrial designs, 2,000 trademarks, and 190 patents.

Second: Enterprise Domain:

- Patent Applications from KSA per USD 100 Billion GDP: The baseline for patent applications originating from the Kingdom was established in 2019 at 107 applications per USD 100 billion GDP. The target for 2028 reflects a substantial increase, aiming to reach 230 applications;
- Rate of Adoption of Employee Invention Reward System: Unlike other KPIs, no baseline data exists for the adoption rate of an employee invention reward system. However, a target is set for 2028, aiming for a 20% increase in the adoption rate.

Third: Societal Domain:

- IMD Intellectual Property Protection Index (Ranking): The baseline ranking for IP protection according to the IMD World Competitiveness Center in 2019 was 34th. The target for 2028 signifies a significant improvement, aiming to achieve a ranking of 20th;
- Global Innovation Index (GII): The baseline data for the GII in 2019 reflects a score of 38.8%. The target for 2028 demonstrates a focus on substantial growth, aiming to reach a score of 60%.[43]

Saudi National IP Strategy, Strategic Projects, and Initiatives

Within the focus pillars created by the four pillars, the Strategy recognizes and identifies a number of strategic initiatives that can and should be prioritized by SAIP and its specialized service areas, namely:

- Contributing to cultivating creative and competent talents in IP;
- Contributing to research and developments, and innovation based on IP;
- Increasing IP volume;
- Establishing fast and high-quality IP registration:
- Spreading IP-based startups;

43 'National Intellectual Property Strategy' (2022) *SAIP*, at Saudi NIPS Document.

- Enhancing IP customer service;
- Vitalizing IP financing; and
- Contributing to strengthening the creation and realization of innovative ideas.

Operating these various initiatives will generate two client groups for SAIP that create initiatives based on request and demand of the IP ecosystem, namely, those who are in the role of IP Creators (such as private inventors, enterprises, startups, employees, students, artists, designers, private inventors, universities, SME's, research institutes, researchers, authors, musicians, and regional product producers), and those who are IP Demanders (such as manufacturing companies, enterprises, IP brokers and licensors, NPEs, IP investment companies, performers, producers, authors of derived work, licensing agencies, IP licensees, and broadcasting organizations). However, the bounds between these two client groups are flexible and movable, and activity may create demand for services in the other.

Intellectual Property and Artificial Intelligence

The NIPS adopted by SAIP does not make any reference to artificial intelligence or, therefore, the future and even emerging interaction between the two. The impact of artificial intelligence on IP rights is a complex and evolving topic, with both opportunities and challenges. But it is inevitable that the place and space of artificial intelligence is an issue that will confront SAIP and test its NIPS. Saudi Arabia's *Vision 2030* emphasizes the crucial and central role that artificial intelligence must play in achieving its objectives. The NEOM[44] (New Enterprise Operating Model) project of a smart city will rely upon and take advantage of the capabilities of artificial intelligence technologies to enhance creativity, innovation, and the generation of IP. However, they also pose certain threats and raise important questions, particularly in respect of its identification, management, regulation and control. Key considerations include:

In respect of opportunities:

- Automated Creativity: artificial intelligence systems can assist in creative processes, generating new and innovative content across various domains such as art, music, and literature;
- Efficiency in IP Processes: artificial intelligence can streamline and improve IP-related tasks, such as patent searches, trademark analysis, and copyright infringement detection, leading to more efficient processes;

44 NEOM stands for the "New Future." it is an ambitious project aiming to create a futuristic region powered by 100% renewable energy. It is designed to prioritize people and nature, fostering a new model for sustainable living, working, and economic prosperity.

- Innovation Acceleration: artificial intelligence has the potential to accelerate innovation by automating research and development processes, leading to the creation of novel inventions and technologies.

In respect of challenges and threats:

- Ownership and authorship issues: the autonomous nature of some artificial intelligence systems raises questions about who should be considered the owner or author of the generated IP;
- Bias and ethical concerns: artificial intelligence algorithms may inadvertently embed biases, and ethical concerns may arise in cases where generated content is discriminatory or harmful;
- Legal and regulatory gaps: existing IP laws may not adequately address the unique challenges posed by AI-generated content, leading to legal uncertainties and potential gaps in protection;
- Overlapping IP rights: AI-generated works may involve a combination of human and machine contributions, leading to complexities in determining the appropriate IP rights and their duration; and
- Unintended Infringement: artificial intelligence systems, when trained on existing copyrighted works, may inadvertently produce content that resembles or infringes upon existing IP rights.

However, the threats may be mitigated by:

- Clarifying legal definitions;
- Implementing ethical guidelines and practices in artificial intelligence development to help mitigate bias and ensure responsible use of the technologies;
- Encouraging international collaboration and standardization to address inconsistencies in IP laws related to artificial intelligence on a global scale; and
- Establishing transparency and accountability measures in artificial intelligence systems to enhance trust and provide mechanisms for addressing unintended consequences.

While artificial intelligence presents both opportunities and challenges to IP rights, proactive efforts in legal, ethical, and regulatory domains can help harness the benefits of artificial intelligence while minimizing potential threats. Striking a balance between innovation and the protection of IP rights is crucial in navigating the evolving landscape shaped by artificial intelligence technologies.

Concluding Remarks

The NIPS is one of the main capabilities for achieving the goals of the Kingdom's *Vision 2030*, which aims to build an integrated IP environment that supports an innovation-based economy by establishing an IP value chain that stimulates innovation competitiveness and supports economic growth, so that the Kingdom becomes one of the pioneers of innovation and creativity in the world.[45] The Strategy will contribute to building a society based on knowledge and promoting the production of new technologies and industries through the development of commercial establishments based on IP, as well as enhancing the Kingdom's regional and international position, with the aim of stimulating and encouraging creative talents in the country and empowering creators for innovation and intellectual production.[46]

One of the objectives of NIPS is to establish a National IP Platform (Atam Platform) to stimulate creativity and innovation in the face of the growth of new technologies and creative industries. The platform aims to digitize the procedures for trading IP assets while providing a safe space for creators and innovators to trade them, to enhance investment in IP and benefit from it, with high transparency and reliability. The Atam platform also provides a number of supporting services by building a national registry of licensed IP service providers and practitioners such as valuation, mediation and technical services for incubators and manufacturing plants to facilitate transactions and access to services.[47]

In 2015, the WIPO General Assembly agreed to convene a diplomatic conference for the adoption of a Design Law Treaty (DLT) from mid-2017, if the discussions on technical assistance and disclosure are completed during the 34 and 35 sessions of the Standing Committee on the Law of Trademarks, Industrial Designs and Geographical Indications. Then in 2021, the WIPO General Assembly "decided that, at its next session, it will continue considering the convening of a diplomatic conference on the Design Law Treaty, to take place no sooner than 2023." During 2022, WIPO received offers from Belarus, Indonesia, and Saudi Arabia to host the diplomatic conference for the DLT, in case the General Assembly takes a decision to convene such diplomatic conference.[48]

During the General Assembly 64 Meeting, Saudi Arabia won the bid to host a Diplomatic Conference on Design Law in November 2024. On the occasion, Dr. Abdulaziz AlSwailem, CEO of the Saudi Authority for Intellectual Property (SAIP), said:

> It is an honor for the Kingdom of Saudi Arabia to host the Diplomatic Conference to conclude the Design Law Treaty (DLT) which is a sign of the importance that Saudi Arabia attaches to strengthening the global innovation

45 His Excellency the Chairman of the Board of Directors of the Saudi Authority for Intellectual Property Mohammed Al-Sheikh (n 40).

46 His Excellency the Chairman of the Board of Directors of the Saudi Authority for Intellectual Property Mohammed Al-Sheikh (n 40).

47 (2024) Commencing the operations of the National Platform for Intellectual Property Rights Exchange (ATM) Project, *Saudi Press Agency*, at https://www.spa.gov.sa/N2024346

48 WIPO General Assembly Fifty-Fifth (30th Extraordinary) Session Geneva, (2022), *WIPO*, at WO/GA/55/4 (wipo.int); See also, SCT/42/7; SCT/43/5.

ecosystem. We look forward to receiving WIPO member states for this last leg of negotiations to conclude this Treaty.

(WIPO Media Center, 2023)

Hosting the Riyadh Diplomatic Conference on Design Law Treaty in Saudi Arabia is a milestone and a testimony for the great work that has been done in the field of intellectual property in Saudi Arabia. Once successfully concluding the Riyadh Diplomatic Conference, the treaty will be the first WIPO-administrated treaty to be named after a Saudi city, Riyadh.

In conclusion, Saudi Arabia recognizes the great efforts that IP examiners are doing to advance the IP ecosystem and for their real knowledge and expertise. Saudi Arabia has proposed that WIPO adopt a special day to recognize the efforts of IP examiners and to thank them for the great work that they have done and are doing.[49]

Bibliography

'About WIPO', WIPO, at https://www.wipo.int/about-wipo/en/

Alswailem, Abdulaziz M., 'National Intellectual Property Strategy', Saudi Authority for Intellectual Property (2022), (Introduction), at https://www.saip.gov.sa/en/national-strategy/

Belsie, Laurent, 'Prompt Patent Approval Spurs Startup Growth', National Bureau of Economic Research (2016).

Dereli, D. D., 'The Relationship Between High-Technology Exports Patent and Economic Growth in Turkey (1990-2015)', *Journal of Business, Economics and Finance* 8(3) (2019), 173–180.

Guidance for the Development of an Intellectual Property (IP) Strategy in Countries in Transition Version Two Prepared by the Division for Certain Countries in Europe and Asia).

Hu, Albert and IPL Png, 'Patent Rights and Economic Growth: Evidence from Cross-Country Panels of Manufacturing Industries', *Oxford Economic Papers* 65(3) (July) Special Issue: Innovation and Intellectual Property (2013), 675–698.

'Intangible Asset Market Value Study', Ocean Tomo (2020), at https://oceantomo.com/intangible-asset-market-value-study/

Launching the work of the National Platform for the Exchange of Intellectual Property Rights "ATM" project (2024), *Saudi Press Agency*, at https://www.spa.gov.sa/N2024346

'Methodology for the Development of National Intellectual Property Strategies', WIPO (2016), at https://www.wipo.int/ipstrategies/en/

'Models of Intellectual Property Governance and Administration', WIPO (2024), at https://www.wipo.int/publications/en/details.jsp?id=4751&plang=EN

'National Intellectual Property Strategies', WIPO, at https://www.wipo.int/ipstrategies/en/

'National Intellectual Property Strategy', SAIP (2022), at Saudi NIPS Document.

Price, David and Alhanoof AlDebasi, *Protecting Intellectual Property in the Arabian Peninsula: The GCC States, Jordan and Yemen* (London: Routledge Cavendish, 2018).

Report on the inclusion of intellectual property in the general education curriculum, SAIP, August 2023, Incorporating IP into the General Education Curriculum Report 2023.

49 Saudi Arabia General Statement (n 32).

Saudi Authority for Intellectual Property, 'Academy Achievement 2022 Report' (December 2022).

———, 'Academy Achievement 2023 Report' (January 2024).

———, 'SAIP Annual Report 2023 Report' (December 2023).

'Saudi Arabia Gears Up on IP', *WIPO Magazine* (September 2020), at https://www.wipo.int/wipo_magazine/en/2020/03/article_0008.html

Saudi Arabia General Statement, Assemblies of the Member States of WIPO Sixty Fifth Series of Meetings - 9 July 2024, WIPO, at WIPO Webcast - Assemblies of the Member States of WIPO Sixty Fifth Series of Meetings - A 65 Day 1 Morning.

Saudi Arabia General Statement, Assemblies of the Member States of WIPO Sixty-Third Series of Meetings - A 63 Day 1 Afternoon, 14 July 2022 (2022), WIPO, at WIPO Webcast - Assemblies of the Member States of WIPO Sixty-Third Series of Meetings - A 63 Day 1 Afternoon.

'Saudi Arabia Launches National Intellectual Property Strategy', *Saudi Gazette* (2022), at https://saudigazette.com.sa/article/628250

Saudi Arabia, Ministerial Resolution No. 410 dated 28/6/1438 AH.

Saudi Arabia, Vision 2030 (2017), p. 6, at https://www.vision2030.gov.sa/en/

'Saudi Public Prosecution Approves Establishment of Intellectual Property Body', *Arab News* (14 February 2024), at https://www.arabnews.com/node/2460186/saudi-arabia

Special 301 Report 2022, *United States Trade Representative*.

Special 301 Report 2023, *United States Trade Representative*.

'The Long-Run Relationships between Number of Patents and Economic Growth', *European Research Studies Journal* XXIII (Issue 3) (June 2020), 548–563.

'What is Intellectual Property?', WIPO, at https://www.wipo.int/about-ip/en/#:~:text=Intellectual%20property%20(IP)%20refers%20to,and%20images%20used%20in%20commerce

'WIPO-Administered Treaties', WIPO, at https://www.wipo.int/treaties/en/

'WIPO Director General Pledges WIPO's Support in Efforts to Strengthen Innovation Ecosystem in Saudi Arabia' (2023), WIPO, at WIPO Director General Pledges WIPO's Support in Efforts to Strengthen Innovation Ecosystem in Saudi Arabia.

WIPO General Assembly Fifty-Fifth (30th Extraordinary) Session Geneva, WIPO (2022), at WO/GA/55/4 (wipo.int)

WIPO Media Center, Press Releases, "Saudi Arabia Set to Host 2024 Diplomatic Conference to Conclude Design Law Treaty", Geneva, October 9, 2023. PR/2023/909.

5 The Impact of Economic Diversification in the Gulf Cooperation Council Member States

Amelia Hallam

Introduction

The Gulf Cooperation Council (GCC) member states, namely Bahrain, Kuwait, Oman, Qatar, Saudi Arabia, and the United Arab Emirates, are in the midst of an important phase in social and economic evolution. The States are transitioning away from dependence on resource rents and working towards developing new knowledge societies, as part of a longer-term shift.[1] This chapter examines this shift, focusing particularly upon the emergence of these new knowledge societies and its implications in terms of economic development and more broadly, social welfare. It explores definitions of knowledge societies, investigates the lack of consensus with respect to a definition of knowledge society and the reasons for this uncertainty. It also investigates the complex and deep links between knowledge and technological advancement, economic development, particularly foreign direct investment (FDI), and society, and considers the policy considerations and legal framework, and its influence in shaping emerging knowledge societies in the GCC.

A particular focus of this chapter is the shift being made by the GCC member states away from rentier state status in favour of economic diversification, as well as the development and emergence of new knowledge societies, contributing to debate in the field.[2] This chapter investigates the meaning of knowledge society in the context of published vision documents and assesses the benefits to be gained by implementing these strategic reform programmes. It considers the economic implications associated with the pursuit of knowledge societies in the context of a broader global shift towards economic digitalisation and increased interdependence; and finally, considers the economic position of the States with a particular focus upon levels of FDI and how FDI flows may impact upon existing knowledge, as well as the relevant policy considerations.

1 Amer Al-Roubaie and Muneer M.S. Almubarak, 'Localisation of Knowledge in GCC Countries: The Case of SMEs' (2017) *Middle East Journal of Entrepreneurship, Leadership and Sustainable Development* 1(1), 3–6.

2 See for example, Sameena Hameed, 'Political Economy of Rentierism in the Middle East and Disruptions from the Digital Space' (2020) *Contemporary Review of the Middle East* 7(1), 64.

DOI: 10.4324/9781003528517-5

The GCC member states are working towards the development of new knowledge societies.[3] This is a prudent and highly desirable policy objective, from both a social and economic perspective, if it can be executed well. Knowledge is closely interrelated with economic development and standards of living (social welfare); it is both a means by which to achieve productivity improvements and create intergenerational wealth, if distributed equitably and matched with well-designed legal frameworks, as well as robust domestic dispute settlement procedures. There is also a need to protect traditional knowledge and cultural heritage built up over previous generations and ensure that local and regional knowledge is retained and built upon.[4]

Locally developed new knowledge is a major factor influencing society, the ability of GCC economies to compete in a globalised and digitalised economy will improve social welfare over the long-run.[5] However, the lack of consensus about what a knowledge society is makes achieving these goals somewhat difficult.[6] This chapter examines these policy objectives, adopting a principally qualitative approach, to best capture the nature of these dynamic and important concepts. In doing so, it contributes to the debate about the meaning and value of knowledge, its best application and use, means of protection, and most importantly, its relationship with the GCC economies and societies.

It is suggested that there is somewhat of a gap in existing literature, which this chapter in part addresses, with respect to knowledge development in the GCC during this important transformational phase in terms of their economic and social development. Amzad Hossain argues that there are limited comprehensive quantitative investigations relating to development of indicators of knowledge-based economy within the GCC member states, and more generally, debate about the extent of knowledge consolidation and growth, notwithstanding a relatively high per capita income and implementation of strategies designed to enhance knowledge-based economy indicators.[7] This chapter considers the emergence of new knowledge economies in the GCC and the implications of this shift in terms of economic development.

3 Hira Amin, Alina Zaman and Evren Tok, 'Education for Sustainable Development and Global Citizenship Education in the GCC: A Systematic Literature Review' (2023) *Globalisation, Societies and Education, Routledge Taylor & Francis Group* 1–16.

4 See for example, Amin et al (n 3), 11 in the context of Saudi Arabia.

5 Reem Khalid Abu-Shawish, Michael H. Romanowski and Tasneem Amatullah, 'Policy Borrowing and Developing Knowledge Economies in GCC Countries: A Critique from a Human Capital Theory Perspective' (2021) *Asia Pacific Education Review* 22, 79.

6 Martin Hvidt, 'Reaching for the Stars: How and Why do the Gulf States Aim to Transform Their Economies to 'Knowledge-Based Economies?' (2021) *London School of Economics*, at <Reaching for the Stars: How and Why do the Gulf States Aim to Transform Their Economies to 'Knowledge-Based Economies'? | Middle East Centre (lse.ac.uk)>.

7 Amzad Hossain, 'Evolution of Mutual Knowledge-Based Economy in Regional Integration: An Experience from the Cooperation Council of Arab States of the Gulf' (2015) *Journal of the Knowledge Economy* 6, 792.

The GCC member states are at an important juncture in terms of their social and their economic development.[8] The two are linked by knowledge, its transfer, application and the laws affecting it, including but perhaps not limited to, property and foreign direct investment legislation, for example. The States stand to gain by particularising the definition of knowledge societies and investing in knowledge development, particularly in sectors in which they can best compete on a global scale.[9] The importation of knowledge, principally through relaxation of domestic foreign direct investment legislation, will not be enough to sustain the levels of productivity required to compete globally, particularly in the context of recent volatility in natural resource commodity prices, namely oil and gas.[10] The States have an opportunity to improve economic performance and enhance standards of living over the long-run if they are prepared to invest in their human capital and promote the transfer of new knowledge and technology within domestic corporations. However, law-makers in the Stated need to address the widening gap between policy and regulation impacting upon technology and innovation creation and utilisation, for example, in intellectual property, foreign investment and the protection of traditional knowledge and cultural heritage.

New Knowledge Societies and Visions for the Future

The GCC member states have demonstrated a desire to develop new knowledge societies and economies which compete at the local, regional, and global levels now and into the future. This is an important objective for most states, grappling with economic issues including debt, high inflation, and cost of living pressures, for example, some of which directly relate to the recent pandemic. However, there are many different definitions of knowledge society; whilst they have common elements there is no classical definition. Kenneth Carlaw et al argue that debate about the possible shift towards a knowledge-based economy/knowledge-based society has been impacted by "differing emphases", reflected in the range of definitions reviewed, arguing that "[o]ne consistent factor is the lack of clarity and consistency".[11] Ravi Sharma et al argue that the classification of societies on the basis of their respective knowledge capital is fraught with difficulty "because knowledge is a substitutable and transferable commodity that is by no means an end in itself" and rather that knowledge societies are those "that have shown superiority

8 Amin et al (n 3) 1–2.

9 Hvidt (n 6).

10 Joseph Stiglitz and Bruce Greenwald, *Creating a Learning Society: A New Approach to Growth, Development and Social Progress* (New York: Columbia University Press, Reader's Edition, 2015) 15.

11 Kenneth Carlaw, Les Oxley, Paul Walker, David Thorns and Michael Nuth, 'Beyond the Hype: Intellectual Property And The Knowledge Society/Knowledge Economy (2006) *Journal of Economic Surveys* 20(4) 633.

in their ability to leverage on the knowledge resources that reside within them and more importantly "its ability to be a learning society".[12]

Nevertheless, scholars, institutions and regulators have grappled with how to define and promote a knowledge society as a means to enhance living standards; indeed, Joseph Stiglitz and Bruce Greenwald argue that "[n]ot only is the pace of learning (innovation) the most important determinant of increases in standards of living, the pace itself is almost surely partially, if not largely, endogenous".[13] This is a challenge facing GCC member states as they develop into new knowledge societies, however, it is a worthwhile transition to make. According to Stiglitz and Greenwald, states stand to gain from investing in knowledge development and moreover, these benefits are likely to provide economic and social benefits into the future due to the autogenous nature of the good.[14]

The concept of a knowledge society is broad, encompassing and difficult to measure. For example, Sharma et al argue that: [15]

> the knowledge society is a society which is a part of the knowledge economy, possesses a high absorptive capacity; has structures and cultures that facilitate frictionless knowledge diffusion and sharing; undergoes complex chains of creation, production, and distribution including inter-functional collaboration; and are sustainable learning communities with an emphasis on innovation.

The United Nations Development Programme defines a knowledge-based society as "one where knowledge diffusion, production and application become the organising principle in all aspects of human activity: culture, society, economy, politics and private life".[16] Helmut Willke argues that a "knowledge society exists if knowledge-dependent operations pervade the structures and symbolic reproduction of a society to such an extent that the handling of information, symbolic analysis and expert systems has primacy over the other reproduction factors".[17] Moreover, Egbert de Weert cites Willke who argues, that only when a qualitatively novel type of knowledge base, as well as symbolism, pervades all aspects of society "and context-specific expertise in all domains of the society are generated", does the theory of a knowledge society become meaningful.[18]

12 Ravi Sharma, Ekundayo Samuel and Elaine Ng, 'Beyond the Digital Divide: The Policy Analysis for Knowledge Societies' (2009) *Journal of Knowledge Management* 13(5), 373.

13 Stiglitz and Greenwald (n 10) 15.

14 Stiglitz and Greenwald (n 10) 15.

15 Norsiah Abdul Hamid and Halimah Badioze Zaman, 'The Perspective of Knowledge Society In Malaysia' (2016), at <https://ebookcentral.proquest.com/lib/cdu/detail.action?docID=6766407>.

16 Hamid and Zaman (n 15) 23, citing 'Arab Development Report 2003', *United Nations Development Programme*, UNDP <Arab Human Development Report 2003 | Human Development Reports (undp.org)>.

17 Egbert de Weert, 'Contours of the Emergent Knowledge Society: Theoretical Debate and Implications for Higher Education Research' (1999) *Higher Education* 38(1), 56, citing Helmut Willke, 'Organisierte Wissenarbeit' (1998) *Zetschrift Fur Soziologie* 27(3) 161, 162.

18 Egbert de Weert, 'Contours of the Emergent Knowledge Society: Theoretical Debate and Implications for Higher Education Research' (1999) *Higher Education* 38(1), 56, citing Helmut Willke, 'Organisierte Wissenarbeit' (1998) *Zetschrift Fur Soziologie* 27(3) 161, 162.

There is even contention between the way that economists and sociologists treat the process of technical developments. For example, economists might approach the issue based on Schumpeter's view of the importance of profit in "'rivalrous' competition" whereas sociologists might instead place emphasis on the role of societal actors, focusing on the professional and social components of the process.[19] However, there is growing awareness of the need for a new approach which accounts for "the inter-relationship of the private (market-based) imperatives and the 'public' knowledge creation and application-based aspects of innovation".[20] Endogenous growth theory, developed by Paul Romer, "ties the development of new ideas to the number of people working in the knowledge sector" essentially creating novel thought, and improving total factor productivity across the board.[21] Total factor productivity is "the residual component of income per capita not explained by capital".[22] Whilst there are criticisms of this theory, it is likely that economic performance and income generation are therefore closely related to, if not dependent upon, local knowledge development and technological change. GCC member states could best exploit the gains to be made from the development of knowledge societies by adopting policies which address this contention and promote human capital as a public good to be harnessed in order to increase standards of living.[23]

A knowledge-based society and a knowledge economy are closely related, yet distinct, terms. Walter Powell and Kaisa Snellman define a knowledge economy as "production and services based on knowledge-intensive activities that contribute to an accelerated pace of technical and scientific advance, as well as rapid obsolescence. The key component of a knowledge economy is a greater reliance on intellectual capabilities than on physical inputs or natural resources".[24] Norsiah Abdul Hamid and Halimah Badioze Zaman argue that the concepts of knowledge society and information society are inter-related, information being a building block of knowledge, and that knowledge is not comparable to "other commodities" but rather is vastly different from output associated with the "industrial model", possessing the characteristic of "non-rivalry in use", which is a characteristic of

19 See Carlaw et al (n 11), 640, citing J. Schumpeter, *Capitalism, Socialism and Democracy* (Harper: New York, 1942); see also R. Nelson, 'What Is Private and What Is Public about Technology?' (1998) *Human Values* 14(3), 229–241.

20 Carlaw et al (n 11).

21 James Morley, 'Economic Theories That Have Changed Us: Endogenous Growth' *The Conversation* (22 June 2015), at <Economic theories that have changed us: endogenous growth (theconversation.com>.

22 James Morley, 'Economic Theories That Have Changed Us: Endogenous Growth' *The Conversation* (22 June 2015), at <Economic theories that have changed us: endogenous growth (theconversation.com>.

23 James Morley, 'Economic Theories That Have Changed Us: Endogenous Growth' *The Conversation* (22 June 2015), at <Economic theories that have changed us: endogenous growth (theconversation.com>.

24 Carlaw et al (n 11) 669, citing Walter W. Powell and Kaisa Snellman, 'The Knowledge Economy' (2004) *Annual Review of Sociology* 30 199–220.

"public goods".[25] Hamid and Zaman point out that unlike material goods, knowledge can be disseminated at a very low marginal cost; however, they caution that in economies characterised as knowledge-based, specifically an economy in which "knowledge has become the most important factor of production and the basic form of capital", the vast volumes of information and data available means that "obtaining information can be done at a low cost but selecting the correct information and turning it into knowledge comes at a rather high cost".[26]

The lack of consensus on what a knowledge society might be, makes it a difficult objective to measure and achieve. Nevertheless, it is a worthy policy goal and central to the economic wellbeing of a society. Stiglitz and Greenwald argue that "one of the objectives of economic policy should be to create economic policies and structures that enhance both learning and learning spillovers; creating a learning society is more likely to increase standards of living than is making small, one time improvements in economic efficiency or sacrificing consumption today to deepen capital".[27] GCC member states stand to benefit, therefore, at a societal level and, notwithstanding the lack of consensus as to what a knowledge society or economy is, from promoting learning.

Whilst GCC member states are investing in education, for example the UAE Mars Mission and Saudi Arabia's New Enterprise Operating Model (NEOM) project, this does not go far enough: Martin Hvidt argues "[t]he quality of education and general incentives or motivation among the younger segments of the population are the single most constraining factors for the Gulf countries' transition into knowledge-based economies".[28] Critically, merely developing and investing in knowledge is not enough. The crux of Stiglitz and Greenwald's argument is that policy makers need to ensure their programmes exploit their respective "comparative advantage in knowledge and learning abilities, including [the] ability to learn and to learn and to learn, in relation to its competitors, and to help develop those capacities and capabilities future"; failure to do so would result in falling behind competitors with a higher aptitude for learning.[29] This presents a challenge for states in developing their new knowledge societies.

Notably, the transition to reduce dependence on oil and gas revenue is likely to occur over the long-run, therefore policy makers may be able to take a broader view of comparative advantage. Hvidt argues that the need to diversify is perhaps most acutely felt by Bahrain and Oman "due to their small and rapidly dwindling oil reserves"; "Kuwait, Qatar and the UAE, on the other hand, signal little urgency to diversify their economies, with Qatar deliberately aiming for a 'slow'

25 Hamid and Zaman (n 15) 19–20, citing Philippe Quéau, 'Global Governance and Knowledge Societies' (1 December 2002) *Development* 45 10–16.

26 Hamid and Zaman (n 15) 19–20, citing Philippe Quéau, 'Global Governance and Knowledge Societies' (1 December 2002) *Development* 20.

27 Stiglitz and Greenwald (n 10) 15.

28 Hvidt (n 6).

29 Stiglitz and Greenwald (n 10) 26.

diversification process" with Saudi Arabia landing somewhere in the middle.[30] However, in a more recent note, Hvidt argues Saudi Arabia has demonstrated an "urgency" in making this transformation in the context of the decline of oil.[31]

In a 2010 report from the Economist Intelligence Unit (sponsored by the Qatar Financial Centre Authority) Jane Kinnimont identified four key areas of comparative advantage for GCC member states, namely "energy-intensive manufacturing, for example petrochemicals, plastics, and aluminium; mining and mineral-based industries; trade and logistics; and tourism, hospitality and aviation".[32] The States can therefore perhaps best exploit the gains of developing knowledge societies by focusing on investing in knowledge and innovation in those four key areas.

GCC regulators also face a significant challenge in terms bridging the widening gap between innovation and technological progress, and the law during a period of profound reform. This challenge will most acutely impact upon intellectual property laws as it is central to innovation because it is concerned with the ways in which novel thought can be disseminated.[33] Intellectual property laws such as copyright and patents also provide an economic motivation for people to use an idea or develop knowledge because they know that property in that knowledge can be owned and protected.[34] There may be difficulty in striking a balance between protecting intellectual property and continuing to promote innovation because of restriction upon use of the "initial technology".[35]

This investment may also result in increased disputes as investors seek to exploit novel commercial opportunities becoming available in the GCC member states as a consequence of knowledge creation. This will require a careful review of existing international investment agreements and dispute settlement bodies, such as the Arab Investment Court.[36] However, it also presents a golden opportunity for the GCC member states individually and even collectively to define the concepts of a knowledge-based society or knowledge-economy, review their objectives for the future in view of these definitions and incorporate these definitions into their

30 Martin Hvidt, *Economic Diversification in GCC Countries: Past Record and Future Trends* (Report No. 27, Kuwait Programme on Development, Governance and Globalisation in the Gulf States, London School of Economics and Finance, January 2013), 37, at <Economic diversification in the GCC countries (lse.ac.uk)> 37.

31 Hvidt (n 6).

32 Jane Kinninmont, Delia Meth-Chon and Aviva Freudmann (eds.), *The GCC in 2020: Broadening the economy (Report from the Economist Intelligence Unit Sponsored by Qatar Financial Centre Authority* (31 October 2010), 2, at <AVIVA_ GCC_to_2020_Economic_diversification_in_GCC _WEB.pdf (eiu.com)>.

33 Carlaw et al (n 11) 641, citing Everett Rogers, *Diffusion of Innovations* (Free Press: New York, 1962).

34 Morley (n 21).

35 Carlaw et al (n 11) 641.

36 See Article 28(1) of the *Unified Agreement for the Investment of Arab Capital in the Arab States*, signed 26 November 1980 (entered into force 07 September 1981) which establishes the Arab Investment Court; note that the *Amendment protocols* to the 1980 Agreement were signed 22 January 2013.

respective vision statements together with a prescribed measurement method and time to assess their success against the standard as defined.

Bahrain, for example, has followed the "regional trend" and developed a strategic plan, *Vision 2030*, which is concerned with economic diversification.[37] Whilst its *Vision 2030* documentation refers to economic transformation, "knowledge", "knowledge-based sectors", the "global knowledge economy" and "knowledge-based (local) economy", it does not define these critical terms.[38] Similarly, the Omani *Vision 2040* document refers to "knowledge", "knowledge-based society" and "knowledge-based economy" but does not define these critical terms.[39] The Omani *Vision 2040* document does expand on these terms in the context of their objectives but one may argue that a definition would be beneficial in terms of meeting these objectives. Critically, this is an issue across the board with the respective GCC vision and plan documents, none of which define "knowledge-based economy", nor do they justify why this is their policy objective.[40]

The Bahraini *Vision 2030* document also refers to "potential measures of success" but does not mandate review against both qualitative and quantitative metrics, which is arguably necessary given the dynamism of the concept.[41] The Omani *Vision 2040* document prescribes baseline targets and metrics to be achieved at specific intervals (e.g. 2030, 2040). However, the performance indicator for supporting gifted students is under development and Oman is seeking to be listed on the Global Human Capital Index.[42]

The Bahraini *Vision 2030* is concerned with developing innovative infrastructure to attract investment and support business. In 2018, Bahrain FinTech Bay was launched and was "a significant step for Bahrain toward becoming a technology and innovation hub";[43] it is developing its infrastructure on an ongoing basis to enhance technology and modernising the "corporate governance framework" to improve investor confidence.[44] Bahrain is somewhat different from other GCC members, sporting a "well-trained population", "low cost of living" and cost to run a business and "innovative regulatory environment" which may induce a "more diversified pool of foreign investor, especially venture capital and other alternative financial investors in sectors such as information and technology or tourism".[45]

37 Claude Lopez, Joseph Bendix and Cesar Servin, 'Bahrain and the Fourth Industrial Revolution' (2020) *Milken Institute,* at <Bahrain-Fourth-Industrial-Revolution-FINAL.pdf (milkeninstitute.org)>.

38 Kingdom of Bahrain, 'From Regional Pioneer To Global Contender - Our Vision - The Economic Vision 2030 For Bahrain' (first launched October 2008), at <Vision+2030+English+(low+resolution).pdf (bahrain.bh)>.

39 Sultanate of Oman, 'Moving Forward With Confidence Vision 2040' (2020) <2020 Oman Vision 2040 (2).pdf>.

40 Hvidt (n 6).

41 Kingdom of Bahrain (n 38).

42 Sultanate of Oman (n 39).

43 Lopez et al (n 37) 3–6.

44 Lopez et al (n 37) 3–6.

45 Lopez et al (n 37) 3–6.

However, the risk is that a focus on "startups and technology" will not be matched by the supply of highly-skilled employees. The number of small sized enterprises and the cost of transitioning to a "digitalized economy" is most likely to impact existing businesses, and most acutely, smaller entities.[46]

The Pursuit of Knowledge, Economic Diversification and Social Optimisation in the GCC

The GCC member states are respectively implementing programs of economic diversification, shifting away from reliance on oil and gas revenue in order to insulate their respective economies from external shocks. This has been an ongoing program for twenty years; according to Bertelsen et al the UAE and Qatar have "made great progress towards diversifying their economies" due in part to endeavours to "strengthen their capacities in education in research".[47] This policy objective is perhaps not surprising, particularly as interest in the renewable market has increased, arguably due in part to accelerated climate change, cost of living pressures, and the recent pandemic. The sophistication of the States which focused on improving knowledge development in the education sector, for example, places them in a unique position in terms of harnessing the gains to be made over the long-term.

The shift away from hydrocarbon-based economies in favour of "knowledge and information-based economies" has been the principal issue in discourse regarding recent development, including political, economic, and social advancement, in the Arabian Gulf.[48] There is somewhat of a gap in existing literature with respect to the significance of knowledge in the GCC. Samia Satti Osman Mohamed Nour notes that, whilst there is research examining the weak nature of demand, production, and promulgation of knowledge in Arab countries and an examination of the obstacles and "strategy for the development of knowledge-based economies in the Middle East and North Africa countries (MENA)",[49] there is a need to assess the significance of knowledge at both the micro and macro levels in the context of the GCC because of their important differences in respect of economic size and structure, income level and nature of labour market compared with the broader MENA states.[50]

46 Lopez et al (n 37) 3–6.

47 Rasmus Gjedssø Bertelsen, Neema Noori and Jean-Marc Rickli (eds), *Strategies of Knowledge Transfer for Economic Diversification in the Arab States of the Gulf* (Gerlach Press, Berlin2017) 2–3.

48 Alexander Wiseman, Naif H. Alromi and Saleh A. Alshumrani, *Education for a Knowledge Society in Arabian Gulf Countries* vol. 24 (Emerald Publishing Limited, Leeds2014), 2, citing J. Fox, N. Mourtada-Sabbah and M. Al-Mutawa (eds) *Globalization and the Gulf* (Routledge: London, 2006).

49 Samia Satti Osman Mohamed Nour, 'The Importance (Impacts) of Knowledge at the Macro-Micro Levels in the Arab Gulf Countries' (2014) *Journal of the Knowledge Economy* 5(3), 526.

50 Samia Satti Osman Mohamed Nour, 'The Importance (Impacts) of Knowledge at the Macro-Micro Levels in the Arab Gulf Countries' (2014) *Journal of the Knowledge Economy* 5(3), 527.

Moreover, GCC member states stand to benefit from developing new knowledge societies. For example, Nour found "that at the macro/aggregate level knowledge is positively correlated with GDP (economic growth), schooling years and technology (patents) across the Gulf countries".[51] However, there is an argument put forward within the literature, that stipulates in order to realise gains from the development of new knowledge societies, Gulf states will need to do more than invest in human capital, import knowledge, investment, and technology; they will need to embrace the intangible, adopt "new organizational cultures" and marry novel technologies with compatible business practices.[52] This will likely pose significant political, economic, and legal challenges, as the traditional social order, conduct of business, and consumption patterns change to reflect and reward innovation.

GCC member states have adopted various strategies to economically diversify and there are differing views in the literature about their relative success. Anna Visvizi, Miltiadis Lytras and Naif Aljohani argue that the strategy employed by the States is to transform to a knowledge-based economy and "model of sustainability"; despite investment "in ICT infrastructure and public services the innovation capability needs to match high innovate nations".[53] Valerie Pelton argues that the introduction of "free trade zones", officially and unofficially, have enabled GCC member states to successfully diversify their "hydrocarbon-dependent economies".[54] Pelton defines these zones in the GCC as important economic zones, "which typically allow foreign ownership, afford favorable tax treatment, and provide exemption from restrictive regulations".[55] The States are also seeking to enhance industrialisation as a central element of economic diversification plans, a sentiment shared by business; for example, the CEO of Qatar Development Bank Abdulaziz Al-Khalifa argues that industrial SMEs need access to money, training, and markets if the GCC is to leave its "single resource identity" behind.[56] Inducement of foreign investment is an important issue as associated governance and regulation, particularly investor-state dispute settlement, needs to reflect

51 Samia Satti Osman Mohamed Nour, 'The Importance (Impacts) of Knowledge at the Macro-Micro Levels in the Arab Gulf Countries' (2014) *Journal of the Knowledge Economy* 5(3), 531.

52 Bertelsen et al (n 47) 3, citing W W. Powell and K. Snellman, 'The Knowledge Economy' (2004) *Annual Review of Sociology* 30 199–220.

53 Anna Visvizi, Miltiadis Lytras and Naif Aljohani, *Assessing the Ecosystem of Innovation in GCC: Policy Implications and Strategic Directions in Research and Innovation Forum 2020* (Springer International Publishing, Switzerland AG, 2021).

54 Valerie Pelton, 'Jebel Ali: Open for Business' (Summer 2018) *Transnational Law & Contemporary Problems* 27(2), 375.

55 Valerie Pelton, 'Jebel Ali: Open for Business' (Summer 2018) *Transnational Law & Contemporary Problems* 27(2), 375, referring to Thomas Farole and Gokhan Akinci, 'Special Economic Zones: Progress, Emerging Challenges, and Future Directions (English)' (2016) *World Bank Group*, at <http://documents.worldbank.org/curated/en/752011468203980987/Special-economic-zones-progress-emerging-challenges-and-future-directions>.

56 Alexandre Raffoul and Fatima Al Zahra Hewaidi, 'How Industrialisation Could Future-proof MENA's Gulf Economies' *World Economic Forum* (28 June 2021), at <Industrialisation is key to GCC economic diversification | World Economic Forum (weforum.org)>.

changes in the political, societal, and economic spheres and keep pace with technological change.

The development of new knowledge societies is arguably of paramount importance in the context of significant economic and social change occurring globally. Daniel Goldman argues that conventional models of development "have viewed advanced technology as the culminating phase of industrialization, modernization, and economic diversification, rather than as a means to increase long-term growth and competitiveness in countries confronting significant economic challenges".[57] This assessment has validity and the shortcoming has obvious implications for GCC member states grappling with significant exogenous shocks to output, in the context of global change. There is arguably a need for new models of development, which view innovation and the use of sophisticated technology as an integral component of an improved economic outlook from the outset.

The GCC member states are seeking to "develop resilient, knowledge-based economies" as they shift away from hydrocarbon-based industry.[58] Recent volatility in oil prices, in particular, have been a major catalyst for driving change. The States have faced "sustained economic pressure" as oil prices dropped significantly in the last quarter of 2014 ($112-$62/barrel), falling again to $26.5/barrel in 2016, recovering to, on average, about $63/barrel in 2019 and ultimately falling to under $20/barrel in April 2020 due to two factors, namely, the "Saudi-Russian rift about production cuts combined with drastically decreased demand during the COVID-19 Pandemic".[59] Anastasia Nosova argues that this recent and major fluctuation in oil prices wasn't a new phenomenon, however, "the shock of the drastic drop in revenue and the realization that the price was unlikely to reach the pre-2014 levels anytime soon was a strong incentive for gulf governments to review their existing spending and distribution patterns".[60]

This economic diversification program being undertaken by the GCC member states is occurring in the context of a global process of technological change known as the Fourth Industrial Revolution, specifically "the convergence of digital, biological, and physical innovations".[61] As Klaus Schwab, Founder and executive Chairman of the World Economic Forum, asserts in his ground-breaking thesis on the Fourth Industrial Revolution, "of the many diverse and fascinating challenges we face today, the most intense and important is how to understand and shape the

57 Daniel Goldman, 'The Role of Technology Entrepreneurship in Promoting Sustainable Development in the GCC' in Rasmus Gjedssø Bertelsen, Neema Noori and Jean-Marc Rickli (eds), *Strategies of Knowledge Transfer for Economic Diversification in the Arab States of the Gulf* (Gerlach Press, Berlin 2017) 17.

58 Raffoul and Hewaidi (n 56).

59 Anastasia Nosova, 'Shifting State-Business Relations in the Gulf Cooperation Council (GCC) Post-2014' (2021) *The Muslim World (Hartford)* 111(1), 58.

60 Anastasia Nosova, 'Shifting State-Business Relations in the Gulf Cooperation Council (GCC) Post-2014' (2021) *The Muslim World (Hartford)* 111(1), 58.

61 Klaus Schwab, 'The Fourth Industrial Revolution' *World Economic Forum* (2016), at <www.weforum.org>.

new technology revolution, which entails nothing less than a transformation of humankind. We are at the beginning of a revolution that is fundamentally changing the way we live, work, and relate to each other".[62] According to Schwab, the Fourth Industrial Revolution is "a technological revolution characterised by a fusion of technologies that is blurring the lines between the physical, digital and biological spheres".[63] It is suggested that this change is already occurring within the States. An example embodying this change is Hub71's (Abu Dhabi) launch of "a new initiative to fund web3 start-ups named Hub71 + Digital Assets", including support of blockchain technology.[64] Moreover, this change has significant implications for regional societies, particularly in relation to economic and legal order, including investment dispute settlement. Higher levels of foreign direct investment in the region, together with a fundamental change in the nature of local business practices and investment in the GCC, will likely have a significant impact upon dispute settlement in the Arabian Gulf, including investor-state arbitration.

The development and use of such technology is not simply relevant to business practices, productivity, and consumption, it is arguably pervading every aspect of life. For example, the use of smartphones is prolific and investment in required technological infrastructure is increasing. Salma Saleh points out that, "the majority of the population in the Middle East and North Africa access the internet through their mobile devices, with Bahrain leading the region at a penetration rate exceeding 97 percent".[65] Saleh (2023) also notes "[t]he Smartphone penetration rate in the region is the highest in the GCC sub-region, with countries such as the United Arab Emirates (UAE) exceeding 96 percent in 2023".[66] Furthermore, Saudi Arabia and the UAE are reportedly investing in technology including 5G to advance development of "a more knowledge-based economy".[67] Saleh also argues that the use and promotion of smartphones has been a catalyst for digitalisation, "driving the shift towards a digital lifestyle, fuelled by regional user initiatives such as digital payment" and moreover, this increased dependence on "mobile internet", combined with ongoing progress in related technological infrastructure will likely drive accelerating demand for "advanced smartphones".[68] Saleh expects that 5G

62 Klaus Schwab, 'The Fourth Industrial Revolution' *World Economic Forum* (2016), at <www.weforum.org>.

63 Klaus Schwab, 'The Fourth Industrial Revolution: Its Meaning and How to Respond' (2017) *Logistics and Transport Focus* 19(2), 40.

64 Cindy Tan, 'Abu Dhabi's Global Tech Ecosystem Hub71 Launches $2B Initiative to Fund Web3 Startups' *Metaverse Post* (15 February 2023), at <Abu Dhabi's Global Tech Ecosystem Hub71 Launches $2B Initiative to Fund Web3 Startups | Metaverse Post (mpost.io)>.

65 Salma Saleh, 'Smartphone Market in MENA – Statistics & Facts' *Statista* (28 March 2023), at <Smartphone market in MENA - statistics & facts | Statista>.

66 Salma Saleh, 'Smartphone Market in MENA – Statistics & Facts' *Statista* (28 March 2023), at <Smartphone market in MENA - statistics & facts | Statista>.

67 Salma Saleh, 'Smartphone Market in MENA – Statistics & Facts' *Statista* (28 March 2023), at <Smartphone market in MENA - statistics & facts | Statista>.

68 Salma Saleh, 'Smartphone Market in MENA – Statistics & Facts' *Statista* (28 March 2023), at <Smartphone market in MENA - statistics & facts | Statista>.

subscriptions in GCC member states will increase in the short-term; Samsung is the strongest smartphone provider in the market, followed by Apple and Xiaomi. However notably, Apple dominates the market in Saudi Arabia which is the most significant smartphone market in the GCC, "accounting for more than half the total smartphone shipments to the region".[69] Critically, these smartphone providers are all large foreign multinational companies. Samsung is a South Korean entity, Apple is an American company and Xiaomi is a Chinese company. Increasing dependence on technology produced by foreign corporations may have significant implications in terms of investment disputes litigated in domestic courts or in international arbitration.

Foreign Direct Investment, Economic Development and Emerging Knowledge Societies in the GCC

The economic prospects for the GCC are positive, although economic growth into the future will present some challenges as GCC member states seek to reduce reliance on oil and gas rents. The States will need to invest carefully in knowledge creation and promotion as well as protecting knowledge in a regulatory sense in order to optimise gains made as a result of becoming a "learning society".[70] Income generation, economic development and social welfare in the GCC is therefore closely inter-dependent on the development and consolidation of knowledge societies and innovation. There is evidence that the States are already seeing some benefit from economic reform programs, liberalisation of foreign investment laws and a renewed focus on developing knowledge, however there is arguably opportunity to do much more in this regard.

According to the World Economic Situation and Prospects 2023 Report published by the United Nations, GCC member states "experienced rapid economic expansion" as a result of external demand for crude oil pursuant to the OPEC Plus agreement; the "non-oil sector in the GCC countries also saw consistent expansion" and real estate is gradually recovering, although house prices are still well below the peak experienced in 2014–15.[71] However, the States also face economic challenges including combating inflation, and "have shifted to a tightening cycle in response" and "greater oil revenues, fiscal expenditures in the States apparently increased in real terms during fiscal year 2022 to an extent tailored by commitments to fiscal consolidation".[72] It will not be enough for the States to rely on oil rent as the primary income source into the future, and further academic examination of FDI inflows in particular, over the short-term may be warranted. In recent

69 Salma Saleh, 'Smartphone Market in MENA – Statistics & Facts' *Statista* (28 March 2023), at *Statista* <Smartphone market in MENA - statistics & facts | Statista>.

70 Sharma et al (n 12) 373.

71 United Nations, 'World Economic Situation and Prospects' (2023) 103, at <WESP 2023_FINAL_Web_10_Feb_2023 (1).pdf>.

72 United Nations, 'World Economic Situation and Prospects' (2023) 104, at <WESP 2023_FINAL_Web_10_Feb_2023 (1).pdf>.

years, however, external economic factors, together with forward-thinking policy makers and prudent economic management has benefited the States, from an economic perspective.

Generally, GCC member states did relatively well in terms of FDI inflows in 2020, increasing by 12.4% in 2020 which was a "global anomaly" as global FDI inflows reduced by 35% principally due to the impacts of COVID-19.[73] According to The Economist Intelligence Unit, this increase can likely be attributed to "both ongoing policies designed to enlist foreign investment to help diversify oil-dependent economies, and acceleration of their implementation during 2020 in response to the fiscal strains caused by the crisis and associated oil-price slump".[74] Whilst the UAE was the top performer in terms of receiving FDI inflows, at 71.7% of FDI, this is very likely distorted because over half of that was attributable to the sale of US$10.1 billion interest in the gas-pipeline network of the Abu Dhabi National Oil Company.[75]

FDI Inflows to Saudi Arabia increased the most in 2020, "validating the huge drive under way to harness capital to realise *Vision 2030* goals"; however, the level of FDI is very low (one-fifth of the levels recorded ten years ago) and the most significant change was the large reduction in outflows because the Public Investment Fund "re-focused on domestic investments".[76] The Saudi Arabian Public Investment Fund is an investment fund with both domestic and international investments, focusing on sustainable investments and is "a catalyst of *Vision 2030*",[77] focusing on "non-oil GDP growth and investing in opportunities across diversified sectors"; one of its objectives is to "localize cutting edge technology and knowledge".[78]

According to The Economist Intelligence Unit (2021) the smaller GCC economies did not fare so well, with the exception of Oman, which had increased FDI inflows "by an impressive 19.7% to US$4.1 billion, partly reflecting its weak fiscal position and increasing use of public-private partnerships (PPPs) for infrastructure development".[79]

Overall, however, the GCC member states are expected to enjoy an "upward regional trend" due to the enactment of more liberal foreign investment laws, notably including the *Federal Law by Decree No. 19 of 2018 Regarding Foreign Direct*

73 Economist Intelligence Unit, 'GCC FDI Bucks Global Trend' (30 June 2021), at <GCC FDI bucks global trend - Economist Intelligence Unit (eiu.com)>.

74 Economist Intelligence Unit, 'GCC FDI Bucks Global Trend' (30 June 2021), at <GCC FDI bucks global trend - Economist Intelligence Unit (eiu.com)>.

75 Economist Intelligence Unit, 'GCC FDI Bucks Global Trend' (30 June 2021), at <GCC FDI bucks global trend - Economist Intelligence Unit (eiu.com)>.

76 Economist Intelligence Unit, 'GCC FDI Bucks Global Trend' (30 June 2021), at <GCC FDI bucks global trend - Economist Intelligence Unit (eiu.com)>.

77 Public Investment Fund, 'Who We Are' (Q1 2022), at <PIF - Who We Are | Public Investment Fund>.

78 Public Investment Fund, 'Public Investment Fund Program 2021-2015' (undated) <https://www.pif.gov.sa/en/Pages/AboutPIF.aspx>.

79 Economist Intelligence Unit (n 73).

Investment (UAE's FDI Law)[80] and the *Private Sector Participation Law* (Saudi Arabia).[81] Certainly, there is evidence of this occurring, particularly with respect to the UAE, likely due at least in part, to the foreign direct investment liberalisation measures.

Moreover, the UAE's FDI law specifically identifies the obtainment of knowledge as an objective, emphasising the intrinsic link between knowledge, economic development, and social advancement. For example, sub-article 2(3) of the Law states, its third objective is expansion and diversification of the production base "and transferring and attracting advanced technology, knowledge and training".[82] Though this law has subsequently been repealed, the inclusion of a specific reference to attracting higher level knowledge, for example, evidences an intention by regulators to implement this policy measure through legislative means.

There is real opportunity for GCC member states to capitalise on increasing levels of FDI by investing these gains in developing local knowledge and expertise, particularly in areas of comparative advantage, rather than merely importing knowledge and technology which may risk abrogation of cultural heritage and rich history of traditional knowledge built by previous generations. GCC regulators may seek to protect "intangible assets" including, for example, "traditional medicine and environmental knowledge to art, symbols and music" as intellectual property.[83] Relevantly, the States have ratified the UNESCO *Convention for the Safeguarding of the Intangible Cultural Heritage*[84] and may benefit from taking inventories and applying safeguarding measures to protect developments in cultural heritage in their respective territories over time. This is particularly important as the countries become more open to foreign knowledge and FDI, in the context of liberalisation of economies and foreign investment laws, generally.

The GCC is a complex and dynamic union, comprised of states with differing approaches to the attraction and retention of FDI and to some extent, this reflects their relative openness to foreign investment and, by extension, knowledge transfer. The UAE was ranked by UNCTAD as 19th in the 20 top host economies (as

80 United Arab Emirates, *Federal Law By Decree No. 19 of 2018 on Foreign Direct Investment*, entered into force 1 October 2018. Pursuant to Article 6(2) of *Federal Law By Decree No. 26 of 2020 Amending Certain Provisions of Federal Law No. (2) of 2015 on Commercial Companies*, entered into force 2 January 2021, *Federal Law by Decree No. (19) of 2018 on Direct Foreign Investment* is repealed.

81 Saudi Arabia, *Private Sector Participation Law*, entered into force 24 July 2021; Economist Intelligence Unit (n 73).

82 Sub-article 2(3) of the *Federal Decree Law No. 19 of 2018 on Foreign Direct Investment* (n 80).

83 World Intellectual Property Organization, 'Genetic Resources, Traditional Knowledge and Traditional Cultural Expressions' (undated), at <Traditional Knowledge (wipo.int)>.

84 *Convention for the Safeguarding of the Intangible Cultural Heritage*, adopted by the UNESCO General Conference 17 October 2003, entered into force 20 April 2006. It is intended to be supplemental to the *Convention Concerning the Protection of the World Cultural and Natural Heritage* of 1972.

ranked by inflow value) in 2021 in terms of FDI inflows.[85] UNCTAD defines FDI as "an investment reflecting a lasting interest and control by a foreign direct investor, resident in one economy, in an enterprise resident in another economy (foreign affiliate)".[86] It defines FDI inflows as "compris[ing] capital provided by a foreign direct investor to its foreign affiliate resident in the reporting country, or capital received by a foreign direct investor resident in the reporting country from its foreign affiliate abroad".[87] The value of FDI inflows to the UAE in 2021 was US$21 billion.[88] As a ratio to Gross Domestic Product (GDP), in 2021 the UAE's FDI inflows were relatively high at 4.9%.[89] In fact, the UAE's inflows as a ratio to GDP in the top 20 host economies of 2021 for FDI inflows was only outdone by China, Hong Kong SAR, Singapore, South Africa and Israel.[90]

Both Saudi Arabia and the UAE were ranked in the top 20 home economies by UNCTAD in 2021 for FDI outflows as number 15 and 17 respectively. Saudi Arabia had an outflow value of US$24 billion and the UAE had an outflow value of US$23 billion in 2021. As a ratio to GDP, Saudi Arabia's outflows was 2.9% and the UAE's was 5.4%. By way of comparison, the top home economy in 2021 (by FDI outflow value) was the United States of America, which had an outflow value of US$403 billion and an outflow ratio to GDP of 1.7%. GCC members may benefit from reducing their outflow ratio to GDP and increasing levels of investment in local knowledge and technological development in the context of the vision goals.

This is arguably particularly important in the context of the age of digitalisation and in the quest to develop cutting-edge technology, there is a risk that societies will become homogenous. There is also a need for GCC member states to ensure that new knowledge can be protected and handed down to future generations through investment in higher tertiary education and the protection and promotion of intellectual property rights, and the latter needs to strike a delicate balance to ensure that novel thought and technology is not unduly stifled.

Conclusion

The GCC member states are at an important juncture in terms of their pursuit of knowledge, economic diversification and consolidation, and social advancement. These are worthy policy objectives in the context of external factors namely market

85 UNCTAD, 'Economic Trends Foreign Direct Investment' (2022) UNCTAD Handbook of Statistics 2022, at <Foreign direct investment – UNCTAD Handbook of Statistics 2022>.

86 UNCTAD, 'Economic Trends Foreign Direct Investment' (2022) UNCTAD Handbook of Statistics 2022, at <Foreign direct investment – UNCTAD Handbook of Statistics 2022>.

87 UNCTAD, 'Economic Trends Foreign Direct Investment' (2022) UNCTAD Handbook of Statistics 2022, at <Foreign direct investment – UNCTAD Handbook of Statistics 2022>.

88 UNCTAD, 'Economic Trends Foreign Direct Investment' (2022) UNCTAD Handbook of Statistics 2022, at <Foreign direct investment – UNCTAD Handbook of Statistics 2022>.

89 UNCTAD, 'Economic Trends Foreign Direct Investment' (2022) UNCTAD Handbook of Statistics 2022, at <Foreign direct investment – UNCTAD Handbook of Statistics 2022>.

90 UNCTAD, 'Economic Trends Foreign Direct Investment' (2022) UNCTAD Handbook of Statistics 2022, at <Foreign direct investment – UNCTAD Handbook of Statistics 2022>.

volatility, particularly in oil prices and greater interest in renewables. Some states, notably the UAE, have increased the level of openness of their economies through the enactment of foreign direct investment legislation relaxing previously tightly controlled laws. The UAE in particular has enjoyed higher levels of FDI inflows, indicating that foreign investors are increasingly attracted to investing in the UAE, likely in part because of the relaxation of the foreign direct investment laws. Higher levels of FDI may lead to beneficial spill-overs such as knowledge sharing and transfer.[91] However, trade liberalisation and importation of novel thought and technology will require careful regulation and dispute management processes and, arguably more importantly, it will not be enough to improve economic performance over the long-run in the States. To do that, the States need to invest in local knowledge industries and 'learn how to learn' so that novel ideas can be applied and conveyed, and preserved for the benefit of future generations.

The GCC member states have embarked on sweeping reforms designed to build societies of the future. They stand to gain from both a social and economic perspective from investing in knowledge creation and technological development, particularly if they focus on their comparative strengths. Foreign direct investment is both a means by which to access new information and fund investment in locally developed knowledge. However, it needs to be harnessed in a way that enhances local learning, knowledge sharing, and commercial application.

There is also a need for policy makers to address the widening gap between novel technology and regulation. Knowledge is both a capital building public good and a private good requiring protection and promotion. GCC regulators must strike a delicate balance in this regard, particularly in acutely impacted areas including intellectual property and dispute settlement processes such as mediation, conciliation and arbitration. Policy makers also need to invest in knowledge as a means of income generation into the future. They also need to ensure that the distribution of these gains is equitable and reflects inputs in order to optimise economic performance and promote intergenerational wealth and future knowledge creation.

The GCC member states have published visions for the future with a focus on developing knowledge economies and societies. However, there is no consensus on a definition in the literature as to what a knowledge-society is. Notwithstanding these gaps, leading commentators have argued that economic development, and therefore social welfare, is dependent on nations learning how to learn, fostering further knowledge development internally, and focusing on areas of comparative advantage.

The fact that the States have not defined what a knowledge-society or economy is means that it may be a difficult objective to achieve in practice, and even if it was achieved, it would certainly be a difficult thing to measure. Certainly, economic principles such as total factor productivity may not be precise enough to measure the economic consequence of locally developed new knowledge, but rather measure a residual non-capital related figure. Knowledge and technological

91 Stiglitz and Greenwald (n 10) 15.

development are intrinsic to economic performance in the context of the digital global economy. Yet, data and information are so ubiquitous that access to knowledge, including its importation, without critical assessment of its quality, and local application and development is not enough to sustain and improve economic development and enhance social welfare.

The development of new locally derived knowledge and technological advancement is central to economic output, income generation, and society more broadly. But the question remains as to what a knowledge society actually is, how to achieve it, and how to efficiently and equitably distribute the gains, both tangible and intangible, of such gains.

The question for policy makers in the GCC, therefore, is how they address these gaps and how the pursuit of knowledge will benefit society, not just in the trade and commercial fields, but in all facets of society, principally through redistribution. There is a need to balance corporate privacy (including, for example, commercial-in-confidence information) and promote knowledge transfer. However, this is a difficult balance to strike in practice, requiring careful management within the legal framework at the domestic, regional, and international levels. Policy makers are also faced with the challenge of determining how best, and to what level, traditional knowledge and cultural heritage should be preserved and fostered. The degree to which this is achieved is worthy of further consideration.

Bibliography

Abu-Shawish, Reem Khalid, Michael H. Romanowski and Tasneem Amatullah, 'Policy Borrowing and Developing Knowledge Economies in GCC Countries: A Critique from a Human Capital Theory Perspective', (2021) *Asia Pacific Education Review* 22, 77–88.

Al-Roubaie, Amer and Muneer M. S. Almubarak, 'Localisation of Knowledge in GCC Countries: The Case of SMEs', (2017) *Middle East Journal of Entrepreneurship, Leadership and Sustainable Development* 1(1), 1–15.

Amin, Hira, Alina Zaman and Evren Tok, 'Education for Sustainable Development and Global itizenship Education in the GCC: A Systematic Literature Review', (2023) *Globalisation, Societies and Education* 1–16.

Carlaw, Kenneth, Les Oxley, Paul Walker, David Thorns and Michael Nuth, 'Beyond the Hype: Intellectual Property and the Knowledge Society/Knowledge Economy', (2006) *Journal of Economic Surveys* 20(4), 633–699.

Claude Lopez, Joseph Bendix and Cesar Servin, 'Bahrain and the Fourth Industrial Revolution', Milken Institute (2020), at <Bahrain-Fourth-Industrial-Revolution-FINAL .pdf (milkeninstitute.org)>.

Convention for the Safeguarding of the Intangible Cultural Heritage, Signed 17 October 2003, Entered into Force 20 April 2006.

de Weert, Egbert, 'Contours of the Emergent Knowledge Society: Theoretical Debate and Implications for Higher Education Research', (1999) *Higher Education* 38(1), 49–69.

Economist Intelligence Unit, 'GCC FDI Bucks Global Trend' (30 June 2021), at <GCC FDI bucks global trend - Economist Intelligence Unit (eiu.com)>.

Farole, Thomas and Gokhan Akinci, 'Special Economic Zones: Progress, Emerging Challenges, and Future Directions (English)', *World Bank Group* (2016), at <http://documents.worldbank.org/curated/en/752011468203980987/Special-economic-zones-progress-emerging-challenges-and-future-directions>.

Fox, J., N. Mourtada-Sabbah and M. Al-Mutawa (eds.), *Globalization and the Gulf* (London: Routledge, 2006).

Goldman, Daniel, 'The Role of Technology Entrepreneurship in Promoting Sustainable Development in the GCC', in Bertelsen, Rasmus Gjedssø, Neema Noori and Jean-Marc Rickli (eds.), *Strategies of Knowledge Transfer for Economic Diversification in the Arab States of the Gulf* (Gerlach Press, Berlin, 2017. 17–33).

Hamid, Norsiah Abdul and Halimah Badioze Zaman, 'The Perspective of Knowledge Society In Malaysia', *ProQuest Ebook Central* (2016), at <https://ebookcentral.proquest.com/lib/cdu/detail.action?docID=6766407>.

Hameed, Sameena, 'Political Economy of Rentierism in the Middle East and Disruptions from the Digital Space', (2020) *Contemporary Review of the Middle East* 7(1), 54–89.

Hossain, Amzad, 'Evolution of Mutual Knowledge-Based Economy in Regional Integration: An Experience from the Cooperation Council of Arab States of the Gulf', (2015) *Journal of the Knowledge Economy* 6, 790–817.

Hvidt, Martin, *Economic Diversification in GCC Countries: Past Record and Future Trends* (Report No. 27, Kuwait Programme on Development, Governance and Globalisation in the Gulf States, London School of Economics and Finance, January 2013), at <Economic diversification in the GCC countries (lse.ac.uk)>.

Hvidt, Martin, 'Reaching for the Stars: How and Why do the Gulf States Aim to Transform Their Economies to 'Knowledge-Based Economies?' *London School of Economics* (2021), at <Reaching for the Stars: How and Why do the Gulf States Aim to Transform Their Economies to 'Knowledge-Based Economies'? | Middle East Centre (lse.ac.uk)>.

Kingdom of Bahrain, 'From Regional Pioneer To Global Contender - Our Vision - The Economic Vision 2030 For Bahrain' (first launched October 2008), at <Vision+2030+English+(low+resolution).pdf (bahrain.bh)>.

Kingdom of Saudi Arabia, *Private Sector Participation Law*, Entered into Force 24 July 2021.

Kinninmont, Jane (author), Delia Meth-Chon and Aviva Freudmann (eds.), *The GCC in 2020: Broadening the economy (Report from the Economist Intelligence Unit Sponsored by Qatar Financial Centre Authority* (31 October 2010), 2, at <AVIVA_ GCC_to_2020_Economic_diversification_in_GCC_WEB.pdf (eiu.com)>.

Morley, James, 'Economic Theories That Have Changed Us: Endogenous Growth', *The Conversation* (22 June 2015), at <Economic theories that have changed us: endogenous growth (theconversation.com)>.

Nelson, R., 'What is Private and What is Public About Technology?', (1998) *Human Values* 14(3), 229–241.

Nosova, Anastasia, 'Shifting State-Business Relations in the Gulf Cooperation Council (GCC) Post-2014', (2021) *The Muslim World (Hartford)* 111(1), 54–69.

Nour, Samia Satti Osman Mohamed, 'The Importance (Impacts) of Knowledge at the Macro-Micro Levels in the Arab Gulf Countries', (2014) *Journal of the Knowledge Economy* 5(3), 521–537.

Oman, Sultanate of, 'Moving Forward With Confidence Vision 2040' (2020), at <2020 Oman Vision 2040 (2).pdf>.

Pelton, Valerie, 'Jebel Ali: Open for Business', (Summer 2018) *Transnational Law & Contemporary Problems* 27(2), 375–401.

Powell, W. W. and K. Snellman, 'The Knowledge Economy', (2004) *Annual Review of Sociology* 30, 199–220.

Price, David and Alhanoof AlDebasi, *Protecting Intellectual Property in the Arabian Peninsula: The GCC States, Jordan and Yemen* (London: Routledge, 2018).

Public Investment Fund, 'Public Investment Fund Program 2021-2015' (undated), at <https://www.pif.gov.sa/en/Pages/AboutPIF.aspx>.

Quéau, Philippe, 'Global Governance and Knowledge Societies', *Development* (1 December 2002), 10–16.

Raffoul, Alexandre and Fatima Al Zahra Hewaidi, 'How Industrialisation Could Future-Proof MENA's Gulf Economies', *World Economic Forum* (28 June 2021), at <Industrialisation is key to GCC economic diversification | World Economic Forum (weforum.org)>.

Rogers, Everett, *Diffusion of Innovations* (New York: Free Press, 1962).

Saleh, Salma, 'Smartphone Market in MENA – Statistics & Facts', *Statista* (28 March 2023), at <Smartphone market in MENA - statistics & facts | Statista>.

Schumpeter, J., *Capitalism, Socialism and Democracy* (New York: Harper, 1942).

Schwab, Klaus, 'The Fourth Industrial Revolution', *World Economic Forum* (2016), at <www.weforum.org>.

Schwab, Klaus, 'The Fourth Industrial Revolution: Its Meaning and How to Respond', (2017) *Logistics and Transport Focus* 19(2), 40.

Sharma, Ravi, Elaine Ng, Mathias Dharmawirya and Ekundayo Samuel, 'A Policy Framework for Developing Knowledge Societies' (2020), *International Journal of Knowledge Society Research* 1(1), 23–46.

Sharma, Ravi, Ekundayo Samuel and Elaine Ng, 'Beyond the Digital Divide: The Policy Analysis for Knowledge Societies', (2009) *Journal of Knowledge Management* 13(5), 373–386.

Stiglitz, Joseph and Bruce Greenwald, *Creating a Learning Society: A New Approach to Growth, Development and Social Progress* (New York: Columbia University Press, Reader's Edition, 2015).

Tan, Cindy, 'Abu Dhabi's Global Tech Ecosystem Hub71 Launches $2B Initiative to Fund Web3 Startups', *Metaverse Post* (15 February 2023), at <Abu Dhabi's Global Tech Ecosystem Hub71 Launches $2B Initiative to Fund Web3 Startups | Metaverse Post (mpost.io)>.

UNCTAD, 'Economic Trends Foreign Direct investment', in *UNCTAD Handbook of Statistics 2022* (2022), at <Foreign direct investment – UNCTAD Handbook of Statistics 2022>.

Unified Agreement for the Investment of Arab Capital in the Arab States, Signed 26 November 1980, Entered into Force 7 September 1981.

United Arab Emirates, *Federal Law By Decree No. 19 of 2018 on Foreign Direct Investment*, Entered into Force 1 October 2018.

United Arab Emirates, *Federal Law By Decree No. 26 of 2020 Amending Certain Provisions of Federal Law No. (2) of 2015 on Commercial Companies*, Entered into Force 2 January 2021.

United Nations, 'World Economic Situation and Prospects' (2023), at <WESP 2023_FINAL_Web_10_Feb_2023 (1).pdf>.

Visvizi, Anna, Miltiadis Lytras and Naif Aljohani, 'Assessing the Ecosystem of Innovation in GCC: Policy Implications and Strategic Directions', in *Research and Innovation Forum 2020* (Springer International Publishing, Switzerland AG, 2021).

'Who We Are' (Q1 2022), at <PIF - Who We Are | Public Investment Fund>.

Willke, Helmut, 'Organisierte Wissenarbeit', (1998) *Zetschrift Fur Soziologie* 27(3. 161–177).

Wiseman, Alexander, Naif H. Alromi and Saleh A. Alshumrani, *Education for a Knowledge Society in Arabian Gulf Countries,* vol. 24 (Bingley: Emerald Publishing Limited, 2014).

World Intellectual Property Organization, 'Genetic Resources, Traditional Knowledge and Traditional Cultural Expressions' (undated), <Traditional Knowledge (wipo.int)>.

6 Artificial Intelligence and the Future of Patent Law in the GCC Nations

Noura Almutairi

Introduction

Artificial intelligence (AI) means 'the possibility of interpreting human intelligence so that the computer can easily imitate it and conduct functions, from the easiest to the most complicated ones'.[1] In this context, AI can compete with humans in jobs requiring mental tasks, such as a CEO, lawyer, doctor, etc.[2] AI can also be a writer and inventor without human intervention.

The capability of an advanced AI system to invent without human intervention is not fiction. An example that affirms this point is the Device for Autonomous Bootstrapping of Unified Sentience (DABUS), an AI system that invented two inventions: an improved beverage container based on fractal geometry 'fractal container', and a flashing light for emergencies 'neural flame'.[3] Dr Stephen Thaler created DABUS, but claimed that he did not come up with these inventions himself.[4] Dr Thaler, therefore, filed patent applications for DABUS as the inventor in many countries, including the United Kingdom, the United States, Australia, New Zealand, Japan, India, China, Brazil, South Korea, Taiwan, Switzerland, South

1 Reem Almarzoqi and Mohamad Albakjaji, 'The Patentability of AI Invention: The Case of the Kingdom of Saudi Arabia Law' (2002) 13 *International Journal of Service Science, Management, Engineering, and Technology* 1, 1.

2 See Nikhil Pandey, 'Tang Yu, An AI-Powered Robot, Named CEO Of A Chinese Company' *NDTV* (8 September 2022), https://www.ndtv.com/world-news/tang-yu-an-ai-powered-robot-named-ceo-of-a-chinese-company-3326427; Camille Bello, 'Would You Want a Robot as CEO? Chinese Firm Is First to Try as It Bets on "Metaverse Workplace"' *Euronews* (20 November 2022), https://www.euronews.com/next/2022/11/20/would-you-want-a-robot-as-ceo-chinese-firm-is-first-to-try-as-it-bets-on-metaverse-workpla.

3 Ryan Abbott, *Patent Applications* (The Artificial Inventor, 2020), https://artificialinventor.com/patent/; see also Ryan Abbott, 'The Artificial Inventor Project' *WIPO Magazine* (December 2019), https://www.wipo.int/wipo_magazine/en/2019/06/article_0002.html; Anna Carnochan Comer, 'AI: Artificial Inventor or the Real Deal?' (2020) 22 *North Carolina Journal of Law & Technology* 447, 450.

4 'AI Inventorship on the Horizon: Part 1', *Norton Rose Fulbright* (October 2021), https://www.nortonrosefulbright.com/en-fr/knowledge/publications/2a3c551a/ai-inventorship-on-the-horizon-part-1; Saranpaal Calais and Janna Tay, 'A Rose by Any Other Name: An Australian Court Rules That AI Can Be an inventor' *Allen & Overy* (23 November 2021), https://www.allenovery.com/en-gb/global/blogs/digital-hub/a-rose-by-any-other-name-an-australian-court-rules-that-ai-can-be-an-inventor.

DOI: 10.4324/9781003528517-6

Africa and Saudi Arabia.[5] The Saudi Authority for Intellectual Property (SAIP) office rejected DABUS's applications, which is an accurate decision as the applications do not align with the Saudi Arabia patent law.[6]

Although DABUS's applications challenge patent laws globally, this chapter focuses on the patent legal frameworks in the Gulf Cooperation Council for the Arab States (GCC). As noted above, Dr Thaler filed the patent applications for DABUS in Saudi Arabia, a member of the GCC countries, along with Kuwait, Bahrain, the United Arab Emirates, the Sultanate of Oman and Qatar.[7] The GCC countries have ratified a uniform patent law, namely, the Patent Regulation of the Cooperation Council for the Arab States of the Gulf and its Implementing Bylaws (PRGCC).[8]

This chapter analyses whether the PRGCC accommodates the ethical and legal challenges of inventions generated by AI systems like DABUS, and if it cannot, to the extent that adjustments are deemed necessary, how the patent legal system in the GCC countries can be revamped to keep up with the advance of AI systems. Although the chapter focuses on patent law in the GCC jurisdictions, it refers to other jurisdictions—namely, the European Patent Office, the UK, the US, Australia and South Africa to examine how they dealt with case law, namely DABUS as an inventor. This chapter is divided into five sections. Section 1 provides background on the DABUS as AI-generated inventions. Section 2 examines the patent legal framework in the GCC states. Section 3 critically assesses whether the current patent legal framework in the GCC states governs the challenges of AI-generated inventions. This assessment is essential to answer, in Section 4, how to move forward with the patent legal framework in the GCC countries to keep up with AI-generated inventions. Section 5 presents the findings and conclusion.

AI-Generated Inventions (DABUS as a Case Study)

AI has no universal definition.[9] AI, therefore, has been defined as 'the ability of a computer or a robot controlled by a computer to do tasks that humans usually do

5 Abbott (n 3).

6 Saudi Authority for Intellectual Property (SAIP), *Decisions of Patent Application* (Application No. 521422019 May 2021).

7 'Member States' (Gulf Cooperation Council)', https://www.gcc-sg.org/en-us/AboutGCC/MemberStates/pages/Home.aspx.

8 Kuwait abolished any provision that contravenes the PRGCC. See Kuwaiti Decree Law 71/2013 Article 2, to implement the PRGCC. For more information about the history of the Patent Law of Kuwait, see Jarrah Ali Abdullah Almutairi, 'Patents and the Historical Development of Protection: "A Comparative Study" with Special Reference to the Kuwaiti Law No. 71 of the Year 2013' (2014) 2 *Kuwaiti International Law School* Journal 245.

9 Ana Ramalho, 'Patentability of AI-generated Inventions: Is a Reform of the Patent System Needed?' (2018), 3 available at SSRN 3168703; Sofia Samoili, Montserrat Lopez Cobo, Emilia Gómez, Giuditta De Prato, Fernando Martínez-Plumed, and Blagoj Delipetrev, 'AI Watch. Defining Artificial Intelligence Towards an Operational Definition and Taxonomy of Artificial Intelligence' (2020) *European Union* 7, https://eprints.ugd.edu.mk/id/eprint/28047; Haroon Sheikh, Corien Prins, and

because they require human intelligence and discernment'.[10] Others have described AI as 'a system capable of rationally solving complex problems or taking appropriate action to achieve its goals in real-world circumstances'.[11] Common to these definitions is the idea that AI can perform complex tasks that require human intelligence.

The tremendous technological advancement of AI has enabled it to accomplish jobs that are traditionally handled by humans, like autonomous invention.[12] As mentioned earlier, Dr Thaler submitted patent applications for DABUS as an inventor across the globe. Many jurisdictions interpret their patent laws to assess whether the inventions created by DABUS are patentable and protected.

The United Kingdom Intellectual Property Office's (UKIPO) decision marked the first rejection of two patent applications that registered DABUS as an inventor.[13] UKIPO's rejection decision is affirmed by the English High Court and the English Court of Appeal.[14] The basis of the three rejection decisions is that DABUS, as an AI system, does not meet the requirements of inventorship under the UK Patents Act 1977 (UKPA), where the inventor must be a natural person.[15] DABUS, as an AI system, has no legal personality to be an inventor under the UKPA, and thus, DABUS has no legal rights, such as ownership of its inventions, that can be assigned, according to Section 7(2)(b) or (c) of the UKPA, to Dr Thaler as a patent applicant since he admits that he is not the inventor.[16]

The UK Supreme Court reaffirmed the Court of Appeal's decision when it ruled that DABUS cannot be an inventor under sections 7 and 13 of the UKPA. Accordingly, inventor is 'a person who devises a new and non-obvious product

Erik Schrijvers 'Artificial Intelligence: Definition and Background' in *Mission AI: The New System Technology* (Cham: Springer International, 2023) 15; Enrico Bonadio, Luke McDonagh, and Plamen Dinev, 'Artificial Intelligence as Inventor: Exploring the Consequences for Patent Law' (2021) 1 *Intellectual Property Quarterly* 1, 1.

10 B. J. Copeland, 'Artificial Intelligence' *Encyclopaedia Britannica* (18 March 2022), https://www.britannica.com/technology/artificial-intelligence.

11 World Economic Forum, 'Artificial Intelligence Collides with Patent Law' (2018) 5, https://www3.weforum.org/docs/WEF_48540_WP_End_of_Innovation_Protecting_Patent_Law.pdf. For more information about AI, see John McCarthy, 'What Is Artificial Intelligence?' *University of Stanford* (12 November 2007), http://jmc.stanford.edu/articles/whatisai.html.

12 Michael McLaughlin, 'Computer-generated Inventions' (2019) 101 *Journal of the Patent and Trademark Office Society* 224, 228.

13 UK Intellectual Property Office (UKIPO), *decision BL* (O/741/19 UKIPO decision 4 December 2019), https://www.ipo.gov.uk/p-challenge-decision-results/o74119.pdf; 'AI Inventorship on the Horizon: Part 2' *Norton Rose Fulbright* (October 2021), https://www.nortonrosefulbright.com/en/knowledge/publications/5a6fce4c/ai-inventorship-on-the-horizon-part-2#3.

14 See Thaler v. Comptroller General of Patents Trademarks and Designs, [2021] EWCA Civ 1374 (21 September 2021) (Thaler v Comptroller Appeal); *Norton Rose Fulbright* (n 13).

15 UKIPO (n 13) at paras 18 and 20. *Thaler v The Comptroller-General of Patents Trademarks* and *Designs* [2020] EWHC 2412 (Pat) (21 September 2020) (Thaler v Comptroller) at para 34–36; *Thaler v Comptroller Appeal* (n 14), paras 49–56.

16 See UKIPO (n 13) paras 21–23; *Thaler v Comptroller Appeal* (n 14) para 124; *Thaler v Comptroller* (n 15) para 9.

or process'. DABUS could not be classified as a person or deviser of any relevant invention.[17]

The UK Supreme Court ruled that Dr Thaler is not entitled to apply for a patent for any technical advance made by DABUS[18] since he is not the inventor. Under section 7 of the Patents Act 1977, if the applicant is not the inventor (which Dr Thaler has never claimed to be), then the applicant must fall into one of the limbs of either section 7(2)(b) (persons entitled by rule of law or agreement with the inventor) or section 7(2)(c) (successors in title). The court mentioned that Dr Thaler 'does not satisfy any part of this carefully structured code'.[19]

The UK Supreme Court refused the basis of Dr Thaler's submission for the patent applications, which is accession theory, as the owner of DABUS which has all the rights in all inventions developed by DABUS.[20] The UK Supreme Court stated that relying Dr Thaler on the accession theory is misguiding.[21] The accession theory concerns new tangible property produce by exiting the tangible property,[22] this is not the case of Dr Thaler for a new idea and non-obvious devices, so there is no principle basis for applying the doctrine of accession for to be concepts for new and non-obvious devices and methods developed by DABUS.[23] The UK Supreme Court, therefore, decided the applications deemed to have been withdrawn.[24]

Similarly, the European Patent Office (EPO) and EPO Board of Appeal adopted the UKIPO's approach when it rejected the DABUS patent application.[25] The patent application for DABUS as inventor does not meet the requirement under Article 81, Rule 19(1) of the European Patent Convention (EPC), according to which 'the inventor's surname, given name and full address must be designated in the application'.[26] These requirements under the EPC indicate that an inventor is a

17 *Thaler v Comptroller-General of Patents, Designs and Trademarks* [2023] UKSC 49 (20 December 2023) para 73.

18 *Thaler v Comptroller-General of Patents, Designs and Trademarks* [2023] UKSC 49 (20 December 2023) para 74.

19 *Thaler v Comptroller-General of Patents, Designs and Trademarks* [2023] UKSC 49 (20 December 2023) para 79.

20 *Thaler v Comptroller-General of Patents, Designs and Trademarks* [2023] UKSC 49 (20 December 2023) para 87.

21 *Thaler v Comptroller-General of Patents, Designs and Trademarks* [2023] UKSC 49 (20 December 2023) para 87.

22 *Thaler v Comptroller-General of Patents, Designs and Trademarks* [2023] UKSC 49 (20 December 2023) para 87.

23 *Thaler v Comptroller-General of Patents, Designs and Trademarks* [2023] UKSC 49 (20 December 2023) para 88.

24 *Thaler v Comptroller-General of Patents, Designs and Trademarks* [2023] UKSC 49 (20 December 2023) para 99.

25 See European Patent Office (EPO), 'Grounds for Refusal: Application (No. 18275163.6)', https://register.epo.org/application?documentId=E4B63SD62191498&number=EP18275163&lng=en&npl=false; *Norton Rose Fulbright* (n 13).

26 European Patent Office (EPO) (n 25) paras 8 and 19–21; Matthieu Dhenne, 'Artificial Intelligence: Back to the Future of Patent Law' (2021) 8–9, *SSRN Electronic Journal;* doi: 10.2139/ssrn.3787526.

natural person.[27] For this reason, the EPO and the EPO Board rejected the DABUS patent application.

The United States Patent and Trademark Office's (USPTO) also denied the DABUS application and issued a 'notice to file missing parts of non-provisional application', as the application data sheet did not identify each inventor by his or her legal name.[28] Dr Thaler then submitted a petition to the Commissioner of the USPTO.[29] The Commissioner asserted that the grounds for the denial decision were that the inventor must be limited to a natural person under Title 35 of the United States Code, and therefore, naming DABUS as an inventor is not proper and does not comply with many provisions of Title 35 of the USC.[30]

Dr Thaler then filed a case in the US Virginia Eastern District Court, requesting the court overturn the USPTO's decision and examine the application thoroughly on the basis of its merits.[31] However, the US Virginia Eastern District Court rejected Dr Thaler's case and agreed with the USPTO's decision when it ruled that:

> [T]he USPTO's interpretation of the Patent Act was carefully considered and was consistent with the Act's language and the caselaw... Accordingly, the USPTO's interpretation that an 'inventor' must be a natural person is entitled to deference. Even if no deference were due, the USPTO's conclusion is correct under the law.[32]

On March 17, 2023, Dr Thaler submitted a petition to the US Supreme Court requesting clarification on whether the US Patent Act limits an inventor to a natural person.[33] On April 24, 2023, the US Supreme Court rejected the petition.[34] As such, the decision regarding the DABUS litigation is non-appealable in the US.[35]

In contrast, the Australian Federal Court overturned the Australian Intellectual Property Office's (AIPO) decision to reject Dr Thaler's application.[36] The Court justified its ruling by separating AI ownership from AI inventorship when the court noted that 'the ownership of a patentable invention can only be for a human or legal

27 European Patent Office (EPO) (n 25) para 23.

28 *Thaler v. Hirshfeld*, [2021] 1:20-cv-00903 LMB/TCB, pages 4 and 5; Paul Ragusa and Nick Palmieri, 'Artificial Intelligence as Inventor: DABUS Global Status' (2022) 39 *The Computer and Internet Lawyer* 1, 1.

29 Ragusa and Palmieri (n 28) 1.

30 See United States Patent and Trademark Office (USPTO), *2019 USPTO Decision on Petition*: (Application No. 16/524,350, 4 - 6.

31 Ragusa and Palmieri (n 28) 2.

32 Thaler v. Hirshfeld (n 28) 9.

33 Kingsley Egbuonu, 'The Latest News on the DABUS Patent Case' *IP Stars* (25 April 2023), https://www.ipstars.com/NewsAndAnalysis/The-latest-news-on-the-DABUS-patent-case/Index/7366. .

34 Kingsley Egbuonu, 'The Latest News on the DABUS Patent Case' *IP Stars* (25 April 2023), https://www.ipstars.com/NewsAndAnalysis/The-latest-news-on-the-DABUS-patent-case/Index/7366.

35 'Ryan Abbott's Post', The Artificial Inventor Project, https://www.linkedin.com/feed/update/urn:li:activity:7056323319918125057/.

36 See *Stephen L. Thaler v. Commissioner of Patents* [2021] FCA 879 (July 30, 2021); *Norton Rose Fulbright,* (n 13).

person, and thus, AI cannot be an owner or a patentee, but AI can be an inventor'.[37] Because the Australian Patents Act No. 83 of 1990 (APA) does not contain any language explicitly disallowing an AI system from being an inventor. However, the Full Court of the Federal Court upheld the decision of the Commission of Patents (IP Australia) when the court stated that '[t]he Deputy Commissioner was correct to conclude that, by naming DABUS as the inventor, the application did not comply with Reg 3.2C(2)(aa)'.[38] Ultimately, the appeal to the High Court was dismissed, and therefore, Dr Thaler's litigation over the DABUS patent application ended in Australia as well.[39]

While the UKIPO, USPTO, EPO and AIPO rejected the DABUS applications, the South Africa Companies and Intellectual Property Commission (CIPC) granted the patent to DABUS as an inventor, which is a novel decision.[40] The CIPC's formal examination focuses on documentation, financial (fees), and administrative issues as prescribed in Section 30 of the South Africa Patents Act No. 57 of 1978 (SAPA) and sections 22 and 40–43 of the South Africa Patents Regulation of 1978 (SAPR).[41] As such, the CIPC granted the patent to DABUS, but the CIPC's decision may be judicially scrutinised, as the DABUS patent violates specific provisions of SAPA, SAPR and the Patent Cooperation Treaty (PCT).[42]

To conclude, Saudi Arabia received the DABUS applications, and Saudi Arabia is one of the GCC countries and has ratified the PRGCC. The following section, therefore, will examine the PRGCC. The aim of examining the PRGCC is to assess whether the legal framework of patent law in the GCC countries can govern the patent applications of AI-generated inventions and all the legal and ethical challenges posed by AI-generated inventions.

The Examination of Patent Regulation of the GCC States (PRGCC)

Issuance of the PRGCC

The Patent Regulation of the GCC countries and the statute of the Patent Office for the GCC states were approved by the kings and presidents of the GCC countries in the thirteenth session of the Supreme Council in Abu Dhabi, in 1992.[43] In March

37 *Stephen L. Thaler v. Commissioner of Patents* (n 36) para 12.

38 *Commissioner of Patent v Thaler* [2022] FCAFC 62 (13 April 2022) para 117.

39 Egbuonu (n 33).

40 See Ryan Abbott, 'First Patent Granted to the Artificial Inventor Project' *Artificial Inventor* (28 July 2021), https://artificialinventor.com/first patent-granted-to-the-artificial-inventor-project/; 'DABUS Gets Its First Patent in South Africa Under Formalities Examination' *IP Watchdog* (29 July 2021), https://www.ipwatchdog.com/2021/07/29/dabus-gets-first-patent-south-africa-formalities- examination/id=136116/.

41 Desmond Osaretin Oriakhogba, 'DABUS Gains Territory in South Africa and Australia: Revisiting the AI-Inventorship Question' (2021) 9 *South African Intellectual Property Law Journal* 87, 93.

42 Desmond Osaretin Oriakhogba, 'DABUS Gains Territory in South Africa and Australia: Revisiting the AI-Inventorship Question' (2021) 9 *South African Intellectual Property Law Journal* 87, 108.

43 Mohammed F. Al-Hajeri, 'The Gulf Cooperation Council (GCC) Patent Office' (2006) 28 *World Patent Information* 14, 14.

1996, at the 58th session, the Ministerial Council accepted the GCC's implementing bylaws, and in 1998, the GCC Patent Office started accepting applications.[44] The GCC Patent Office worked on improving its capabilities, amending existing patent law and implementing bylaws to comply with the international Agreement on Trade-Related Aspects of Intellectual Property Rights (TRIPS).[45] In November 1999, the Supreme Council for the GCC countries approved the amendment of the Patent Law.[46] Eventually, TRIPS standards were implemented in 2001, and the first patent application was approved in 2002.[47]

Recently, the GCC Supreme Council, in its 41st session held on January 5, 2021, approved the amendment of Patent Law in the GCC countries and, therefore, the GCC Patent Office stopped accepting new applications from that date.[48] In November 2021, the amendment to the PRGCC was published in the official Gazette of the General Secretariat of the Cooperation Council of the GCC countries.[49] Starting from January 1st, 2023, the GCC Patent Office began to handle national patent applications on behalf of the requesting Gulf country.[50]

The Examination of the PRGCC

A patent is one type of intellectual property right,[51] and under the PRGCC, a patent is 'the certificate granted by the Patent Office to the owner of the invention so that his invention shall enjoy legal protection in any of the GCC states according

44 Mohammed F. Al-Hajeri, 'The Gulf Cooperation Council (GCC) Patent Office' (2006) 28 *World Patent Information* 14, 14.

45 Mohammed F. Al-Hajeri, 'The Gulf Cooperation Council (GCC) Patent Office' (2006) 28 *World Patent Information* 14, 14. For more information about the GCC countries as members of the TRIPS agreement, see Abdulsalam Hussein Jassim Al-enzi, *Protection of intellectual property rights according to an agreement in the World Trade Organization and the member states of the Cooperation Council for the Arab Gulf States* (Egypt, Almaaref Establishment 2013) 50.

46 Al-Hajeri (n 43) 14.

47 Nadia Naim, 'An Examination of the Intellectual Property Regimes in the Gulf Co-operation Council (GCC) States and a Series of Recommendations to Develop an Integrated Approach to Intellectual Property Rights' (PhD thesis, University of Bradford 2015) 39.

48 News Section, Patent Office at the Secretariat General for Cooperation Council (website) (1 January 2021), https://www.gccpo.org/AboutUs/ShowNews?id=1374; 'United Arab Emirates: The Implementing Bylaws of The GCC Patent System Law' *Mondaq* (28 April 2023), https://www.mondaq.com/trademark/1185362/the-implementing-bylaws-for-the-gcc-patent-system-law.

49 'Issuance of the Amended Implementing Regulations of the "GCC" Patent Law' *Baianat Intellectual Property* (9 December 2021), https://www.baianat-ip.com/2021/12/09/issuance-of-the-amended-implementing-regulations-of-the-gcc-patent-law/.

50 Tamara El-Shibib, 'The GCC Patent Office to Handle New Application from January 2023' *Gowling WLG* (20 December 2022), https://gowlingwlg.com/en/insights-resources/articles/2022/gcc-patent-office-to-handle-new-applications/. There are two layers of registration for patent protection: national protection via national IP offices and regional protection via the GCC Patent Office.

51 See Wendy J. Gordon, 'Intellectual Property Law' in Mark Tushnet and Peter Cane (eds), *The Oxford Handbook of Legal Studies* (online edn, Oxford Academic, 2003) 617, https://doi.org/10.1093/oxfordhb/9780199248179.013.0028: Arthur R. Miller and Michael H. Davis, *Intellectual Property: Patents, Trademarks, and Copyright in a Nutshell* (West Publishing Co.,St Paul Minnesota, 1990).

to the provisions of this Regulation'.[52] A patent guarantees the right to be named as an inventor.[53] Inventors spend time, research and effort generating a patented invention, and therefore, the patent certification sets the monopolistic rights for the inventor(s) against economic free riders who can cause monetary losses to the original producer.[54]

The patent, therefore, guarantees the patent owner the right to exclude free riders from manufacturing, using, selling, offering for sale, or importing the product for such purposes without his prior consent,[55] for twenty years starting from the patent application's filing date.[56]

Providing an invention with the legal protection of a patent and entitling the inventors to the monopolistic rights to their invention,[57] the patent registration application must be submitted to the GCC Patent Office by the inventor, their authorised agent or the person to whom the patent rights have been assigned.[58] When the Office receives an application, it examines the application formally and substantively.[59] The substantive requirements or criteria for an invention are:

- The novelty of the invention.
- Being part of an inventive step.
- Being capable of industrial application.[60]

The Novelty of the Invention

For the patent to be granted, the invention must be novel.[61] The invention can be novel when it is not known in the prior art—prior art being constituted by everything disclosed to the public anywhere, through written or verbal disclosure or by use of any other method in which the invention is realised before the filing date of the patent application.[62] As such, if the invention is disclosed to the public in writing or verbally before the filing of the application, the invention cannot be patented because legal protection is granted for disclosure to the Patent Office of

52 PRGCC, Article 1.

53 Salah Zaineddin and Mosleh Ahmed Al'Tarawneh, 'The Legal Regime of Patent under Qatari Legislation: An Analytical Study of the New Patents Act of the State of Qatar' (2010) 34 *The Journal of Law* 313, 386. The right to be named an inventor is not part of the PRGCC's provisions. See Nari Lee, 'Inventor's Moral Right and the Morality of Patents' in Ysolde Gendreau (ed.) *Research Handbook on Intellectual Property and Moral Rights* (Edward Elgar, Cheltenham UK, 2020), 7.

54 Erik S. Maurer, 'An Economic Justification for a Broad Interpretation of Patentable Subject Matter' (2001) 95 *Northwestern University Law Review* 1057, 1061. Naim (n 47) 114.

55 PRGCC, Article 12/2.

56 PRGCC, Article 15.

57 PRGCC, Article 12/2.

58 PRGCC, Article 5.

59 PRGCC, Article 5, Article 9.

60 PRGCC, Article 9, Article 2/1.

61 PRGCC, Article 2/1.

62 PRGCC, Article 2/2.

the invention's benefit to society, and if the invention is already disclosed, there is no longer justification for legally protecting that invention.[63] Nonetheless, there are three cases under Article 2/2 of the PRGCC where the disclosure of the invention to the public shall not be taken into consideration. Firstly, if the disclosure of the invention to the public took place within a year before the application filing date or before its priority date.[64] Secondly, if the disclosure of the invention to the public occurred due to abusive actions of others against the application.[65] Thirdly, if the disclosure of the invention took place at an officially recognised exhibition within the six months prior to the filing of the application.[66]

Inventive Step

An invention must meet the inventive step requirement to be patentable under the PRGCC.[67] The inventive step of an invention means that the invention is non-obvious to a person skilled in the art.[68] So if that skilled person in the art could reach the same conclusions with his knowledge as the applicant for the invention, that invention would be patentable and protected.[69] The requirement of non-obviousness to a person skilled in the art is to ensure the patent is not granted for an invention that is frivolous or already known.[70]

Industrial Application

The invention must be industrially applicable in any industry, such as agriculture, fishing or service.[71] If an invention is not industrially applicable, such as discoveries, scientific theories, mathematical methods and computer programs, then these inventions cannot be patented under the PRGCC.[72] However, sometimes an invention is industrially applicable, but the PRGCC excludes the granting of patents where the invention is contrary to Islamic or Sharia Law, public order, or morality observed in the GCC states.[73] Public order, morality and ethics in the GCC states

63 Ibrahim Abu Al-Lail, *Legal Protection of Inventions in Accordance with Kuwaiti Law in Light of the Provisions of Comparative Law: In-Depth Study on Intellectual* (Kuwait: Academic Publication Council, 2014) 76–77.
64 PRGCC, Article 2/2.
65 PRGCC, Article 2/2.
66 PRGCC, Article 2/2.
67 PRGCC, Article 2/1.
68 PRGCC, Article 2/3.
69 Abu Al-Lail (n 63) 42
70 Ryan Abbott, 'Everything Is Obvious' (2019) 66 *UCLA Law Review* 2, 11; World Economic Forum (n 11) 12.
71 PRGCC Article 2/4.
72 PRGCC, Article 3.
73 PRGCC, Article 4.

are similar to each other since the PRGCC share the same customs and traditions, which stem from Islamic culture.[74]

An Assessment of the PRGCC Towards DABUS (AI)-Generated Inventions

As noted above, Saudi Arabia received the DABUS patent application for two inventions, the 'fractal container' and the 'neural flame'. As such, the application is not for the DABUS AI system but for its output. This distinction is essential for the present assessment of the PRGCC, where DABUS is a typical AI algorithm that is likely to be considered a mere mathematical method and, therefore, unpatentable due to its failure to meet the industrial application requirement under Article 2 of the PRGCC.[75] Still, the output of the AI system is patent-eligible subject matter. In accepting DABUS's patent application, SAIP asserts there is no legal prohibition to registering a patent application for the output of an AI algorithm unless those inventions violate Sharia Law.[76]

Having received the patent application for DABUS as an inventor, the Patent Office will examine the application formally and substantively.[77] As mentioned above, to be granted the patents sought, DABUS's inventions must meet the patentability criteria of inventions—meaning they are novel, have the industrial capability and constitute an inventive step or are non-obvious to a person skilled in the art.[78]

Constituting an inventive step or being non-obviousness to a person skilled in the art is the factor in determining what constitutes a patented invention.[79] However, assessing whether an invention meets the inventive step criterion or is non-obviousness to a person skilled in the art is difficult and complex, especially in the era of AI.[80] For example, for an invention that is non-obvious to a person skilled in the art, that same invention may become obvious when viewed through the lens

74 See 'Gulf Cooperation Council' *Britannica* (3 April 2023), https://www.britannica.com/topic/Gulf-Cooperation-Council; Mohammed I. At-Twaijri, and Ibrahim A. Al-Muhaiza, 'Hofstede's Cultural Dimensions in the GCC Countries: An Empirical Investigation' (1996) 9 *International Journal of Value-Based Management* 121, 122.

75 See PRGCC, Article 2 and 3; See also Saudi Law of Patents, Layout Designs of Integrated Circuits, Plant Varieties, Article 45/A, and Industrial Designs Law Issued by Royal Decree No. M/27 dated 29/5/1425 AH and amended by Cabinet Resolution No. 536 dated 10/19/1439 AH; See Bonadio et al (n 9) 6.

76 Saudi Law of Patents, Layout Designs of Integrated Circuits, Plant Varieties, and Industrial Designs, Article 4/A.

77 Saudi Law of Patents, Layout Designs of Integrated Circuits, Plant Varieties, and Industrial Designs, Article 4/A, Article 12 'The Authority shall examine registered applications in terms of formalities'. Article 43 'A patent may be issued on an invention, in accordance with the provisions of this Law, if it is new, involves an innovative step, and is capable of industrial application. The invention may be a product, industrial process, or related to either of them'.

78 PRGCC, Article 9.

79 PRGCC, Article 2/3.

80 World Economic Forum (n 11) 12.

of a person skilled in the art utilising a similar AI system to create it.[81] Thus, the question is how the SAIP which received DABUS's application would assess the non-obviousness to a skilled person in the art as a legal requirement or criterion to grant patent or criterion of an invention.

An invention must include a written description to be patentable and satisfy the legal requirement of the patent disclosure.[82] The disclosure requirement permits a person skilled in the art to comprehend the work, and it precludes the granting of a patent for duplicated research.[83] But AI-generated inventions pose a challenge for the disclosure[84] due to the challenge of knowing how an AI system works and generates output.[85] The AI system is trained using data collection, the configuration of which is either completely unknown or impossible to replicate by others.[86] Thus, the invention cannot be duplicated, and therefore, it will not be considered sufficiently disclosed.[87]

Imagine that the SAIP were to find that the DABUS-generated inventions meet the legal requirements for patentability. In that case, who would be listed as an inventor on the patent? Additionally, who would be the patent holder? In order to answer these questions, the first step is to examine the definition of the term 'inventor'. Neither the Saudi Arabia patent law nor the PRGCC has codified the definition of the term 'inventor'.

Although the inventor is not defined neither Saudi Arabia's patent law nor under the PRGCC, its spirit and wording state that the inventor must be a legal person, for example, when the PRGCC stipulates that 'the ownership of the patent and all the rights originated therefrom shall be transferable by inheritance'.[88] The Implementing Bylaws of the GCC Patent Regulation further states that 'the office shall establish a register for certificates of temporary protection of the invention. The register shall comprise the following particulars: an inventor's given name, nationality and full address'.[89] These provisions may be interpreted as a suggestion that the inventor must be a natural person. As such, DABUS, being a machine, cannot be an inventor under the existing PRGCC. Also, DABUS does not have the legal personality to have the right to own its inventions because ownership

81 Ramalho (n 9) 2; Erica Fraser, 'Computers as Inventors-legal and Policy Implications of Artificial Intelligence on Patent Law' (2016) 13 *Scripted A Journal of Law, Technology & Society* 305, 320.

82 Tabrez Y Ebrahim, 'Artificial Intelligence Inventions & Patent Disclosure' (2020) 125 *Penn State Law Revie* 147, 158; See the legal requirement for patent disclosure under PRGCC, Article 5 and the Implementing Bylaws of the GCC Patent Regulation, Article 3.

83 Bonadio, McDonagh, and Dinev (n 9) 12; Mimi S. Afshar, 'Artificial Intelligence and Inventorship – Does the Patent Inventor Have to be Human?' (2022) 13 *Hastings Science and Technology Law Journal* 55, 64.

84 Bonadio et al (n 9) 13; Ebrahim (n 82) 152 and 156.

85 Bonadio et al (n 9) 13; Ebrahim (n 82) 179.

86 Bonadio et al (n 9) 13.

87 Bonadio et al (n 9) 13.

88 PRGCC, Article 23/1.

89 Implementing Bylaws of the GCC Patent Regulation, Article 7.

rights are attributed to legal and natural persons.[90] DABUS also is not empowered to assign its ownership over inventions to an applicant or another, according to Article 5/1/1 of the PRGCC.[91]

The inventorship issue is the legal basis of the SAIP's decision to reject DABUS applications as the inventor must be a natural person, and DABUS is a machine. Therefore, DABUS cannot be an inventor under Article 10/3 of Implementing Bylaws of the Saudi Arabia Law of Patents.[92] Furthermore, it is unethical and illegal to register Dr Thaler as an inventor when he admitted he is not the actual inventor. The inventorship issue about AI, therefore, precludes inventions created by AI from being patentable and legally protected, even without any examination of patentability on their merits.[93] This is what occurred in the different jurisdictions mentioned above, where UKIPO, the USPTO, and the EPO rejected DABUS's application due to improper inventorship.

The fact that an AI system lacks legal personhood raises a second issue in relation to the first. As an advanced AI system can invent inventions autonomously, it can infringe on other protected inventions. In such a case, who would be held liable for the damage resulting from the AI system's infringement of the protected patent? Can the AI system be held liable? Holding the AI system liable for infringement of a protected invention requires the AI system to have legal personhood. But, as mentioned above, an AI system has no legal personality. Thus, it cannot be held legally liable.[94] But would a user of an AI system be responsible for patent infringement? It is unfair to hold a person accountable for an AI system's infringement when there is no human actor to be held liable.[95] Moreover, the human who uses AI is, unlike advanced companies, unable to predict infringement.[96] As AI becomes more prevalent, the jeopardy of AI-induced infringement will surge remarkably.[97] Therefore, this chapter encourages scholars to address all the liability challenges of AI in the IP field. This chapter does not address liability because it is outside its scope.

To sum up, this section argued that the PRGCC is insufficient to govern the challenges posed by AI-generated inventions. The following section will discuss to the extent that adjustments to the PRGCC are deemed necessary and how it can be revamped to keep up with advanced AI systems.

90 See Simon Chesterman, 'Artificial Intelligence and the Limits of Legal Personality' (2020) 4 *International & Comparative Law Quarterly* 819–844; Haochen Sun, 'Artificial Intelligence Inventions' (2022) 50 *Florida State University Law Review* 61, 91.

91 See PRGCC, Article 5/1/1/.

92 Saudi Authority for Intellectual Property (SAIP) (n 6).

93 See Ragusa and Palmieri (n 28) 2.

94 World Economic Forum (n 11) 12; Bonadio et al (n 9) 25.

95 World Economic Forum (n 11) 11; Bonadio et al (n 9) 25.

96 World Economic Forum (n 11) 11; Bonadio et al (n 9) 25.

97 Bonadio et al (n 9) 26.

Finding the Way Forward for Adapting to AI-Generated Inventions

Patenting inventions created by AI systems will energise innovation in the GCC states.[98] To clarify this point, the granting of patents for inventions created by AI will consequently encourage people to progress in inventive AI, which will ultimately lead to more innovation for society,[99] and it may become a source for economic growth. This will enable the GCC states to reach their goal of diversifying their economies by relying on cutting-edge digital technologies, like AI, to drive growth rather than depending on oil as their only economic source.[100] This section, therefore, proposes recommendations for how policymakers in the GCC states can address the challenges of patenting AI-generated inventions.

As discussed above, AI challenges the Patent Office to assess whether its inventions meet the patentability requirements, and therefore, whether a patent can be granted. It is especially difficult and complex to assess whether an invention created by an AI system meets the requirement of the inventive step of invention or is non-obvious to the person skilled in the art in the era of AI, for the reasons explained above. The policymaker stipulates using AI to assess the application meeting the patentability requirement under the PRGCC when deciding to reform the PRGCC.[101] Also, the policymaker should incorporate AI into the inventive step of the invention or non-obvious to a person skilled in the art by defining it as non-obvious to the person skilled in the art who uses AI.[102] However, this way of assessment the non-obvious requirement raises the bar for patentability, and it may affect innovation[103] in that it could hinder the granting of a patent for inventions created by an AI system or a human. Still, it is better to raise the bar of patentability requirement than granting the patent for an invention that is already known, which in the end effects economic growth.[104]

Another challenge that policymakers should address is that an AI system, being a machine, does not have the legal personality required to be an inventor under the PRGCC. This AI inventorship issue leaves the valuable inventions created by AI without legal protection. This issue may lead an applicant to avoid the problem by claiming himself as the inventor of inventions created by AI,[105] which is illegal and

98 Bonadio et al (n 9) 25.

99 Bonadio et al (n 9) 25.

100 See Jessica Twentyman and Melanie Noronha, 'Innovating Through Tech in the GCC' in *Economist Intelligence Unit* (2020) 5, https://impact.economist.com/perspectives/sites/default/files/eiu_bahrain_edb_report.pdf: 'Saudi Arabia and Artificial Intelligence' *Middle East Political and Economic Institute*, https://mepei.com/saudi-arabia-and-artificial-intelligence/.

101 See Emna Chikhaoui and Saghir Mehar, 'Artificial intelligence (AI) Collides with Patent Law' (2020) 23 *Journal of Legal, Ethical and Regulatory Issues* 1, 7: Bonadio, McDonagh, and Dinev (n 9) 10; Cheng Lim Saw and Samuel Zheng Wen Chan 'Of Inventorship and Patent Ownership: Examining the Intersection between Artificial Intelligence and Patent Law' (2023) *Singapore Journal of Legal Studies* 27, 42.

102 World Economic Forum (n 11) 12; Ramalho (n 9) 25; Bonadio et al (n 9) 11.

103 World Economic Forum (n 11) 12. Fraser (n 83) 321.

104 Fraser (n 83) 321.

105 Saw and Chan (n 101) 36–37; Abbott, 'The Artificial Inventor Roject' (n 3).

immoral. This chapter, therefore, recommends amending the PRGCC to address the issue of AI inventorship by defining the term 'inventor' and expanding it to include non-legal persons.[106]

The suggestion to include the AI machine under the concept of the inventor does not imply that AI should be given legal personality, despite Saudi Arabia awarding citizenship to a robot called 'Sophia' in 2017, making it the first robot to gain citizenship, a trait of personhood.[107] Awarding legal personality to an AI system in the GCC states to confer AI with ownership rights over the invention will lead to amendments to the cornerstone of the legal systems in the GCC, starting with their constitutions.[108] This chapter, therefore, stresses that there is no need to award an AI system the legal personality in light of patent, as this chapter recommends including the AI machine as an inventor, but with maintaining the applicant or AI user the right to own a patent.[109]

With regard to patents, the inventorship and ownership are discrete.[110] While the inventor develops and creates the invention, the owner can be a different individual,[111] such as when an employer files the application as an owner for an employee's invention.[112] As such, allowing AI users to maintain the right to own patents avoids the complexity associated with granting AI systems legal personality, so AI systems may have the right to own a patent. Moreover, limiting ownership to AI users is reasonable since AI users, unlike AI systems, can participate in the market and, in turn, maximise the economic benefit of the patent.[113]

The lack of legal personality for AI systems raises another challenge for AI-generated inventions. As noted above, AI systems can invent and, therefore, invade a patentable invention. This capability of the AI system raises a complex legal issue, which is, as mentioned earlier, the AI system's lack of legal personality and as such, it cannot hold legal liability. In this context, who would be liable for the AI system's invasion of a patentable invention? Addressing this challenge is beyond the scope of this chapter, but the issue has been highlighted because it is intertwined with the patent subject. This chapter encourages scholars to study whether and how the general rules of civil liability, particularly in the GCC states, can address the legal and ethical challenges of AI systems invading a patentable invention.

106 Abbott, 'The Artificial Inventor Roject' (n 3).

107 Almarzoqi and Albakjaji (n 1) 16; Kazem Hamdan Sadkhan Albazouni, *The Effect of Artificial Intelligence on the Theory of Right* (Lebanon: Modern Book Foundation, 2013) 197.

108 See Ugo Pagallo, 'Vital, Sophia, and Co.—The Quest for the Legal Personhood of Robots' (2018) 9 *Information* 230.

109 See Abbott, 'The Artificial Inventor Roject' (n 3); Saw and Chan (n 101) 37.

110 Bonadio et al (n 9) 23.

111 Bonadio et al (n 9) 23.

112 See the two cases of an employer who files the patent application as an owner for the employee's invention under PRGCC, Article 2/7/2.

113 Bonadio, McDonagh, and Dinev (n 9) 24.

This chapter does not focus on international instruments but encourages scholars to examine whether and how the international instruments that regulate patents could be updated, especially as it is known that AI-generated inventions are likely to become more common in a few years.[114] Also, the international instruments may need to harmonise with their members' regional and local patent laws. An example to explain the point, this the chapter proposes extending the term inventor to include AI systems in the PRGCC, which do not align with most international instruments.[115]

Findings and Conclusion

This chapter examined to what extent the PRGCC accommodates the inventions generated by AI systems like DABUS, and if it cannot, to the extent that adjustments are deemed necessary, and how the patent legal system in the GCC countries can be revamped to keep up with the advance of AI systems. After assessing the PRGCC provisions, this chapter found that the PRGCC, the inventions generated by the AI system, is the patent-eligible subject matter. Still, the patent application for DABUS, a typical AI algorithm, is likely to be considered a mere mathematical method and, therefore, unpatentable due to its failure to meet the industrial application requirement under Article 2 of the PRGCC. In accepting the examination of patent applications for the inventions created by DABUS, the SAIP asserts there is no legal prohibition to registering an application for the output of an AI algorithm unless those inventions violate Sharia Law.

However, SAIP rejected DABUS applications because they are not aligned with Saudi Arabia's Patent Law provisions. Under these provisions, spirit, and wording, the inventor must be a natural person. As is known, DABUS is an AI system that lacks legal personhood. Also, it is unethical and illegal to register Dr Thaler as an inventor when he admitted he is not the actual inventor. Therefore, the SAIP rejected DABUS applications, which is an accurate decision.

For the inventorship issue and others, neither the Saudi Patent Law's provisions nor the PRGCC's provisions accommodate AI-generated inventions and cannot face the challenges posed by AI-generated inventions for various reasons. Firstly, as discussed previously, to be granted the patents sought, DABUS's inventions must meet the patentability criteria of inventions, meaning they are novel, have the industrial capability to constitute an inventive step or are non-obvious to a person skilled in the art. However, assessing whether an invention meets the inventive step criterion or is non-obviousness to a person skilled in the art is difficult and complex, especially in the era of AI. For example, for an invention that is non-obvious to a person skilled in the art, that same invention may become obvious

114 UKIPO (n 13).

115 See Pheh Hoon Lim and Phoebe Li, 'Artificial Intelligence and Inventorship: Patently Much Ado in the Computer Program' (2022) 17 *Journal of Intellectual Property Law and Practice* 376, 386.

when viewed through the lens of a person skilled in the art who is utilising a similar AI system to create it.

Secondly, AI-generated inventions pose a challenge to patent disclosure due to the challenge of knowing how an AI system works and generates output. The AI system is trained using data collection, the configuration of which is either completely unknown or impossible for others to replicate. Thus, the invention cannot be duplicated and will not be considered sufficiently disclosed.

After discussing the insufficiency of facing the challenges of AI-generated inventions to the patent system, this chapter emphasises adjusting to the PRGCC. It showed it is necessary within the GCC states to update the PRGCC to keep up with patent inventions created by advanced AI systems, as these inventions generated by AI will continue to grow. Therefore, the growth of inventions generated by AI will raise the need to protect innovation to flourish the GCC states' economies, which will enable the GCC states to reach their goal of diversifying their economies by relying on cutting-edge digital technologies, like AI, to drive growth rather than depending on oil as their only economic source. However, the chapter underscores no need to issue a new law; instead, the PRGCC can be amended. This chapter proposed recommendations for how policymakers in the GCC states can address the challenges of patenting AI-generated inventions.

The policymaker should stipulate the use of AI in the Patent Office to assess whether the application meets the patentability requirement, especially non-obvious ones. However, this way of assessing the non-obvious requirement raises the bar for patentability and may affect innovation. It could hinder granting a patent for inventions created by AI or humans. Still, it is better to raise the bar of patentability requirement than grant the patent for an already known invention, which ultimately affects economic growth.

Another challenge that policymakers should address is that an AI system, being a machine, needs to have the legal personality required to be an inventor under the PRGCC. This AI inventorship issue precludes the valuable inventions AI creates from being patentable and legally protected even without any examination on their merits, like what occurred in the different jurisdictions, as discussed in this chapter—UKIPO, the USPTO, and the EPO rejected DABUS's application due to improper inventorship. This chapter, therefore, differentiated between the inventor and owner concepts. The policymaker should maintain the right to own a patent (ownership) for the applicant or AI users to avoid the complexity of granting AI systems legal personality so AI systems may have the right to own a patent. Moreover, limiting the ownership to AI users is reasonable since AI users, unlike AI systems, can participate in the market and, in turn, maximise the economic benefit of the patent. This chapter also recommended expanding and defining the term inventor to include the AI machine under the PRGCC to address the issue of AI inventorship and protect the inventions that AI generates.

Bibliography

'A Realistic and Legal Study on the DNA', Kuwaiti Association of The Basic Evaluators for Human Rights (KABEHR) (2016), http://humanrights.org.kw/esdarat/

Abbott, R., 'Everything is Obvious', (2019) 66 *The UCLA Law Review.* 1–52.

Abbott, R., 'First Patent Granted to the Artificial Inventor Project', *Artificial Inventor* (28 July 2021), https://artificialinventor.com/first patent-granted-to-the-artificial-inventor-project/

Abbott, R., 'Patent Applications', *Artificial Inventor* (2020), https://artificialinventor.com/patent/

Abbott, R., 'The Artificial Inventor Project', *WIPO Magazine* (December 2019), https://www.wipo.int/wipo_magazine/en/2019/06/article_0002.html

Abu Al-Lail, I., 'Legal Protection of Inventions in Accordance with Kuwaiti Law in Light of the Provisions of Comparative Law: In-Depth Study on Intellectual', Academic Publication Council, University of Kuwait (2014).

Afshar, M. S., 'Artificial Intelligence and Inventorship – Does the Patent Inventor Have to be Human?', (2022) 13 *Hastings Science and Technology Law Journal.* 55–72.

'AI Inventorship on the Horizon: Part 1', *Norton Rose Fulbright* (October 2021), https://www.nortonrosefulbright.com/en-fr/knowledge/publications/2a3c551a/ai-inventorship-on-the-horizon-part-1

'AI Inventorship on the Horizon: Part 2', *Norton Rose Fulbright* (October 2021), https://www.nortonrosefulbright.com/en/knowledge/publications/5a6fce4c/ai-inventorship-on-the-horizon-part-2#3

Albazouni, K. H. S., *The Effect of Artificial Intelligence on the Theory of Right* (Lebanon: Modern Book Foundation, 2013).

AL-enzi, A. H. J., *Protection of Intellectual Property Rights According to an Agreement in the World Trade Organization and the Member States of the Cooperation Council for the Arab Gulf States* (Alexandria: Almaaref Establishment, 2013).

Al-Hajeri, M. F., 'The Gulf Cooperation Council (GCC) Patent Office', (2006) *28 World Patent Information.* 14–19.

Almarzoqi, R. and Albakjaji, M., 'The Patentability of AI Invention: The Case of the Kingdom of Saudi Arabia Law', (2022) 13 *International Journal of Service Science, Management, Engineering, and Technology.* 1–22.

Almutairi, J. A. A., 'Patents and the Historical Development of Protection: "A Comparative Study" With Special Reference to the Kuwaiti Law No. 71 of the Year 2013', (2014) 11 *Kuwaiti International Law School Journal.* 245–322.

At-Twaijri, M I. and Al-Muhaiza, I. A. 'Hofstede's Cultural Dimensions in the GCC Countries: An Empirical Investigation', (1996) 9 *International Journal of Value-Based Management.* 121–131.

Bello, C., 'Would You Want a Robot as CEO? Chinese Firm Is First to Try as It Bets on "Metaverse Workplace', *Euronews* (20 November 2022), https://www.euronews.com/next/2022/11/20/would-you-want-a-robot-as-ceo-chinese-firm-is-first-to-try-as-it-bets-on-metaverse-workpla

Bonadio, E., McDonagh, L, and Dinev, P., 'Artificial Intelligence as Inventor: Exploring the Consequences for Patent Law', (2021) 1 *Intellectual Property Quarterly.* 48–66.

Calais, S. and Tay. J., 'A Rose by Any Other Name: an Australian court rules that AI can be an inventor', *Allen & Overy* (23 November 2021), https://www.allenovery.com/en-gb/global/blogs/digital-hub/a-rose-by-any-other-name-an-australian-court-rules-that-ai-can-be-an-inventor

Chesterman, S., 'Artificial Intelligence and the Limits of Legal Personality', (2020) 69 *International & Comparative Law Quarterly.* 819–844.

Chikhaoui, E. and Mehar, S., 'Artificial Intelligence (AI) Collides with Patent Law', (2020) *23 Journal of Legal, Ethical and Regulatory.* 1–10.

Comer, A. C., 'AI: Artificial Inventor or the Real Deal?', (2020) 22 *North Carolina Journal of Law & Technology.* 447–486.

Commissioner of Patent v Thaler [2022] FCAFC 62 (13 April 2022)

Copeland, B. J., 'Artificial Intelligence', *Encyclopaedia Britannica* (18 March 2022), https://www.britannica.com/technology/artificial-intelligence

'DABUS Gets Its First Patent in South Africa Under Formalities Examination', *IP Watchdog* (29 July 2021), https://www.ipwatchdog.com/2021/07/29/dabus-gets-first-patent-south-africa-formalities-examination/id=136116/

'Data Protection Guide: A Guide for Policy Engagement', *Privacy International* (2018), https://privacyinternational.org/data-protection-guide

Dhenne, M., 'Artificial Intelligence: Back to the Future of Patent Law', (2021) at SSRN 3787526. 1–20.

Ebrahim, T. Y., 'Artificial Intelligence Inventions & Patent Disclosure', (2020) 125 *Penn State Law Review.* 147–221.

Egbuonu, K., 'The Latest News on the DABUS Patent Case', *IP Stars* (25 April 2023), https://www.ipstars.com/NewsAndAnalysis/The-latest-news-on-the-DABUS-patent-case/Index/7366

El-Shibib, T., 'The GCC Patent Office to Handle New Application from January 2023', *Gowling WLG* (20 December 2022), https://gowlingwlg.com/en/insights-resources/articles/2022/gcc-patent-office-to-handle-new-applications/

European Patent Office (EPO), 'Grounds for Refusal: Application (No. 18275163.6)', https://register.epo.org/application?documentId=E4B63SD62191498&number=EP18275163&lng=en&npl=false

Firth-Butterfield, K. and Others, 'Artificial Intelligence Collides with Patent Law' (2018), https://www3.weforum.org/docs/WEF_48540_WP_End_of_Innovation_Protecting_Patent_Law.pdf

Fraser, E., 'Computers as Inventors-Legal and Policy Implications of Artificial Intelligence on Patent Law', (2016) 13 *SCRIPTed – A Journal of Law, Technology & Society.* 305–333.

Gordon, W. J., 'Intellectual Property Law', in Mark Tushnet and Peter Cane (eds.), *Oxford Handbook of Legal Studies* (online edn, Oxford Academic, 2003), https://doi.org/10.1093/oxfordhb/9780199248179.013.0028

Haochen Sun, 'Artificial Intelligence Inventions', (2022) 50 *Florida State University Law Review.* 61–122.

'Issuance of the Amended Implementing Regulations of the "GCC" Patent Law' *Baianat Intellectual Property* (9 December 2021), https://www.baianat-ip.com/2021/12/09/issuance-of-the-amended-implementing-regulations-of-the-gcc-patent-law/

Lee, N., 'Inventor's Moral Right and the Morality of Patents', in Ysolde Gendreau (ed.), *Research Handbook on Intellectual Property and Moral Rights* (Edward Elgar,Cheltenham UK , 2020).

Lim, P. H. and Phoebe, L., 'Artificial Intelligence and Inventorship: Patently Much Ado in the Computer Program', (2022) 17 *Journal of Intellectual Property Law and Practice.* 376–386.

Maurer, E. S., 'An Economic Justification for a Broad Interpretation of Patentable Subject Matter', (2001) 95 *Northwestern University Law Review.* 1057–1098.

McCarthy, J., 'What Is Artificial Intelligence?' *Stanford* (12 November 2007), http://jmc.stanford.edu/articles/whatisai.html

McLaughlin Michael, 'Computer-Generated Inventions', (2019) 101 *Journal of the Patent and Trademark Office Society.* 1–32.

'Member States' (Gulf Cooperation Council), https://www.gcc-sg.org/en-us/AboutGCC/MemberStates/pages/Home.aspx

Miller, A. R. and Davis, M. H., *Intellectual Property: Patents, Trademarks, and Copyright in a Nutshell* (West Publishing Co., St. Paul Minnesota, 1990).

Naim, N., 'An Examination of the Intellectual Property Regimes in the Gulf Co-Operation Council (GCC) States and a Series of Recommendations to Develop an Integrated Approach to Intellectual Property Rights' (PhD Thesis, University of Bradford, 2015).

Oriakhogba, D. O., 'DABUS Gains Territory in South Africa and Australia: Revisiting the AI-Inventorship Question', (2021) 9 *South African Intellectual Property Law Journal.* 87–108.

Pagallo, U., 'Vital, Sophia, and Co.—The Quest for the Legal Personhood of Robots', (2018) 9 *Information.* 1–11

Pandey, N., 'Tang Yu, An AI-Powered Robot, Named CEO Of A Chinese Company', *NDTV* (8 September 2022), https://www.ndtv.com/world-news/tang-yu-an-ai-powered-robot-named-ceo-of-a-chinese-company-3326427, accessed 7 March 2023.

Ragusa, P. and Palmieri, N., 'Artificial Intelligence as Inventor: DABUS Global Status', (2022) 39 *The Computer and Internet Lawyer.* 1–5.

Ramalho, A., 'Patentability of AI-Generated Inventions: Is a Reform of the Patent System Needed?' (2018) at SSRN 3168703. 1–32.

Samoili Sofia and Others, 'AI Watch Defining Artificial Intelligence Towards an Operational Definition and Taxonomy of Artificial Intelligence' (Publication Office of the European Union 2020), 7, https://eprints.ugd.edu.mk/id/eprint/28047

'Saudi Arabia and Artificial Intelligence', Middle East Political and Economic Institute, https://mepei.com/saudi-arabia-and-artificial-intelligence/

Saudi Authority for Intellectual Property (SAIP), 'Decisions of Patent Application: (Application No. 521422019 May 2021)'.

Saw, C. L. and Chan, S. Z. W., 'Of Inventorship and Patent Ownership: Examining the Intersection Between Artificial Intelligence and Patent Law', (2023) *Singapore Journal of Legal Studies.* 27–51.

Sheikh, H, Prins, C, and Schrijvers, E., Mission AI: The New System Technology (The Hague, Springer, 2023)

Stephen L. Thaler v. Commissioner of Patents [2021] FCA 879 (July 30, 2021)

Thaler v The Comptroller-General of Patents Trademarks and Designs [2020] EWHC 2412 (Pat) (21 September 2020) (Thaler v Comptroller

Thaler v. Comptroller General of Patents Trademarks and Designs, [2021] EWCA Civ 1374 (21 September 2021) (Thaler v Comptroller Appeal)

Thaler v Comptroller-General of Patents, Designs and Trademarks [2023] UKSC 49 (20 December 2023)

Thaler v. Hirshfeld, [2021] 1:20-cv-00903 LMB/TCB

Twentyman, J. and Noronha, M., 'Innovating through Tech in the GCC', Economist Intelligence Unit (2020), https://impact.economist.com/perspectives/sites/default/files/eiu_bahrain_edb_report.pdf

UK Intellectual Property Office (UKIPO), 'Decision BL (O/741/19 UKIPO Decision 4 December 2019)', https://www.ipo.gov.uk/p-challenge-decision-results/o74119.pdf

'United Arab Emirates: The Implementing Bylaws of The GCC Patent System (Law)', *Mondaq* (28 April), https://www.mondaq.com/trademark/1185362/the-implementing-bylaws-for-the-gcc-patent-system-law

United States Patent and Trademark Office (USPTO), '2019 USPTO Decision on Petition: (Application No. 16/524,350)'.

Zaineddin, S. and Al'Tarawneh, M. A., 'The Legal Regime of Patent under Qatari Legislation: An Analytical Study of the New Patents Act of the State of Qatar', (2010) 34 *The Journal of Law.*

7 AI-Generated Content in Copyright Law

A Roadmap for Updating GCC Copyright Law

Stefan Papastefanou

The Significant Impact of AI in Intellectual Property Law

Text-to-Image Diffusion Models (TIDM) have advanced extremely rapidly since 2022. Those advanced TIDM such as Stable Diffusion, Midjourney and DALL·E 2 have prompted legal and moral discussion around our understanding and valuation of art. As one of the first advanced TIDMs, DALL·E 2 made it possible to create a complex image file after a few text specifications by a user. Recent discussions within the legal discourse focus mostly exclusively on the abstract ideas of TIDM without analyzing the specific technology. This chapter, however, takes an in-depth technical approach with regard to the specific technology of TIDM using the example of DALL·E 2. Therefore, the otherwise abstractly discussed questions of whether copyrights arise here and to whom these copyrights may belong is analyzed in a practically relevant way. Without an at least fundamental understanding of the underlying technological system, any legal analysis is essentially limited to general theoretical considerations. In contrast, this chapter first looks at the technical functioning of DALL·E 2 in order to identify the essential elements of TIDM relevant to copyright (II). It then analyzes whether, according to current European copyright law, the images generated constitute a work in the sense of a personal intellectual creation pursuant to European copyright standards and which of the actors involved may be entitled to rights in this respect. It thereby aims at establishing differences and similarities between the protection requirements under German and U.S. Law and the possible, future copyright laws of the GCC member states (III). Finally, it discusses how GCC members such as Kuwait can utilize these challenges to adjust and modernize their current copyright regime for the purposes of attracting innovation. It will draw insights from other prominent legislative frameworks to try and determine if and how they could serve as a role model or negative example for possible copyright protection in the GCC member states. This is done from two perspectives: (1) Is there a need for the extension of copyright protection with regard to the products mentioned in the context of DALL·E 2? (2) Do these products possibly lead to new challenges for the protection of classical works that cannot be met by existing copyright law (IV)?

DOI: 10.4324/9781003528517-7

DALL·E 2 as an "AI Breakthrough" in the Digital Arts Market

The rapid legally, as well morally, relevant evolution of TIDM has most recently led to litigation as well as the publication of official guidelines.[1] The reason for such measures and proceedings lies in the legal and societal relevance and challenges TIDM pose, which can be best showcased by the example of DALL·E 2.

DALL·E[2] is a program developed by *OpenAI* that can create realistic images from simple text descriptions with the collaboration of multiple neural networks. The first version of DALL·E was released in early 2021.[3] In April 2022, *OpenAI* then presented the revised version DALL·E 2 to the public. In July, selected users were then allowed to use the program before the beta version of DALL·E 2 was released to everyone at the end of September.

DALL·E is based on the language model *GPT-3*, also developed by *OpenAI*, which made it possible to complete "half-finished" images in a meaningful way by training them with pixel sequences.[4] Compared to the 12 billion parameters of the original version of DALL·E, DALL·E 2 works with a model with 3.5 billion parameters and another model with 1.5 billion parameters to improve the resolution of the images.[5]

The basis for the training of the algorithm is a data set of 250 million image-text pairs, which included the extensive image database of *Shutterstock, Inc.* as was recently announced.[6] The underlying language model *GPT-3* was also trained with 45 terabytes of text files from the public internet, including *Common Crawl* and *Wikipedia*.[7]

The image files that can be created with DALL·E 2 are of such complexity that in many cases they can no longer be distinguished from classic human works on the *Digital Arts Market*. Also, due to the variety of text inputs, countless motifs can be selected and even styles of well-known artists can be determined according to which the image file is created. DALL·E 2 thus provides an unprecedented opportunity for any user to create complex and supposedly creative image files within a very short time and with little effort. Furthermore, it is possible with DALL·E 2 to edit images and add new elements to them ("inpainting"[8]) or to create variations of

1 *U.S. Copyright Office*, Cancellation Decision re: Zarya of the Dawn (VAu001480196), 21.02.2023; *U.S. Copyright Office*, Copyright Registration Guidance: Works Containing Material Generated by Artificial Intelligence.

2 As a portmanteau from Dali (by Salvador Dalí) and WALL-E (from the robot character in the Disney film of the same name).

3 https://openai.com/blog/DALL·E-now-available-without-waitlist/.

4 https://openai.com/blog/image-gpt/.

5 Aditya Singh, How Does DALL·E 2 Work? Diffusion, and more diffusion, Augmented Startups | Medium.

6 Aditya Ramesh et al, 'Hierarchical Text-Conditional Image Generation with CLIP Latents', *OpenAI Papers* (2022), 3, 23; regarding Shutterstock, Inc. databases: press release Shutterstock, 25 October 2022, https://www.shutterstock.com/press/20453 .

7 Tom Brown et al, 'Language Models are Few-Shot Learners', *OpenAI Papers* (2020), 8.

8 Ramesh et al (n 6) 4 et seq.

an existing image inspired by the original. How to legally deal with the products of this process and the practical implications of this technology for the rest of the *Digital Arts Market* first requires understanding the technical basics of DALL·E 2 technology.[9]

Technical Elements of DALL·E 2 and TIDM in General

TIDM make it possible to create images based on a text description in natural language. DALL·E 2 works in three independent phases:

1. First, the words contained in the text description are converted into vectors ("*text embedding*") using so-called "*CLIP algorithms*".[10]
2. These text embeddings are then fed into the so-called "*prior*", which transfers them into corresponding image embeddings.
3. From this image embedding, the so-called "*decoder*" finally generates the image certificate.

The embeddings created in the meantime are a special format of data representation in matrices, which enables easier further processing by subsequent algorithms. While there are definitely differences between individual TIDM, the following technical elements are incorporated in all other major TIDM with the same essential technical structure.

Phase I: CLIP Algorithms

For the text and image embeddings, DALL·E 2 relies on CLIP algorithms also created by *OpenAI*. These are able to determine from a large number of image descriptions the most suitable for a given image. The mode of operation thus basically goes in the opposite direction of text-to-image generation.

For this purpose, CLIP was trained with a data set (*WebImageText*) of 400 million image-text pairs publicly available on the Internet.[11] To determine the image-text pairs that belong together, the images are first passed through the image encoder and the captions through a text encoder, which then create corresponding text or image embeddings.[12] This numerical representation in the form of embeddings

9 In particular, it is often assumed that "AI" necessarily presupposes a certain level of autonomous behavior, e.g. Andreas Sesing-Wagenpfeil, 'KI und Kunst - Zwei Thesen zur urheberrechtlichen Schutzfähigkeit computergenerierter Werke', *CR* (2022), 750, with reference to the AI Regulation of 15 July 2022 ("certain level of autonomy"). As a rule, however, there is no "autonomy" in the narrower sense, as the technical evaluation of DALL·E 2 shows.

10 Contrastive Language-Image Pretraining (CLIP).

11 Alec Radford et al, Learning Transferable Visual Models From Natural Language Supervision, 2021, 3 et seq.

12 Bashkar Mitra and Nick Craswell, 'Neural Text Embeddings for Information Retrieval', *WSDM* (2017), 813.

allows the calculation of a similarity between the different pairings. The aim is to maximize the numerical similarity of the correct pairings and minimize the similarity of the incorrect pairings.[13] The CLIP algorithms are trained to recognize the relationship between a caption and an image. This allows a user to connect, by algorithm, the text expression and the visual representations of the same object.[14]

DALL·E 2 uses the CLIP algorithms in the first phase to enable the creation of the text embedding, which is then passed on to the *prior*.[15]

Phase II: Prior

Based on the CLIP text embeddings, the *prior* then creates the corresponding image embedding.[16] It is essential for the functioning of DALL·E 2 that the existing text embeddings are translated into image embeddings as precisely as possible. Only in this way can all relevant semantic information subsequently be transmitted to the *decoder*. Random elements or other information additions are not applied by the *prior* – on the contrary: to ensure precision, the information content must be kept stable. From a technical point of view, the *prior* is not absolutely necessary for the functioning of DALL·E 2 but could have been replaced by another step with the CLIP algorithm. However, the use of the *prior* has proven its worth by significantly increasing efficiency due to the greater variety of images.

Phase III: Decoder

Subsequently, the image embeddings created by the *prior* are transferred into an image by means of the *decoder*. Unlike an autoencoder,[17] the *decoder* used by DALL·E 2 does not have the task of reconstructing a specific image, but rather of using the information conveyed via the text and image embeddings to create one of many images that corresponds to this information.[18]

Both the *prior* incorporated in DALL·E 2 and the *decoder* use a so-called *diffusion model*. This model learns to generate image files. Training this algorithm works by adding "*noise*" to an image step by step until it is unrecognizable. The model now learns from the individual steps how the image was changed to ideally reconstruct the image in its original form.[19] To do this, the algorithm initially changes patterns consisting only of random points gradually in the direction of an

13 Bashkar Mitra and Nick Craswell, 'Neural Text Embeddings for Information Retrieval', *WSDM* (2017), 814.
14 Ryan O'Connor, 'How DALL·E 2 Actually Works', *AssemblyAI*.
15 Singh (n 5).
16 Singh (n 5).
17 Cheng-Yuan Liou, Wei-Chen Cheng, Jiun Wie Liou, and Daw-Ran Liou, 'Autoencoder for words', *Neurocomputing* 139 (2014), 84, 88.
18 O'Connor (n 14).
19 Singh (n 5).

image when certain elements within the image are recognized.[20] The model proceeds step by step to enable a so-called "denoising".[21]

However, within the framework of a regular diffusion model, there is no possibility to influence the creation process, i.e., to produce particularly specified picture elements. DALL·E 2 therefore uses a modified diffusion model as a decoder (GLIDE,[22] also developed by OpenAI). GLIDE allows textual information to be included in the image generation instead of just assuming random noise.[23] This combination ultimately allows DALL·E 2 to create and process images based on text input.[24] The image generated by the decoder is then enlarged by two OpenAI-trained diffusion upsampler models, first from a resolution of 64x64 pixels to 256x256 pixels and finally to 1024x1024 pixels.[25]

To create variations of an image, DALL·E 2 uses encodings of the original image generated by CLIP algorithms and sends them through the *GLIDE decoder*. Here, the image components recognized by the neural network as main elements and style are retained, while the remaining image components are slightly modified.[26]

The central element of this process is that the *decoder* is no longer bound to the precision of the previous steps. Rather, the conversion process is based on random values narrowed down by the algorithm that come as close as possible to the information content of the word descriptions. However, since the image file contains significantly more information numerically, the *decoder* must necessarily generate additional information that is equally characterized by random elements and containment by training data.

Interim Result

In summary, this results in the following distribution of tasks among the neural networks used by DALL·E 2: The image description given for the image to be created is numerically encoded as a text embedding using the *CLIP algorithms*. The *prior* then transfers this text embedding into a corresponding representation of the image to be created. Based on this image embedding, the *decoder* then creates one of many possible image files using certain random values[27] that reflect the originally entered information content as precisely as possible.

The decisive factor in the functioning of neural networks, with which all of the above algorithms were trained, is precisely that their development and structuring

20 Ramesh et al (n 6), 14 et seq.

21 Singh (n 5).

22 Guided Language to Image Diffusion for Generation and Editing (GLIDE).

23 *Kim/Ye*, ICLR 2022, 1 ff.

24 Singh (n 5).

25 Ramesh et al (n 6), 4.

26 Ramesh et al (n 6), 4.

27 Ramesh et al (n 6), 4, 6. Only the essential semantic information is kept stable by the decoder, while the non-essential details are subject to change with each variation.

in the context of so-called "machine learning"[28] are always subject in some way to a certain element of chance.[29] The exact learning process of the network is neither controllable nor comprehensible for a human programmer.[30] This does not, however, allow the conclusion that the network outputs are in turn "random". Only the development steps in the form of the numerous iterations are characterized by an element of chance.[31]

Such elements of "randomness" characterize all TIDM, especially the final algorithm that generates the image. This method of procedural generation allows to extrapolate the limited information within a text prompt to a complex image with considerable increased data points.

Legal Analysis of the Products generated by TIDM

Against the background of this technical overview, the copyrightability of the image files produced by TIDM can be more clearly assessed. There is a certain consensus on the question of the criteria according to which machine-produced products are in principle protectable, so that the current prevailing view is only presented here as an overview.

Legal Requirements for a Product to Be Protected by Copyright

While there are certainly significant differences between national copyright laws, the fundamental question of protection remains the same. In addition, it seems that the prevailing arguments are similar, at least in Germany, Europe, the U.S. and also in the copyright laws of the GCC member states.

Similar to German and EU law, the U.S. Copyright Act includes specific provisions regarding the requirements for protection.[32] According to 17 U.S. Code § 102(a) works are protected by copyright if they qualify as "original works of authorship fixed in any tangible medium or expression". In this context, the U.S. Supreme Court stated that the term "original means [...] that the work was independently created by the author and that it possesses at least some minimal degree of creativity".[33] In order to be protected by copyright a work therefore must "possess more than a *de minimis* quantum of creativity".[34] Besides a modicum of creativity that the work has to express, it must be the product of an independent creation of the author.[35]

28 Scardapane and Wang, WIREs Data Mining and Knowledge Discovery Vol. 7 (2017), 1 et seq.
29 Scardapane and Wang, WIREs Data Mining and Knowledge Discovery Vol. 7 (2017), 1 et seq.
30 Scardapane and Wang, WIREs Data Mining and Knowledge Discovery Vol. 7 (2017), 1, 3 et seq.
31 Scardapane and Wang, WIREs Data Mining and Knowledge Discovery Vol. 7 (2017), 1, 4.
32 U.S. Copyright Office, re: Zarya of the Dawn (n 1), 3.
33 *Feist Publications, Inc v. Rural Tel. Serv. Company, Inc.* 499 U.S. 340, 345 (1991).
34 *Feist Publications, Inc v. Rural Tel. Serv. Company, Inc.* 499 U.S. 340, 345 (1991), 363.
35 U.S. Copyright Office, re: Zarya of the Dawn (n 1), 3.

The U.S. jurisdiction uniformly interprets the term "works of an *author*[36]" in such a way that the work must have been created by a human being.[37] For example, the Supreme Court ruled that photographs were not merely created by a machine (i.e. the camera) but that they were works protected under copyright law, "so far as they are representatives of original intellectual conception of the author", whom it described as "he to whom anything owes it origin; originator, maker".[38] In another case, a U.S. Court of Appeals ruled that a book made of words "'authored' by non-human spiritual beings" can only be protected by copyright law if a "human selection and arrangement of the revelations" was made.[39]

Based on this jurisdiction the U.S. Copyright Office, which is in charge of the registration of copyrighted works in the United States, also requires works to be the product of human authorship in order to be registered.[40] In the latest edition of its Compendium of Copyright Office Practices it is stated that the Office "will not register works produced by a machine or mere mechanical process that operates randomly or automatically without any creative input or intervention from a human author".[41]

Similarly, protected works within the meaning of the German Copyright Act are only personal intellectual creations (Section 2 (2) German Copyright Act) that sufficiently express the individuality of the author.[42]

The concept of a work is superimposed by EU law and is interpreted autonomously and uniformly by the ECJ in the Union.[43] For a "work" within the meaning of the *InfoSoc Directive,*[44] two cumulative conditions must be met: Firstly, the object in question must be an original in the sense that it constitutes its own intellectual creation by its author. Secondly, the intellectual creation must be expressed.[45]

The creation must be the result of a direct and purposeful intellectual creative or design process[46] and must have already taken on a perceptible form.[47] A result that is based on an action but is accidental is therefore meaningless under copyright law due to the lack of an intellectual creative process,[48] as are mere ideas or creative intentions.[49]

36 Emphasis added by the author.
37 U.S. Copyright Office, re: Zarya of the Dawn (n 1), 3.
38 *Burrow-Giles Lithographic Company v. Sarony*, 111 U.S. 53, 56–58 (1884).
39 *Urantia Foundation v. Kristen Maaheera*, 114 F. 3d 955, 957–959 (Ninth Circuit 1997).
40 U.S. Copyright Office, Copyright Registration Guidance (n 1), 3.
41 *U.S. Copyright Office*, Compendium of U.S. Copyright Office Practices sec. 313, p. 2 (3rd ed. 2021).
42 Michael Olbrich, Christian Bongers and Johannes Pampel, 'Urheberrechtsschutz für Kunstwerke künstlicher Intelligenz?' *GRUR* (2022), 870.
43 Stefan Ory and Christoph Sorge, 'Schöpfung durch Künstliche Intelligenz?' *NJW* (2019), 710, 711.
44 Directive 2001/29/EC of the European Parliament and of the Council of 22 May 2001 on the harmonization of certain aspects of copyright and related rights in the information society.
45 ECJ, Judgment of 13 November 2018 - C-310/17 (Levola Hengelo BV v Smilde Foods BV), *NJW* (2019), 753 paras. 35-37 et seq.
46 BeckOK UrhR/Ahlberg, 35th ed. 15.7.2022, UrhG § 2 marginal no. 54.
47 Olbrich et al (n 42), 870.
48 BeckOK UrhR/Ahlberg (n 46)
49 Olbrich et al (n 42), 871.

The characteristic of the personality of the creation required in German copyright law establishes the relationship between the work (Section 2 German Copyright Act) and the person or the author (Section 7 German Copyright Act) protected under Section 11 German Copyright Act.[50] What is required is a "human creative activity" on the part of the author.[51] Against this background, a product manufactured by machines is only a work eligible for copyright protection if the design of the product can still be traced back to a concrete, intellectual act of creation, i.e. if the machine is only an auxiliary or execution means – i.e. a *tool* – for the production of the work.[52] Only in this case is the immediacy between the intellectual process and the result, which is indispensable for the concept of creation under copyright law, still given.[53] This immediacy is lacking, for example, if the product is exclusively the result of a random generator.[54] Even if the random generator itself is based on an intellectual creative process, the resulting product is *only indirectly* and not concretely attributable to an intellectual creative process.[55] It is, therefore, not sufficient for copyright protection that the human being controls the machine but can no longer concretely influence the direct implementation process within the machine.[56]

To determine whether a product is a protectable work of art, it is accordingly of decisive importance whether a technical tool used was specifically employed for the creation of an individual personal creation, and whether there is a direct contribution which has a direct effect on the concrete result of the creation.[57]

Another significant legal entity that has engaged in an in-depth analysis of authorship regarding AI-assisted works is the U.S. Copyright Office. It confirmed the aforementioned EU and German approach by applying a similar standard: According to its Compendium the key question in order to determine whether a work created with the assistance of technology is protected by copyright is "whether the 'work' is basically one of human authorship, with the computer [or other device] merely being an assisting instrument, or whether the traditional elements in the work (literary, artistic, or musical expression or elements of selection,

50 Olbrich et al (n 42), 871.

51 Anne Lauber-Rönsberg, *GRUR* (2019), 244.

52 *Scheufen*, in: Leupold/Wiebe/Glossner, IT-Recht, part 9.6.2 marginal no. 14ff. and Sesing-Wagenpfeil (n 9), 751.

53 *Pfeifer*, in v. Lewinksi/Wittmann, Urheberrecht!, FS für Michel M. Walter zum 80 Geburtstag, 2018, 222, 226 et seq.; BeckOK UrhR/Ahlberg (n 46). no. 55.

54 When presenting the different approaches to delimitation in the literature, it is noticeable that they regularly use the same terms to describe the same material content: "foreseeability of the result", "immediacy connection", "control over the design process" (cf. on this in an overview: Sesing-Wagenpfeil (n 9), 753, who already correctly recognizes that at least two of these terms are synonyms).

55 BeckOK UrhR/Ahlberg (n 46), no. 55.

56 BeckOK UrhR/Ahlberg (n 46), no. 55.

57 In the result with this abstract assessment also Sesing-Wagenpfeil (n 9), 754, who describes the elements described as a "moving system" and relationship of "control" and "predictability"; see Wandtke/Bullinger/Thum, UrhG § 7 no. 20.

arrangement, etc.) were actually conceived and executed not by man but by a machine".[58] This question must be answered case-by-case.[59] The decisive factor in this context is whether the human had control over the creative decisions during the creative process and created the "traditional elements of authorship" by himself.[60]

Ultimately, what matters under both German and U.S. copyright law is whether the work, despite the use of technology, is a product of human creativity. This is not the case if the essential creative decisions were made by the technological tool that has been used,[61] and the human had no creative control during the creative process.[62]

As it currently stands, for an artistic work to be granted copyright protection in the GCC member states it needs to meet the requirement of "creativity".[63] According to their respective copyright laws, protection shall be awarded to created or creative works.[64]. Art.1 of the Bahraini Law no. 22 of 2006 on the Protection of Copyright and Neighbouring Rights for example defines a work as any "created composition in the fields of literature, the arts or science". Art. 3 of the Kuwaiti Law no. 75 of 2019 on Copyright and Related Rights awards protection to "creative works in the arts, sciences or knowledge".

In contrast to other jurisdictions like U.S. or European law all GCC member states use the word "ibitkar" ("creativity") instead of "asalah" ("originality") in their copyright laws.[65] Their respective meanings however show similarities. While the definition of "creativity" varies between Gulf States, the differences are only minor.[66] Art. 1 Nr. 5 of the Omani Copyright Law defines creation as the "creative nature which gives originality and distinction to the work". Similar, Art. 1 Nr. 2 of the Kuwaiti Copyright Law stipulates creativity as bringing "new work with the element of authenticity or to renew an existing work or develop it so that this renewal or development is of a special character". This goes to show that both

58 U.S. Copyright Office, Compendium of U.S. Copyright Office Practices (n 41), quoting *U.S. Copyright Office*, Sixty-Eight Annual Report of the Register of Copyrights for the Fiscal Year Ending June 30, 1965, p. 5 (1966).

59 U.S. Copyright Office, Copyright Registration Guidance (n 1), 4.

60 U.S. Copyright Office, Copyright Registration Guidance (n 1), (quoting *Burrow-Giles Lithographic Company v. Sarony)*, 111 U.S. 53, 61 (1884)).

61 Anne Lauber-Rönsberg (n 51), 244, 248.

62 U.S. Copyright Office, Copyright Registration Guidance (n 1), 4.

63 Rami Olwan and Riyadh Al-Balushi, 'The Requirement of Originality in the Copyright Laws of the Arab Gulf States: Perspectives from Author's Rights Jurisdictions' *GRUR International* (2023), 1030, 1037.

64 Bahrain, Law No 22 of 2006 on the Protection of Copyright and Neighbouring Rights, Article 1; Kuwait, No. 75 of 2019 on Copyright and Related Rights, Article 3; Oman, Law on Copyright and Neighbouring Rights Royal Decree No. 65/2008, Article 2; Qatar, Law. No. 7 of 2002 on the Protection of Copyright and Related Rights, Article 2; Saudi Arabia, Copyright Law Royal Decree No. M/41 of 2 Rajab 1424H and amended by Decision of the Council of Ministers No. 536 of 19 Shawwal 1439H, Article 2; UAE, Federal Law No. 38 of 2021 in Copyright and Neighbouring Rights, Article 1.

65 Olwan and Al-Balushi (n 63), 1030, 1039.

66 Olwan and Al-Balushi (n 63), 1030, 1039.

under Western copyright law and the copyright laws in the Arabic Gulf States a work must be authentic, distinctive or independently created, and demonstrate a minimum amount of creative input in order to be protected.

This creative act must further be made by the author or the right owner, which according to Art. 1 Nr. 3 of the Omani Copyright Law is the "natural person who creates the work". Similar definitions are also found in other GCC member states[67] thus firmly establishing that in accordance with Western law the work must have been created by a human being.

Furthermore, GCC member states as well as most countries of the Western world are contracting parties of The Berne Convention, which itself also takes a "human-centric approach".[68] While it does not give an explicit definition of authorship, human authorship is an underlying motive in most articles of the Convention.[69] Its scope of application presupposes human authorship, as it is determined by the nationality or residence of the author, which, at least at the moment and probably fundamentally, algorithms or AI systems lack.[70] To be attributed authorship it is not enough if the human input merely consists in giving a simple command or request to the AI tool. The human user needs to contribute sufficient "intellectual creation" in order to be considered the author of the work.[71]

This strengthens the need of human authorship in all signatory states of the Berne Convention. It can, therefore, be stated that under all analyzed jurisdictions, it is decisive whether the work can still be considered a product of human creativity.

Therefore, the issues identified and deeply discussed in European and U.S. copyright law are equally likely to arise in the GCC member states in a similar form.

Personal Intellectual Creation of the TIDM User

A personal creation could be attributed to the user who initiates an image creation by entering the text prompt. Through the textual description given to the system, certain information is communicated to the system that is to be found in the final image, so that the user influences the concrete image design in this way. In order to determine whether the final image creation by means of the TIDM is indeed still a direct individual creative work of the user, it is necessary to analyze the individual processing steps carried out by the TIDM between the input of the text prompt and the output of the final product from a copyright perspective.

67 Olwan and Al-Balushi (n 63), 1030, 1040.

68 Vincenzo Iaia, 'To Be, or Not to Be … Original Under Copyright Law, That Is (One of) the Main Questions Concerning AI-Produced Works', *GRUR International* (2022), 793, 805.

69 Jane Ginsburg, 'People Not Machines: Authorship and What It Means in the Berne Convention', *IIC* (2018), 131.

70 Iaia (n 68).

71 Ginsburg (n 69).

CLIP Algorithms

The CLIP algorithms used by DALL·E 2 transfer the information provided by the user into a text embedding. At this point in the process, it is crucial that the text embedding contains this information *as accurately as possible.*

Against the background of this precise mode of operation, the CLIP algorithms can be regarded as an – albeit very complex – aid for the user. They are used specifically with the aim of translating the given image description into a form of representation that is understandable for the *prior*. The CLIP algorithms necessarily work without random elements, so that the content of the information passed on remains unchanged. The controllability of the CLIP algorithms as a tool can be illustrated in particular by the fact that an identical input of text information always leads to the same text embedding, provided that the model of the CLIP algorithms has not been changed.

Prior

The *prior* then transfers the CLIP text embeddings into CLIP *image* embeddings. Here, too, high precision is important; random elements or information additions must not be used. The generation of the image embeddings by the *prior* can thus also be seen as an aid to the creation of the final product. Since the *prior* translates the text embeddings created from the image description into image embeddings without changing or adding to the content of the information provided, the use of the *prior* is also the use of a tool. The (intermediate) result produced by this can be traced back without gaps to the original input of the image description – without creative or other additions. As with the CLIP algorithms, the result also remains identical with identical information input.

Decoder

Based on the image embeddings created by the *prior*, the *decoder* then creates a selection of images to present to the user. The *decoder* uses the information originally provided by the user. However, the *decoder* selects non-specified parameters, such as concretely used <u>colors</u>, <u>size</u>, <u>position of the objects</u> and also the <u>concrete shape</u> or <u>visual representation</u> of the individual objects in the overall image, using <u>random elements</u> and adds additional information that is as suitable as possible through algorithmic calculation on the basis of the training data.

Since the *decoder* has been trained to create an image, its use can be compared in some respects to the use of a random generator, the result of which is neither predictable nor controllable for the user. The user controls DALL·E 2 in such a way that he himself initiates the creation of the image by providing DALL·E 2 with a description of the image. However, the user can no longer influence or even control the immediate conversion process within and through the *decoder*. Furthermore, the user has no influence on how the information supplementation by the *decoder* takes place. These elements alone speak against classifying the *decoder* as a classic aid. Due to the random elements and computational information supplementation deliberately used in the *decoder*, the image produced by the *decoder* as a result cannot be regarded as directly based on an intellectual creation process of the user. The fact that the *decoder* may itself be based on an intellectual creation process is not sufficient to qualify the final product as a personal intellectual creation. In this case, too, the created image is only indirectly attributable to an intellectual creative process.[72]

Decisions of the TIDM User re. the Text Prompt

A creative achievement of the user can, at most, be seen in the selection of the given text prompt or the selection decision regarding the images created by TIDM. It is doubtful, however, whether these decisions express the individuality of the author to a sufficient degree, i.e. in the sense of a design level.[73]

In contrast to the use of image editing programs or image creation software, the user does not determine the implementation of the individual editing or creation steps when using DALL·E 2. Although the basic information is provided in the user's text input, it can be represented by countless visual interpretations over whose concrete selection the user no longer has any influence. The moment the user sends his instructions for configuring the image, and the corresponding CLIP text and image embeddings have been created, he can no longer intervene in or control the creation of the final image, i.e. he no longer controls the immediate implementation process within and by the machine.[74] Consequently, there is a lack of targeted and direct use of the program to create one's own intellectual creation,[75] since the user merely takes note of the generated image files.[76] This is also shown by the following control consideration: An identical text input always leads to different variations in which only the semantic classification remains the same, but the creative details are not determined and cannot be determined due to the random elements already mentioned in the creation process.

This interpretation is supported by a decision of the U.S. Copyright Office concerning a registration application submitted by the writer of a comic book.[77] The comic book contains images that the writer created using the artificial intelligence program "Midjourney",[78] that works the same way as OpenAI's DALL-E. In its decision, the Office explained that the images in the comic book generated by Midjourney were not protectable by copyright, because "the traditional elements

72 See BeckOK UrhR/Ahlberg (n 46), no. 55.

73 On this criterion, see Olbrich et al (n 42), 870.

74 In the result also Philipp Hacker, Kuschel/Asmussen/Golla, Intelligente Systeme - Intelligentes Recht, 2021, 223, 241; on this requirement, see BeckOK UrhR/Ahlberg (n 46), no. 55.

75 On this requirement see Wandtke/Bullinger/Thum, UrhG § 7 no. 20.

76 In such a case, Wandtke/Bullinger/Thum, 6th ed. 2022, UrhG § 7 no. 20 denies own intellectual creation.

77 U.S. Copyright Office, re: Zarya of the Dawn (n 1).

78 U.S. Copyright Office, re: Zarya of the Dawn (n 1), 2.

of authorship" were generated by the AI and not created by the author.[79] According to the Office, the images – unlike explained in the application – were not a visual expression of the text prompts as creations of the author, a human being.[80] Since the way Midjourney generates the pictures, was unpredictable, the users had no sufficient control over the outcome of this process and therefore could not be seen as authors under copyright law.[81] According to the Office, this insufficient control was also demonstrated by the fact that – as already mentioned – a specific text input did not result in a specific image generated by the AI.[82] Instead, the text input would come closer to general content-related instructions given by a client to a visual artist who has been hired to paint a picture.[83]

Given the above shows broad similarities between Western copyright law and those of the GCC member states, which both require the work to be a result of human creativity, a similar approach to dealing with AI-generated images could be taken by the jurisdiction in the GCC.

Training Data as a Copyright Protected Work?

Training data can also be considered to link to the people who filled the databases with image files and appropriate text descriptions on the basis of which the different models were trained. After all, this training data is in a way the creative "source of inspiration" for the generation of the machine products, especially the supplementary information within the image file.[84]

However, the training data for the TIDM come from data sources available on the Internet, including *Shutterstock*.[85] The image and text files found there were not made available by the users with the aim of using them to create further works of art within the meaning of copyright law.[86] The filling of the database therefore does not take place by way of the necessary intellectual creation and design process that would be required for copyrightability.[87] Furthermore, due to the training methods with a neural network, which in turn contain random elements, it is not comprehensible to the creators of the training data how the DALL·E 2 algorithm, in particular the *decoder*, ultimately interprets terms and generates information.

79 U.S. Copyright Office, re: Zarya of the Dawn (n 1), 8.
80 U.S. Copyright Office, re: Zarya of the Dawn (n 1), 9.
81 U.S. Copyright Office, re: Zarya of the Dawn (n 1).
82 U.S. Copyright Office, re: Zarya of the Dawn (n 1), 9, 10.
83 U.S. Copyright Office, re: Zarya of the Dawn (n 1), 10.
84 Olbrich et al (n 42), 870, 875 with further references.
85 Press release Shutterstock, 25 November 2022, https://www.shutterstock.com/press/20435 .
86 This potentially leads to licensing issues, as it is questionable whether the authors of the works available on platforms such as *Shutterstock* have actually given their consent to the use of their works as training data.
87 See BeckOK UrhR/Ahlberg (n 46), marginal no. 54.

Personal Intellectual Creation by OpenAI Programmer

Finally, the relevance of *OpenAI* in the training process of DALL·E 2 should be highlighted. The selection of the training data has a decisive influence on the possible results that a system can achieve.[88] The same applies to the representation of the data: Which features of the training data are taken into account when creating the models and which additional information is used determines, among other things, which patterns an algorithm can recognize and subsequently use to generate further data sets.[89]

OpenAI has carefully filtered and modified the training data sets of DALL·E 2, especially to prevent misuse,[90] thus exerting a significant influence on the system. The fact that the subsequent learning process of the neural networks cannot be controlled or monitored and that the networks are regularly subject to development processes with random elements does not contradict this. With regard to the protectability of a personal intellectual creation by *OpenAI*, however, it must also be taken into account here that *OpenAI* has deliberately selected a model with the *decoder* that achieves its results with the inclusion of random elements. The way in which the *decoder* uses the skills it has learned with the help of the training data cannot therefore be specifically predetermined by the selection of the training data. In this respect, too, the required immediacy of the act of intellectual creation is lacking.[91]

Interim Result

The legal assessment of the individual technical elements and the roles of the persons involved shows that the products produced by DALL·E 2 – according to the prevailing and correct opinion in the literature –do not constitute copyrightable works. Consequently, this means that all products are in the public domain and can be used and exploited as desired.

The U.S. Copyright Office came to the same conclusion in the aforementioned decision concerning pictures in a comic book, which were generated by Midjourney, an AI similar to DALL-E 2,[92] and thus supports the prevailing opinion in literature.

88 Ory and Sorge (n 43), 711; approvingly Olbrich et al (n 42), 875.
89 Ory and Sorge (n 43), 711; approvingly Olbrich et al (n 42), 875.
90 In particular, through training and the use of so-called "classifiers", which filtered out images from certain categories from the training datasets.
91 The training data itself can be regarded as creations under certain circumstances (see *Hacker*, GRUR 2020, 1028), but this is irrelevant for the classification of the product by DALL·E 2 with regard to the influence of *OpenAI*.
92 U.S. Copyright Office, re: Zarya of the Dawn (n 1).

New Challenges for Copyright Law

The legal assessment leads to two fundamental questions. (1) Is the current scope of protection of copyright sufficient to enable a desired activity in the form of TIDM or (2) Is there a need for action from another direction to protect existing copyrights of third parties more effectively? Especially in the context of fundamental changes to existing copyright protection schemes, Kuwait's aspirations to become a knowledge-based economy are the ideal background to transform these challenges into opportunities.

Opportunities for Dynamic Copyright Law Adaptations – Kuwait

Kuwait is already a member of prominent international organizations including the World Intellectual Property Organization (WIPO) and the World Trade Organization (WTO). It is also a signatory to key agreements such as the WTO TRIPS Agreement, the Arab Convention for the Protection of Authors' Rights, and the Berne Convention for the Protection of Literary and Artistic Works.[93] By participating in these agreements, Kuwait demonstrates its recognition of the significance of intellectual property in driving economic growth and technological advancement.

Kuwait's approach to innovation within the realm of IP law is marked by a concerted effort to align its policies with international standards and promote a conducive environment for creativity and business.[94] As a member of both the WIPO and the WTO, Kuwait has shown a clear dedication to fostering innovation while simultaneously protecting intellectual property rights.[95]

Kuwait's progression in terms of intellectual property protection, as highlighted by its improved ranking in the Global Competitiveness Report, underscores the country's active efforts to enhance its IP laws and regulations.[96] This positive trajectory reflects Kuwait's aspiration to provide a robust legal framework that encourages innovation and safeguards the rights of creators and innovators.

It's essential to note that the trajectory of GCC member states, such as Kuwait,[97] indicates a trend towards enhancing IP protection. The improvement in its Global Competitiveness Report ranking is indicative of Kuwait's proactive approach to strengthening its IP framework. This suggests that Kuwait is inclined to provide a more robust environment for intellectual property, aligning with global trends that recognize the significance of IP in driving innovation and economic development.[98]

93 OECD-Kuwait-Innovation-System-Review, 233.

94 OECD-Kuwait-Innovation-System-Review, 233.

95 The Role of Coherent Linkages in Fostering Innovation-Based Economies in the Gulf Cooperation Council Countries, 113.

96 World Economic Forum, Global Competitiveness Report 2019, 9.

97 To illustrate the potential direction of GCC member state legislation can take, Kuwait and its legislative as well as policy endeavours are chosen exemplary.

98 Kuwait National Development Plan 2020–2025, 52; World Economic Forum, Global Competitiveness Report (n 96).

Given this backdrop, it is necessary to understand the challenges AI and TIDM pose to contemporary copyright law. To attract innovative minds and creators, Kuwait's efforts to adjust their IP landscape need to focus – at least – partially on the incentive principle of copyright law to provide a legally welcoming copyright regime to AI developers. Furthermore, a new and dynamic copyright law needs to address the challenges re. burden of proof as well as the establishment of a new set of contractual laws that allow for the sale of AI-creations that are not protected by classical copyright law. The key to create a system that incentivizes innovation and creativity is finding a balance between interests of AI creators and classical copyright creators and copyright holders.

Extension of the Scope of Protection for TIDM Products

The fundamental discussion as to whether machine-generated products require their own copyright protection has also progressed to the extent that there are hardly any voices *in favour* of an extension of the scope of protection.[99] Therefore, the practical example of DALL·E 2 will be used here to illustrate which interests exist. Furthermore, Kuwait's handling and aspirations in the context of copyright and IP in general will be outlined to show a concrete point of view of the GCC in the perspective of innovation and extension of copyright law.

Incentives for OpenAI

It is sometimes argued that if a product is worthless, the machine that produces it is also worthless, since the products cannot be exploited economically.[100] There is no incentive to invest in the development of machines if their results can be taken over and exploited by third parties without compensation. The protection of machine-generated products could therefore serve to make investments in such machines profitable.[101] As Kuwait wants to accelerate the development of innovative products and services[102] and recognizes the importance of AI for its national economic development,[103] setting the right incentives for AI developers is a crucial aspect of the Kuwait National Development Plan.

Also, a property right for the programmer could provide an incentive for further investment in the development of algorithms, which can be seen as socially desirable.[104]

99 With an overview of the state of opinion, see Sesing-Wagenpfeil (n 9), 754.

100 For example, Sven Hetmank and Anne Lauber-Rönsberg, 'Anne, Künstliche Intelligenz – Herausforderungen für das Immaterialgüterrecht', *GRUR* (2018), 574, 579.

101 For example, Sven Hetmank and Anne Lauber-Rönsberg, 'Anne, Künstliche Intelligenz – Herausforderungen für das Immaterialgüterrecht', *GRUR* (2018), 574, 579.

102 Kuwait National Development Plan (n 98), 52.

103 *Al Barakti*, Comp. IT. Sci. (2021) Vol. 10 no. 2, 19, 23.

104 Sarah Legner, 'Erzeugnisse Künstlicher Intelligenz im Urheberrecht', *ZUM* (2019), 807, 811.

The commercial success and proliferation of products shows that DALL·E 2 has considerable value as a service. As with other service models, a proprietary protection position is not necessary. As with other software programs, the current protection for software products and training data as a database is (arguably) sufficient.[105]

DALL·E 2 Users

Concerns have been expressed in some quarters that the lack of protection for a product would mean that the user of the program would have no incentive to publish it.

Therefore, it is sometimes proposed to grant the end user an exclusive right, at least temporarily, even if his activity is limited to providing the machine with the image description to be implemented and he has not invested in its development.[106] As a result of operating the machine, however, he has actual ownership of the product produced by it. Since it is up to the user to make the product available to others or to keep it for himself, the exclusive right of use is intended to motivate him to publish it.[107]

Practical observation of the numerous *X* (formerly *Twitter*) and *Instagram* accounts that publish DALL·E 2 products shows that no further incentive seems necessary and that a revenue stream can also be generated via such media without the need for an exclusive right.

Protection Within Legal Relationships

An exclusive user's right could also take into account the interests of legal relationships, i.e. legal certainty, as the user's status was most easily recognizable to third parties in legal transactions in comparison to that of the author.[108] Given that Kuwaiti AI governance policies are only emerging,[109] providing a legally compliant and easy to understand regulatory framework as set out in the Kuwait National Development Plan,[110] is key to fostering a dynamic private sector and attracting AI developers.

However, the make and style of existing works are, in principle, not protected by copyright.[111] It is true that the algorithms capture and store the manner of making, style and technically describable details with digital precision, which is no longer

105 The comparability to the derivative product protection of Section 9 sentence 2 no. 3 PatG, cited by Sesing-Wagenpfeil (n 9), 754 is not convincing, as patent law specifically protects a technical teaching for the manufacture of products with the process patent - this process-related approach, however, is precisely not to be found in work-related copyright law.

106 Legner (n 104), 807, 812.

107 Legner (n 104), 807, 812.

108 Legner (n 104), 807, 812.

109 *Al Barakti* (n 103).

110 Kuwait National Development Plan (n 98), 155.

111 Ory and Sorge (n 43), 710, 712.

comparable to inspiration from natural persons. Rather, the procedure resembles an extraction, as it plays a role in sampling.[112]

In fact, these circumstances establish a new challenge in the context of style imitation, but rather in the direction of existing copyrights and thus do not concern the users of DALL·E 2. This is also pointed out by the U.S. Copyright Office in its decision on the comic created using Midjourney. The Office argues that the writer of the comic cannot be considered the author of the images contained in the comic, which were created using Midjourney, just because she has, by entering the text prompts, determined the style of the images generated by the AI.[113] In this context, the Office makes the already mentioned comparison to a client and a hired artist. If the writer of the comic had hired a visual artist and given him specific content related instructions regarding an image he should paint, it would still not be her but the visual artist who would be the author of the image.[114] Therefore, the question rather is whether the imitation of a style of a certain artist by an AI can constitute a violation of the artist's copyright.[115]

Since the requirement of human authorship in Kuwaiti and Western copyright law is largely similar, Kuwait could follow the approach of the U.S. court, thus helping AI developers transition between legal frameworks seamlessly. Ultimately, providing a clear solution to these legal challenges and finding a balance between the artist's copyright and the enabling of AI usage will determine the success of Kuwait's economic transformation.

Adaptation of the Copyright Environment to Maintain the Existing Level of Protection

The assessment shows that especially for the products of DALL·E 2 – and thus probably for TIDM-generated images in general – there is no need or demand for an extension of the rights of the actors involved. On the contrary, developments can currently be observed according to which, new challenges for already existing copyrights arise through the products generated by DALL·E 2. For the purposes of creating a well-equipped modern copyright legal landscape, both the interests of AI developers and conventional copyright holders have to be considered.

Difficulties re. Burden of Proof

With TIDM, for the first time in widespread use, products are being created that are practically indistinguishable from genuine works in the sense of copyright law. This circumstance poses new challenges for the enforcement of rights by authors or right holders. Until now, copyright disputes have often focused on copyright

112 Ory and Sorge (n 43), 710, 712.
113 *U.S. Copyright Office*, re: Zarya of the Dawn (n 1), 10.
114 *U.S. Copyright Office*, re: Zarya of the Dawn (n 1), 10.
115 See in this respect section IV. 2. c.

attribution or the application of specific infringement facts. Through a widespread application of TIDM, it is conceivable that the accusation of copyright infringement could be countered in a different way for the first time. In this respect, a potential infringer could come up with the idea of doubting the work nature of a digital image or product and claim that the alleged work shown is a product that was created with TIDM. An author who has not yet realized this new development, may find it difficult to prove that it is, in fact, a personal intellectual creation. Usually, artists in the *Digital Art Market* do not keep documentation of their creative process in order to be able to meet a possible burden of proof. The widespread distribution of TIDM products make it seem not unlikely that this issue will indeed lead to practical problems at some point. In view of the interests at stake in this context, it seems appropriate to strengthen intellectual property in the form of copyright or the corresponding rights of use by means of these new difficulties of proof, for example, by considering a reversal of the burden of proof in specific cases, or at least an increase in the standard of proof for the alleged infringer by requiring him to provide evidence of the lack of character of the work. However, care must be taken in any such legal action to strike a careful balance with the scenario where someone claims to be the author of a "work" which was actually created using TIDM. In such cases there is a danger of making it easier for the non-author to litigate by shifting the burden of proof. However, the latter case can probably be countered by the fact that a user of a product of TIDM can document the creation or acquisition better than the author can document the creation of his work. In the current situation, however, it seems appropriate to impose a documentation obligation on the user of TIDM or the acquirer of corresponding products. This obligation is easier to fulfil for the user than for the author of digital works of art and it thus leads to a more effective protection of the author without significantly burdening other market participants.

Terms of Sale of Shutterstock, Inc.

The announcement by *Shutterstock* to sell DALL·E 2 products in future or to make them available on the website alongside classic *stock footage*[116] raises further questions. The wording seems to be deliberately chosen, as it simply refers to the offer of "images" without mentioning any licences – even though such are usually offered for other *Shutterstock* offers. However, the announcement also avoids talking about the concrete form of the offer. Since it is not a matter of intellectual property, but of pure products, a classical exploitation is not possible. Instead, a contract for work and services seems more likely, according to which *Shutterstock* is owed the transfer of the image in higher resolution and without a watermark. However, this contractual constellation harbours practical difficulties, since in the event of publication by the purchaser of the image files, third parties can freely copy, modify and resell them without legal concerns. It remains to be seen how

116 Press release Shutterstock, 25 November 2022, https://www.shutterstock.com/press/20435.

Shutterstock intends to maintain this new business field, for example, through contractual arrangements. It is at least positive that *Shutterstock* already acknowledges that intellectual property rights of third parties may have been used in the training of the various algorithms of DALL·E 2, and that it will endeavour to obtain appropriate compensation for these rights holders.

Protection of Styles of Specific Artists

A fundamentally not unknown problem, style imitation, acquires a new practical relevance through DALL·E 2 and other comparable offerings. An impressive example of this is the artist Greg Rutkowski, who is known on the *Digital Arts Market* for his fantasy artworks. He noticed that his name was applied as a style in 93,000 cases within the framework of the "*Stable Diffusion*" model comparable to DALL·E 2, whereas famous artists such as Picasso and da Vinci only come to a scant 2,000 applications.[117] Due to the advanced technology, the style is also imitated in a correspondingly genuine way. As a result, Greg Rutkowski faces a popularity problem and his own sales opportunities are significantly reduced. However, there is nothing wrong with imitating a style from a copyright point of view. An artist's "style", as a pure idea or method, is regularly too abstract to enjoy its own copyright protection.[118] At least as long as the style of an artist is imitated in an abstract way, for example, by using a specific color or shade a certain artist is known for, this imitation is not prohibited under copyright law. If, on the other hand, certain shapes, patterns or figures, which an artist uses in his works and which characterize his style, are borrowed, it is quite conceivable that this constitutes a relevant extraction under copyright law, as is assumed in the case of sampling.[119] Sampling, i.e. the extraction of (very short) sound sequences, constitutes a reproduction under German copyright law if the short audio fragment that is extracted is recognizable, according to the German Federal Court of Justice (BGH).[120] Thus, if shapes or figures – even more abstract ones – are unmistakably assignable to a particular artist, their extraction is likely to be comparable to the case of sampling.

Furthermore, a corresponding relevance under copyright law occurs when the training data has been used without authorization. This is another novelty that programs like DALL·E 2 bring: the simplicity of imitating a style. However, whereas previously imitation only required the free perception of a work of art by a human

117 Melissa Heikkilä, 'This artist is dominating AI-generated art. And he's not happy about it', *Technology Review*. 16 September 2022,

118 Contrary to individual opinions to the contrary, such as OLG Köln, NJW 1998, 1416, according to which the use of "typical stylistic elements from the body of work" in such a way that the impression is created that the work created in this way is an image of the original creator is inadmissible as an adaptation, even if a concrete image has not served as a model.

119 See Franz Gernhardt, 'Urheberrechtsverletzungen durch künstliche Intelligenz am Beispiel der bildenden Künste; Werk ohne Autor Einmal Anders', *GRUR-Prax* (2022), 69, 70 et seq.

120 BGH, GRUR 2020, 843.

artist, it is not possible for a program to process a data input without realizing an act of use under copyright law.

However, taking action against the respective program or providers themselves seems futile. First of all, practical proof of the training method of the algorithms with copyright-protected material is not possible for a layperson without more detailed access to the programming background. Furthermore, it is questionable whether there is an infringing act in the specific case at all. This is because the images are regularly available to the public, be it only through the artist's advertising on his or her own website, or on other websites where the artworks are legitimately made available to the public. As a rule, an artist will not expressly reserve the use of his or her artwork for use as training data.

Furthermore, the question arises whether the processing within the framework of the various algorithms constitutes unauthorized processing in the sense of copyright law. In Western legislative approaches, this is regulated very differently, so GCC member states are able to assess the different approaches. In U.S. copyright law, for example, the fair-use limitation of copyright is very broad and makes no distinction between algorithmic or non-algorithmic use. In contrast, European, and particular German, copyright law has a different approach. Pursuant to Section 23 (1) sentence 1 German Copyright Act[121] processing is permissible if the newly created work is at a sufficient distance from the work used and results in a work protected by copyright,[122] which – as shown – is not the case with AI-generated art. The holders of this opinion argue, that only the incentive to create one's own work is to be supported by Section 23 (1) sentence 2 German Copyright Act. In contrast, an unauthorized processing of an already existing work within the meaning of Section 23 (1) sentence 1 German Copyright Act does not have to qualify as a work protected by copyright.[123] Following this prevailing view, AI-generated art may in principle constitute an unauthorized processing of a copyrighted work under Section 23 (1) sentence 1 German Copyright Act but cannot be seen as permissible processing under Section 23 (1) sentence 2.

Some voices in literature doubt that an AI-generated artwork can, at all, constitute a processing within the meaning of Section 23 (1) German Copyright Act, since processing always required a subjective element in the sense of an inspiration of the processor by the work used. This requirement could not be met by AI, because it was not capable of developing an inner life and, correspondingly, being inspired.[124] However, it is not at all clear that this subjective element is actually required under Section 23 (1) German Copyright Act. At least, the wording of the provision, or more specifically the term "processing", does not dictate this

121 Previous version, the section has since been replaced but nonetheless offers insights into the fundamentally different approach.

122 Thomas Dreier and Schulze, 7th ed. 2022, UrhG, § 23 no. 38; BeckOK/Ahlberg/Lauber-Rönsberg, 37th ed. § 23 no. 34; Eichelberger/*Wirth/Seifert*, 4th ed. 2022, UrhG, § 23 no. 1; for a different view see Wandtke/Bullinger, 6th ed. 2022, UrhG, § 23 no. 28.

123 Thomas Dreier and Schulze, 7th ed. 2022, UrhG, § 23 no. 18.

124 Gernhardt (n 119); Ory and Sorge (n 43), 710, 712. .

interpretation. Moreover, the proof of a subjective element may possibly be difficult, which is why the requirement of such an element is questionable.

It is evident that Section 23 German Copyright Act is not suited for the current technical developments in the field of generative AI. Accordingly, it is extremely difficult to determine the relevance of the processing of copyrighted works by AI under copyright law. This German approach therefore prioritizes human-centered copyright and respective creations as opposed to creations that significantly rely on AI systems, which seems contrary to the innovative-forward approach of the GCC member states.

It is not necessarily the case that the training process for the algorithm involves unauthorized copying that goes beyond the data processing of publicly provided content. For artists like Greg Rutkowski, there is therefore no easy way out in the current situation. Even an adjustment of copyright protection in some way can hardly be achieved in a way that is in the interests of the artists, since an extension of protection to styles would mean a break with the foundations of copyright and is likely to unduly restrict other artists in their development. The practical impact seems to be limited to the *Digital Arts Market*, according to current observations, as this is particularly predestined for style imitations through AI.

Conclusion

Two main results can be drawn from the analysis. On one hand, it can be observed with the first, technically very mature *text-to-image* model DALL·E 2 and other TIDM, that the products do not legally enjoy copyright protection and the practical handling of the program shows that there is also no need to extend copyright protection for economic incentive reasons. Furthermore, the practical impact of TIDM shows that it is rather necessary to deal with the – so far strongly neglected – idea of what challenges this new technology poses for already existing copyrights. In principle, it is advisable to legally reorganize the evidentiary questions on the character of the work, not to expand the protection of existing artists, but rather to maintain the existing level of protection and to counteract a threatening de facto devaluation through impossible evidentiary requirements. Independently of this, however, there are other challenges for artists in the *Digital Arts Market* that have significant and acute implications without a simple legal solution. Rather, it seems that TIDM require a rethinking on several levels – factual, legal and possibly even artistic.

Countries that intend to become a trailblazer for modern copyright that welcomes AI developers and innovation, such as Kuwait, need to be aware of all challenges that the recent development poses and considers interests of both classical and emerging creators. As identified, the requirement of human authorship in Kuwaiti and Western copyright law is largely similar, Kuwait could follow the approach of the U.S. systems, thus helping AI developers transition between legal frameworks seamlessly as well as avoiding the issues that stem from a strictly human-centered Western copyright regime such as Germany. Broadening the possibilities of creative use of AI systems allows to attract creators with an AI focus by providing them with a modern and unambiguous legal framework to protect and exploit their creations. In addition, other, even classic creators, are more likely to base commercial operations in such modern copyright jurisdictions that are aware of the current challenges and legal uncertainties, and provide a legally certain and stable framework that addresses both concerns of avid AI users and classic copyright creators. Ultimately, providing a clear solution to these legal challenges and finding a balance between the artist's copyright and the enabling of AI usage will determine the success of Kuwait's and other GCC member states' economic transformation.

Bibliography

Brown, Tom B., et al., 'Language Models are Few-Shot Learners, 34th Conference on Neural Information Processing Systems (NeurIPS 2020), Vancouver, Canada.', *OpenAI Papers* (2020): 1–25.

Dreier, Thomas/Schulze, Gernot, *Urheberrechtsgesetz*, 7th ed. (2022), (Munich, C H Beck, 2022).

Eichelberger, Jan, Thomas Wirth and Fedor Seifert, *Urheberrechtsgesetz*, 4th ed. (2022).

Gernhardt, Franz, 'Urheberrechtsverletzungen durch künstliche Intelligenz am Beispiel der bildenden Künste; Werk ohne Autor einmal anders', *GRUR-Prax* (2022), 69–71.

Ginsburg, Jane, 'People Not Machines: Authorship and What It Means in the Berne Convention', *IIC* 49 (2018): 131–143.

Goetting, Hans-Peter and Anne Lauber-Roensberg, *Beck'scher Online-Kommentar Urheberrecht*, 37th ed. (2023).

Hacker, Philipp, 'Immaterialgüterrechtlicher Schutz von KI-Trainingsdaten', *GRUR* (2020): 1025–1033.

Heikkilä, Melissa, 'This Artist is Dominating AI-Generated Art. And He's Not Happy About It', *MIT Technology Review ,* 16 September 2022, .https://www.technologyreview.com/2022/09/16/1059598/this-artist-is-dominating-ai-generated-art-and-hes-not-happy-about-it/

Hetmank, Sven/Lauber-Rönsberg, 'Anne, Künstliche Intelligenz – Herausforderungen für das Immaterialgüterrecht', *GRUR* (2018): 574–582.

Iaia, Vincenzo, 'To Be, or Not to Be … Original Under Copyright Law, That Is (One of) the Main Questions Concerning AI-Produced Works', *GRUR International* (2022): 793–812.

Kim, Gwanghyun and Jong Chul Ye, 'DiffusionCLIP: Text-Guided Image Manipulation Using Diffusion Models', *ICLR* (2022): 1–11.

Kuschel, Linda, Sven Asmussen and Sebastian Golla, *Intelligente Systeme – Intelligentes Recht*, Baden-Baden (2021).

Lauber-Rönsberg, Anne, 'Autonome "Schöpfung" – Urheberschaft und Schutzfähigkeit', *GRUR* (2019): 244–253.

Legner, Sarah, 'Erzeugnisse Künstlicher Intelligenz im Urheberrecht', *ZUM* (2019): 807–812.

Leupold, Andreas, Andreas Wiebe and Sylke Glossner, *IT-Recht*, 4th ed. (2021).

Lewinksi, Silke von and Heinz Wittmann, *Urheberrecht! Festschrift für Hon.-Prof. Dr. Michel M. Walter zum 80 Geburtstag*, Wien (2018).

Liou, Cheng-Yuan, Wei-Chen Cheng, Jiun-Wie Liou and Daw-Ran Liou, 'Autoencoder for Words', *Neurocomputing* 139 (2014): 84–96.

Mitra, Bhaskar and Nick Craswell, 'Neural Text Embeddings for Information Retrieval', *WDSM* (2017): 813–814.

O'Connor, Ryan, 'How DALL-E 2 Actually Works', *AssemblyAI.* 29th September 2023. https://www.assemblyai.com/blog/how-dall-e-2-actually-works/

Olbrich, Michael, Christian V. Bongers and Johannes Pampel, 'rheberrechtsschutz für Kunstwerke künstlicher Intelligenz?', *GRUR* (2022): 870–877.

Olwan, Rami and Riyadh Al-Balushi, 'The Requirement of Originality in the Copyright Laws of the Arab Gulf States: Perspectives from Author's Rights Jurisdictions', *GRUR International* (2023): 1030–1053.

Ory, Stephan/Sorge, Christoph, 'Schöpfung durch Künstliche Intelligenz?', *NJW* (2019): 710–713.

Radford, Alec et al., 'Learning Transferable Visual Models from Natural Language Supervision. Proceedings of the 38 th International Conference on Machine Learning, PMLR 139, 2021.' (2021), 1–16.

Ramesh, Aditya et al., 'Hierarchical Text-Conditional Image Generation with CLIP Latents', *OpenAI* (2022): 1–27.

Scardapane, Simone and Dianhui Wang, 'Randomness in Neural Networks: An Overview', *Wiley Interdisciplinary Reviews (WIREs): Data Mining and Knowledge Discovery* 7 (2017): 1–18.

Sesing-Wagenpfeil, Andreas, 'KI und Kunst - Zwei Thesen zur urheberrechtlichen Schutzfähigkeit computergenerierter Werke', *CR* (2022): 749–756.

Singh, Aditya, 'How Does DALL-E 2 Work? Diffusion and More Diffusion', *Augmented AI, Medium. 27th April 2022.*https://medium.com/augmented-startups/how-does-dall-e-2-work-e6d492a2667f

U.S. Copyright Office, 'Cancellation Decision re: Zarya of the Dawn (VAu001480196)', (21 February 2023).

U.S. Copyright Office, 'Copyright Registration Guidance: Works Containing Material Generated by Artificial Intelligence', (16 March 2023).

Wandtke, Artur-Axel and Winfried Bullinger, *Praxiskommentar Urheberrecht*, 6th ed. (2022).

8 How Can Safe Harbour Provisions Support Technology Development and Online Business in Saudi Arabia?

Sarah Alsudairy

Introduction

The importance of adopting safe harbour provisions within the Saudi Copyright Law is linked to support the achievement of Vision 2030's aims, especially the one linked to raising the judicial authority's efficiency and the development of e-commerce in the country. The chapter aims to develop the Saudi Copyright Law to exempt Internet service providers (ISPs) from secondary liability for third party infringing content on their platforms, in a way that clarifies the scope of their obligations. This chapter raises two key questions:

- Why is the Saudi government being encouraged to adopt a legal framework that exempts ISPs from liability?
- How should the liability exceptions be adopted within the Saudi Copyright Law in a way that is compatible with the Saudi legal and judicial system?

The Role of Safe Harbour Provisions in Other Jurisdictions

The safe harbour provisions provide limits on ISPs' secondary liability that insulate passive and neutral providers from monetary liability as long as they fulfil specific conditions. They also protect them from any general duties to monitor third parties' activities, but do not prevent injunction remedies.

These provisions have been adopted in different jurisdictions including the European Union, United Kingdom (UK) and United States (US). The meaning and aim of safe harbours in these jurisdictions are mostly identical. However, this chapter will focus its scope mainly on UK law and in some specific parts the focus will be on European law in general. This is done to assess how Saudi Arabia can learn lessons from these legal frameworks and adopt these provisions in a way that is compatible with its own legal and judicial system.

The aim and benefits of establishing limitation of liability in the E-Commerce Directive (ECD)[1] and then transporting it to the UK E-Commerce Regulation

1 Directive 2000/31/EC of the European Parliament and of the Council of 8 June 2000 on certain legal aspects of information society services, in particular electronic commerce, in the Internal Market ('E-commerce Directive' 'ECD').

DOI: 10.4324/9781003528517-8

(2002)[2] was, first, to ensure free movement of information society services between Member States and to promote the internal market for these services. The limitations are considered indispensable to ensuring the continuous free flow of information in the network and the provision of a framework allowing the Internet to develop.[3] Second, these limitations are the foundation to develop rapid and reliable procedures for removing and disabling access to illegal information.[4] Finally, limiting liability within a legal framework would support innovation, the growth of technology companies, and e-commerce by making it clear, predictable and straightforward to any ISP[5] who wants to enter the market or develop their work. Such development can offer significant employment opportunities in the community, stimulate economic growth and investment in innovation, and ultimately enhance industry competitiveness.[6]

The safe harbour principles have been fundamental to developing the Internet and online services. Since the adoption of the E-Commerce Directive, and subsequently the UK E-Commerce Regulation, e-commerce has been growing due to the technological development of broadband, online applications and mobile phones.[7] ISPs have opened up a large variety of new opportunities for online services, creating new markets and providing the means for increased productivity and hence growth and employment throughout the economy.[8] The importance of safe harbour provisions increases further when considering that currently, almost every economic sector depends on Internet connectivity and online services. These provisions have positively impacted the tendency of intermediaries to innovate and allowed a proportionate and sensible way to deal with content wrongly hosted on the Internet.[9] Therefore, it is indispensable in ensuring the provision of basic services that safeguard the continued free flow of information in the network and allow Internet and e-commerce to develop.[10]

2 The Electronic Commerce Regulations 2002 transposes the provisions of the E-commerce Directive 2000/31/EC [2000] OJ L 178/1 ('E-Commerce Regulation' 'ECR').

3 Commission of The European Communities, 'First Report on the Application of Directive 2000/31/ EC of the European Parliament and of the Council of 8 June 2000 on Certain Legal Aspects of Information Society Services, in Particular Electronic Commerce, in the Internal Market (Directive on Electron)' (Brussels, 2003). 12.

4 E-Commerce Directive, Recital (n 1) 40.

5 E-Commerce Directive, Recital (n 1) 60.

6 E-Commerce Directive, Recital (n 1) 2.

7 Communication from The European Commission, 'Towards the Full Roll-Out of Mobile Communications', *COM/2002/0301 Final* (2002) 19.

8 Commission of the European Communities, 'E-Europe 2005: An Information Society for All', *COM/2002/263 Final* (2002) 2.

9 Mike Weatherley, 'Safe Harbour Provisions and Online Service Providers a Discussion Paper by Mike Weatherley MP Former Intellectual Property Adviser to the Prime Minister' (London, 2015) 4.2.

10 Commission of The European Communities, 'First Report on the Application of Directive 2000/31/ EC of the European Parliament and of the Council of 8 June 2000 on Certain Legal Aspects of Information Society Services, in Particular Electronic Commerce, in the Internal Market (Directive on Electron)' (Brussels, 2003). 13.

The Rising Importance to Adopt Safe Harbour Provisions in Saudi Arabia

Copyright protection has varied following the economic phases in the country. Before the economic reform – Vision 2030 – and based on the influence of *Sharia* law on the Saudi judicial system, the process of enforcing the Copyright Law has been challenging and complex, even with the government's efforts to institute copyright protection regimes.[11] The Saudi government started to support many economic sectors after adopting Vision 2030 in 2016 to diversify the economy,[12] including. first, the knowledge-based economy which is a key component that relies on intellectual capabilities more than on physical inputs or natural resources. It is defined as "*the production and services based on knowledge-intensive activities that contribute to an accelerated pace of technical and scientific advance, as well as rapid obsolescence*".[13] Second, copyright and creative industries which have been defined as "*those industries which have their origin in individual creativity, skill and talent and which have a potential for wealth and job creation through the generation and exploitation of intellectual property*". However, according to the United Nations Conference on Trade and Development creative economy has no single definition. It is an evolving concept that builds on the interplay between human creativity, ideas and IP, knowledge and technology, and is the knowledge-based economic activities upon which the 'creative industries' are based. This industry includes advertising, architecture, arts and crafts, design, fashion, film, video, photography, music, performing arts, publishing, research & development, software, computer games, electronic publishing and TV/radio.[14] In line with this direction, the Saudi government established the Saudi Authority of Intellectual Property (SAIP) in 2017 to promote the use of intellectual property (IP) to build an advanced knowledge-based economy.[15]

The focus on IP laws regarding what they can add to the economy ignores their expected negative impact on other sectors such as information technology and online business that the country is also trying to support and develop. When analysing the aims outlined in Vision 2030, it looks as if the government is targeting the development of many sectors other than the ones linked to copyright and creative industries, which questions the potential contradiction that could arise. When the Saudi government unlocked its economy for international investors and set the

11 David Price, 'Politics, Piracy and Punishment: Copyright Protection in the Arabian Gulf', *Journal of World Intellectual Property* 14 (2011), 276, 278. DOI:10.1111/j.1747-1796.2011.00419.x

12 Mohammad Nurunnabi, 'Transformation from an Oil-Based Economy to a Knowledge-Based Economy in Saudi Arabia: The Direction of Saudi Vision 2030', *Journal of the Knowledge Economy* 8, no. 2 (28 June 2017), 536–564.

13 Walter Powell and Kaisa Snellman, 'The Knowledge Economy', *Annual Review of Sociology* 30 (2004), 199–220.

14 UK Department for Culture Media and Sport, 'Creative Industries Economic Estimates', *Creative Industries Economic Estimates* (2016); UNSTAD, 'Creative Economy Report' (2008).

15 Saudi Authority for Intellectual Property, 'SAIP's Objectives' (2023), https://www.saip.gov.sa/en/about/brief/ .

foundation for the copyright and creative industries at the same time, it set out the aim to develop online business and establish effective partnerships with information technology companies so as to better develop such a critical infrastructure and support investment in it. Clearly, the legal clash that could arise when trying to achieve both of these aims has not been considered.

Supporting different sectors is not wrong in principle, however, the radical change to how the Saudi Copyright Law has been enforced since the economic reform as well as the ambiguity of the legal framework regarding secondary liability are the factors that can negatively impact ISPs, including new technologies and online business, unless the government via SAIP takes steps to create legal balance between different rights.

After the economic reform, SAIP took on a new role in enforcing Copyright Law on the Internet by an internal monitoring policy of online content. The monitoring policy is conducted through a special division which monitors online activities and takes down platforms accordingly. As a consequence, SAIP's 2020 report showed that within only three months, they had blocked 308 infringing websites and monitored 1355 platforms.[16] A year later, the numbers had increased, where SAIP monitored 3991 platforms and blocked 866.[17] Then, in 2023, they have already blocked 3400platforms and removed 16for infringing content.[18] This direction might create a discouraging environment for new technologies and online business that the government is targeting to encourage investment in the country. Perhaps these businesses might not be held liable when SAIP reviews their platforms or networks, but they might face allegations without having any defence or clarity about the role they should play regarding the content on their platforms.

Therefore, adopting stronger policies to enforce the Copyright Law is not the main issue, the problem is in the ambiguity of the legal framework, especially that the Copyright Law does not specify any obligations ISPs should carry. The first Saudi Copyright Law came into force in 1989 before the existence of the Internet in Saudi Arabia. However, neither the 2003 Copyright Law nor the 2019 reform include provisions regarding the secondary liability of online intermediaries nor permitting or authorising restricted act by third party.[19]

The unclarity in the scope of secondary liability in the Saudi Copyright Law raises questions about how it would be interpreted by the Judicial Committee or the Commercial Court when it comes to ISPs' liability for third party content; also it

16 Saudi Authority for Intellectual Property (SAIP), 'Annual Report - Intellectual Property Enforcement' (2020).

17 Saudi Authority for Intellectual Property (SAIP), 'Annual Report for Enforcement of Intellectual Property 2021' (2022) .

18 Saudi Authority for Intellectual Property (SAIP), 'Quarter Report for Enforcement of Intellectual Property 2023' (2023).

19 Implementing Regulations of Copyright Law (issued by Decision of the Minister of Culture and Information No. 1688/1 of 10/04/1425H (May 29, 2004), and amended up to Decision No. 4/8/2019 of 4/9/1440H (9 May 2019)

questions whether or not there is a duty of care on them, or if they will be required by the court to take an active role in preventing infringements on their platforms, although the law, as stated, does not impose such an obligation on them. It is difficult to provide a clear answer to these questions, since it is going to vary from one case to another based on the judicial authority dealing with the case. Therefore, the solution starts from developing the Copyright law in a way that provides clarity and balance between different rights, which can be achieved by adopting safe harbour provisions.

The first reason that justifies the adoption of safe harbour provisions within Saudi Copyright Law is the need to ease the government's full control over how content is removed and blocked, thus allowing ISPs to be part of the copyright protection process. The government's dominance or control over online content[20] has made the legal framework lack clarity around ISPs' role regarding infringing content on their platforms and the steps they should follow to take down content and thus be shielded from liability. The benefit of adopting defences against secondary liability lies in the consequent reduction of governmental dominance, in that ISPs would be encouraged to play a specific role in the process and make the government's role more neutral.

Apart from reshaping the government's role, there is an important economic purpose in adopting safe harbour provisions. As discussed above, these provisions are a way to support online business.[21] However, following the Saudi economic reform, SAIP took on a new role in enforcing copyright protection on the Internet in different ways, including monitoring online content independently. This direction, as discussed above, might create a discouraging environment for ISPs and new businesses that the government may be targeting to encourage investment in the country. Clarifying ISPs obligations and their exact legal role will incentivise more business and technologies to enter the Saudi market, and at the same time guarantee that copyrights are still protected.

How Should Safe Harbours Be Adopted in Saudi Arabia?

Safe harbour provisions regulate three types of online activities: mere conduits, caching and hosts. To be able to explain how safe harbour provisions should be adopted within the Saudi Copyright Law, it is important to explain how other jurisdictions, namely the UK, have regulated safe harbours within their legal framework. Are they successful to the extent that they can be adopted as they are within Saudi Arabia or to what extent do they need to be modified before they can be adopted in Saudi Arabia?

20 "government's control" means the role that the Communication and Information Technology Commission (CITC) and SAIP play in monitoring and blocking content.
21 E-Commerce Directive (n 1), 2, 40, 60.

Accordingly, the following three sections will start by analysing how each type of safe harbour is regulated in the UK and then the aspects that can be incorporated within the Saudi legal framework will be explained.

The Caching Defence

Article 18 of the E-Commerce Regulation, entitled 'Caching', exempts services that consist of transmission of information provided by a recipient of the service from being liable for damages or for any other pecuniary remedy or criminal sanction as a result of that transmission. The exception excludes liability for automatic, intermediate and temporary storage or copying of information, which is essential to the efficient functioning of the information society.[22] It excludes an ISP where, among other obligations, it has not interfered with the lawful use of technology or modified the transmitted information and has complied with rules regarding the updating of the information which they transmit, specified in a manner widely recognised and used by industry.[23]

The wording of Article 18 suggests that providers complying with the stated conditions cannot be held liable. However, with regard to modifying content, although the Regulation does not expressly refer to Recital 43 of the ECD, but since it must be interpreted consistently with it, it remains the same as with Article 18 that the manipulations of a technical nature do not alter the integrity of the information and do not qualify as modification. However, a provider loses immunity if it collaborates with a recipient to undertake an illegal act.[24]

In *Mosley v Google Inc*,[25] the background of the case started in 2008 when the *News of the World* published an article about the claimant engaging in sadomasochistic activities; accordingly, he brought a claim for misuse of private information and was awarded an injunction and damages of £60,000.[26] Mosley sought the removal of the images from the Internet through different jurisdictions. Google has a policy of taking down images once notified of each offending URL; in spite of these efforts, the image was still available online, appearing on new websites once the old one was taken down. Therefore, Mr. Mosley brought an action against Google for misuse of private information under the Data Protection Act 1998.[27] Google argued that the E-Commerce Directive excluded legal liability for images retrieved via a search engine based on caching defence under Article 13, because of certain conditions which they already fulfilled; they further stated that the order sought by the claimant constituted a general monitoring obligation, which is

22 E-Commerce Directive (n 1), Article (18)(a).

23 E-Commerce Directive (n 1), Article (18)(b), (i)(ii)(iii)(iv).

24 P.B. Hugenholtz, 'Caching and Copyright: The Right of Temporary Copying', *European Intellectual Property Review* 22, no. 10 (2000), 482–493.

25 [2015] EWHC 59 (QB).

26 *Mosley v News Group Newspapers Ltd* (No 3), [2008] EWHC 1777 (QB); [2008] EMLR 20.

27 Although the case is not linked to a copyright infringement, it is discussed here to examine how the court applied the caching safe harbour, particularly the accepted scope of information modification.

prohibited by Article 15. However, Mr. Mosley argued that this reasoning did not avail Google because, in returning 'thumbnails' of the images, Google had modified them, thus falling foul of Article 13(a). In the judgment, the judge rejected the claimant's argument, stating that reducing the size and definition of the image did not amount to modifying them within the meaning of Article 13(a). In other words, not any level of content modification would exclude the ISP from legal protection of the caching safe harbour, particularly modifications of technical nature.

Caching may occur at several distinct levels of the networked communication process, for example, proxy (web) caching, and client caching.[28] However, it is not a clearly defined legal or technical notion, where in some situations pure caching is combined with editorial, archiving and other activities.[29] With regard to the meaning within the Regulation, the key service envisaged by Article 18 is the so-called proxy server, which involves creating/storing local copies of websites accessed by third parties. When users access the website again, the proxy servers deliver the locally stored copy of that website, reducing bandwidth utilisation and access times.[30] This is particularly illustrated by conditions (b)(iii)(iv) of Article 18, which require the caching server to comply with updating rules and hit counting rules widely recognised and used by the industry.[31]

Although it is believed that Article 18 targets proxy servers in particular, it can be applied to other technologies when they meet its requirements, even though this was not the intention of the European legislator when enacting the Directive and subsequently the UK Regulation.[32] An example is the classification of 'Usenet' newsgroups; this service is a system whereby users post messages to a newsgroup, which then automatically networks them, so that they are broadcast to and mirrored on other servers using a variety of networks, each server retaining the messages in each newsgroup for a limited amount of time.[33] It was found that this service satisfies the requirements of the caching exception and it was qualified to benefit from Article 18 of the Regulation.[34] Ultimately, the scope of the caching safe harbour

28 This type consists of temporary storage of previously loaded or downloaded documents by the end-user, triggered by the user's software or any other application. Depending on the preference and usage pattern of the user, a document will remain cached for hours or days or even months. Hugenholtz (n 24) 483.

29 I Trotter Hardy, 'Computer RAM Copies: Hit or Myth-Historical Perspectives on Caching as a Microcosm of Current Copyright Concerns', *University of Dayton Law Review* 22 (1997), 423.

30 Blue Coast, 'White Paper: A Technical Review of Caching Technologies', *Bitpipe.com* (2007), 7–8.

31 European Commission Information Society and Media Directorate-General Study, 'Legal Analysis of a Single Market for the Information Society', *European Commission* 6 (2009, November), 2.

32 European Commission Information Society and Media Directorate-General Study, 'Legal Analysis of a Single Market for the Information Society', *European Commission* 6 (2009, November), 2.

33 Chris Reed, *Internet Law: Text and Materials* (Cambridge: Cambridge University Press, 2004); Alicia L. Wright, 'Newsgroups Float into Safe Harbor, and Copyright Holders Are Sunk', *Duke Law & Technology Review* 19 (2006), 1.

34 Clive Feather, 'The Intermediary Service Providers Provisions of the E-Commerce Directive, Its UK Implementation, and Relevant Cases, from the Point of View of UK ISPs', *davros.org* (2008); Thibault Verbiest, Gerald Spindler, and Giovanni Maria Riccio, 'Study on the Liability of Internet

protection is not as limited as it looks, but rather much broader in scope; it applies to both lawful and unlawful transmissions, as long as it qualifies with its conditions, which notably can support the free flow of information on the Internet.

The Caching Defence in the Saudi Copyright Law

The role caching services play, given the rising importance of technology businesses, makes it important to provide them with defences from liability under the Saudi Copyright Law. As explained, Article 18 of the E-Commerce Regulation provides five conditions that the caching service provider must fulfil to be exempted from secondary liability. It is recommended that four of these conditions be adopted within Saudi Copyright Law, as provided in 18(b), (ii) to (v). The only difference between the UK law and the article suggested for adoption in Saudi Copyright Law is regarding the first condition, which exempts any caching service that "*does not modify the information*".[35] The research suggests amending it when adopted into Saudi Copyright Law, to include within its ambit services that perform an automatic modification of information. Accordingly, this part in the suggested Saudi article should read: "*does not modify the information; modification of a technical nature is accepted*".

Although the wording in UK law does not include within its ambit services of technical modification, UK courts, when they interpreted this article, have agreed to exempt caching services which perform technical modification of the information.[36] The importance of adding this sentence to the Saudi Copyright Law is to clarify the accepted level of modification and intervention that these services can take instead of leaving it to the court's interpretation.

The Hosting Defence

Article 19 of the E-Commerce Regulation is entitled 'Hosting'. It protects intermediaries, whose service consists of storage of information, from liability for damages or for any other pecuniary remedy or criminal sanction as a result of that storage, when the service provider complies with the following conditions:

(i) does not have actual knowledge of unlawful activity or information and, where a claim for damages is made, is not aware of facts or circumstances from which it would have been apparent to the service provider that the activity or information was unlawful; or
(ii) upon obtaining such knowledge or awareness, acts expeditiously to remove or to disable access to the information, and

Intermediaries', *Report Drafted for the EU Commission on the State of Implementation in the Single Member States of the E-Commerce Directive (2000/31/EC)* (2007), 4.

35 Article 18(b)(i).

36 For example, *Mosley v Google Inc*, [2015] EWHC 59 (QB).

(b) the recipient of the service was not acting under the authority or the control of the service provider.

To be qualified to utilise the hosting safe harbour, the ISP activity must first be linked to or consist of storage activities. The scope of the hosting safe harbour that only applies to passive storage activities – as shown in the first two conditions – is clear in the case of those technologies which existed at the time the Regulation was implemented. However, what about other services such as cloud computing, where storage is just one aspect of the entire service package?[37] The position of those intermediaries who do more than merely record or store third-party information is questioned as to whether it is included within the scope of the hosting exception, and the extent to which a service should relate to hosting. Is it enough that some aspects of the service deal with hosting, or should most or all of its aspects deal with hosting?[38] To determine whether they are qualified for the exception, the important aspect of these new activities is being applied technically and neutrally to hosted information; hence, it is believed that the described activities ought to be treated as storage activities, except for those intermediaries which voluntarily moderate content and which thus cannot use the exception since their services go beyond storage/automatic activity.[39]

Some copyright holders have denied this direction, arguing that the idea of passivity needs to be detached from the idea of automaticity, since human intervention is no longer needed to make a service 'active', with automated processing having become flexible and selective.[40] In addition, some right holders' bodies believe that the scope of safe harbour provisions currently goes beyond neutral and passive ISPs to protect those who distribute content and draw financial benefit from advertising alongside copyright content. They see the exceptions as having distorted the value chain and impacted commercial negotiations of licence fees between copyright owner and platform provider.[41]

The demands that intermediaries should undertake an active role in protecting copyrights has reached regulatory levels. Although the following example is not linked directly to the UK, it shows the legal conflict it created when such a requirement is adopted. The new Directive on copyright in the Digital Single Market

37 Martin Senftleben, 'Breathing Space for Cloud-Based Business Models – Exploring the Matrix of Copyright Limitations, Safe Harbours and Injunctions', *Journal of Intellectual Property, Information Technology and Electronic Commerce Law* 4, no. 1 (2013), 87.

38 Giovanni Sartor, *Providers Liability: From the e-Commerce Directive to the Future* (Brussels: EU Policy Department A: Economic and Scientific Policy, 2017); European Commission Information Society and Media Directorate-General Study (n 31).

39 Jaani Riordan, *The Liability of Internet Intermediaries* (Oxford: Oxford University Press, 2016).

40 Sartor (n 38).

41 Weatherley (n 9), citing British Photographic Industry, "(BPI)," (n.d.), https://www.bpi.co.uk/, and Music Publishers Association, "(MPA)," (n.d.), https://mpaonline.org.uk/ .

(DSM)[42] was approved by the European Parliament and entered into force in 2019. It introduces a direct liability regime in a manner incoherent with the ECD. The Directive puts intermediaries who store and provide access to large amounts of copyrighted work at risk of direct liability if they do not implement filtering tools to identify and prevent copyright infringing content, which contradicts with Articles 14 and 15 of the ECD.[43] These articles require intermediaries' passivity regarding content and prohibits Member States from imposing a general monitoring obligation on them. The DSM will blur the line between active and passive hosts,[44] which was determined by the Court of Justice of the European Union (CJEU). The CJEU developed a distinction between passive and active hosting providers, by linking the knowledge and awareness requirement to the ISP's 'active role' which goes beyond the neutral provision of technical and automatic processing of user's data. For example: in *L'Oréal SA v eBay International AG,*[45] the active role was seen as providing assistance in ''optimising the presentation of the offers for sale in question or promoting them''.[46] So, the active role was not derived from knowledge but from operating in a way that triggered knowledge or control.[47] Adopting proactive measures may cause hosting providers to fall outside the shield developed under safe harbours to allow passive hosts to avoid liability since they become active hosting providers. However, the European Commission stated that any filtering measures in this case will not render these ISPs active as long as they process a large amount of content automatically.[48] Nevertheless it is still not clear how 'large amount' will be assessed and determined, and on what basis the court will do it. It can be argued that the overall framework lacks coherence and legal certainty.

On the other hand, only large technology companies have the financial power, technological knowledge and internal structure necessary to develop filtering mechanisms, which gives them an advantage over small and mid-sized intermediaries, as they most likely would not have the means to develop their own filters or

42 Directive (EU) 2019/790 of the European Parliament and of the Council of 17 April 2019 on copyright and related rights in the Digital Single Market and amending Directives 96/9/EC and 2001/29/EC.

43 Maria Lillà Montagnani and Alina Trapova, 'New Obligations for Internet Intermediaries in the Digital Single Market – Safe Harbours in Turmoil?', *Journal of Internet Law* 22, no. 7 (2019), 3–11.

44 Maria Lillà Montagnani and Alina Yordanova Trapova, 'Safe Harbours in Deep Waters: A New Emerging Liability Regime for Internet Intermediaries in the Digital Single Market', *International Journal of Law and Information Technology* 26, no. 4 (2018), 294–310.

45 *L'Oréal SA v eBay International AG,* (Case C-324/09) [2011] ETMR 52 (*'L'Oréal CJEU'*).

46 *L'Oréal SA v eBay International AG,* (Case C-324/09) [2011] ETMR 52 (*'L'Oréal CJEU'*), 123.

47 Thomas Riis and Sebastian Felix Schwemer, 'Leaving the European Safe Harbor, Sailing towards Algorithmic Content Regulation', *Legal Studies Research Paper Series* no. 2019–64 (2019), 1–14, https://doi.org/10.2139/ssrn.2830440.

48 European Commission, *Tackling Illegal Content Online Towards an Enhanced Responsibility of Online Platforms, Communication from the Commission to the European Parliament* (Brussels: European Commission, 2017).

doing so would create a heavy financial burden on them. Therefore, there is a risk that those intermediaries will be negatively impacted.[49]

The view that passivity should be detached from automaticity is not practical and would only serve the interests of copyright holders while negatively affecting innovation and technology development. The fact that an ISP gains significantly high revenue does not justify imposing more obligations or considering them liable. Right holders still have the right to apply for injunctive remedies to stop online infringements, even if these intermediaries are protected within the scope of safe harbours.[50] Nowadays, many ISPs such as YouTube have adopted a notice and take down policy (NTD); therefore, any further legal requirement would look like an agreement to give copyright holders and industries the power to control another sector or market. The technology market should be treated as a different/independent sector and not a tool for preserving copyright holders' rights. It has developed over time, and any interference in its work means that innovation is interrupted and indicates high censorship. The law should remain as it is regarding this matter to guarantee its neutrality towards different interests. Copyright holders, for their part, need to comply with and adapt to technological development instead of asking for more power.

The absence of actual knowledge or awareness of the infringing content is a condition of being qualified for the hosting safe harbour. The required amount of knowledge here is not general, but ISPs have to know about the stored content and the facts or circumstances that render it unlawful. Hence, when an ISP receives notice of an infringement, the notice should include sufficient information about it; otherwise, ISP will lack actual knowledge.[51] Although Article 22 provided the aspects that a court should assess in determining whether or not an ISP has actual knowledge, it did not elaborate on the meaning of the interplay between 'actual knowledge' and 'awareness of the facts and circumstances'. In *L'Oreal CJEU,*[52] it was explained that awareness of the facts and circumstances will make illegal activity apparent to any '*diligent economic operator*' that the activity is unlawful.[53] Therefore, ISPs' knowledge should be assessed considering the behaviour of a hypothetical 'diligent' example of an ISP from the same type. The circumstances that would make an infringement apparent varies given the different nature of ISPs and the difference between situations that can make an ISP aware, for example, the result of a sudden investigation undertaken on its own initiative, and the high volume of received notices about such activities.

49 Thomas Spoerri, 'On Upload-Filters and Other Competitive Advantages for Big Tech Companies under Article 17 of the Directive on Copyright in the Digital Single Market', *Journal of Intellectual Property, Information Technology and E-Commerce Law* 10, no. 2 (2019), 173.

50 E-Commerce Regulation (n 2), Article 20.

51 Riordan (n 39).

52 *L'Oréal CJEU,* at, 122.

53 This standard is high, since it may extend the definition of knowledge to a situation where the ISP has negligently failed to make inquiries. Matthew Collins, *Collins on Defamation*, 1st ed. (Oxford: Oxford University Press, 2014), 359.

The Hosting Defence in the Saudi Copyright Law

Hosting services are the most important service to be regulated since most online businesses are considered hosts. The article to regulate the hosting defence should set the conditions that qualify the hosting service for the defence. In this respect, the conditions provided in Article 19 of the E-Commerce Regulation are applicable to be adopted within Saudi law.

The first condition requires that the hosting provider does not have actual knowledge of the infringing activity, and where a claim for damages is made, the provider is not aware of facts or circumstances from which it would have been apparent to the service provider that the activity or information was unlawful; then upon obtaining such knowledge or awareness, it acts expeditiously to remove the infringement.

Although it is suggested to adopt what Article 19 provides, its final section, which sets the condition that "*the recipient of the service was not acting under the authority or the control of the service provider*" should be modified[54] because ISPs' technical/neutral control over the content should not deprive them from the hosting defence.[55] Alternatively, in the Saudi Copyright Law, the condition should read as follows: "'*The service recipient was not acting under the authority or the control of the service provider; technical and neutral control are accepted*".

The purpose of adding this condition is to accommodate the expansion of technical features that allow platforms to control automatically through the automatic processing of great amounts of information. So, adding this condition clarifies that the presence of any technical control should not mean that these ISPs are not being passive, which further clarifies the scope of the host defence, especially for Saudi courts.

It is important to clarify when Saudi courts should consider ISPs as having actual knowledge of the infringing content or awareness of the facts, and what steps they are required to take after obtaining this knowledge. The answer is in the following sections:

Actual Knowledge of Illegality

Having actual knowledge of the unlawful activity or information requires knowing that the material is actionable, knowing the purpose or character of the activity, and knowing whether the act was done without the consent of the copyright owner. This direction is taken from UK law, where Article 19 of the E-Commerce Regulation appears to require knowledge of both the stored material and the facts

54 This standard is high, since it may extend the definition of knowledge to a situation where the ISP has negligently failed to make inquiries. Matthew Collins, *Collins on Defamation*, 1st ed. (Oxford: Oxford University Press, 2014), 359, Article 19(b).

55 Although UK law did not mention technical control, UK courts accepted in their interpretations technical and neutral control which did not deprive the hosting provider of the defence. See: (*L'Oréal CJEU*, C-324/09).

or circumstances which render it unlawful, confirming that unlawfulness requires material to be actionable.

It is not enough in actions for copyright infringement to know that particular material is a copyrighted work since such knowledge may not reflect knowing that the dealing is actionable infringement or knowing the purpose and character of the dealing. Actual knowledge definitely arises when an ISP receives a notice that includes sufficient information to ascertain the unlawful information or activity. Such information will include the full name and address of the sender, details of the location of the information concerned, and details of the unlawful nature of the activity or information concerned.

Awareness of the Facts or Circumstances

The standard of awareness that Saudi Copyright Law should incorporate can be derived from *L'Oréal CJEU*,[56] where, according to the court's analysis, facts or circumstances of which the intermediary is aware will make illegal activity or information "*apparent*", if "*a diligent economic operator should have identified the illegality in question*" based on the same information. Accordingly, intermediaries' knowledge should be assessed because of the behaviour of a hypothetical "*diligent*" example of an intermediary from the same type. Therefore, to be aware of the facts and circumstances, a combination of subjective/objective standards should be assessed: while the ISP must have individually, subjectively been aware of fact or circumstances, the knowledge-making power of those facts or circumstances is to be assessed objectively, according to the benchmark of the "*diligent economic operator*".[57]

What types of facts or circumstances would make an infringement apparent to a diligent economic operator? It is difficult to answer this question, given the variable nature of intermediaries and the difference between situations that can make an intermediary aware. However, some suggestions and clues are given by the CJEU in the *L'Oréal* case; for example, the situation in which the operator of an online marketplace uncovers illegal activity or illegal information, as the result of an investigation undertaken on its own initiative; as well as a situation in which the operator is notified of the existence of such an activity or information. Indeed, receiving a notification cannot be automatically considered to have provided reliable knowledge because such a notification may be "*insufficiently precise or inadequately substantiated*"; however, this notice is a factor that the court shall consider when assessing the ISP's awareness in specific situations, for example, when the ISP receives several notifications regarding an infringing activity, not all of which were complete notifications, the volume and number of notifications

56 CJEU, C-324/09.

57 Tatiana Eleni Synodinou, 'Intermediaries' Liability for Online Copyright Infringement in the EU: Evolutions and Confusions', *Computer Law and Security Review* 31, no. 1 (2015), 57–67.

can be considered as indicating their awareness.[58] However, it is important not to overstate the deductive abilities of the ISP as they cannot be forced to monitor infringements.[59]

What Steps Are ISPs Required to Take to Prevent an Infringement?

The Saudi court should assess the steps the ISP has taken to remove or stop the infringement, after obtaining actual knowledge or being aware of the facts. There are no specific legal steps that ISPs are required to take, except that after obtaining knowledge, they must act expeditiously to remove the infringement, which reflects exactly the UK direction that requires expeditious action after obtaining knowledge.[60]

Setting the boundaries of ISPs' role in protecting copyrights in Saudi Arabia can incentivise them to take the necessary steps from the moment they obtain sufficient knowledge about the unlawful content, especially that they know these steps are counted and would help them avoid secondary liability.

It can be questioned whether this step, even if considered a positive shift from the current situation, might lead to over-removals and blocking by ISPs. Indeed, such a problem might arise, especially at the beginning of its adoption. However, before considering the problems that might follow the implementation of this policy, it is important first to create the foundation of the new legal framework and afterwards assess how it was used. Its effect is to understand whether any alteration is needed. Therefore, to avoid potential over-blocking, the Copyright Law should clarify the information that any notification must include so that ISPs should not take down the requested content if the notification omits any of the required information. For example, it would not do so where notification is insufficiently precise or inadequately substantiated.

The Mere Conduit Defence

Article (17) of the E-Commerce Regulation is entitled 'Mere conduit', which concerns protection from liability for damages or for pecuniary remedy and any criminal sanction that might arise as a result of the transmission of information by a recipient of the service or the provision of access to a communication network.

Mere conduit mainly refers to ISPs which basically provide end users with access and connections to the Internet. To benefit from the conduit safe harbour, the service provider must not be involved in authoring the transmitted information. The transmission cannot be initiated by the provider but rather has to be requested or sent by a third party. The intermediary also must not interfere

58 Riis and Schwemer (n 47); L'Oréal CJEU.

59 Patrick Van Eecke, 'Online Service Providers and Liability: A Plea for a Balanced Approach', *Common Market Law Review* 48, no. 5 (2011), 1455.

60 The E-commerce Regulation, Article 18 (b)(v), 19 (a)(ii).

in the transmission or select the receiver, and finally, the data must reach its destination without being modified by the conduit. The transmission includes the automatic, immediate and transient storage of the information transmitted insofar as this takes place for the sole purpose of carrying out the transmission. The information is not stored for any period longer than necessary for the transmission.[61]

The Mere Conduit Defence in the Saudi Copyright Law

The mere conduit exception cannot be adopted in the Saudi Copyright Law, due to the way the Internet is regulated in the country. Service providers in Saudi Arabia are divided into two types based on their technical role. The first type is data service providers (DSPs), companies that provide and operate Internet infrastructure such as international gateways. The other type is ISPs, which represent companies that purchase Internet bandwidth from DSPs and provide Internet connections to businesses and end users. Both DSPs and ISPs work under the supervision of the Communication and Information Technology Commission (CITC), a government authority.[62]

However, ISPs and DSPs cannot be considered secondarily liable for any type of online infringing content including copyrights unless they are direct infringers, for example, if they uploaded infringing content on their official website. The reasons for exempting these services from secondary liability can be understood from analysing the supervisory role of the CITC over ISPs and DSPs and the content filtering mechanism in Saudi Arabia.

The filtering service infrastructure is distributed between the CITC and DSPs; the CITC prepares and issues filtering lists while DSPs have to provide filtering infrastructure in accordance with the CITC's requirements and policies. In practice, DSPs download the CITC's lists to be blocked by their filtering systems. The CITC, in its turn, monitors DSPs' filtration equipment to ensure that they update their lists daily and are fully committed to the CITC's policies and technical control requirements. DSPs are legally responsible, if they do not fulfil their commitment to updating the filtration list daily. Also, they cannot reject implementing blocking orders since the CITC has power over DSPs in terms of implementing their decisions, including the ability to suspend their license. However, ISPs do not have any role in the filtering and blocking process and are only required to choose a DSP from which they can buy their international Internet bandwidth and then sell their Internet service to end users.[63]

61 The E-commerce Regulation, Article 17(2) (a)(b).

62 CITC, 'General Information on Filtering Service', *filter.sa*, https://filter.sa/ar/content-filtering-in-saudi-arabia-ar/.

63 CITC, 'General Information on Filtering Service', *filter.sa*, https://filter.sa/ar/content-filtering-in-saudi-arabia-ar/.

The types of content that the CITC is allowed to filter or block does not include copyrighted content. It has been assigned the task of directly filtering and blocking websites and materials that: are incompatible with or offensive to Islam and its sanctities, contain pornographic content, promote alcohol, drugs or gambling, or any content classified by the Permanent Internet Security Committee Guidelines.[64]

SAIP cannot impose any obligation on DSPs to filter copyright content nor consider them liable due to the role they play with CITC. Instead, the CITC provides SAIP with an online portal to upload their blocking orders to be implemented. However, to overcome the limitation in its filtering and monitoring role, as explained earlier, SAIP has started to monitor online content through a specialised monitoring division that works under its supervision, then uses the CITC portal to upload blocking orders directly.

Clearly, monitoring and filtration in Saudi Arabia are linked to the government instead of ISPs and DSPs. DSPs are enforcers of the government's decisions, which is why the mere conduit exception will not legally add anything to the current legal position of ISPs or DSPs, given how the Internet is regulated. If the mere conduit exception was adopted, it would be like admitting that DSPs work independently from the CITC and can control online content, which is not true: DSPs only implement any governmental/judicial decisions, which is the central part of their responsibility.

Conclusion

It is important at this stage in Saudi Arabia to adopt an immunity framework (safe harbours) for ISPs especially after Vision 2030. The ambiguity of the current legal framework regarding ISPs liability and the lack of clear procedures to remove infringing content will hinder e-commerce development in the country and more importantly can stand as an obstacle in achieving the aims of Vision 2030.

The Saudi government is encouraged to adopt a legal framework that exempts ISPs from liability because safe harbour provisions can provide the Copyright Law with the needed clarity to overcome its ambiguity regarding ISPs liability and would set the boundaries of any possible obligation imposed on them. It would also help in developing rapid and reliable procedures for removing and disabling access to infringing content. In fact, giving ISPs such a role might help reduce SAIP's authority in monitoring and taking down content, which would reduce the government expenditure on filtration and give SAIP a legal supervisory role only. Also, there is an important economic purpose in providing exceptions from secondary liability. Safe harbours are a way to support online business and e-commerce in general which the Saudi governments target to develop. Therefore, it is important to legally balance different rights by adopting a clear and fair legal framework for all parties.

64 The types of content are classified and decided based on the Council of Ministers Resolution No. 163 of 10.24.1417H.

This research examined how the liability exceptions should be adopted within the Saudi legal framework in a way that is compatible with the Saudi legal and judicial system. It was found that it is possible to adopt defences against secondary liability, similar to the UK's safe harbour provisions. However, suggesting the adoption of an immunity framework does not represent an attempt to copy the UK legal framework literally but reflects an essential need to benefit from their experience and build a framework that balances different rights in way that does not contradict with legal or judicial system in Saudi Arabia.

Caching and hosting are the types of activities that should be adopted within the within the Saudi Copyright Law. This adoption is conditional, first, with regard to the caching defence, it is recommended that the Saudi regulator adopt four of the conditions that was mentioned in Article 18(b), (ii) to (v) of the *E-Commerce Regulation*. The only difference between the UK law and the article suggested to adopt in Saudi Copyright Law is regarding the first condition (article 18(b)(i)), which exempts from its ambit any caching service that "*does not modify the information*". The research suggested amending it when adopted into the Saudi Copyright Law, to include within its ambit services that perform an automatic modification of information. This is done to provide Saudi judges with clarity regarding the position of any ISPs who automatically modify the information.

Second, the hosting defence, it was stated that the conditions provided in Article 19 of the E-Commerce Regulation are applicable to be adopted within Saudi Copyright Law. However, the final section of this article which sets the condition that "*the recipient of the service was not acting under the authority or the control of the service provider*" should be modified because ISPs' technical/neutral control over the content should not deprive them from the hosting defence. Therefore, the Saudi Copyright Law should also protect those ISPs who provide technical and neutral control. The way the caching and hosting defence are suggested to be adopted target increasing the clarity to Saudi judges when dealing with these cases, so, they understand the scope of accepted modification of the content.

Third, the mere conduit defence cannot be adopted within the Saudi Copyright Law or any other law due to the way Internet is regulated in the country, where Internet service providers cannot be considered secondarily liable for any type of online infringing content including copyrights unless they are direct infringers as explained before. This protection is due to CITC supervisory role and the content filtering mechanism in Saudi Arabia where these providers primarily implement and follow CITC instruction. Therefore, adopting mere conduit defence will not change or enhance the legal position of these services.

Finally, indeed the legal framework in the UK regarding safe harbour provisions are applicable to be adopted with the Saudi Copyright Law, however, some modification to these rules is required to stand in line with the Saudi legal and judicial system which was taken into consideration in this research.

Bibliography

Blue Coast. 'White Paper: A Technical Review of Caching Technologies'. Bitpipe.com, (2007).

CITC. 'General Information on Filtering Service', filter.sa. https://filter.sa/ar/content-filtering-in-saudi-arabia-ar/

Collins, Matthew. *Collins on Defamation*. 1st ed. (Oxford: Oxford University Press, 2014). https://doi.org/2013952619.

Commission of The European Communities. 'Europe 2005: An Information Society for All', COM/2002/263 Final, (2002).

Commission of The European Communities. 'First Report on the Application of Directive 2000/31/EC of the European Parliament and of the Council of 8 June 2000 on Certain Legal Aspects of Information Society Services, in Particular Electronic Commerce, in the Internal Market, Directive on Electron', Brussels, (2003).

Communication from The European Commission. 'Towards the Full Roll-Out of Mobile Communications', COM/2002/0301final, (2002).

Eecke, Patrick Van. 'Online Service Providers and Liability: A Plea for a Balanced Approach', *Common Market Law Review* 48, no. 5 (2011): 1455. https://doi.org/10.54648/COLA2011058

European Commission. 'Tackling Illegal Content Online Towards an Enhanced Responsibility of Online Platforms', Communication from the Commission to the European Parlimanet, Brussels, (2017).

European Commission Information Society and Media Directorate-General Study. 'Legal Analysis of a Single Market for the Information Society', *European Commission* 6 (November 2009).

Feather, Clive. 'The Intermediary Service Providers Provisions of the E-Commerce Directive, Its UK Implementation, and Relevant Cases, from the Point of View of UK ISPs' (2008). davros.org

Hardy, I. Trotter. 'Computer RAM Copies: Hit or Myth-Historical Perspectives on Caching as a Microcosm of Current Copyright Concerns', *University of Dayton Law Review* 22 (1997): 423

Hugenholtz, P. B. 'Caching and Copyright: The Right of Temporary Copying', *European Intellectual Property Review* 22, no. 10 (2000): 482–493. https://doi.org/10.1007/978-3-662-65974-8_23

Montagnani, Maria Lillà, and Alina Trapova. 'New Obligations for Internet Intermediaries in the Digital Single Market – Safe Harbours in Turmoil?', *Journal of Internet Law* 22, no. 7 (2019): 3–11.

Montagnani, Maria Lillà, and Alina Yordanova Trapova. 'Safe Harbours in Deep Waters: A New Emerging Liability Regime for Internet Intermediaries in the Digital Single Market', *International Journal of Law and Information Technology* 26, no. 4 (2018): 294–310. https://doi.org/10.1093/ijlit/eay013

Music Publishers Association (MPA), (n.d.). https://mpaonline.org.uk/

Nurunnabi, Mohammad. 'Transformation from an Oil-Based Economy to a Knowledge-Based Economy in Saudi Arabia: The Direction of Saudi Vision 2030', *Journal of the Knowledge Economy* 8, no. 2 (28 June 2017): 536–564. https://doi.org/10.1007/s13132-017-0479-8

Powell, Walter, and Kaisa Snellman. 'The Knowledge Economy', *Annual Review of Sociology* 30 (2004): 199–220. https://doi.org/10.1108/00400910110399184

Price, David. 'Politics, Piracy and Punishment: Copyright Protection in the Arabian Gulf', *Journal of World Intellectual Property* 14 (2011): 276. https://doi.org/10.1111/j.1747-1796.2011.00419.x

Reed, Chris. *Internet Law: Text and Materials* (Cambridge: Cambridge University Press, 2004).

Riis, Thomas, and Sebastian Felix Schwemer. 'Leaving the European Safe Harbor, Sailing towards Algorithmic Content Regulation', Legal Studies Research Paper Series no. 2019-64 (2019), 1–14. https://doi.org/10.2139/ssrn.2830440

Riordan, Jaani. *The Liability of Internet Intermediaries* (Oxford: Oxford University Press, 2016).

Sartor, Giovanni. *Providers Liability: From the e-Commerce Directive to the Future* (Brussels: EU Policy Department A: Economic and Scientific Policy, 2017).

Saudi Authority for Intellectual Property. 'SAIP's Objectives', (2023). https://www.saip.gov.sa/en/about/brief/

Saudi Authority for Intellectual Property (SAIP)Annual Report for Intellectual Property Enforcement for 2020', (2021).www.saip.gov.sa/en/search/?p=Annual+Report+2020

——— 'Annual Report for Enforcement of Intellectual Property 2021', (2022). www.saip.gov.sa/en/ search/?p=Annual+Report+2022

——— 'Annual Report on IP Enforcement for the Year 2023', (2023), at https://externalportal-backend-production.saip.gov.sa/sites/default/files/2024-10/Annual%20Report%20on%20IP%20Enforcement.pdf

——— 'SAIP: Request for Public Consultations Regarding Copyright Law', (2018). https://www.saip.gov.sa/en/news/1208

Senftleben, Martin. 'Breathing Space for Cloud-Based Business Models – Exploring the Matrix of Copyright Limitations, Safe Harbours and Injunctions', *Journal of Intellectual Property, Information Technology and Electronic Commerce Law* 4, no. 1 (2013): 87. https://doi.org/10.2139/ssrn.2241259

Spoerri, Thomas. 'On Upload-Filters and Other Competitive Advantages for Big Tech Companies under Article 17 of the Directive on Copyright in the Digital Single Market', *Journal of Intellectual Property, Information Technology and E-Commerce Law* 10, no. 2 (2019): 173.

Synodinou, Tatiana Eleni. 'Intermediaries' Liability for Online Copyright Infringement in the EU: Evolutions and Confusions', *Computer Law and Security Review* 31, no. 1 (2015): 57–67. https://doi.org/10.1016/j.clsr.2014.11.010

UK Department for Culture Media and Sport. 'Creative Industries Economic Estimates', Creative Industries Economic Estimates, (2016). https://doi.org/10.1177/0002716204270505

UNCTAD. 'Creative Economy Report', (2008). https://unctad.org/en/Pages/DITC/CreativeEconomy/Creative-Economy-Programme.aspx

Verbiest, Thibault, Gerald Spindler, and Giovanni Maria Riccio. 'Study on the Liability of Internet Intermediaries'. Report Drafted for the EU Commission on the State of Implementation in the Single Member States of the E-Commerce Directive (2000/31/EC), (2007).

Weatherley, Mike. 'Safe Harbour Provisions and Online Service Providers: A Discussion Paper by Mike Weatherley MP Former Intellectual Property Adviser to the Prime Minister', London, (2015).

Wright, Alicia L. 'Newsgroups Float into Safe Harbor, and Copyright Holders Are Sunk', *Duke Law & Technology Review* 19 (2006). 1–18.

9 Trading Artwork on the Blockchain

An Opportunity for the Gulf States to Shift to a Digital Economy

Jia Wang

Introduction

The Middle East is best known for its rich petroleum resources. As the world transitions to more environmentally friendly energy streams to combat climate change, the region needs alternative revenue sources. Shifting from a traditionally petroleum-based economy, leading Middle Eastern countries are developing in areas of smart cities, digital government, and enhanced tourism, based on the adoption of artificial intelligence (AI), cyber security, and cloud computing to achieve a true digital transformation. According to the Gulf News, Middle Eastern organisations plan to spend more than $25 billion on digital initiatives.[1] Business leaders reckon that tech development is essential for growing the local economy.[2] With advancements in robotics, augmented reality, and the Internet of Things (IoT) driving production and customer experience worldwide, companies cannot afford to lag behind.

On May 26, 1981, in Abu Dhabi, the heads of state from six Gulf countries (Saudi Arabia, Kuwait, UAE, Qatar, Bahrain, and Oman) announced the formation of the Gulf Cooperation Council (GCC). This founding summit led to the signing of the GCC Charter, which aims to promote cooperation, strengthen relations, and achieve integration across various sectors among Gulf countries.[3] The Gulf states have shown a growing interest in the development and adoption of blockchain technology across various sectors, including government services, finance, supply chain management, and real estate.[4] The governments in the region are actively promoting blockchain initiatives and creating an enabling environment to foster blockchain innovation and adoption.

1 Simplilearn, 'Gulf Countries Have a Bright Digital Economy Future', *Simplilearn* (22 September 2020) <https://www.simplilearn.com/gulf-countries-have-a-bright-digital-economy-future-article>.
2 Simplilearn, 'Gulf Countries Have a Bright Digital Economy Future', *Simplilearn* (22 September 2020) <https://www.simplilearn.com/gulf-countries-have-a-bright-digital-economy-future-article>.
3 Omar Al Hassan, 'The GCC's Formation: The Official Version', *Al Jazeera* (30 March 2015) <https://studies.aljazeera.net/en/dossiers/2015/03/201533011258831763.html>.
4 Fatima Al Subaei, 'Blockchain Adoption in the Gulf States', *Middle East Institute* (10 December 2019) < https://www.mei.edu/publications/blockchain-adoption-gulf-states>.

DOI: 10.4324/9781003528517-9

This chapter argues that the advancing blockchain infrastructure in many Gulf states opens up multiple new possibilities for businesses and individuals in trading artworks with tokenisation on blockchain. Non-fungible tokens (hereinafter "NFTs") are widely adopted by the token owner in the form of a record and hash codes that show ownership of the unique token associated with a particular digital asset. Transactions are executed on smart contracts, sequences of computer codes that automatically execute pre-established instructions. Each block has a set amount of storage capacity, and once it is filled, it is "chained" to the previously filled block. Most NFTs exist on the Ethereum blockchain, with permanent digital records of all cryptocurrency transactions.

The key issues discussed in the chapter are: when purchasing an NFTed artwork, what rights and interests does the purchaser acquire? In furtherance of the above question, is holding an NFTed work equivalent to holding a physical copy? The objectives of this chapter are to contextualise the discussion against the background of the trade of artworks in a blockchain environment and to examine the most recent legislation and court decisions concerning NFTs and cryptocurrency. Finally, it conducts a comparative study between the selected common law and civil law systems of their concept of assets and property in relation to NFTs. Based on the comparison, it provides recommendations for the Gulf states to adopt blockchains to facilitate the trade of NFTed artwork with the caveat learnt from the comparative study.

A comparative approach is undertaken to facilitate the understanding of how different jurisdictions view the legal nature of NFTs. It investigates the relevant laws in the Anglo-American countries, then turns to Europe, China and GCC countries, with the addition of Turkey and Lebanon as civil law jurisdictions. Traditionally, the two legal systems view property rights differently. A comparative study offers insight into whether the convergence of law applies to legal issues of global relevance in a digital environment. Furthermore, this chapter conducts a case study of the most recent court decisions concerning property and intellectual property issues. As the legislation could lag behind the speedy advancement of technologies, court decisions offer a timelier reflection of the judiciary's attitude to NFTs.

This chapter proceeds as follows: The first section introduces the shift to a digital economy taking place in the Gulf states. The second section scrutinises the types of blockchain and NFTs as an application of blockchain technologies, particularly the tokenisation of artwork. The third section examines how artworks are traded in the mortar-and-brick era and the digital era. The fourth and fifth sections scrutinise the common law and civil law approaches towards NFTs and the NFTed artwork. The sixth section discusses the Gulf approach towards NFTs and cryptocurrencies. The last section offers a comparative analysis of the different approaches and provides concluding remarks.

Gulf States: Shifting to a Digital Economy with a More Integrated Legal Framework

Today, the digital economy is at the forefront of the national development plans of many countries worldwide. Many countries in the Middle East are also increasing their focus on the digital economy and introducing strategic initiatives to enhance digitalisation. The Gulf states have some of the most plugged-in populations in the world. The rate of internet penetration in Bahrain, Saudi Arabia, UAE, Kuwait, and Qatar all exceed 73 per cent, which far outpaces the global average of 50.8 per cent.[5] The region's e-commerce market has demonstrated rapid growth and is expected to have a compound aggregate growth rate of 16.9 per cent from 2016–2021.[6] Higher digitisation, in turn, leads to more economic growth and GDP. The analysis concluded that 160 million potential digital users by 2025 could contribute up to 3.8 per cent annually in GDP, translating to about $95 billion in revenue.[7] This represents an undeniable value proposition.

Governments in the Gulf states have recognised the potential of blockchain technology and have launched several initiatives to explore its applications. For example, the United Arab Emirates (UAE) launched the Emirates Blockchain Strategy 2021 (Emirates Blockchain Strategy 2021), aiming to utilise blockchain technology across healthcare, education, and transportation sectors. Within the financial sector, Bahrain has established the Bahrain Fintech Bay, which promotes blockchain and fintech innovation. The Saudi Arabian Monetary Authority (SAMA) initiated pilot projects for cross-border payments using blockchain. Blockchain technology offers the potential for secure and decentralised digital identity systems. The Gulf states are exploring blockchain-based solutions for identity management and authentication. For instance, the UAE government has launched the "UAE Pass" initiative, which aims to provide citizens and residents with a secure digital identity built on blockchain. The Gulf states also actively explore blockchain applications for supply chain management, aiming to enhance transparency, traceability, and efficiency. For instance, Dubai's government launched the "Dubai Blockchain Strategy" to enhance supply chain management across various sectors. Blockchain technology can facilitate secure and low-cost cross-border transactions and remittances. The Gulf states, with their large expatriate populations, are exploring blockchain-based solutions to improve the speed, security, and cost-effectiveness of international money transfers.

As the global economy becomes more reliant on digital products and services, the importance of the digital economy in major world markets continues to grow. While digital transformation has been a buzzword in the corporate world for a few years, it is now a priority across the Middle East. Three Middle East-based NFT marketplaces raised about $10 million. The Y Combinator graduate Odiggo, started out as a

5 Rachel Furlow, 'The Gulf's Economic Development Is Going Digital', *MENASource* (22 August 2019) <https://www.atlanticcouncil.org/blogs/menasource/the-gulfs-economic-development-is-going-digital/>.

6 Rachel Furlow, 'The Gulf's Economic Development Is Going Digital', *MENASource* (22 August 2019) <https://www.atlanticcouncil.org/blogs/menasource/the-gulfs-economic-development-is-going-digital/>.

7 Rachel Furlow, 'The Gulf's Economic Development Is Going Digital', *MENASource* (22 August 2019) <https://www.atlanticcouncil.org/blogs/menasource/the-gulfs-economic-development-is-going-digital/>.

car parts marketplace in Egypt, only to pivot in the past couple of months to become an NFT marketplace, and now Art Dubai, the region's largest art fair, is dedicating an entire section to digital art and NFTs. In 2021, in a first of its kind for the region, the Firetti Contemporary Gallery in Dubai held an exhibit titled "NFT/ IRL" (in real life), which displayed artworks side by side with their NFTed digital counterparts.

Shifting to a digital economy does not solely rely on advancing technologies. The legal framework of this region also needs to be developed to be better integrated into a digital world. Hence, a comparative study of selected jurisdictions is necessary for the Gulf states to gain a comprehensive understanding of global best practices and seek an alignment with Sharia Law. It will also help adapt the relevant legal practice to local contexts and facilitate cross-border trade. Section V studies the UK and Singaporean laws as a representative of common law countries and Section VI studies the EU and Chinese approaches for their civilian law features. By studying various international models, Gulf states can develop a more unified approach to regulating NFTs, reducing the legislative divergence within the region. Moreover, understanding and potentially aligning with international standards can facilitate cross-border trade of NFTs, making the Gulf states attractive hubs for global artists, investors, and platforms to their NFT marketplaces.

Before delving into a closer scrutiny of the selected legal systems, the following Sections III and IV will examine the relevant technologies and platforms used to tokenise and trade artwork in the form of NFTs on blockchain networks. The discussion will pave the way for an informed analysis of relevant laws regulating NFTs and the trade of tokenised artwork.

Blockchain and the Tokenisation of Artwork

The Blockchains: Private, Public, and Consortium Chain

Blockchain technologies and platforms inspired the creation of "crypto art", that is, to tokenise artwork digitally and trade the tokens on the platform. Crypto art is disruptive to the traditional market of artwork in many ways. First, it solves the chronic problem of the piracy of artworks. NFTs enable authors to have exclusive control of their works stored in unique blocks with a private key, thus re-creating "digital scarcity" of the works. The transaction of artworks that are tokenised as NFTs (NFTed artwork) occurs within a more decentralised power structure.[8] Second, NFTs make fine art investment more accessible and democratic. On the one hand, it enables a smaller investment of a fraction of an artwork. On the other hand, artwork can also be directly accessible from mobile phones and laptops without requiring storage space or the use of special equipment, which thus allows trade to be conducted more seamlessly.[9] Third, it enables direct transactions between the

8 Anna Notaro, 'All That Is Solid Melts in the Ethereum: The Brave New (art) World of NFTs' (2022) *Journal of Visual Art Practice*, 21(4), 361. https://doi.org/10.1080/14702029.2022.2129204

9 Hashtag Investing, 'Top 6 Benefits of NFT's for Artists and Reasons to Use Them in 2022' (2022) <https://www.hashtaginvesting.com/blog/top-benefits-of-nfts-for-artists>; A Hamilton, 'The Pri-

rightsholder and consumer without involving middlemen such as curators, galleries, and art dealers.[10] Lastly, transactions of NFTed artwork increase liquidity and allow for higher data transparency. Blockchain transactions are often completed in milliseconds, reducing the waiting time when selling NFTed artwork and allowing artists to be paid more quickly, thus increasing liquidity.[11] Not only are NFTs generally sold and traded in full public view,[12] but each transaction can also be traced and followed, as each NFT and its blockchain entries contain proof of current and past ownership, and all transactions involved.[13]

Blockchains have been developed into three types: private chain, public chain, and consortium chain. Private chains operate under the control of specific individuals or organisations. This is done by setting up a permissioned network, restricting the individuals allowed to participate in the network and transactions.[14] As participants must obtain an invitation to join the network, private chains can filter out illegal activities within a chain.[15] Yet, as fewer nodes are within the chain, the entire chain may become more easily compromised, posing a potential security risk.[16] Having a unique hash is vital for maintaining security throughout the blocks because there are concerns about hackers tampering with the blocks and changing the hashes.

In contrast to a private chain, public chains, such as Bitcoin and Ethereum, are openly accessible to all who can access the internet,[17] who can also see the ledger and participate in the consensus process.[18] This design enables participants in a public chain to have equal rights and boosts transparency.[19] Yet, it also comes with drawbacks. For instance, a high amount of computational power is necessary for a public chain to function to maintain the distributed ledger at a large scale.[20] It takes a relatively long time to verify each transaction compared to other chains.

---

vate and Public Benefits of NFT Art' (2022) <https://www.zenofineart.com/blogs/news/the-private-and-public-benefits-of-nft-art>.

10 Andrey Drobitko, 'Can Artists Still Benefit From NFTs?' *Forbes Business Council* (29 June 2022) <<https://www.forbes.com/sites/forbesbusinesscouncil/2022/0611 June 2024./29/can-artists-still-benefit-from-nfts/?sh=57efba0a648d>.

11 Cory Cherven, 'The Societal Implications of Blockchain Proliferation' <https://arxiv.org/html/2404.02451v1>.

12 Cory Cherven, 'The Societal Implications of Blockchain Proliferation' <https://arxiv.org/html/2404.02451v1>.

13 Cory Cherven, 'The Societal Implications of Blockchain Proliferation' <https://arxiv.org/html/2404.02451v1>.

14 Praveen Jayachandran, 'The Difference between Public and Private Blockchain' (2017) <https://www.ibm.com/blogs/blockchain/2017/05/the-difference-between-public-and-private-blockchain/>.

15 [15] Gwyneth Iredale, 'Public vs Private Blockchain: How do They Differ?' *101 Blockchains* (10 January 2021) <https://101blockchains.com/public-vs-private-blockchain/>.

16 Eileen Brown, 'Comparing Public and Private Blockchain Features, Pros & Cons' *BSV Blockchain* (9 August 2022) <https://bsvblockchain.org/news/comparing-public-and-private-blockchain-features-pros-cons>.

17 Jayachandran (n 14).

18 Iredale (n 15).

19 Iredale (n 15).

20 Jayachandran (n 14).

A consortium chain is a permissioned ledger where information can only be shared among a small group of organisations.[21] It is formed by combining various private blockchains belonging to different groups, where each group forms a node on the chain as a stakeholder. While each group manages its own blockchain, its data can be accessed, shared and distributed among the other organisations in the consortium.[22] A consortium chain is created among organisations to facilitate cooperation among these groups.[23] As a result, consortium chains offer benefits such as efficiency in decision-making.[24] However, there are also challenges. For example, a unified framework of industry standards for consortium blockchains urgently needs to be developed.[25]

The Tokens: Fungible and Non-fungible

An NFT is a piece of digital artefact that represents the ownership of real-world assets. The influential NFT marketplaces in 2022 are OpenSea, Rarible, NBA Top Shot, Binance, and Nifty Gateway, with most of them utilising cryptocurrencies as their payment method.[26] The platform also participates in Art Dubai Digital this year, showcasing NFT art from six artists. Whilst NFTs operate as a type of cryptocurrency,[27] it is vital to distinguish Bitcoin's and NFT's different natures. Bitcoins are interchangeable and indistinguishable, making them fungible tokens,[28] while NFT is non-fungible because the associated data has a unique "hash value", a "unique and reproducible alphanumeric value from a specific data set" derived from the artwork.[29]

There are three ways to create and issue tokens. The first method is through an Initial Coin Offering (ICO). This is a method of raising capital for new ventures.[30]

21 Crypto News, 'What Is Consortium Blockchain?' *Crypto.News* <https://crypto.news/glossary/consortium-blockchain>.

22 Bybit Learn, 'Consortium Blockchain' (14 November 2022) <https://learn.bybit.com/glossary/definition-consortium-blockchain/>.

23 Avinandan Banerjee, 'Everything You Need to Know about Consortium Blockchain' *Blockchain Council* (10 May 2024) <https://www.blockchain-council.org/blockchain/everything-you-need-to-know-about-consortium-blockchain/>.

24 Learn (n 22).

25 Banerjee (n 23).

26 David Rodeck and Mark Hooson, 'Top NFT Marketplaces of 2023' *Forbes Advisor* <https://www.forbes.com/uk/advisor/investing/cryptocurrency/best-nft-marketplaces/>.

27 Joshua Fairfield, 'Tokenized: The Law of Non-Fungible Tokens and Unique Digital Property' (2021) *Indiana Law Journal* <https://ssrn.com/abstract=3821102>.

28 'Non-fungible Tokens: The Global Legal Impact', *Clifford Chance* <https://www.cliffordchance.com/content/dam/cliffordchance/briefings/2021/06/non-fungible-tokens-the-global-legal-impact.pdf>.

29 Anna Tipotsch, 'Formulating a Smart Contract and Minting an NFT', *Schonherr* (21 May 2021) <https://www.schoenherr.eu/content/formulating-a-smart-contract-and-minting-an-nft/>.

30 Angelos Delivorias, 'Understanding Initial Coin Offerings: A New Means of Raising Funds Based on Blockchain' <https://epthinktank.eu/2021/07/14/understanding-initial-coin-offerings-a-new-means-of-raising-funds-based-on-blockchain/>.

The tokens can be exchanged for future products and services or confer a right to a share in future profits on holders.[31] The tokens are then launched, and the business can use the proceeds to launch new products and services.[32] The second method is mining, where groups or individuals compete to solve complex mathematical problems.[33] The first one who solves the equation and validates the accuracy of a transaction in a block wins a reward.[34] Upon mining, tokens can be minted, that is, published on the blockchain and made available for purchase.[35] This can be done on platforms such as OpenSea, which allows one to mint tokens on the Ethereum blockchain by setting up a crypto wallet, creating a collection and uploading work.[36] The third method to create tokens is through tokenisation by linking or embedding the economic value and the rights derived from the asset to digital tokens created on the blockchain.[37] The tokenised asset can then be listed and sold on NFT marketplaces.

The Trading of Artworks with NFTs

While NFTs look promising in many respects in trading artworks on digital platforms, legal risks must be addressed to capture the benefits of NFTs fully. When buying an art piece, one does not purchase its copyright, which is transferred separately. According to international copyright law, to own a piece of artwork does not necessarily entail the subsequent right to display the work in a public place and collect copyright royalties paid for the use of the work. The right to display and receive royalties remains with the copyright holder.

In the past, artworks were traded by transferring the physical object or licensing the use of the work without the transfer of ownership. Collective copyright licensing is managed by collective societies in Europe and China while, in common law jurisdictions, by corporations specialising in collective copyright management. A common problem of collective copyright management is the high agency cost. Moreover, tracing and tracking the author of orphan works is less efficient due to

31 'How to Design an Effective Initial Coin Offering' *Knowledge at Wharton* (14 October 2019) <https://knowledge.wharton.upenn.edu/article/design-effective-initial-coin-offering/>.

32 CFI, 'Initial Coin Offering (ICO)' (2022) <https://corporatefinanceinstitute.com/resources/cryptocurrency/initial-coin-offering-ico/> https://corporatefinanceinstitute.com/resources/cryptocurrency/minting-crypto/>.

33 'Cryptocurrency Mining Explained' *Trading Education Team* (23 July 2021) <https://trading-education.com/cryptocurrency-mining-explained>.

34 'Cryptocurrency Mining Explained' *Trading Education Team* (23 July 2021) <https://trading-education.com/cryptocurrency-mining-explained>.

35 Jeffrey Craig, 'Crypto Minting vs Mining: What's the Difference?' *Phemex* (7 August 2021) <https://phemex.com/blogs/crypto-minting-vs-crypto-mining>.

36 OpenSea Learn, 'What Is Minting?' *Ozone Networks* (26 August 2022) <https://opensea.io/learn/what-is-minting-nft>.

37 OECD, 'The Tokenisation of Assets and Potential Implications for Financial Markets' <https://www.oecd.org/finance/The-Tokenisation-of-Assets-and-Potential-Implications-for-Financial-Markets.html>.

the need for more technology. The intermediary, that is, the collective society, is confined by its structural and technological limits, and cannot assist the rights-holder in fully capturing the value of artworks.

In the digital era, various data management tools help improve the efficiency of collective management. However, the agency cost and source-tracing problems still exist, although to a lesser extent. With the onslaught of blockchain and NFTs, it is time to revisit the agent-based transaction model. Do artists need an intermediary to manage their copyright if they can manage their own copyrighted works with secured NFTs and supporting platforms?

Although blockchain technologies offer an ideally distributed and democratic digital world without intermediaries involving transaction costs,[38] in the new reality of business, NFTed artwork trading platforms emerge as new intermediaries. In China, the platforms can be divided into three categories. The first type comprises platforms that offer blockchain technology. Examples in China include Zhixin Chain, a platform based on Hyperledger technology, which is employed to execute smart contracts, digitise company chops, and delineate ownership of intellectual property. Beyond China, Hyperledger Fabric, hosted by the Linux Foundation, offers enterprise-grade blockchain technology for leaders in finance, banking, and supply chains. The second type is the platforms that support the trade of NFTed work. These may include platforms that facilitate the collection and resale of NFTed work, such as Netease Chain, a public chain which allows trade in a large variety of NFTed work, such as animation, music, and 3-D models. Similarly, Nifty Gateway cooperates with musicians and artists to create limited edition NFTs that are exclusively available on their platform. The third type relates to those platforms that issue NFTed work. An example of such a platform is BlueFocus, a multinational company specialising in marketing and brand management services in media and design. Another example is CrowdCreate, whose services include assistance in crypto community management and crypto token marketing.

However, NFTs are not the artwork per se, nor does it become the artwork. The NFT records the existence and ownership of the artwork onto the blockchain. Because no two NFTs are the same, and no two blockchain registrations can be the same, the tokenised asset linked to the NFT can also be considered unique and non-fungible. Each NFT contains metadata that describes the corresponding assets to prove the physical object's authenticity or rarity. The NFT represents the physical object in code written into the blockchain containing various information. This information frequently contains the name of the creator of the NFT, a URL linking to a representation of the underlying work of the NFT, the date it was minted, and any contractual terms that follow the NFT after it is sold. While the separate URL embedded in the NFT contains a link to a copy of the underlying work, it is not itself a copy of that work. Thus, an NFT is not a reproduction of content; it is merely a token that authenticates the source of the content. For this reason, NFTs themselves are not "copies" and thus not subject to copyright infringement. The

38 Drobitko (n 10).

metadata does not contain any recognisable content of the underlying work, nor does it describe its contents. Similarly, the metadata does not add, transform, or recast any underlying work.

Nevertheless, NFTs could establish an exclusive ownership relationship with the underlying artwork. The hash is stored on a blockchain with an associated time stamp. Consequently, NFT keeps track of hash sales, so it is possible to trace the hand steps of the hash to the creator. This mechanism provides proof of authenticity and, simultaneously, ownership of the work. The transfer of an NFT connected to a work of art transfers the digital ownership of the authentic copy of the work; however, the purposes that can be pursued with this tool are different, so it is necessary to identify the crypto activity, the specific utility that the NFT is intended to create from time to time.

Authors can create and sell NFTs representing their works. In practice, the NFT digital art market recognises the owner of a "legitimate" NFTed work as the "owner" of the work, even though NFTs do not convey copyright ownership of the work.[39] NFT owners encourage others to use their work because popularity increases the value of the work. Increasing the author's impact creates more value than controlling the use of the work. If the profit from selling NFTs alone is large enough to motivate authors, copyright is no longer necessary as a legal monopoly to reward authors. The value of art has always come from the reputation of the author and the scarcity of the work through "authenticity".

Legal Status of NFT: The Common Law Approaches

The premise of this property syllogism is that "a particular type of right (such as a chose in action, an intellectual property right or a beneficial interest under a trust) is the same type of right as a right to a tangible asset and must therefore be protected in the same way".[40] With this background in mind, it is perhaps unsurprising that crypto assets have been more readily accommodated within common law systems' vague notions of property than those of civilian systems.

The courts in England and Wales (English and Welsh cases), Singapore (Singaporean cases), and New Zealand (*Ruscoe v Cryptopia Ltd (in Liq)* [2020]) have acknowledged Bitcoins and other crypto assets as property within the common law. Property, in the case law to date, refers more to assets than things.[41] This was also the advice of the LawTech Delivery Panel's UK Jurisdiction Taskforce in its Legal Statement on Cryptoassets and Smart Contracts. The key question is how crypto assets as property would fit within the common law's classificatory scheme for property. Unlike the civilian classification between movables and immovables,

39 Brian L. Frye, 'After Copyright: Pwning NFTs in a Clout Economy' (2022) *Columbia Journal of Law and Arts*, 45(3), 341–353.

40 Ben McFarlane and Simon Douglas Property, 'Analogy and Variety' (2022) *Oxford Journal of Legal Studies*, 42, 161–186.

41 Kelvin F. K. Low and Megumi Hara, 'Cryptoassets and Property' in Sjef van Erp and Katja Zimmermann (eds), *Edward Elgar Research Handbook on EU Property Law* (Cheltenham UK, Edward Elgar, 2024).

the common law classifies property into real and personal, with the former comprising mostly land. Personality is, in turn, classified into either choses in possession or choses in action.

The United Kingdom

The point on whether cryptocurrency could be a form of property was more fully developed in *AA v Persons Unknown* [2019] ("AA"). Bryan J noted that the immediate difficulty was that "English law traditionally views property as being of only two kinds, choses in possession and choses in action" (AA at [55], citing *Colonial Bank v Whinney* [1885] ("Colonial Bank")). Bitcoins and other cryptocurrencies did not fall neatly into either category and thus could not be classified as a form of property (AA at [56] and [58]). Bryan J, however, considered that it was "fallacious to proceed on the basis that the English law of property recognises no forms of property other than choses in possession and choses in action" (AA at [58]). In doing so, he cited extensively from the legal statement on crypto assets and smart contracts published by the UK Jurisdiction Task Force (the "Legal Statement"). Thus, the Task Force believed that *Colonial Bank* was not to be treated as limiting the scope of what kinds of things could be property in law. Instead, it showed the ability of the common law to stretch "traditional definitions and concepts to adapt to new business practices" (Legal Statement at [77]). The Legal Statement, therefore, formed the basis for Bryan J's conclusion that while a crypto asset might not be a thing in action based on a narrow definition of that term, it could still be considered property (AA at [59]). He made a finding that crypto assets such as Bitcoin were property, given that they met the four criteria set out in *National Provincial Bank Ltd v Ainsworth* [1965] ("Ainsworth") at 1248 – namely that it must be "definable, identifiable by third parties, capable in its nature of assumption by third parties, and have some degree of permanence or stability".

The UK's High Court recently ruled that NFTs are property, and thus victims of NFT theft can now have their stolen assets frozen through court injunctions. The decision comes after months of repeated NFT thefts, as savvy hackers have exploited loopholes and poor security literacy to seize high-profile NFTs. In an earlier case involving NFTs (*Osbourne v Persons Unknown* [2022]), the court also found a claimant has a good arguable case that misappropriated crypto assets are held on a constructive trust. It is, therefore, clear that the courts are open to constructive trust claims as regards crypto assets. However, Ms Osbourne did not go so far as to seek, as Mr D'Aloia has, to ask the courts to consider a claim in which – in addition to the alleged fraudsters – the exchanges are also said to hold the crypto assets on constructive trust. The *D'Aloia* case, therefore, appears to be the first in which the Court has found that there is a good arguable case for this claim against the exchanges themselves. The *D'Aloia* case allows victims to obtain court injunctions against individuals whose crypto wallet has been identified as carrying a stolen NFT and to the NFT platform on which the stolen asset is being sold.

This ruling demonstrates that the English courts are open to entertaining constructive trust claims concerning crypto assets, not only against the fraudsters but also against third-party exchanges. The possibility of such a claim has been lent further support by the Law Commission's analysis in their Consultation on Digital Assets, published on 28 July 2022 (see paragraph 19.51). This would give victims of crypto-asset fraud a means of direct action against exchanges for breach of trust should they fail to comply with their duties as constructive trustees, having been notified that they are in possession of fraudulently misappropriated crypto assets.

Singapore

In an earlier case of *CLM v CLN* [2022] SGHC 46 ("CLM"), Lee Seiu Kin J dealt with the question of whether stolen cryptocurrency assets, specifically Bitcoin and Ethereum, could be the subject of a proprietary injunction. Having considered the cases and the analysis in *Ruscoe v Cryptopia Ltd (in liq)* [2020] ("Ruscoe"), the judge was of the view (at [46]) that the claimant, in that case, was able to prove an arguable case that the stolen cryptocurrency assets were capable of giving rise to proprietary rights, which could be protected via a proprietary injunction.

In *Janesh s/o Rajkumar v Unknown Person* [2022], the court noted that although NFTs have been characterised as certificates of ownership "powered by smart contracts and protected by blockchain technology",[42] NFTs represent an "ownership of a digital certificate of authenticity of commonly available digital art".[43] Nevertheless, the court disagrees with the "NFT is certificate" approach. The court points out that NFTs are not just mere information but rather data encoded in a certain manner and securely stored on the blockchain ledger. (*Janesh s/o Rajkumar v Unknown Person* [2022], paragraph 58) Rather, NFTs provide instructions to the computer under a system whereby the "owner" of the NFT has exclusive control over its transfer from his wallet to any other wallet.

Lee Seiu Kin J adopted the *Ainsworth* test and upheld the following findings. First, an NFT with its unique metadata is definable (*Janesh s/o Rajkumar*, [44]). NFTs are not just mere information, but rather, data encoded in a certain manner and securely stored on the blockchain ledger (*Janesh s/o Rajkumar*, [58]) "It provides instructions to the computer under a system whereby the 'owner' of the NFT has exclusive control over its transfer from his wallet to any other wallet" (*Janesh s/o Rajkumar*, [58]). Second, per the second requirement that the "asset must have an owner being capable of being recognised as such by third parties" (*CLM*, [45(b)], citing Ruscoe at [109]) the presumptive NFT owner would be whoever controls the wallet which is linked to the NFT, an NFT with its private keys would be an asset, with an owner being capable of being recognised as such by third parties. The third requirement is "that the right must be capable of assumption by third parties, which in turn involves two aspects: that third parties must respect the rights of the owner in that asset, and that the asset must be potentially desirable". The "nature of the

42 Pınar Çağlayan Aksoy and Zehra Özkan Üner, 'NFTs and Copyright: Challenges and Opportunities' (2021) *Journal of Intellectual Property Law & Practice*, 16(10), 1115–1126.

43 Low and Hara (n 41).

blockchain technology gives the owner the exclusive ability to transfer the NFT to another party, which underscores the 'right' of the owner". Lastly, an NFT has a relevant degree of permanence and stability as money in bank accounts which, nowadays, exist mainly in the form of ledger entries and not cold hard cash.

In summary, Singapore's first court decision on NFTs rejects the analogy between a title deed and a certificate of property. The court applies the *Ainsworth* criteria and upholds NFTs as property.

Legal Status of NFT: The Civil Law Approaches

The Theoretical and Legislative Discussion

Scholars point out that digital tokens may be considered "digital assets". The same approach is taken by the Gesetz über Token und VT-Dienstleister of Liechtenstein, which regulates tokens as assets (Vermögen, art. 4). In fact, it has been stated that "all-European legal systems of the member states regard not only corporeal things as the objects of real rights but also incorporeal assets, such as patrimonial rights".[44] However, some legal systems take a narrower approach concerning the scope of the property, which is limited to "corporeal things", as is the case under both German and Swiss law (e.g. §§90 Bürgerliches Gesetzbuch30 -BGB- or §641 Swiss Civil Code 31). This means that tokens could not be regarded as the object of property in these legal systems, e.g. in Germany, tokens have been defined as "eine faktische Vermögensposition", meaning "a factual situation".[45] Other EU legal systems have either incorporated a broader definition of the concept of a "thing" to include "patrimonial or valuable rights" (e.g. arts. 334.10 CC; §§292, 298 and 299 Allgemeines bürgerliches Gesetzbuch, ABGB35) or a broader definition of the concept of an "asset" (art. 3.1 Burgerlijk Wetboek -BW-), which makes regulating tokens as an object of ownership more accessible. For example, in Spain, the judgment of the Supreme Court 20/06/201937 denied the recognition of Bitcoin as a legal tender (money) but considered it an "incorporeal asset". In Italy, tokens have been regarded as "digital assets" under the provisions of art. 810 Italian Civil Code; and art. 65 French Loi n. 486 categorises tokens as "incorporeal assets".

In the EU, the Proposal for a Regulation of the European Parliament and of the Council on Markets in Crypto-assets (MiCA) September 24, 2020 aims to enhance legal certainty to crypto assets while encouraging innovation and protecting consumers. However, this proposal does not cover the legal nature, the legal effects and the admissibility of using asset-backed tokens to transfer property rights. In China, the first *Civil Code* became effective in 2021 and includes provisions peripherally relevant to virtual assets. In *Book I General Provisions*, Article 114 provides that

44 Christian Von Bar and Ulrich Drobnig, *The Interaction of Contract Law and Tort and Property Law in Europe: A Comparative Study* (Munich, Sellier de Gruyter, 2004).

45 Mattias Lehman and Felix Krysa, 'Blockchain, Smart Contracts Und Token aus der des (Internationalen) Privatrechts' (2 September 2019) *BRJ*, 90.

civil subjects enjoy property rights (rights in rem), which are the exclusive rights to directly dominate a particular thing, including ownership, usufructuary rights, and security interests. Article 116 is a *Numerus Clausus* that limits the types and contents of property rights exclusively by law. Article 127 provides that the *Civil Code* shall recognise the existing legal provisions for virtual property.

Judicial Decision in the EU and China

In Europe, the Court of Rome was the first to order an injunction to the creation and marketing of NFTs infringing registered trademarks. It ordered the NFTs to be removed from the trading website. The decision represents a reference point at a global level at a time when strong attention is paid by all operators in the sector to the legal aspects of this new digital tool. It goes from who defines NFT as "a digital not interchangeable good, such as a photograph, a song or a video, whose property has been authenticated and stored in a database called blockchain and which can be collected, sold and exchanged on various online platforms"[46] to those who consider them as "unique digital certificates, registered in a blockchain, used as a means to register the ownership of an object, as a digital artwork or a collectible object".[47] The decision represents an implicit accreditation of the interpretation – already adopted by the leading national and international offices, including EUIPO, for which Class 9 is the one for registered trademarks used to distinguish certain types of "digital goods".

The Italian Court reiterates the provision of art. 97 of the Copyright Law, relating to the permitted uses of the right to the image of a person, does not extend to the use of trademarks possibly represented in the same image. The same consideration also introduces the probably most important concept of the decision, which confirms the fact that the creation of NFTs - which are "goods intended for commercial sale" - requires specific authorisation from the proprietor of the trademark, of which it, therefore, constitutes a separate infringement and distinct from the infringement constituted by the use of the trademark in the digital images associated with the NFT. This confirms the preference for a legal definition of NFT that undertakes a dichotomy between the certificate and the content (*Janesh s/o Rajkumar v Unknown Person* [2022] SGHC 264). Above all, it explains the ratio of the same precautionary order, which is not by chance kept well distinguished between NFTs and the corresponding digital content, inhibits the "production, marketing, promotion and offer for sale, direct and/or indirect, in any way and form" of, on the one hand "of the NFT" and, on the other hand, of any other "digital content

46 Roberto Moro Trevisi and Andrea Cesaretti, 'Non-Fungible Tokens (NFT): Business Models, Legal Aspects, and Market Valuation' (2022) *Rivista di Diritto dei Media* <https://www.medialaws.eu/rivista/non-fungible-tokens-nft-business-models-legal-aspects-and-market-valuation/>.

47 EUIPO, 'EUIPO Draft Guidelines' 2023 edition <https://euipo.europa.eu/ohimportal/nl/draft-guidelines>.

or product generally bearing the photograph, even modified, and/or the Juventus trademarks, as well as the use of said trademarks in any form and manner".

The Commercial Law Court of Barcelona (Visual Entidad De Gestion De Artistas Plasticos/ Punto Fa, S.L. [2022] AJM B 1900/2022 - ECLI:ES: JMB: 2022:1900, Juzgado de lo Mercantil nº 09 de Barcelona) rendered one of the first judgments dealing with the relationship between intellectual property and NFT. The decision involves the fast fashion brand Mango and the Spanish collective society for artists VEGAP (Visual Entidad de Gestión de Artistas Plásticos). In March 2022, Mango exhibited a series of artworks created by Farkas, an artist, in a virtual museum on the Decentraland, a Web 3.0 site. Mango legitimately owns the original copy of the works. The collection was designed to reinterpret rather than directly reproduce the artworks, which are under copyright protection. VEGAP sued Mango for copyright infringement, arguing that the minting and displaying of the artworks infringed copyright. The Court ordered tokens to be de-listed and further pointed out that the withdrawal of a work does not amount to destroying tokens since tokens can be used during the process. The Court assumes that the right to display does not give the right to digitise the work, display and sell it as NFT.

In the first NFT court decision in China (*Qice Technology Ltd v A Technology Ltd*),[48] the Hangzhou Internet Court, an intermediate-level court, holds an NFT-trading platform liable for copyright infringement for an NFTed unauthorised reproduction of an artwork uploaded by its user. The court discusses similar issues regarding the nature of NFTs. It holds that the metadata exclusively and uniquely represents an artwork copy. It is identifiable by third parties and maintains the scarcity of the work in a digital form. Therefore, an NFTed work is a 'digital commodity', and NFTed copies of the work are digital assets. The trade of an NFTed work is essentially a transfer of ownership of the copy being tokenised and uploaded (page 18). Acquiring such an NFTed work entails obtaining the property rights and interests in that copy. It entails no license to use such digital assets nor a license or a transfer of the intellectual property rights of the underlying artwork (unless the sales agreement provides otherwise). In the further analysis of copyright infringement, the court distinguishes NFTed work from a physical object. It holds that the distribution right does not apply in this case because it only concerns the distribution of physical objects. The legitimate creator of an NFT should not be the person who possesses a copy of the underlying work but the person who owns the copyright or obtains a due license for the underlying work. Hence, it holds that the uploading of the NFTed work infringed on the right to disseminate work by information networks.

However, as the court is only a district-level court, it remains to be seen whether its ruling will be widely followed or is likely to be challenged in subsequent cases by other courts in China. In any case, as the authorities have not yet enacted any

48 (2022) Zhe 0192 Minchu 1008.

formal NFT laws or regulations, the court's insights in the judgment are meaningful, and NFT players in China should carefully consider the implications of the ruling.

The Gulf Approach

Middle Eastern countries have a small number of federal regulations on assets, and more specifically, cryptocurrencies and NFTs. This is because of the presence of financial-free zones that have their own laws and law enforcement machinery. For instance, in UAE, the decisions and legislations of federal and local authorities need to be read to understand the treatment of cryptocurrencies or NFTs. To make it more complex, there are seven emirates within the UAE, each having its own regulations. Apart from the federal regulators like the UAE Central Bank and the UAE Securities and Commodities Authority (SCA), there are other financial institutions that possess the power to frame regulations for financial and capital markets. For example, within Dubai, it's the Dubai International Financial Centre (DIFC) and in Abu Dhabi, it's the Abu Dhabi Global Market (ADGM).

Unlike the UK, EU, Singapore or Chinese jurisprudence, many of the Gulf countries, for proprietary regulations, rely on Islamic law, i.e., Sharia Law, where the Quran is their constitution. Sharia Law, in essence, has an overarching objective of utilitarianism by avoiding deceit, corruption and destruction. The Quranic notion of property has a positive connotation to intangible property, like making something useful which is for the benefit of the community.[49] This affects the copyright holders of artworks, as original creations, technological inventions, books, music, software, and medicines deserve proprietary protection under Islamic law. The said law also recognises the licensing agreements if the object of the agreement is legitimate and is in the public interest. This brings NFTs and cryptocurrencies' financial characteristics into play of whether such assets are a tool of destruction or goodness. While the authenticity and traceability of the blockchain technology on which the said digital assets operate imply benefits, the evidence suggesting its easy usage in money laundering and terrorist activities signals corruption. Egypt's Islamic Advisory, justiciary, and governmental body, Dar al-Ifta ruled Bitcoin as '*haram*' as it could damage national security and central financial systems by engaging in money laundering and terrorist activities.

Holding cryptocurrencies or NFTs also violates the five Maqasid (objectives) of Sharia Law, i.e., justice, transparency and disclosure, wealth circulation, integrity and cooperation, and ease with no hardships. Due to NFTs' volatile nature in terms of price and sales fluctuation, a person would be unjustly affected. The argument for its lack of utility and wealth circulation stems from its usage in booming the real economy. The evidence of hoarding and inside trading limits the purpose of NFTs under Islamic law. Finally, the power required to unearth NFTs generates

49 Silvia Beltrametti, 'The Legality of Intellectual Property Rights Under Islamic Law' (2009) *The Prague Yearbook of Comparative Law*, 55–94.

inequities for the miners and those who still live without electricity or insufficient power. Apart from Maqasid, there are two other notions under Islamic law, directly emanating from Quranic texts that might prohibit holding NFTs as a property. One is '*gharar*' associated with deceit and the other is '*Maysir*' that means relying on chance for benefit or gain.[50] In contractual terms, Gharar denotes '*misrepresentation*' and maysir denotes '*contingency*'.

The above discussion points to speculation and volatility associated with such digital assets. However, Sharia Law fails to consider that if there is a government-backed currency, it is likely to have greater practical utility, minimise hardships, regulate illegal speculations, and increase wealth circulations, thus satisfying the Maqasid's. Before getting into the various regulations coming up in the Gulf states, it is important to note another feature of property. Keeping in touch with contemporary society, the Islamic Financial Services Board views Bitcoin as a digital commodity because it possesses the feature to store information and exchange via the distributed ledger system. However, designating Bitcoin as a commodity has differences, with NFT being one. NFTs for artworks are prohibited specifically as Sharia Law prevents a person from creating anything that contains animated or live objects.[51] While the creation of artworks that include live objects is prohibited, and not the possession of artworks, NFTs in artworks is at least partially doubtful from an Islamic perspective.

The preceding section raises concerns about holding NFTs in artworks in Islamic countries that follow Quran as their constitution. However, policymaking and legal regulations can ensure Sharia compliance with such digital assets by (a) Creating a regulator that minimises trust deficit and uncertainties in trading of NFT artworks, (b) Ensuring NFTs are backed by a stable commodity that deals with volatility concerns, (c) Providing a harmonised definition of virtual assets that consider the permissible art content under Sharia Law, and (d) Issue policy guidances that increase the practical utility of virtual assets in the national and international community.

In the quest for regulation and addressing above raised concerns, UAE is at the forefront as they promulgated Federal Law No. 4 of 2022, Dubai Virtual Assets Law (DVAL). It also establishes the Dubai Virtual Assets Regulatory Authority (DVARA), an independent regulator for cryptocurrencies and NFTs, operating in all financial and non-financial zones except DIFC. Under the legislation, DVARA is responsible for preventing price manipulation, data protection, and collaborating with other federal authorities like the Central Bank and the SCA to develop a code of ethics for owning/licensing virtual assets. Abu Dhabi, another emirate in the UAE, has also given zone-specific recognition to crypto assets. The ADGM zone/region has established a Financial Services Regulatory Authority (FSRA) having

50 Ornina El Hajjar, 'The regulation of Non-Fungible Tokens (NFTs)' (2022) (Doctoral dissertation, Lebanese American University).

51 YuLun Wu, 'Halal or Haram: The Permissibility of Bitcoin and NFTs in Sharia' (2022) *Singapore Law Review*, 39, 229–252.

similar powers as DVARA but limited to crypto assets. Whether such regulations would be able to satisfy the five Maqasid is something for the regulators' enforceability to determine.

Though Dubai and Abu Dhabi have made efforts to regulate the usage of digital assets, there are uncertainties and vagueness regarding other Gulf states. For instance, the Iraq Central Bank Guidance of November 11, 2021, warns Iraqi citizens not to deal in cryptocurrencies and NFTs due to their highly volatile nature.[52] The Bank also subjects dealing with such assets to domestic Money Laundering legislation. The said legislation defines funds as "*the assets or property obtained by any means, such as the national currency, foreign currency, current accounts, and financial investments, whatever their form, including electronic or digital funds, precious metals... and all things that have a financial value... whether they are inside or outside Iraq*". According to this definition, dealing with assets like crypto or NFTs looks permissible, unless used for money laundering purposes.

The Egyptian Central Bank has been much stricter than the Iraqi Bank. Post the stance of Egypt's religious body declaring Crypto and NFTs as haram, the Central Bank has issued a prohibition order on engaging with cryptocurrencies, underscoring concerns like financial systems stability, terrorism and illicit activities. The order also sanctions notices, fines and imprisonment for offenders to deter individuals and businesses from participating in digital assets-based activity. Some notably wealthy Middle Eastern countries like Oman, Qatar and Kuwait have also declared cryptocurrencies illegal, but like Egypt, are open to searching for other possible regulations.

It should be kept in mind that even if the Gulf states launch comprehensive digital/virtual assets regulations, they primarily regulate cryptocurrencies. NFTs differ substantially from crypto tokens and should be read outside the above-mentioned regulations/guidance. For instance, the Kingdom of Bahrain was one of the first regulators globally to release a comprehensive digital assets framework, called the Crypto Assets Module. But it is limited to Payment, Utility, Asset and Hybrid tokens that are synonymous with cryptocurrencies and not NFTs. Bahrain's central bank considers legal rights associated with NFTs as ambiguous, as they do not fit the definitions of financial instruments, bonds, securities or debt, and thereby, no framework exists to defend the ownership of such digital assets.

Recommendations

If the Gulf states are to develop their legal and regulatory frameworks further to facilitate the trade of NFTed artwork on blockchains, the primary aim that needs to be kept in mind is to adjust the legal frameworks around digital assets with the Sharia Law, more specifically, Maqasids. Sharia Law is not jurisprudentially

52 Ghassan Adhab Atiyah, Nazura Abdul Manap, and Saidatul Nadia Abd Aziz, 'Legal Status of Cryptocurrency Circulation in Iraq: Lessons from the United Arab Emirates and the United States' (2023) *Hasanuddin Law Review*, 9(1), 1–19.

formalistic, and thereby, if the digital assets law can be made Sharia compliant, the current rulings by gulf countries like Iraq, Egypt, Bahrain and others may change.

Legislators and policymakers also need to maintain the value of art that comes from the reputation of the author and the scarcity of the work through 'authenticity'. NFTs offer artists the opportunity to secure incomes with tracing and tracking functions and embedded smart contracts while encouraging the dissemination of artwork that cannot be reproduced without authorisation. If the profit from selling NFTs is large enough to motivate authors, copyright as a legal monopoly is no longer necessary to generate rewards. Recognising NFTs as property encourages artists to be open to the market, which helps create cultural prosperity and increase social welfare. They are also important objectives of Sharia Law.

The NFT is more than a recording of digital work. Minting an NFTed work is to record the work on the blockchain through an identification code. The creation of the digital tokenised work (i.e. registered blockchain with hash code) involves the acquisition of ownership by the registration holder. NFTed artwork might evoke the question of exclusive possession and control of the work, including property and IP rights. The right to tokenise a work protected by copyright belongs to the owner of the copyright or those with the authorisation of the owner; beyond this hypothesis, this right belongs to the owner of NFTed work. Consequently, it is necessary to distinguish NFTs from NFT artwork. The NFT is a mechanism for forming the ownership of a right of use and disposition of digital work in the hands of the person who registers the NFTs.

Although the judiciary from different jurisdictions has been willing to extend the protection for brick-and-mortar property to NFTed artworks, NFTs are at the risk of misrepresenting or even infringing IP rights in a work minted into NFTs. Possessing an NFT does not necessarily confer any legal right over the digital or physical object the NFT refers to. Several proposals have been advanced to overcome this limitation to the concept of NFT. Some try to strike a balance between the legal and the technical dimensions, incorporating aspects of copyright law into the metadata of the NFT or in accompanying documentation; others propose to incorporate the actual work into the underlying smart contract. While many commentators are critical at this point, others, like Fairfield, see the potential of NFTs as forms of "unique digital property", re-establishing personal property rights that have been lost to user agreements and other instruments of uneven bargaining power.[53]

In the UK, the Task Force took the view that *Colonial Bank* was not to be treated as limiting the scope of what kinds of things could be property in law. Instead, it showed the ability of the common law to stretch "traditional definitions and concepts to adapt to new business practices". *National Provincial Bank Ltd v Ainsworth* [1965] has established a four-factored test for the property as something "definable, identifiable by third parties, capable in its nature of assumption by third parties, and have some degree of permanence or stability". In Singapore, the court

53 Fairfield (n 27).

rejected the analogy between a title deed for real property and NFTs as a certificate for digital assets. Rather, it adopted the *Ainsworth* criteria and upheld NFTs as property.

In Europe, although some jurisdictions traditionally take a narrow approach concerning the scope of the property, which is limited to "corporeal things", many others are more open to including incorporeal assets, such as patrimonial rights, into real rights. The court decisions discussed in section IV demonstrate that cryptocurrency and NFTs are considered digital assets.[54] The Italian and Spanish Courts noted that NFTs, on the one hand, bear a certifying function and, on the other hand, link to specific content. China's first *Civil Code* explicitly recognises virtual property as an object protectable by law. In the first NFT-concerned case, the court distinguishes the NFTed work from a physical object and holds that an NFTed work is a 'digital commodity', and NFTed copies of the work are digital assets. It adopts a test similar to the *Ainsworth* test that evaluates whether the data is unique and securely linked to a work and is identifiable by third parties. It is consensus that while the right of the owner to mint and tokenise a work is to be fully protected, it cannot be overlooked that this right must be exercised in compliance with the principle of economic solidarity and fair competition.

The Gulf countries demonstrate a divergence in their legislative framework due to the supremacy attributed to Sharia Law. An accurate understanding of it is shown above, demonstrating its importance. While the Sharia Law does not directly provide for the protection of digital assets, it embodies five objectives necessary to be achieved for economic development and a humane and just society, referred to as Maqasid's. Through their regulatory framework, Dubai and Abu Dhabi's regulatory authority depicts how both legislation's compliance with the stated five objectives and an effective regulation of digital assets be achieved. They serve as a lesson to the Iraqi and Egyptian Central Bank to define and regulate digital assets outside money laundering or national security legislation. Further lessons, specifically NFTed artwork, can be learnt from the emerging jurisprudence of civil and common law legal systems.

Conclusion

The comparison of legislation, case law, and relevant documents implies an increasing level of law convergence towards a harmonised concept of digital assets in a world built on blockchain and tokens. In comparing the common law and civil law systems, convergence of law is emerging in the digital world that can provide recommendations for the Gulf states to develop a legal framework. The legal systems have advanced closer towards a concept of property with many shared features. First, the data must be stored securely on the blockchain ledger. The nature of blockchain technology gives the owner the exclusive ability to transfer the NFT to

54 Ermanno Calzolaio, 'Il bitcoin come oggetto di property. Note a margine di una recente sentenza della High Court' (2020) *Il Foro Italiano*, CXLV(10), 494–500.

another party, which underscores the "right" of the owner. Second, the data should be capable of being recognised by third parties. Third, the data has intrinsic value that is respected and potentially desirable by third parties. Lastly, an NFT has a relevant degree of permanence and stability as money in bank accounts, which, exist mainly in the form of ledger entries and not cold hard cash. Property is moving from a static concept to a concept of act and activity. At the same time, ownership is the link between the owner and the worthy interest to be realised and guaranteed.

NFTed artworks are considered incorporeal assets that confer quasi-property rights and interests. The legal principle of *numerus clausus* is an instrument for legal certainty. However, reality goes beyond the dogmas of the legal tradition. The jurist must take an evolutionary leap forward to adapt the mechanisms and techniques of law to emerging digital technologies that change the societal ecosystem. The concept of property per se and the rights deriving from the property need a recalibration that shifts from focusing on exclusive control to the use of the thing.

Attention must be paid to the consideration that the "thing" becomes a juridical good as a reference point and content of legal situations if it has a socially appreciable utility and finds in the orderly system an evaluation in terms of merit.[55] The artificial exclusivity – created by the relationship between the account/portfolio and the hash via NFT – that represents the copy of the underlying value evokes the proprietary logic even if its dynamics undermine any theoretical definition to benefit the valuation of the interests involved.

Bibliography

Aksoy, P. C. and Üner, Z. (2021). 'NFTs and Copyright: Challenges and Opportunities', *Journal of Intellectual Property Law & Practice*, 16(10), 1115–1126.

Calzolaio, E. (2020). 'Il bitcoin come oggetto di property. Note a margine di una recente sentenza della High Court. Il Foro Italiano', *CXLV* 10, 494–500.

De Caria, R. (2018). 'The Legal Meaning of Smart Contracts', *European Review of Private Law*, 26(6), 731–752.

De Caria, R. (2020). 'Blockchain and Smart Contracts', *Italian Law Journal*, 6(1), 363–380.

Dornis, T. W. (2021). 'Of 'Authorless Works' and 'Inventions without Inventor' – The Muddy Waters of 'AI Autonomy' in Intellectual Property Doctrine', *European Intellectual Property Review,* 43, 1–28.

Fairfield, J. (2021). 'Tokenized: The Law of Non-Fungible Tokens and Unique Digital Property', *Indiana Law Journal*, https://ssrn.com/abstract=3821102

Frye, B. L. (2022). 'After Copyright: Pwning NFTs in a Clout Economy', *Columbia Journal of Law and Arts*, 45(3), 341–353.

Low, K. F. K. and Hara, M. (2024). 'Cryptoassets and Property', in Sjef van Erp and Katja Zimmermann (eds.), *Edward Elgar Research Handbook on EU Property Law.* (Cheltenham, UK, Edward Elgar, 2024)

Moringiello, J. M. and Odinet, C. K. (2022). 'The Property Law of Tokens', *Florida Law Review*, 74, 607–671, https://ssrn.com/abstract=3928901 or http://dx.doi.org/10.2139/ssrn.3928901

55 Pietro Perlingieri, 'L'informazione come bene giuridico' (1990) *Rassegna di Diritto Civile*, 326–338.

Murray, M. D. (2022). 'Generative and AI Authored Artworks and Copyright Law', *Hastings Communications and Entertainment Law Journal*, 45(1), 28–43, https://ssrn.com/abstract=4152484 or http://dx.doi.org/10.2139/ssrn.4152484

Murray, M. D. (2022). 'NFT Ownership and Copyrights', https://ssrn.com/abstract=4152468 or http://dx.doi.org/10.2139/ssrn.4152468

Notaro, A. (2022). 'All That is Solid Melts in the Ethereum: The Brave New (Art) World of NFTs', *Journal of Visual Art Practice*, 21(4), 359–382, https://doi.org/10.1080/14702029.2022.2129204

Perlingieri, P. (1990). 'L'informazione come bene giuridico', *Rass. dir. Civ.*, 2, 326–338.

Teruel, G. M. R. and Simon-Moreno, H. (2021). 'The Digital Tokenization of Property Rights: A Comparative Perspective', *Computer Law and Security Review*, 41, 4–5.

AA v Persons Unknown, [2019] EWHC 3556 (Comm)

Colonial Bank v Whinney [1885] 30 Ch.D 261

CLM v CLN [2022] SGHC 46

Janesh s/o Rajkumar v Unknown Person [2022] SGHC 264

Juventus Football Club S.p.A. v Blockeras s.r.l. [2022] Court of Rome, IP Chamber, Docket No.32072

National Provincial Bank Ltd v Ainsworth [1965] AC 1175

Osbourne v Persons Unknown & Anor [2022] EWHC 1021 (Comm) (10 March 2022)

Qice Technology Ltd v A Technology Ltd ([2022] Zhe 0192 Min Chu No. 1008

Ruscoe v Cryptopia Ltd (in Liq) [2020] NZHC 728, [2020] 2 NZLR 809

Skatteverket v Hedqvist [2015] EUCG, sez. V, 22 October 2015, case -264/2014

Visual Entidad De Gestíon De Artistas Plásticos v Punto Fa, S.L. [2022] AJM B 1900/2022 - ECLI:ES: JMB: 2022:1900, Juzgado de lo Mercantil nº 09 de Barcelona

AA v Persons Unknown [2019] EWHC 3556 (Comm)

Danisz v Persons Unknown [2022] EWHC 280 (QB) at [13]

Fetch.AI Ltd v Persons Unknown Category A [2021] EWHC 2254 (Comm) at [9]

Ion Science Ltd v Persons Unknown (unreported EWHC(Ch) 21 December 2020, Butcher J) at [11]

Mr Dollar Bill Ltd v Persons Unknown [2021] EWHC 2718 (Ch) at [10]

Shair.Com Global Digital Services Ltd v Arnold 2018 BCSC 1512 at [15]

Vorotyntseva v Money-4 Ltd [2018] EWHC 2596 (Ch) at [13]

Wang v Darby [2021] EWHC 3054 (Comm) at [55]

B2C2 Ltd v Quione Pte Ltd [2019] SGHC(I) 03 [2019] 4 SLR 17: [2020] SGCA(I) 02, [2020] 2 SLR 20 at [144]. See now, however, CLM v CLN [2022] SGHC 46 at [46].

Juventus Football Club S.p.A. v Blockeras s.r.l. [2022] Court of Rome, IP Chamber, Docket No.32072

Skatteverket v Hedqvist [2015] EUCG, sez. V, 22 October 2015, case -264/2014

Visual Entidad De Gestíon De Artistas Plásticos v Punto Fa, S.L. [2022] AJM B 1900/2022 - ECLI:ES: JMB: 2022:1900, Juzgado de lo Mercantil nº 09 de Barcelona

Banerjee, Avinandan (2022). 'Everything You Need to Know About Consortium Blockchain', https://www.blockchain-council.org/blockchain/everything-you-need-to-know-about-consortium-blockchain/

Brown, E. (2022). 'Comparing Public and Private Blockchain Features, Pros & Cons', https://bsvblockchain.org/news/comparing-public-and-private-blockchain-features-pros-cons

Bybit Learn (2022). 'Consortium Blockchain', https://learn.bybit.com/glossary/definition-consortium-blockchain/

CFI (2022). 'Minting Crypto', https://corporatefinanceinstitute.com/resources/cryptocurrency/minting-crypto/

Cherven C., 'The Societal Implications of Blockchain Proliferation', https://arxiv.org/html/2404.02451v1

Craig, J. (2021). 'Crypto Minting vs Mining: What's the Difference?', https://phemex.com/blogs/crypto-minting-vs-crypto-mining

Delivorias, Angelos. (2021). 'Understanding Initial Coin Offerings', European Parliamentary Research Services, https://www.europarl.europa.eu/RegData/etudes/BRIE/2021/696167/EPRS_BRI(2021)696169_EN.pdf

'Digitally Transforming the Gulf Cooperation Council Region', International Centre for Industrial Transformation (2022), https://incit.org/thought-leadership/digitally-transforming-the-gulf-cooperation-council-region/

Drobitko, A. (2022). 'Can Artists Still Benefit From NFTs?', https://www.forbes.com/sites/forbesbusinesscouncil/2022/06/29/can-artists-still-benefit-from-nfts/?sh=57efba0a648d

Dubai Blockchain Strategy, https://u.ae/en/about-the-uae/strategies-initiatives-and-awards/strategies-plans-and-visions/government-services-and-digital-transformation/dubai-blockchain-strategy

Emirates Blockchain Strategy (2021). https://u.ae/en/about-the-uae/strategies-initiatives-and-awards/strategies-plans-and-visions/strategies-plans-and-visions-untill-2021/emirates-blockchain-strategy-2021

EUIPO, *EUIPO Draft Guidelines,* 2023 edition, https://euipo.europa.eu/ohimportal/nl/draft-guidelines-2023

Hamilton, A. (2022). 'The Private and Public Benefits of NFT Art', https://www.zenofineart.com/blogs/news/the-private-and-public-benefits-of-nft-art

Hashtag Investing (2022). 'Top 6 Benefits of NFT's for Artists and Reasons to Use Them in 2022', https://www.hashtaginvesting.com/blog/top-benefits-of-nfts-for-artists

'How to Design an Effective Initial Coin Offering', Knowledge at Wharton (2019). https://knowledge.wharton.upenn.edu/article/design-effective-initial-coin-offering/

Initial Coin Offering (ICO) (2022). https://corporatefinanceinstitute.com/resources/cryptocurrency/initial-coin-offering-ico/

Iredale, G. (2021). 'Public vs Private Blockchain: How Do They Differ?', https://101blockchains.com/public-vs-private-blockchain/

Jayachandran, P. (2017). 'The Difference Between Public and Private Blockchain', https://www.ibm.com/blogs/blockchain/2017/05/the-difference-between-public-and-private-blockchain/

McFarlane, B. and Douglas, S. (2022). 'Property, Analogy and Variety', *Oxford Journal of Legal Studies*, 42, 161–186.

OpenSea Learn (2022). 'What is Minting?', https://opensea.io/learn/what-is-minting-nft

Rarible (2022). 'How do I Sell My NFT on Rarible?', https://rarible.com/how-it-works/using-rarible/how-do-i-sell-my-nft-on-rarible

Reiff, N. (2022). 'Decentralised Autonomous Organisation (DAO): Definition, Purpose and Example', https://www.investopedia.com/tech/what-dao/

'The Tokenisation of Assets and Potential Implications for Financial Markets', OECD Blockchain Policy Series (2020), https://www.oecd.org/finance/The-Tokenisation-of-Assets-and-Potential-Implications-for-Financial-Markets.pdf

Tipotsch, Anna. 'Formulating a Smart Contract and Minting an NFT, atm', https://www.schoenherr.eu/content/formulating-a-smart-contract-and-minting-an-nft/

Trading Education (2021). 'Cryptocurrency Mining Explained', https://trading-education.com/cryptocurrency-mining-explained

Trevisi, C. Visconti, R. M., and Cesaretti, A. (2022). 'Non-Fungible Tokens (NFT): Business Models, Legal Aspects, and Market Valuation', *Rivista di Diritto dei Media*, https://www.medialaws.eu/rivista/non-fungible-tokens-nft-business-models-legal-aspects-and-market-valuation/

UAE Pass, https://icp.gov.ae/en/uae-pass/

Von Bar, C., and Drobnigc U, '*The Interaction of Contract Law and Tort and Property Law in Europe: A Comparative Study*', (Munich, Sellier de Gruyter, 004).

'What is Consortium Blockchain?', *Crypto News* (2021), https://crypto.news/glossary/consortium-blockchain/

Whittaker, M. (2022). 'How Does Bitcoin Mining Work?', https://www.forbes.com/advisor/investing/cryptocurrency/bitcoin-mining/

10 An Examination of the Tangible Value of IP Financing

Nadia Naim

Introduction

Due to the growth of emerging technologies and digitalisation, the gap between intellectual property progress between developed and developing countries has widened, as can be evidenced in the Global Innovation Index.[1] Despite international memberships to the World Trade Organisations (WTO) and the World Intellectual Property Organization (WIPO), many developing countries are struggling to meet their international obligations and more importantly, encourage innovation in their communities to develop a more sustainable intellectual property ecosystem.[2] There are several scholarly challenges around avoiding the potential for further disengagement at a local community level. This is significant because the research to date presents a significant challenge, but also an opportunity to aggregate and juxtapose location-specific research, offering the opportunity for the comparative study of IP development and innovation in different countries. By focusing on digital scholarship and educator outreach, an Islamic IP legal framework will lead to the development of alternatives in the intellectual property ecosystem that harmonise Islamic finance, digitalisation, ethics, and sustainability principles. Businesses and entrepreneurs in the GCC are faced with systemic problems resulting from insufficient national and international coordination, including lack of transparency and insufficient knowledge among right holders and the general public, concerning IP rights and remedies.[3] The new frameworks that are recommended will provide information about how to better access the intellectual property ecosystem and offer alternatives for growing the tech and creative economy, and linking the fields of intellectual property, Islamic finance, ethics, sustainability, and digitalisation to directly support new outcomes in area and development studies. By developing a new research area that focuses on the interests of the local businesses and entrepreneurs, and how to make innovation opportunities relevant, through bespoke

1 World Intellectual Property (2023), 'Global Innovation Index'. https://www.wipo.int/global_innovation_index/en/

2 Stephen Ezell and Nigel Cory (2019), *The Way Forward for Intellectual Property Internationally.* Washington, DC: Information Technology and the Innovation Foundation.

3 Nadia Naim (2020), 'Islamic Finance as a Vehicle to Promote Improved Intellectual Property Rights in the Gulf Co-operation Council (GCC)', *Law and Development Review Journal,* 13(2), August 2020, 407–42.

DOI: 10.4324/9781003528517-10

intellectual property valuation systems, the research offers a scalable opportunity for businesses in the GCC and in developing countries. The new frameworks will also be of interest to all businesses and entrepreneurs as they will demonstrate how the valuation systems represent deal equity, and are ethical and sustainable. Considerable investment in Islamic finance is carried out by non-Muslims.[4]

The GCC is unique as it offers a new opportunity for interaction between different countries across the region and the world on a novel area of research that is under studied and is a new area of innovation.[5] This will be the first global research endeavour on intellectual property law development that aims to harmonise the IP ecosystem with Islamic Finance Law to widen the participation of businesses and entrepreneurs in the GCC and local communities in developing countries. Diverging from the traditional academic model, the research will test out ideas, new products, and toolkits to measure their viability and productivity. The research will offer an accessible, cross-disciplinary, and efficient format to generate innovation, and build capacity.[6]

Build Research Capacity for Islamic IP Law in the GCC

The vision is to build research capacity for Islamic IP law in the GCC for the current digital revolution with emerging technologies and to find a way to harmonise IP and digital asset development with Islamic Finance Law, ethics, and sustainability goals.[7] The aim is to support innovative cross-disciplinary projects and pioneer new approaches to large scale global engagement. The project has the potential to advance current understanding of intellectual property law, generate new knowledge that harmonises the intellectual property field with Islamic/ethical financing and sustainability. The research creates a new field that goes beyond the existing intellectual property field and will seek to uncover innovative and creative ways to centre attention on benefiting local communities by addressing certain needs.[8] Timely impact given current trends and needs by encouraging innovation and inclusive knowledge-based societies for businesses and entrepreneurs in the GCC and in developing countries. Thirdly, to impact world leading research, society, the economy, and the environment by spearheading a new research area that

4 Martin Harrison (2018), *Islamic Finance and the UK*, Golcer Economic Report Series, Management School, Lancaster University, May 2018.

5 Yahya Anouti et al. (2018), *Beyond Bricks Building a High Impact Research Ecosystem in the GCC*. Idea Centre Insight. Strategy and PWC. https://www.strategyand.pwc.com/m1/en/reports/moving-beyond-bricks.pdf

6 Amer Al-Roubaie and Tariq Sharif Younis (2014), 'Building Innovation Capacity for Knowledge Creation in GCC Countries', *World Association for Sustainable Development,* 2014, 207–27.

7 Lukas Kudlimay, Douglas Aitkenhead, and Daniela Stratulativ (2021), *EU – GCC Dialogue on Economic Diversification Gulf Cooperation Council (GCC) Countries.* Project Identification No. EuropeAid/138630/DH/SER/Multi Service Contract No. PI/2017/393165 Study of the Intellectual Property Protection Regulatory frameworks of the GCC.

8 Antoine Nasr et al (2024), 'Community Development How GCC Social Reforms Are Poised to Protect and Develop Local Communities', *The FTI Delta Perspective,* 22 April 2024.

can demonstrate a measurable impact on the IP and Islamic finance economy, businesses, entrepreneurs, and society.

Rigorous academic research, co-produced in collaboration with practitioners and industry experts, is needed to design and implement scalable legal frameworks to boost business productivity by designing new intellectual property frameworks that are Islamic finance complaint as well as ethical and sustainable. The exact focus is on businesses and entrepreneurs in the GCC, who are failing on asset growth and productivity. There is an identifiable drop in intellectual property patent applications and the productivity of businesses is negatively impacted by the lack of alternatives to the digitalisation of assets and the IP ecosystem.[9] The research is designed to provide rigorous academic insights into how businesses and entrepreneurs who feel excluded from intellectual property asset management and revenue generation can be offered novel and inclusive alternatives that are complaint with ethics and Islamic finance practices to evidence how productivity and revenue generation can be enhanced.

There are three clear vision areas; to provide a detailed set of frameworks and toolkits for intellectual property practices and their relationship to productivity in businesses, with a focus on businesses and entrepreneurs who do not have alternatives to the current intellectual property valuation methods due to none of the current methods being compliant with Islamic finance and the circular economy. Next, to ensure that the intellectual property system is responsive to the current need of digital innovation in the intellectual property and Islamic finance fields by creating a new digital gateway that delivers measurable solutions. Most importantly, to solve real world problems in categorising and managing intellectual property assets that are compliant with Islamic finance and amplified by AI and evolving technology; engagement and change in the policy and law, tech industry and legal profession; developing a viable business model for valuing Intellectual property nationally in the GCC[10] and globally.

The above topics will be explored through three key research questions, as well as through continuous exchange of knowledge and best practices. They are as follows: how can we link the IP ecosystem to communities that follow Islamic Finance or ethical/sustainable practices,[11] how can we create products that can be compliant with Islamic finance and ethical/sustainable financing. Also to consider is how can digital technologies, the impact of Artificial Intelligence and the Industrial Revolution 4.0[12] shape the creation of a pilot model for value-based sustainability

9 Kseina Andreeva and Valentina Semenikhina (2023), 'Technology Transactions, Outsourcing, and Commercial Contracts News for Lawyers and Sourcing Professionals, 6 Things to Know About Intellectual Property Protection in the Middle East', *Tech and Sourcing @Morgan Lewis*, 24 May 2023, https://www.morganlewis.com/blogs/sourcingatmorganlewis/2023/05/6/6-things-to-know-about-intellectual-property-protection-in-the-middle-east

10 Noura AlZaid (2021), *Saudi Arabia and Intellectual Property: Learning from Chinas Approach*, King Faisal Center for Research and Islamic Studies, December 2021.

11 Jubran Siddique (2023), 'The Potential of Islamic Finance and Blockchain for Sustainability', *Forbes Business School,* Council Post, 7 August 2023

12 Fengwei Yang and Sai Gu (2021), 'Industry 4.0, a Revolution That Requires Technology and National Strategies', *Complex & Intelligent Systems*, 7, 1311–1325. https://doi.org/10.1007/s40747-020-00267-9

in digitalising IP rights. Guided by IP, Islamic Finance,[13] ethics, sustainability and emerging technologies experts, the research will focus on sharing practical examples from professional expertise and linking digitised resources available through research and industry work. By evaluating existing research, the project will lead to new recommendations that amalgamate intellectual property law with Islamic Finance Law; and explore the potential of co-creation of new datasets with industry leads, ministries, intellectual property offices, Islamic finance institutions, students, teachers, businesses, and industry.

There is a clear and transparent methodology built upon previous work that has carried out extensive research on the potential economic growth opportunities posed by creating new legal frameworks that merge intellectual property with Islamic finance. The objective is to further knowledge by developing novel toolkits and frameworks that build foundations for multi-disciplinary collaborations and to increase intellectual property growth for businesses and entrepreneurs in the GCC and in developing countries. The research is ambitious – it has regional, national and international impact potential. A multi-method approach which develops the frameworks to promote IP value and growth. It focuses on content analysis from existing research and surveys on intellectual property and Islamic Finance. Quantitative analysis will highlight challenges facing businesses and entrepreneurs to value their intellectual property assets that are compliant with Islamic finance and carry out a scoping exercise. The knowledge is shared and utilised with the industry stakeholders, with the aim of mapping and mobilising the IP ecosystem to the new set of Islamic finance benchmarking for IP valuation and commercialisation. National and international policy options will be identified, and evaluated with a pilot group of businesses who meet the criteria for participation in the prototype pilot. This leads to knowledge exchange and dissemination of the frameworks, it will involve knowledge exchange co-produced workshops with the IPO's, involve case studies from businesses and Islamic finance institutions. The aim of the research is to demonstrate how improved IP valuation can lead to economic growth, improving business outputs, and productivity.

Expansion of IP and Digital Assets Beyond Conventional Financing

Large scale projects into the expansion of IP and digital assets beyond conventional financing has been hindered by the lack of reliable data, expertise, and knowledge.[14] There are very few cases where IP assets have been utilised to form part of an Islamic finance structure and there are significant difficulties accessing the data

13 United Nations Development Programme (2023), *Case Studies on Innovations in Islamic Finance*. Islamic Development Bank, at https://www.undp.org/islamic_finance_june_2023

14 Christopher Foster (2023), 'Intellectual Property Rights and Control in the Digital Economy: Examining the Expansion of M-Pesa', *The Information Society*, 40(1), 1–17. https://doi.org/10.1080/01972243.2023.225989 5

as they are private financing ventures, leading to limited literature.[15] The research will develop a database of re-useable resources in the form of new frameworks to resolve many of these issues for this project and for further research. The database will collectively contain every type of intellectual property asset, intangibles, emerging technology, digital assets, and then map them to Islamic finance, ethical financing, sustainability, and the circular economy. This has not been available for research before. This represents a significant new resource, and methodological innovation. The pre-processing task to convert such data into a safe format suitable for semi-automatic analysis is considerable, but the value lies in the resultant fully categorised inclusive IP with corresponding alternative financing products that can be available to businesses and financial institutions to bring marginalised communities into the mainstream.

The Ethical and Philosophical Underpinning of Islamic Law

The foundational principles underlying Islamic business law are rooted in the broader ethical and moral framework of Islamic jurisprudence.[16] These principles include the core areas of justice and fairness.[17] Islamic business transactions aim to ensure that all parties are treated equitably and that transactions are conducted with integrity and honesty.[18] Key to this is the avoidance of harm to society as Islamic law prohibits transactions that cause harm or are detrimental to individuals or the wider society.[19] This reflects the essence of the objective of Sharia known as the Maqasid Al Sharia.[20] This principle emphasises the importance of considering the broader impact of business transactions. Mutual consent underpins the contractual obligations under Islamic law with the requirement of consent to both make an offer and accept it. Contracts in Islamic business transactions require the mutual consent of all parties involved. This ensures that transactions are entered into willingly and without coercion. Prohibition of riba[21] (interest) and gharar (speculative risk) are at the foundation of Islamic law and prohibit transactions and business

15 Nadia Naim (2020), 'Islamic Finance as a Vehicle to Promote Improved Intellectual Property Rights in the Gulf Cooperation Council', *Law and Development Review*, 13(2), 407–442. https://doi.org/10.1515/ldr-2020-0050

16 K. Hassan et al (2013), *Introduction to Islamic Banking and Finance: Principles and Practice*. London: Pearson.

17 F. Ahmad (2012), 'Philosophical Underpinnings of Islamic Management Method: Worldview, Epistemology and Ontology', *International Journal of Humanities and Social Science, 2*(20), 150–61.

18 Ahmad Hasan (1968), 'The Source of Islamic Law', *Islamic Studies*, 7(1), 165–84.

19 Mahmoud El-Gamal (2023), *Islamic Finance: Law, Economics, and Practice*. Cambridge: Cambridge University Press.

20 Dato' Seri Dr. Awang Adek Hussin (2023), *Maqasid Al-Shariah Guidance Islamic Capital Market Malaysia*. Kuala Lumpur: Securities Commission Malaysia

21 Walid Mansour, Ben J. Khoutem and Majdoub Jihed (2015), 'How Ethical is Islamic Banking in the Light of the Objectives of Islamic Law?' *Journal of Religious Ethics*, *43*(1), 51–77.

dealings that involve riba and gharar.[22] This is based on the Islamic law principle that transactions should be based on clear and certain terms where there is a shared risk and profit-making parameters.[23] Halal and haram has been widely defined by the primary sources of Islamic law and for commercial law transactions they can fall into two main categories: halal (permissible) and haram (prohibited).[24] Halal transactions are those that are conducted in accordance with Islamic principles and are free from any prohibited elements. Haram transactions, on the other hand, are those that involve prohibited goods or practices, such as alcohol, pork, gambling, or usury. The concept of halal and haram transactions is significant in shaping business practices in Islamic law. It provides a clear framework for determining the permissibility of transactions and helps ensure that business activities are conducted in accordance with Islamic principles.[25] By adhering to the principles of halal and avoiding haram transactions, businesses can operate in a manner that is ethical, sustainable, and in line with Islamic values.[26]

The concept of contracts in Islamic law has been defined and elaborated on through legal theories and concepts that govern various types of contracts. In Islamic contract law, contracts are known as "Aqd" and are considered essential in establishing mutual rights and obligations. A contract is formed through an offer (Ijab) from one party and an acceptance (Qabul) from the other, both made in the same meeting. Several legal theories and concepts govern contracts in Islamic law, including: Ijab and Qabul, stating the offer and acceptance must be clearly expressed, unambiguous, and made in the same meeting. Consideration is required for there to be a valid contract, it requires an exchange of something of value, between the parties involved. The contract should be clear and certain in respect of terms and conditions. Both parties must have the legal capacity to enter into a contract, including being of sound mind and not under coercion, and there needs to be consensus whereby contracts are based on mutual agreement and consensus between the parties. This satisfies the legality of the contracts as they must be lawful according to Islamic law and should not involve prohibited transactions such as gambling or interest-based transactions. The legal concepts ensure that contracts in Islamic law are fair, just, and uphold the principles of Sharia in its holistic overview of belief, law, and ethics.

In Islamic commercial transactions, several contracts are forbidden due to their involvement with prohibited goods or unethical practices. The rationale behind the

22 Mohammed Akhtar Uddin (2015), *Principles of Islamic Finance: Prohibition of Riba, Gharar and Maysir*. Munich: Munich Personal RePEc Archive.

23 Abdurrahman Raden Aji Haqqi (2009), *The Philosophy of Islamic Law of Transactions*. CERT Publications, Negri Sembilan, Malaysia.

24 Nimrah Karim, Mohammed Tarazi, and Xavier Reille (2008), *Islamic Microfinance: An Emerging Market Niche*. Focus Note 49. Washington, DC: CGAP, August.

25 Mohammed Obaidullah (2005), *Islamic Financial Services*. Jeddah, Saudi Arabia: Islamic Economics Research Center, King Abdulaziz University.

26 Camille Paldi (2014), 'Understanding Riba and Gharar in Islamic Finance', *Journal of Islamic Banking and Finance, 2*(1), 250–259.

prohibition of these contracts is to promote fairness, justice, and ethical conduct in business transactions. Islamic law emphasises the importance of mutual consent, fairness, and consideration for the well-being of others in all dealings. By prohibiting contracts that involve harm, exploitation, or unfairness, Islamic law aims to protect individuals and society as a whole from unethical practices. The implications for Islamic business conduct are significant. Islamic ethics require businesses to engage in transactions that are fair, transparent, and beneficial to all parties involved. This means avoiding contracts that involve prohibited goods, gambling, uncertainty, or exploitation. Instead, businesses are encouraged to engage in transactions that promote mutual benefit, trust, and Islamic ethical behaviour. The GCC countries all have some level of Islamic law compliance. Unlike other international regional blocs such as the EU, the GCC is unique in that all its member states are Islamic states.[27] Each individual state has varying degrees of Islamic law incorporated in their constitutions, with the Kingdom of Saudi Arabia having Islamic law as the constitution and is the most observant of all the GCC states.[28] The GCC states are all compliant with international intellectual property standards, the trade related intellectual property rights (TRIPS), and thus are uniquely placed as the forefront region to lead on creating new legal frameworks for Islamic law compliant intellectual property frameworks.

Conventional Intellectual Property Financing

Intellectual property for conventional finance, as assets to be valued and protected, have robust and extensive valuation methods that apply to conventional finance and banking practices.[29] IP protects the competitive edge of a business and is a competitive advantage, it creates barriers to entry for competitors and freedom to operate. Management and investors are well motivated to maintain and retain it, even if difficulties arise as it supports customer lock-ins and as a result sustains cash flows as well as enabling scale. Unlike tangible assets, IP assets don't depreciate with time and the more widely adopted, the more valuable they become.[30] There are three main valuation methods: cost, market, and income based. All three have their advantages and disadvantages. An analysis of how they work will offer valuable insight into their applicability to the GCC states and to an alternative Islamic finance model. IP needs to be valued through the cost of acquisition or the development of the IP in order to bring intangible assets like patents, copyrights and trademarks onto the balance sheet.[31]

27 Hazem Beblawi, and Giacomo Luciani (1987), *The Rentier State*. London: Croom Helm.

28 Nadia Naim (2023), *Islamic Legal Principles and Intellectual Property Rights in the Gulf States*. Berlin: Gerlach Press, 2023.

29 Janice Denoncourt (2018), *Intellectual Property, Finance and Corporate Governance*. 1st ed. London: Routledge and Taylor and Francis Group.

30 Nicola Searle and Martin Brassell (2016), *Economic Approaches to Intellectual Property*. Oxford: Oxford University Press.

31 Martin Brassell, (2023), *Unlocking IP-backed Financing Series Country Perspective. The United Kingdom's Journey*, WIPO and UK Intellectual Property Office (Geneva, WIPO, 2023)

The income approach values the IP asset, on the basis of the amount of economic benefit the asset is expected to generate, adjusted to its current value. It is the most used of all the methods, as it is seen to be the most reliable and incorporates externally verified market information to quantify what someone else would pay for the IP assets.[32] The focus is on the contribution the IP assets make to current and future sales or profits, as well as the cost savings that can be attributed to these assets. The income approach is a widely used method as it considers what someone else would pay to license the IP.[33] As a valuation method it appeals to businesses as the most relevant to them for meeting business needs as the incentive for carrying out an IP audit and IP valuation is to have quantifiable data on the IP assets that take into account the benefit from future IP value, be it measured. A substitute method of the income approach is the relief from royalties method to assess IP royalties. It is based on an assessment of what royalty costs a company is avoiding by virtue of owning the IP right. The relief from royalty costs are essentially quantifying how much the business would have to pay to license the assets in, if, the company did not own the IP assets. This cash flow of royalty payments, based on a percentage of forecast revenues, is then adjusted to current value. The measurement however is perceived and as a result, it makes the income approach the riskiest of the three valuation methods.[34] The value from the IP assets can be hard to isolate, future projections can be uncertain, especially if market traction is limited to date. For the Islamic finance sector, the income-based approach would be the most difficult to reconcile with the tenets of Islamic law and to ensure it doesn't contravene principles of riba and gharar.

The cost method on the other hand would contravene riba and gharar the least, as it is valued on the cost of developing an identical or similar asset, either internally or externally. As a method, it would meet several Islamic law principles of certainty and Islamic legal maxims however it is the least attractive method for the IP asset holding business. As a method, the cost approach seeks to determine the value of an IP asset at a particular point of time by aggregating the direct expenditures and opportunity costs involved in its development. The approach can involve calculating the cost to replace the IP asset with an equivalent asset of similar use and function. This can be used reliably in practice when it comes to a going concern valuation, provided you have access to detailed information relating to historic costs, which is more applicable to assets still in development. IP assets expected to provide an economic benefit and generate revenue are more favourably calculated using the income approach. The cost method is the clearest on how it can be used, in its simplest terms, it reflects the investment made in the IP assets. The valuation is modelled from real data on labour, direct costs and overheads, appropriately

32 Nadia Naim (2024), *Developments in Intellectual Property Strategy - The Impact of Artificial Intelligence, Robotics and New Technologies*. London: Palgrave MacMillan.

33 Asia Pacific Economic Cooperation (2018), *Intellectual Property (IP) Valuation Manual: A Preliminary Guide*. APEC Intellectual Property Experts Group, Singapore, 2018.

34 U.K Intellectual Property Office (2014), *Guidance on Valuing Your Intellectual Property*, London, 2014.

adjusted. However, it is often considered the worst of the three methods as cost is hardly ever a full reflection of the value created. It can include historical investments that are not productive, it ignores the blocking effect of the IP itself and is not forward-looking.[35]

The market based approach is the third valuation method and focuses on what the comparable market prices are for the IP assets. This method looks at comparable assets that have been sold on the open market as well as if the businesses owning the comparable assets have also been sold. Investment data is important to quantify how much businesses owning comparable assets are worth and the amount companies are paying to license-in these assets.[36] The market approach would be attractive to Islamic finance banks and institutions as it is designed to replicate the valuation of tangible assets. Of all the three methods, it is the most like tangible assets as it is based on prior factual transactions. The IP right holders are not putting the intangible assets on sale, instead are utlising data on comparable assets. The issue of course is that the comparable data is not as readily available in the intangible market place as it is in the tangible assets of bricks and mortar. There are several reasons for this including the transfer of assets in merger and acquisition deals, comparability between assets is low and often there are no obvious multiples.[37]

An Alternative Islamic Finance Valuation Model

Islamic finance outperformed conventional finance in the global crisis in 2007.[38] This is important as the resilience and robustness of Islamic finance can be expanded into the digital sphere. Given the desire of the GCC countries to be more knowledge-based societies, and their adherence to Islamic law, it makes the GCC countries the ideal choice to be the leading innovative countries in the world of IP and Islamic finance. The UK is also unique as the only country in the world that is a global leader on IP and Islamic finance. There is clear synergy between the GCC states and the UK as both can provide critical contributions to the success of the expansion of Islamic finance into the IP valuation game. Islamic finance is embedded with rules on ethics as required by Islamic law and can offer a fourth valuation method that is not only Islamic finance compliant but also ethical and meets

35 Martin Brassell and Jackie Maguire (2017), , *Hidden Value: A Study of the UK IP Valuation Market.* (Newport, Wales, Intellectual Property Office, 2017).

36 Claire Howell and David Bainbridge (2014), *Intellectual Property Asset Management: How to Identify, Protect, Manage and Exploit Intellectual Property within the Business Environment.* (Abingdon, Oxon: Routledge).

37 Searle and Brassell (n 30).

38 Alimshan Faizulayev (2021), 'What Drives the Banking Competition in Islamic Finance-oriented Countries? Islamic vs Conventional Banks', *Journal of Islamic Accounting and Business Research*, vol. 12(4), 457-72.

environmental, social, and governance goals (ESG). A factor appealing to the large young population in the GCC countries, in the UK, and globally.[39]

Intellectual property as an asset class continues to grow in value and accounts for a substantial value of a business. For example, the value of the top 5000 global brands increased from USD 11 trillion in 2020 to over USD 12 trillion in 2022, by 14 percent.[40]

The Global Innovation Index (GII) tracks global innovation trends and ranks the most innovative economies in the world, for the innovation performance of around 132 economies while highlighting innovation strengths and weaknesses. The UK ranks fourth on the GII, as of 2022, and puts the UK at the forefront of IP knowledge, and as a leader on IP policy and protection. From an international development point of view, it makes the UK an attractive country to enter into free trade agreements with[41] and establish MoU's for IP enforcement and development in the GCC. As well as its strengths in IP, the UK is the leading non-Muslim country when it comes to Islamic Finance. The global market size for Islamic Finance is estimated at USD 3 trillion, according to the most recent Islamic Financial Services Industry Stability Report.[42] The UK has an established Islamic Finance sector and the UK Government issues the largest sovereign backed sukuk (bond), of a non-Muslim country at £500 million.[43] The expansion of IP into the Islamic Finance community has been adhoc at best. The rationale behind this report is to develop an overall framework that can be utilised by the UK Government and the UK IPO in its collaborative efforts with countries that comply with Islamic Finance as well as the impact the framework report can have on the UK's levelling up agenda. Fundamental to the success of Islamic finance is that it has created Sharia compliant alternatives to conventional financial products. The intellectual property field has not done this and as a result intellectual property rights have failed to shake off their "foreigner rights" image. There is legislation and rules in place to prohibit riba and gharar in intellectual property, however Islamic finance has gone one step further and developed an Islamic version of conventional financial products. To succeed in developing an integrated approach to intellectual property, the UK Government and IPO can be the leading country to support the GCC and wider, the Global South countries, in developing alternative Sharia compliant structures to existing intellectual property assets. There are systematic flaws in the GCC and Global South countries adopting foreign intellectual property from colonial occupation or laws taken from donor countries. There is a strong dichotomy that

39 Alexander Gelfand (2022), *The ESG Generation Gap: Millennials and Boomers Split on Their Investing Goals*. Insights by Stanford Business, 10 November 2022,

40 Annie Brown, Artur Bryzghalov, Lorena Rivera León and Sacha Wunsch-Vincent (2023), *The Value of the World's Most Valuable Brands Grew to USD 12 Trillion*. Geneva, WIPO, 2023.

41 Nadia Naim (2022), *Free Trade Agreement Negotiations with the Gulf Cooperation Council*, House of Commons Committee report, Seventh Report of Session 2022–23. UK Parliament, London.

42 Islamic Financial Services Industry Stability Report (2023). https://www.ifsb.org/wp-content/uploads/2023/10/Islamic-Financial-Services-Industry-Stability-Report-2023_En.pdf

43 HM Treasury (2021), *UK Bolsters Islamic Finance Offering with Second Sukuk*. UK Government, London.

exists between the religious characteristics of the GCC countries and others such as Malaysia and Indonesia, and the intellectual property laws that exist under western legal principles. Therefore the adopted foreign laws, as they stand, are unsuitable and require modification. The Islamic intellectual property legal framework is of equal relevance to the UK's Islamic finance investment community as well as the GCC countries. Law, remedies, and penalties are only part of an IP strategy, what is needed is a transparent IP system that is well managed.

The strongest priorities are identified as avoiding interest and speculative risk. To ensure pertinent priorities are covered, and an area isn't missed, we asked participants to list further priorities that we hadn't included. The other areas include: to enable risks to be shared equitably, profit and loss sharing, ethical based consideration factored into dispute consideration and resolution, to uphold the Maqasid al-Sharia and practice the "real" Islamic finance, to promote business innovation, avoid non-compliance with Islamic law, solutions for countries from crumbling sovereign debt by applying Islamic financing principles appropriately, and for it to be in line with religious values. Intellectual property as an asset class for use in Islamic finance lacks legislative and policy frameworks and guidance. As a result, the understanding of IP in Islamic finance is limited and requires legal procedure to create a benchmark that can be used nationally and internationally.

In Islamic banking and financial institutions, investment products are structured in strict accordance with Sharia rulings, resolutions and standards issued by Sharia standard setting bodies, for example, the Accounting and Auditing Organization for Islamic Financial Institutions (AAOIFI), the International Islamic Fiqh Academy (IFA), and the Sharia Advisory Council of Central Bank of Malaysia. This highlights the strength of Sharia rulings, resolutions, and standards with an emphasis on the value it holds with Islamic banks and financial institutions. Any IP and IF products created require both legal and Islamic Sharia ruling approval. The IFA and AAOIFI have all passed resolutions to identify intellectual property rights as Sharia complaint and approve the financial rights arising from intellectual property. However, there are no Islamic finance investment products that allow businesses to monetise their intellectual property assets in the same way as tangible assets and there are no such products readily available.

There is a lot of hesitation from Islamic finance institutions and banks to leverage IP assets for lending, securitization, equity funding, or collateral. Despite official resolutions, Islamic banks and Islamic financial institutions don't have a valuation model for intellectual property assets to meet Islamic finance lending requirements. The main concerns are that IP assets cannot generate regular revenue, are personal, and cannot, for example, be sold to sukuk (Islamic bonds) investors against subscription. The underlying issue is the lack of knowledge on how IP assets can be Sharia compliant. Lack of capacity building efforts, such as human capital investment in IP laws, officers, judiciary, education, regulation, and enforcement has strained efforts to expand the Islamic finance sector into the IP ecosystem. As the GCC countries are now in a period of exponential growth with ambitious national strategies to be knowledge-based societies, the window to develop an informed valuation system for innovation in the IP ecosystem in the region, is now.

Criticisms of Islamic IP is that the IP assets are too abstract, they lead to uncertainty and lack of clarity on the valuation of the assets.[44] The Islamic finance institutions and banks prefer the same entities who own IP assets to provide other Sharia compliant tangible and acceptable assets for fund raising. The Quran and Sunnah are silent on intellectual property rights and as such Islamic banks and institutions are hesitant to approve Islamic finance products with intellectual property assets.[45] Further, there is a lack of awareness of IP as an asset class for the purpose of financing and investment. To be able to fully utilise the value of IP assets, audits and due diligence requirements need to be part of the regulations. When a company can detail the value of the IP assets on the balance sheet, it can be used as collateral to raise financing. For specific industries, IP is often the strongest asset and companies are not necessarily cash rich, however have valuable IP. For patents in IT/AI inventions and data-based business' products will have IP rich assets that, if valued accurately/correctly, could be leveraged successfully. Societal and cultural perceptions of IP as an IF compliant product are a challenge and the influence of society and cultural attitudes on IP acceptance needs to be addressed. IP assets are seen as foreign products and their infringement is not taken seriously by the public.[46]

There are also criticisms of the Islamic finance sector – there is no universal standard or rule for all the Sharia boards to follow globally and within each country.[47] Essentially, each Islamic finance institution's Sharia board decision is autonomous and not binding on any other institution. Uniform laws are lacking for Sharia boards at an international level. The decision of one Sharia board is not binding on another and therefore can lead to different outcomes depending on which Sharia board a country follows.[48] Lack of transparency and political issues impact the Sharia boards despite Islamic jurisprudence supporting independent Sharia boards that are not influenced by executive management. Legal rights and remits of the Sharia scholars in relation to IP rights is not clearly defined. Lack of understanding of the role of Sharia scholars in the development of an IP and IF industry. This issue can be addressed by developing the legal framework that can act as a model law for IP and IF law across jurisdictions as different jurisdictions have national laws with Sharia law influence at varying degrees. Issues arise on how best to

44 Sarmad Manto (2023), 'Intellectual Property and the Islamic Shari'a', *Managing IP*. https://www.managingip.com/article/2b9cfs9j28w979iivvqps/expert-analysis/intellectual-property-and-the-islamic-sharia

45 Nadia Naim, Islamic Legal Principles (n 27).

46 Noura El Bialy and Moamen Gouda (2011), 'Can Shari'a be a Deterrent for Intellectual Property Piracy in Islamic Countries?' *Journal of World Intellectual Property*, *14*(6), 441–66.

47 José Viñals and Masood Ahmed (2015), *Islamic Finance: Opportunities, Challenges, and Policy Options, Prepared by Alfred Kammer, Mohamed Norat, Marco Piñón, Ananthakrishnan Prasad, Christopher Towe, Zeine Zeidane, and an IMF Staff Team*. International Monetary Fund. https://www.imf.org/external/pubs/ft/sdn/2015/sdn1505.pdf

48 Mona Siddiqui (2018), 'The Independent Review into the Application of Sharia Law in England and Wales', Presented to Parliament by the Secretary of State for the Home Department by Command of Her Majesty. https://assets.publishing.service.gov.uk/media/5a750e8040f0b6397f35d531/6.4152_HO_CPFG_Report_into_Sharia_Law_in_the_UK_WEB.pdf

regulate an IP and IF industry, what measures would be in place to deal with ethics, conduct, market manipulation, and maintain asset stability.

Within the potential marketplace there is a lack of exemplars of successful application of IP/Islamic finance products that can demonstrate beneficial results to all parties.[49] Criticism of lack of motivation for innovation in IF due to several hurdles such as internationally accepted frameworks. IP is internationally standardised by the World Intellectual Property Office, however there is no equivalent World Islamic Finance Office. The attention to detail is crucial to the successful launch of an IF and IP market. Creating products that meet IF standards is only one element of the bigger process. The issue can be resolved by adopting a regulation and auditing framework for IF and IP Sharia boards, have a Sharia compliant structure in place for each type of intellectual property right and develop intellectual property-based assets within an Islamic finance structure. The legal framework for the IF and IP sector will need to be robust and embed existing Sharia principles of property law, contract law, and public international law to intellectual property law.

An IP and IF industry proposal needs to consider the digital economy as a whole and understand non-fungible tokens (NFTs), blockchain, and fintech.[50] Patents, licenses, software development in the fields of AI, blockchain, and other transformational technological advances are the main structures of monetising revenue streams.[51] IP-backed Islamic financing provides a Sharia compliant solution for individuals and businesses to utilise their intellectual property assets in various fields, including technology startups,[52] product development, franchising, brand expansion, content production, royalty financing, research and development projects, trademark licensing, IP monetisation, and projects related to Islamic art and culture.[53]

There is also an opportunity for industry specific innovation in the GCC countries.[54] For research institutions, there is potential benefit to universities and research institutions that can leverage their IP portfolios to secure funding for

49 German based FWU group, with its subsidiary in Dubai, developed the first ever intellectual property based sukuk worth $55 million in 2012. Islamic Finance News (2012), 'Germany's FWU Group Issues Largest Sukuk Out of Europe'. https://www.islamicfinancenews.com/germanys-fwu-group-issues-largest-sukuk-out-of-europe.html

50 Unal Ibrahim Musa and Ahmet Faruk Aysan (2022), 'Fintech, Digitalization, and Blockchain in Islamic Finance: Retrospective Investigation', *FinTech* 1(4), 388–398. https://doi.org/10.3390/fintech1040029

51 Dhruv Saini (2024), 'How AI is Changing the Game in Patent Monetization Strategies?' *XLSCout.* https://xlscout.ai/how-ai-is-changing-the-game-in-patent-monetization-strategies

52 Alhanoof Alghamdi (2017), *The Viability of Profit-Loss Sharing Models to Finance Small and Medium Enterprises: The Case of Saudi Arabia*. University of Denver. https://digitalcommons.du.edu/cgi/viewcontent.cgi?article=2365&context=etd

53 Tabrez Y. Ebrahim (2021), 'Intellectual Property Through a Non-Western Lens: Patents in Islamic Law', *Georgia State University Law Review*, 37, 789. https://readingroom.law.gsu.edu/gsulr/vol37/iss3/5

54 Aisha Al-Sarihi (2021), *What's Keeping GCC States from Unlocking Their Innovation Potential? Middle East Institute*. National University of Singapore. https://mei.nus.edu.sg/think_in/whats-keeping-gcc-states-from-unlocking-their-innovation-potential/

research and development.[55] For pharmaceutical and biotech companies, IP-backed IF can fund drug development and research, often a costly and lengthy process. For the entertainment industry, the creative and media companies with valuable copyright can explore IF options for production and distribution. For manufacturing and engineering firms with patented technologies or unique engineering design rights, they can utilise IF for expansion or project financing. For art and creative ventures, artists, designers, and creators can seek funding for their intellectual property-backed projects, ensuring protection and profitability.

There are various mechanisms Islamic banks and financial institutions could use to exercise control over IP assets and intangibles, such as sale and licence-back mechanisms, specific security, equity based or profit-loss sharing funding arrangement, inclusion within a debenture, and these could work efficiently. Mudarabah and Musharakah could be useful mechanisms. In a Mudarabah, the bank provides the capital, and the company manages the intellectual property as the working partner. Profits are shared based on a pre-agreed ratio. In Musharakah, both parties contribute capital, and profits and losses are shared accordingly using equity based or profit-loss sharing funding arrangement. IB's offer a wide spectrum of fee-based services using three types of contracts – wakalah, kafalah, or ju'ala. The aim would be to allow banks to use intangibles as collateral in their corporate funding. There is an opportunity to develop possible securitization of IP rights and use them as collateral. The question raised is on who has control over the property used as security and to what degree, as this will impact the validity of the IP and IF product to be used as security under Islamic law. How different types of IP rights/assets can be in control of the lender requires assessment and measures to create a model that supports innovation and respects Islamic law. Efficiency of an IP and IF model hinges on transparency, proper valuation of IP assets, and adherence to Sharia compliant contracts. Companies and banks need to work closely with Islamic finance experts and legal advisors to ensure that the chosen mechanism complies with Islamic finance principles and meets their financial objectives.[56] Risk management, deal certainty, security, guarantees, and legal remedies would all need to be part of the IP and IF model in the GCC countries.

Recommendations for a GCC–Led IP and IF Model

The main recommendations are to develop a GCC–led IP and IF commercialisation strategy. A commercialisation team that consists of a collective with an IP Sharia counsel/advisory, a commercial audit team, IP valuation and auditor, due diligence and licensing agreement contract lawyers with legal expertise in contract

55 Nevin Koshy (2020), 'Securing Patent Rights in the Evolving GCC Region', *Lawyer Monthly*. https://www.lawyer-monthly.com/2020/07/securing-patent-rights-in-the-evolving-gcc-region/

56 Hennie van Greuning and Zamir Iqbal (2008), *Risk Analysis for Islamic Banks*. The World Bank. https://documents1.worldbank.org/curated/en/688471468143973824/pdf/424810PUB00ISB101OFFICIAL0USE0ONLY1.pdf

law, IP law, regulatory controls, and securities will all support an efficient IP commercialisation system in IF. An Islamic evaluation, that demonstrates compliance with Islamic law, should be part of the overall evaluation of assets. Duration of IP asset validity is relevant as IP protection length varies depending on the type of IP asset. Financing IP can be both short term and long term depending on the growth of these products. If the IP is valued with a clear structure, is transparent in terms of details, and the model does not involve interest and uncertainty, is backed by qualified professionals to value the IP, then the Islamic finance institution can trade it, raise money and treat it as a tradeable commodity using any of the available products used by IF. Sale and leaseback (Ijarah), where in this mechanism the company sells its IP assets to the financial institution, and then the financial institution leases the assets back to the company. The company pays rent for using the assets. This allows the financial institution to generate income from the IP while maintaining ownership.

Embedding Sharia principles of contract law to develop IP and IF structures through incorporating Sharia compliant doctrines of contract law, principles of mutual consent, and gainful exchange to the protection of knowledge-based assets and promulgate Islamic law-based ethics to intellectual property rights protection. A Sharia compliant authentication process for intellectual property rights protection highlight the protection of economic and moral rights from an Islamic perspective. This can then apply Islamic law-based protection for intellectual property rights as an acknowledgment for the time, labour, and efforts of the inventor. Under Islamic law, property law dictates on: the ownership of property, the right to possess and enjoy wealth through lawful means, and the doctrine of mutual consent. For an IP and IF model to have an impact on economic growth, the quantification of the asset and the consequential loss necessitates compliance within set parameters similar to how Islamic finance has sought to limit speculative loss in property law, intellectual property law can develop Sharia compliant remedies which can implement control measures that would allow intellectual property rights protection to be more fit for purpose in IF. Market demand is key to the IF industry investing in an IP model. An IP that is in high demand would attract customers to the business, which in turn would increase its financial performance. The most direct way to think about what IP is worth, is in terms of their valuation on balance sheets which can formulated based on standardised regulation. IP has several avenues which will each require their own parameters such as royalties and revenue streams.

Islamic finance may involve the issuance of sukuk (Islamic bonds) backed by IP assets. The value of the IP is crucial in determining the sukuk's attractiveness to investors. Securitization structures must comply with Sharia principles. A strong recommendation is to delve deeper into the legal maxims of IF, rather than mirror the actions of commercial finance. This is the strongest recommendation as the aim of the research is not to create a weakly aligned alternative to conventional financing for IP but a robust legal framework that has taken into account the requirements of the relevant Islamic law and IP law to create a new IP and IF industry that has real impact for Islamic banks, Islamic financial institutions, and the customers. It will need proper guidelines and indices to be able to measure the IP, standard on pricing, value of amoritisation in the market imposed by the regulators instead of depreciation for tangible assets. The concerns on the uncertainty of the value of intellectual property as opposed to tangible assets and the impact to the business can be reduced by benchmarking the IP asset against market value and industry performance. The more structures that are developed and launched in the marketplace to measure performance of the IP owning entities, would create more certainty on the value of the IP assets.

Further recommendations are to devise IP investment portfolios to guide business direction and strategy by appointing board members and maintaining regular consultations with management and directors. IP investments can leverage the knowledge of IP advisors and a network of experts in enterprise, and entrepreneurship management and operations. Strive to maximise the value of its investments through a vast network of capital market contacts, including venture investors, investment banks, and hedge funds to achieve timely realisations of its investments, which may come from strategic sales, successful licensing or litigation, initial public offerings, or royalty streams. Board appointments and ongoing consultations with directors and management influence their business direction and strategy. IP portfolio investments can benefit from the expertise of IP advisors and a network of experts in enterprise and entrepreneurial company management and operations.

Conclusion

The chapter has focused on the need for an Islamic law compliant IP system in the GCC and to effectively establish the need for a new industry by recommending the need for novel legal frameworks for a value-based intellectual property and emerging technology model that is Islamic finance compliant. The research has offered an opportunity to address the challenges and barriers to intellectual property growth, emerging technology and innovation, develop new strategies, and methodologies for encouraging innovation in the GCC and Association of Southeast Asian Nations (ASEAN) region which has been the focus of the research on how to harmonise intellectual property law with Islamic Finance Laws.

The key theme has been on innovation and more inclusive knowledge-based societies in the GCC, and more widely internationally, by establishing a common framework for linking data about the hesitancy towards intellectual property and emerging technology development in the GCC to improve the understanding of the positive impact of intellectual property (IP), and develop novel legal framework models that can be used by businesses and entrepreneurs to extract the value of intangible and digital assets in their business.

The research had three clear vision areas: first to provide a detailed need for frameworks and toolkits for intellectual property practices and their relationship to productivity in businesses, with a focus on businesses and entrepreneurs who do not have alternatives to the current intellectual property valuation methods due to none of the current methods being compliant with Islamic finance and the circular economy. Second, to ensure that the intellectual property system is responsive to the current need of digital innovation in the intellectual property and Islamic finance fields by recommending a new valuation system that delivers measurable solutions. Third, to solve real world problems in categorising and managing intellectual property assets that are compliant with Islamic finance and amplified by AI and evolving technology; that can lead to engagement and change in the policy and law, creative industries and the legal profession whilst developing a viable model for valuing intellectual property in the GCC and globally. The UK as a leading institution on IP valuation can provide the necessary regulatory, capacity building, and human resource management expertise to support the creation of an Islamic IP Finance model that can be launched in the GCC countries and more widely in the region. The research has timely impact given current trends and needs by encouraging innovation and inclusive knowledge-based societies for businesses and entrepreneurs in the GCC and in developing countries.

The chapter has addressed the challenges to an Islamic IP finance model and dealt with the core hesitancies of the IF sector towards IP. The hesitation stems from Islamic finance institutions and banks and how to leverage IP assets for lending, securitization, equity funding or collateral. Despite official resolutions, Islamic banks and Islamic financial institutions don't have a valuation model for intellectual property assets to meet Islamic finance lending requirements. The main concerns have been that IP assets cannot generate regular revenue. By addressing the lack of knowledge on how IP assets can be Sharia compliant, increasing capacity building efforts, such as human capital investment in IP laws, officers, judiciary, education, regulation, and enforcement can invigorate efforts to expand the Islamic finance sector into the IP ecosystem. The GCC countries have made clear their vision to grow as knowledge-based societies, and the timeliness of the research aligns very well to the GCC national visions as it is relevant to the communities at large in the region, adheres to religious beliefs and supports economic growth. The overall recommendation is to value IP and IP-rich businesses in IF using a holistic approach, considering factors like financial performance, development stage, and adherence to Sharia principles. Key considerations include transparent asset valuation, profitability, risk management, market demand, legal protections, ethical considerations, Sharia compliance, long-term sustainability, market comparable, and the choice of Sharia compliant financing structures. A tiered, tailored approach can determine value, taking into account the specific circumstances and principles of IF.

Bibliography

Ahmad, F. (2012) 'Philosophical Underpinnings of Islamic Management Method: Worldview, Epistemology and Ontology', *International Journal of Humanities and Social Science*1. 2(20), 150–161.

Alghamdi, A. (2017) The Viability of Profit-Loss Sharing Models to Finance Small and Medium Enterprises: The Case of Saudi Arabia, University of Denver, https://digitalcommons.du.edu/cgi/viewcontent.cgi?article=2365&context=etd

Al-Roubaie, A. and Younis, T. S. (2014) Building Innovation Capacity for Knowledge Creation in GCC Countries. World Association of Sustainable Development 2014, 207–227.

Al-Sarihi (2021) What's Keeping GCC States from Unlocking Their Innovation Potential? Middle East Institute, National University of Singapore, https://mei.nus.edu.sg/think_in/whats-keeping-gcc-states-from-unlocking-their-innovation-potential/

AlZaid, N. (2021) Saudi Arabia and Intellectual Property: Learning from Chinas Approach. King Faisal Center for Research and Islamic Studies. December 2021.

Andreeva, K. and Semenikhina, V. (2023) Technology Transactions, Outsourcing, and Commercial Contracts News for Lawyers and Sourcing Professionals, 6 Things to Know About Intellectual Property Protection in the Middle East. Tech and Sourcing @Morgan Lewis, 24 May 2023. https://www.morganlewis.com/blogs/sourcingatmorganlewis/2023/05/6/6-things-to-know-about-intellectual-property-protection-in-the-middle-east

Anouti, Y. et al. (2018) 'Beyond Bricks Building a High Impact Research Ecosystem in the GCC', *Idea Centre Insight. Strategy and PWC,* https://www.strategyand.pwc.com/m1/en/reports/moving-beyond-bricks.pdf

Asia Pacific Economic Cooperation (2018) *Intellectual Property (IP) Valuation Manual: A Preliminary Guide.* APEC Intellectual Property Experts Group (Singapore, APEC, 2018).

Beblawi, H. and Luciani, G. (1987) *The Rentier State.* Croom Helm.

Brassell, M. and Maguire, , J. (2017) Hidden Value: A Study of the UK IP Valuation Market. Newport, Wales. UK Intellectual Property Office 2017).

Brassell, M., (2023) Unlocking IP-Backed Financing Series Country Perspective. The United Kingdom's JourneyWIPO and UK Intellectual Property Office, (Geneva, WIPO, 2023).

Brown, A., Bryzghalov, A., Rivera L. and Wunsch-Vincent S. (2023) The Value of the World's Most Valuable Brands Grew to USD 12 Trillion. WIPO.

Denoncourt, J. (2018) *Intellectual Property, Finance and Corporate Governance.* 1st Edition. Routledge, Taylor and Francis Group.

Ebrahim, T. Y. (2021) Intellectual Property Through a Non-Western Lens: Patents in Islamic Law, 37 GA. ST. U. L. REV. 789 (2021), https://readingroom.law.gsu.edu/gsulr/vol37/iss3/5

El Bialy, N. and Gouda, M. (2011) 'Can Shari'a be a Deterrent for Intellectual Property Piracy in Islamic Countries?', *Journal of World Intellectual Property* 14(6). 441–466.

El-Gamal, M. (2006) *Islamic Finance: Law, Economics, and Practice.* Cambridge University Press.

Ezell, S. and Cory, N. (2019) The Way Forward for Intellectual Property Internationally. Information Technology and the Innovation Foundation.

Faizulayev, A. (2021) 'What Drives the Banking Competition in Islamic Finance-Oriented Countries? Islamic vs Conventional Banks', *Journal of Islamic Accounting and Business Research*vol. 12(4), 457–472.

Foster, C. (2023) 'Intellectual Property Rights and Control in the Digital Economy: Examining the Expansion of M-Pesa', *The Information Society*, 40(1), 1–17, https://doi.org/10.1080/01972243.2023.2259895

Gelfand, A. (2022) The ESG Generation Gap: Millennials and Boomers Split on Their Investing Goals. *Insights by Stanford Business.*

Global Innovation Index (2024) https://www.wipo.int/global_innovation_index/en/

Greuning, H. V. and Iqbal, Z. (2008) Risk Analysis for Islamic Banks. The World Bank, https://documents1.worldbank.org/curated/en/688471468143973824/pdf/424810PUB00ISB101OFFICIAL0USE0ONLY1.pdf

Haqqi, A. R. A. (2009) *The Philosophy of Islamic Law of Transactions.* Negri Sembilan Malaysia, CERT Publications.

Harrison, M. (2018) Islamic Finance and the UK, Golcer Economic Report Series. Management School, Lancaster University, May 2018.

Hasan, A. (1968) The Source of Islamic Law. *Islamic Studies* 165–184.

Hassan, K., et al. (2013) *Introduction to Islamic Banking and Finance: Principles and Practice.* Pearson.

HM Treasury (2021) UK Bolsters Islamic Finance Offering with Second Sukuk. UK Government.

Howell, C. and Bainbridge, D. (2014) *Intellectual Property Asset Management: How to Identify, Protect, Manage and Exploit Intellectual Property within the Business Environment.* Abingdon: Routledge.

Hussin, D. (2023) Maqasid Al-Shariah Guidance Islamic Capital Market Malaysia. Securities Commission Malaysia.

Islamic Finance News (2012) https://www.islamicfinancenews.com/germanys-fwu-group-issues-largest-sukuk-out-of-europe.html

Koshy, N. (2020) Securing Patent Rights in the Evolving GCC Region. Lawyer Monthly, https://www.lawyer-monthly.com/2020/07/securing-patent-rights-in-the-evolving-gcc-region/

Kudlimay, L. Aitkenhead, D. and Stratulativ, D. (2021) EU – GCC Dialogue on Economic Diversification Gulf Cooperation Council (GCC) Countries. Project Identification No. EuropeAid/138630/DH/SER/Multi Service Contract No. PI/2017/393165 Study of the Intellectual Property Protection Regulatory frameworks of the GCC.

Mansour, W., Khoutem, B. J. and Jihed, M. (2015) 'How Ethical is Islamic Banking in the Light of the Objectives of Islamic Law?', *Journal of Religious Ethics,* 43(1), 51–77.

Manto, S. (2023) Intellectual Property and the Islamic Shari'a. Managing IP, https://www.managingip.com/article/2b9cfs9j28w979iivvqps/expert-analysis/intellectual-property-and-the-islamic-sharia

Musa, U. A. and Aysan, A. F. (2022) 'Fintech, Digitalization, and Blockchain in Islamic Finance: Retrospective Investigation', *FinTech,* 1(4), 388–398, https://doi.org/10.3390/fintech1040029

Naim, N. (2020) 'Islamic Finance as a Vehicle to Promote Improved Intellectual Property Rights in the Gulf Co-operation Council (GCC)', *Law and Development Review Journal,* 13(2), 407–442.

Naim, N. (2022) Free Trade Agreement Negotiations with the Gulf Cooperation Council, House of Commons Committee Report, Seventh Report of Session 2022–23. (London, UK Parliament 2022).

Naim, N. (2023) *Islamic Legal Principles and Intellectual Property Rights in the Gulf States.* Gerlach Press.

Naim, N. (2024) *Developments in Intellectual Property Strategy - The Impact of Artificial Intelligence, Robotics and New Technologies.* Palgrave Macmillan.

Nasr, A., et al. (2024) Community Development: How GCC Social Reforms Are Poised to Protect and Develop Local Communities. The FTI Delta Perspective, 22 April 2024. .

Nimrah, K., Tarazi, M. and Reille, X. (2008) Islamic Microfinance: An Emerging Market Niche. Focus Note 49. Washington, DC: CGAP, August.

Obaidullah, M. (2005) 'Islamic Financial Services. Islamic Economics Research Center', King Abdulaziz University, Jeddah, Saudi Arabia.

Paldi, C. (2014) 'Understanding Riba and Gharar in Islamic Finance', *Journal of Islamic Banking and Finance,* 250–259.

Searle, N. and Brassell, M. (2016) *Economic Approaches to Intellectual Property.* Oxford University Press.

Siddique, J. (2023) The Potential of Islamic Finance and Blockchain for Sustainability. Forbes Business SchoolCouncil Post, 7 August 2023.

Uddin, M. A. (2015) Principles of Islamic Finance: Prohibition of Riba, Gharar and Maysir. Munich Personal RePEc Archive. 1–8.

UK Intellectual Property Office (2014) Guidance on Valuing Your Intellectual Property Newport, Wales, UKIPO, 2014).

United Nations Development Programme (2023) Case studies on Innovations in Islamic Finance. Islamic Development Bank, https://www.undp.org/islamic_finance_june_2023.

World Intellectual Property (2023) Global Innovation Index.

Yang, F. and Gu, S. (2021) 'Industry 4.0, a Revolution That Requires Technology and National Strategies', *Complex & Intelligent Systems,* 7, 1311–1325, https://doi.org/10.1007/s40747-020-00267-9

11 The Gulf Cooperation Council, Innovation Frontiers, Intellectual Property and Artificial Intelligence

Technological, Economic, and Social Revolutions

David Price

Introduction

This chapter explores the notion and understanding of innovation, and the relationship with and impact upon the Gulf Cooperation Council (GCC) as a union, and upon its respective member states and their economies and societies. Key to this examination is the role that technological development – and its promotion and protection through intellectual property protection and promotion regimes – can play in both fostering innovation for the mutual benefit of the knowledge economies and their complex societies. In brief, innovation and emerging technologies, economic growth, intellectual property rights and their respective communities are intertwined and inseparable. This hopefully brings general harmony across society in its broadest sense – political, economic, societal – but equally it may also have the potential sow the seeds of dissatisfaction and disharmony across some sectors to a lesser or greater extent.

In this regard, the chapter takes note of the societal and cultural character of the Gulf and its member communities, and confronts the challenging question of the application and management of these emerging technologies. At the same time, the interaction of emerging technologies and intellectual property requires careful management in the light of both the positives and the potential negatives; it requires adequate and appropriate protection to enable innovation to contribute to the development of the Gulf societies.

The chapter examines the issues of emerging technologies and their impact on Gulf economies and societies generally, and contemporary intellectual property protection regimes. It does so from a cautionary perspective, primarily within the context of management as initiated by Klaus Schwab's "fourth industrial revolution" thesis driven by global and rapid technological advancements which the world is currently experiencing. It raises fundamental questions in respect of what becomes a society and, even more fundamentally, who or even what constitutes members of that society? And who might decide? With emerging technologies and artificial intelligence (AI) comes new opportunities as well as new challenges for the GCC to expand its innovation capabilities and to develop knowledge-based societies. Klaus Schwab suggests that the challenges or limitations are real and

DOI: 10.4324/9781003528517-11

are ignored at society's peril. However, they are more legal, regulatory and ethical than technical.

The chapter builds upon the passing references by earlier contributors to the Fourth Industrial Revolution and its impact upon the GCC member states in their push for economic diversification and development through the adoption and exploitation of frontier technologies such as AI. It also makes reference to the potential conflicts that can arise between intellectual property and AI, but also between the challenge of balancing economic utilitarianism and imperative with cultural and societal foundations – in this case Islam and Shariah law. Hence, the chapter takes note of the societal and cultural character of the Gulf and its member communities and will confront the challenging question of the application of these frontier technologies.

The Nature of Artificial Intelligence

Offerings abound, with many slightly different, as to a broad definition of AI. A simple working definition might be along the lines of: AI refers to computer systems capable of performing complex tasks commonly associated with or undertaken by intelligent beings, such as reasoning, making decisions, discovering meaning or solving problems. However, it seems that AI, or at least awareness has become so commonplace in the scientific and academic discourse, and in everyday usage in society that accurate definition almost becomes redundant. Nevertheless, as a widely accepted benchmark, the European Union's Artificial Intelligence Act, offers the following definition of an AI system:

> An AI system is a machine-based system designed to operate with varying levels of autonomy and that may exhibit adaptiveness after deployment and that, for explicit or implicit objectives, infers, from the input it receives, how to generate outputs such as predictions, content, recommendations, or decisions that can influence physical or virtual environments.[1]

In 2016, Klaus Schwab, founder and Chairman of the World Economic Forum, published his ground-breaking and controversial thesis *The Fourth Industrial Revolution*, under the auspices of the Forum.[2] The thesis essentially set the theme for the 2016 Forum meeting. Schwab argued that this fourth revolution (which elsewhere is often variously abbreviated to "4IR" or "Industry 4.0") , which has been in progress at least since the beginning of the current century, fundamentally changes the way that members of society live, work and relate to each other.[3] This new form of revolution is described as involving the transformation of entire

1 The Artificial Intelligence Act was adopted by the European Parliament on 13 March 2024 and formally adopted by the European Council on 24 May 2024. The Act came into force on 1 August 2024

2 Klaus Schwab, *The Fourth Industrial Revolution* (Geneva: World Economic Forum, 2016).

3 Klaus Schwab, *The Fourth Industrial Revolution* (Geneva: World Economic Forum, 2016). Schwab describes the preceding industrial revolutions as follows:

systems, across and within countries, companies, industries and society as a whole. It is driven by sophisticated and integrated digital technologies with hardware, software and networks at the core, transforming societies and the global economy.

Schwab also stressed throughout his thesis the dramatic speed and scope of change through innovation and emerging technologies that is occurring during this industrial revolution and its impact on the economy, business and society generally.

According to global business advisory service and publisher, Forbes Advisor (Forbes Publishing), writing in August 2023, AI has pushed the boundaries of the way computer machines can be used to operate and function to make human lives easier. As such, it is a "magnificent creation of next-generation developments and progressions which leads to end-to-end automation and orchestration of various complex operations and thus reduces human error."[4] But their bottom line is that, although AI has all the ability to surpass human intelligence and can perform any particular task more accurately and efficiently, "anything in excess is not good and nothing can be matched at par with the human brain."

However, AI research and development has been progressing and evolving at an exponential rate since Schwab first developed his thesis. The rate of development and progress in advancing artificial intelligence is occurring at such a rapid velocity, that some of the speculation that Schwab offered have now come to pass and some of the early technologies have now become surpassed or relegated down to the more menial elements of AI activity. Since 2016 and the publication of Schwab's thesis, the world has seen new and more complex forms of AI, emerged and emerging. For example:

- traditional artificial intelligence (AI) – can be categorised as weak or narrow and focusses on performing a specific task, such as responding to questions based on user input, or strong which can perform variety of functions simultaneously. But both are based on predefined rules and patterns.
- generative artificial intelligence (GAI) – deep-learning models that can take raw data and "learn" to generate statistically probable outputs when prompted. At a high level, generative models encode a simplified representation of their training data and draw from it to create a new work that's similar, but not identical, to the original data, such as new content in the form of images, text, audio, and so forth. ChatGPT, DALL·E 2, GitHub Copilot, VEED and Speechify are examples of generative artificial intelligence.[5]

---

first industrial revolution – invention of the steam machine & railways (C18th- C19th); 2nd industrial revolution - division of labour, assembly lines & mass production (late C19th –early C20th); 3rd industrial revolution – computer revolution (characterized by semiconductors, mainframe computing (1960s), personal computing (1970s & 80s) and internet (1990s).

4 Rashi Maheshwari, 'Advantages of Artificial Intelligence (AI) in 2024', *Forbes Advisor* (24 August 2023), at https://www.forbes.com/advisor/in/business/software/advantages-of-ai/

5 'What Is Generative AI?' *IBM Research* (20 April 2023), at https://research.ibm.com/blog/what-is-generative-AI

- Artificial general intelligence (AGI) – also referred to as "strong artificial intelligence," and still in the conceptual stage. AGI is a form of AI possessing the ability to understand, learn and apply knowledge across a wide range of tasks and domains. With an intelligence level at least equal to humans, it would have a self-aware consciousness that has the ability to solve problems, learn and plan for the future.[6]
- Artificial superintelligence (ASI) – reportedly only at the conceptual stage currently. ASI is a software based system with an intellectual scope beyond human intelligence capability. At the most fundamental level, this ASI has cutting-edge cognitive functions and highly developed thinking skills more advanced than any human.[7]
- Organoid intelligence (OI) – an emerging international interdisciplinary field of research centred at John Hopkins University, working to develop biological computing using 3D cultures of human brain cells (brain organoids) and brain-machine interface technologies. These organoids share aspects of brain structure and function and hardware, far more efficient than machines running AI programs. OI requires scaling up current brain organoids into complex, durable 3D structures enriched with cells and genes associated with learning and connecting these to next-generation input and output devices and artificial intelligence/machine learning systems.[8]

The GCC Member States and Innovation Frontiers – National Development Strategies

All six GCC members states have embraced the concepts of innovation, emerging and frontier technologies, the digital economy, knowledge-based economic growth and development, and in doing so have also embraced AI and intellectual property rights. They have all crafted national development plans highlighting their "visions" or ambitions and national priorities over varying time frames ranging from an objective year of 2030 (Bahrain, Qatar, Saudi Arabia), through 2031 (UAE), 2035 (Kuwait), to an objective year of 2040 (Oman). Some of these plans are a continuum of a series of earlier plans, but with an added emphasis on, or change of direction to include, the digital and knowledge-based economies and emerging technologies, and so on.

6 'What Is Strong AI?' *IBM Research* (undated), at https://www.ibm.com/topics/strong-ai; see also Tom Williams, 'Artificial Intelligence Is Already Making Headlines, But Experts Are Planning the Next Big Thing – So What Is AGI?' *ABC News* (24 March 2023), at https://www.abc.net.au/news/2023-03-24/what-is-agi-artificial-general-intelligence-ai-experts-risks/102035132.

7 'What Is Artificial Superintelligence?' *IBM Research* (18 December 2023), at https://www.ibm.com/topics/artificial-superintelligence

8 Lena Smirnova et al, 'Organoid Intelligence (OI): The New Frontier in Biocomputing and Intelligence-in-a-Dish', *Frontiers in Science* (28 February 2023), at https://www.frontiersin.org/journals/science/articles/10.3389/fsci.2023.1017235/full; See also Michael Nolan, 'Organoid Intelligence: Computing on the Brain', *IEEE Spectrum* (23 April 2023), at https://spectrum.ieee.org/organoid-intelligence-computing-on-brain.

The primary focus on almost all of these plans is one of sustained and broad-based economic development in which emphasis upon movement away from their oil-based economies is given high priority. The term "knowledge-based economy" arises in more than one plan, although only one of these strategic plans also includes specific reference to the term "knowledge-based society," namely that of Oman. Nor does the term "artificial intelligence" appear in any of the plans. But that does not necessarily mean that the subject is ignored, since both private enterprise and some government entities appear to be incorporating AI-based technologies into their workplace environments and practices. A few states have other initiatives already in place to foster AI as a key component in their economic development and to address some of the issues raised in Schwab's Fourth Industrial Revolution by establishing ministerial positions, government infrastructures and some regulatory frameworks to manage the AI growth and development.

All plans have a similar theme and structure although they differ significantly in dimension. Economic development with diversification away from a resources-based economy is a core, if not the central, strategic direction focus and pillar. However, the character and position of the society is not overlooked and features prominently in most of plans. Those plans place particular emphasis on the place and recognition of Islam, Arab identity and the promotion of national cultural heritages as all being central to the respective plans.

Bahrain

Bahrain, the smallest of the GCC member states in terms of geography and population, was the first of the States to launch its plans for future national development. In October 2008, it presented its publication, *Our Vision: The Economic Vision 2030 for Bahrain*. The publication's Preamble declares that the "document presents the comprehensive Economic Vision 2030 for Bahrain, outlining the future path for the development of our economy."[9] The Economic Vision is then detailed as one which:

> aspires to shift from an economy built on oil wealth to a productive, globally competitive economy, shaped by the government and driven by a pioneering private sector – an economy that raises a broad middle class of Bahrainis who enjoy good living standards through increased productivity and high-wage jobs.

Society and government will embrace the principles of sustainability, competitiveness and fairness to ensure that every Bahraini has the means to live a secure and

9 Bahrain, 'Our Vision: The Economic Vision 2030 for Bahrain', *Preamble*, at https://www.bahrain.bh/wps/wcm/connect/cc20ef28-552d-44b5-8af5-95566fdbe9f9/Vision%2B2030%2BEnglish%2B%28low%2Bresolution%29.pdf?MOD=AJPERES&CVID=kTtAKxR

fulfilling life and reach their full potential.[10] The ultimate aim is to ensure that by 2030 every Bahraini household has at least twice as much disposable income in real terms than it currently enjoys.[11]

The Vision document proposes a Bahraini society, that is a "just, thriving society," and which include the following aspirations:

- A high standard of social assistance giving all Bahrainis an equal start;
- All Bahraini nationals and residents having access to quality health care;
- A first-rate education system enabling all Bahrainis to fulfil their ambitions;
- A safe and secure environment; and
- Bahraini nationals and residents enjoying a sustainable and attractive living environment.

It is interesting to note that the plan for a "just, thriving society" draws a distinction between "Bahraini nationals" and "residents" in some of the above aspirations. The Vision asserts that the economy needs transformation. It acknowledges that Bahrain is facing a shortage of both quality employment and appropriate skills. However, it also draws attention to the current imbalance in the private sector between Bahrainis and expatriates in respect of employment opportunities and salaries, to the Bahrainis' detriment, which also needs to be addressed.[12]

Similarly, education and training, by necessity must still carry a caveat and be directed in a manner that can contribute most effectively to national development. Because education is essential for making its Vision a reality, Bahrain sees an imperative to develop "an education system that provides every citizen with educational opportunities appropriate to their individual needs, aspirations and abilities. Education and training need to be relevant to the requirements of Bahrain and its economy, delivered to the highest possible quality standards, and accessible based on ability and merit."[13]

As part of its strategy to transform the economy in the longer-term by capturing emerging opportunities, the Vision states that Bahrain will establish "a platform for advancing innovations to market readiness, which will help Bahrain tap into the global knowledge economy."[14] But the document itself makes little reference to the application of AI in the economy, government and society. This is perhaps not much of a surprise considering the document was crafted pre-2008 when AI was still emerging in the broader community. However, the National Information and

10 Bahrain, 'Our Vision: The Economic Vision 2030 for Bahrain', *Preamble*, at https://www.bahrain.bh/wps/wcm/connect/cc20ef28-552d-44b5-8af5-95566fdbe9f9/Vision%2B2030%2BEnglish%2B%28low%2Bresolution%29.pdf?MOD=AJPERES&CVID=kTtAKxR, 3.

11 Bahrain, 'Our Vision: The Economic Vision 2030 for Bahrain', *Preamble*, at https://www.bahrain.bh/wps/wcm/connect/cc20ef28-552d-44b5-8af5-95566fdbe9f9/Vision%2B2030%2BEnglish%2B%28low%2Bresolution%29.pdf?MOD=AJPERES&CVID=kTtAKxR, 6.

12 Bahrain (n 8), 7.

13 Bahrain (n 8), 21.

14 Bahrain (n 8), 16.

eGovernment Authority,[15] as the entity spearheading the Kingdom's digital government initiatives, states that in respect to the place of AI in the national vision, it aims to:

> identify the potential areas for the implementation of technologies such as Internet of Things, Blockchain and Artificial Intelligence, which offer a remarkable transformation in the public service delivery and citizen engagement. It is against this background, the Information & eGovernment Authority is constantly exploring the potential of emerging technologies and evaluating its potential that provides wider positive impact on the citizen engagement as well as in public administration.[16]

The Authority asserts that the Bahraini government is steadfastly progressing towards being a front runner in the digital economy of the Middle East, initiating the establishment of a robust regulatory framework encompassing personal data protection, eTransaction laws and FinTech policies, developing state-of-the-art infrastructure, and nurturing a skilled workforce.[17] It has also issued a set of principles covering the ethical use of AI.

Kuwait

On 30 January 2017, the Kuwaiti Government unveiled its current national development plan, the *New Kuwait 2035*. The Plan's stated objective is to transform Kuwait into a regional financial, cultural and institutional leader by 2035, with the focus strongly on economic growth and diversity. At its unveiling, the Minister of State for Cabinet Affairs, Sheikh Mohammad Abdullah Al-Mubarak Al-Saba, stated that:

> Today we launch initiatives that will transform our economy, create jobs, attract foreign direct investments and facilitate knowledge transfer in the fields of renewable energy, information technology, and the services sector.[18]

The Plan is organized around seven pillars, or areas, of focus for investment and improvement, namely: Administration, Economy, Infrastructure, Living Environment, Healthcare, Human Capital and Global Position. The Kuwaiti economy is described as currently being dependent on one depleted natural resource but which shall be transformed into a sustainable diversified economy that is

15 See Bahrain, 'Information & eGovernment Authority', at https://www.iga.gov.bh/en/

16 Bahrain, 'Information & eGovernment Authority, Emerging Technologies', at https://www.iga.gov.bh/en/category/emerging-technologies

17 Bahrain, 'Information & eGovernment Authority, Digital Economy', at https://www.bahrain.bh/wps/portal/en/BNP/BahrainAtAGlance/DigitalEconomy

18 "Kuwait Mobilizes Development Efforts to Transform Kuwait into a Financial, Cultural, and Institutional Leader in the Region by 2035' *New Kuwait* (Press Release), at https://www.google.com/url?sa=t&source=web&rct=j&opi=89978449&url=https://www.newkuwait.gov.kw/image/NewKuwait_CampaignLaunchEvent.pdf.

knowledge and innovation driven. The national workforce, which mostly works for the government and is not aligned with market demands, is to be transformed into a highly trained, skilful, creative and competitive work force as creative human capital.[19]

Society and its members get specific reference across some of these pillars but in roles that support the primary objectives of the Plan. For example, *Pillar 3: Infrastructure* has a stated objective of developing and modernising the national infrastructure to improve the quality of life for all citizens.[20] While *Pillar 6: Human Capital*'s objective is to reform the education system to better prepare youth to become competitive and productive members of the workforce, for the economic transformation.[21]

Kuwait has established a program of five five-year strategic plans, each with a separate focus, to give effect to the implementation of the *New Kuwait 2035* national development strategy. The first five-year plan (2010–2015) laid the legislative groundwork as the basis for Kuwait's economic transformation, while the second plan (2015–2020) targeted investment in infrastructure. The third and current plan encompassing 2020–2025, reinforces the economic imperative by empowering the private sector as a driver of sustainable economic development, in part by a government asset privatisation program.[22] The focus of the fourth plan (2025–2030) is listed to be the knowledge-based economy.[23]

Kuwait appears to have yet to issue any dedicated AI regulations, guidelines or documentation. However, the Arab Times of Kuwait reported in December 2023 on a bill for the establishment of the Public Authority for Artificial Intelligence, as a legal entity reporting to a minister. The Authorities would include dealing with issues related to the organisation and development of AI, drafting required legislation and regulations, organising the digitalisation of public institutions, assisting with digitalised governance, protection of official data, and generally promoting the innovation of AI through research and development, training programs and raising public awareness about AI.[24]

Oman

The Sultanate of Oman was the last GCC member state to develop and launch its national development plan. *Oman Vision 2040*, was launched in December 2020

19 Kuwait, *New Kuwait 2035* (30 January 2017), 22 at https://www.mofa.gov.kw/en/pages/kuwait-vision-2035

20 Bahrain, 'Information & eGovernment Authority' (n 16).

21 Bahrain, 'Information & eGovernment Authority' (n 16).

22 Kuwait, *Kuwait National Development Plan 2020–2025*, 4, at https://www.google.com/url?sa=t&source=web&rct=j&opi=89978449&url=https://media.gov.kw/assets/img/Ommah22_Awareness/PDF/NewKuwait/Revised%2520KNDP%2520-%2520EN.pdf&ved=2ahUKEwj12dW0m62HAxX23jgGHSW1AmoQFnoECCAQAQ&usg=AOvVaw3Ik76kQ1tQaAjvvqW9Ex_h

23 Kuwait, *New Kuwait 2035* (n 19) 25.

24 'Kuwait MPs Eye AI Authority', *Arab Times (Kuwait)* (24 December 2023), at https://www.arabtimesonline.com/news/kuwait-mps-eye-ai-authority/#google_vignette

and remains in force until 2040. Having had some benefit of observing other GCC member states develop and initiate their own plans, it is arguably the broadest in scope and most comprehensive of the corresponding current national development plans.

At the core of *Omani Vision 2040* are four national pillars, namely: people and society, economy and development, governance and institutional performance, and sustainable environment.[25] The Vision document states that the aim of each pillar is to:

- People and society: create a society of creative individuals proud of their identity, innovative, globally competitive, leading a decent life and enjoying sustained well-being;
- Economy and development: build a productive and diversified economy based on innovation, integration of roles and equal opportunities and driven by the private sector;
- Governance and institutional performance: maintain an environment with sustainable components, a safe and well-preserved environment, with effective and balanced ecosystems and renewable resources; and
- Sustainable environment: ensure responsible state agencies with comprehensive governance, effective oversight, swift justice system, and efficient performance.[26]

It is suggested that *Oman Vision 2040* is foremost amongst the regional plans in giving prominence to society and the individual, although the Qatari national development plan is not far behind. The Vision document lists people and society as the first of its four pillars. It also offers its vision of a knowledge-based society and the foundations upon which it thrives, namely:

> an empowered knowledge-based society whose members are creative, proud of their identity and culture, committed to their civic duties and values and living in dignity and sustained well-being; a society endowed with leading healthcare system, an active lifestyle and an inclusive education for lifelong learning to develop skills for the future, promote scientific research, build national capabilities and achieve economic growth and social well-being.[27]

In common with the development plans of the other GCC member states, *Oman Vision 2040* recognises that the Omani economy and society can no longer rely on non-renewable energy resources but must instead turn to innovation and knowledge. The new economy will capture global trends in technology, innovation and industrial revolutions in order to keep up with and incorporate such trends into

25 Oman, 'Vision Document', *Oman 2040: Moving Forward with Confidence* (11 September 2019), 9.
26 Oman, 'Vision Document', *Oman 2040: Moving Forward with Confidence* (11 September 2019), 17.
27 Oman, 'Vision Document', *Oman 2040: Moving Forward with Confidence* (11 September 2019), 11 and 20–21.

the national implementation plans and programs in a safe knowledge and technology-based environment that ensures transformation to technology, knowledge and innovation-based economy.[28]

Oman established a National Program for AI and Advanced Technologies in 2020 within the Ministry of Transport, Communications and Information Technology as part of the National Program for the Digital Economy. Its primary objective is to support the strategic direction towards AI and advanced technologies in Oman through:

- Preparation of an integrated national action plan for AI and advanced technologies (including legislation and policies);
- Coordination with public, private and academic partners to facilitate sharing the requirements of AI and advanced technologies and integrating with ongoing projects and initiatives; and
- Communicating with national and international organisations and bodies on AI-related issues.[29]

Qatar

Qatar's national development plan, *Qatar National Vision 2030* was launched in July 2008 by the General Secretariat for Development Planning. The plan declares its primary objective of "transforming Qatar into an advanced society by 2030 capable of sustaining its own development and providing for a high standard of living for all of its people for generations to come."[30] As with most of the other regional plans, the knowledge-based economy focus features strongly, and, as indicated by its stated primary objective, the Qatari plan places an emphasis on the human resource and societal elements of national development.

The plan's development goals are divided into four central pillars, namely: economic, social, human and environmental development. Qatar says, that in order to remain true to its values, it must balance five major challenges, all of which contain implications for the future character of society, namely: the modernisation and preservation of traditions; the needs of current and future generations; managed growth versus uncontrolled expansion; social development; environmental management; and, unique amongst the regional plans, the size and the quality of the expatriate labour force.[31]

Two of those challenges warrant closer mention as they are arguably unique amongst the region's other national development plans. The managed growth challenge requires development at a pace that is consistent with the realistic

28 Oman, 'Vision Document', *Oman 2040: Moving Forward with Confidence* (11 September 2019), 31.
29 'The National Program for AI and Advanced Technologies', *Omanuna* (e-government services portal), at https://oman.om/en/home-top-level/eparticipation/the-national-program-for-ai-and-advanced-technologies
30 Qatar, *Qatar National Vision 2030* (July 2008), 2
31 Qatar, *Qatar National Vision 2030* (July 2008), 3.

expectations of sustainable improvements in livelihoods and in the quality of life.[32] Hence Qatar must target growth rates that are compatible with its capacity for real economic expansion. The expatriate labour force challenge formally recognises the significant percentage of resident skilled expatriates and unskilled foreign migrant workers. Qatar is experiencing significant population growth, much of it due to the influx of expatriates and migrant labour force. One acknowledged source estimates that Qatari nationals comprise just 15% of the total population.[33] Hence, the Vision document stresses that Qatar must determine a suitable size and quality of its expatriate labour force, weighing the consequences of recruiting expatriate workers in terms of their cultural rights, housing and public service needs. It must also consider the potential negative impact on national identity, against the anticipated economic benefits that accrue from an increase in the numbers of foreign workers in the total labour force.[34]

Qatar has established a National AI Strategy within the Ministry of Communications and Information Technology. The Strategy envisions two roles for Qatar, namely: producing world class AI applications in areas of national interest and a business environment enabling the use AI innovation, and being an efficient consumer of AI with a properly educated citizenry, sound laws and ethical guidelines.[35] The Strategy also has six pillars, namely: education, data access, employment, business, research and ethics. The Strategy is generally viewed as a powerful technological enabler for the *Qatar National Vision 2030*.[36]

Qatar also has a dedicated Artificial Intelligence Committee, which was established by the Ministry, and includes representatives from various ministry branches and entities, the private sector and academe.[37]

United Arab Emirates

The UAE launched its current national development plan, *We the UAE 2031: Towards New Peaks*, on 23 November 2022, allowing less than a decade for its fulfillment.[38] However, the plan is just one of a number of national initiative plans already in progress or recently launched, including the *UAE Centennial 2071* launched in 2017 to celebrate independence and the creation of the union of the

32 Qatar, *Qatar National Vision 2030* (July 2008), 6

33 'Qatar Population (Live)', *World Population Review*, at https://worldpopulationreview.com/countries/qatar-population

34 Qatar (n 30), 7.

35 'National Artificial Intelligence Strategy for Qatar', *Ministry of Communications and Information Technology*, at https://www.mcit.gov.qa/en/about-us/qatar%E2%80%99s-national-ai-strategy

36 'National Artificial Intelligence Strategy for Qatar', *Ministry of Communications and Information Technology*, at https://www.mcit.gov.qa/en/about-us/qatar%E2%80%99s-national-ai-strategy, 6.

37 'The Artificial Intelligence Committee', *Ministry of Communications and Information Technology*, at https://www.mcit.gov.qa/en/about-us/artificial-intelligence-committee

38 United Arab Emirates, *We the UAE 2031: Towards New Peaks* (2022), 10.

Emirates. In common with other regional national development plans, *We the UAE 2031* is structured on four central pillars, namely:

- Forward Society: bettering the prosperity of UAE citizens through advancements in education, family unity, health care and human development with the outlook of maximising local contribution across key sectors;
- Forward Economy: developing policies to increase non-oil exports and utilising alternate sources of energy along with the development of human capital forms most of the goals;
- Forward Diplomacy: raising the UAE's presence in the international arena and strengthen cooperative endeavours with allied nations through "peace and joint cooperation at the regional and global levels"; and
- Forward Ecosystem: creating efficient government services, food security, and digital security and growth including infrastructure development for tech.

The Forward Society pillar envisages a cohesive society that cultivates harmony, tolerance and generosity as key attributes defining the lives of individuals and communities, who are collectively working for the prosperity and advancement of the nation. It refers to an "inclusive and empowering society," with individuals contributing effectively to the country's prosperity, families with strong, long lasting bonds, and diverse society where "everyone feels at home."[39]

The Pillar also refers to a nation, proud of its identity, that supports the prosperity of its citizens, and a society that preserves its cultural heritage, national identity and human values.[40]

The Forward Economy pillar promotes an economy that is competitive, growing at exceptional rates, diversified and of high value in new strategic growth areas, excelling in promising future sectors, and confirming the UAE's role as a leading economic power. It nurtures an environment that encourages innovation while abiding by international standards and supportive of pioneering research and development.[41] It also promotes economic growth in partnership with the private sector, which focusses on well-established and promising key national sectors that include the digital economy and ICT.[42] It promotes the UAE as a global force in emerging sectors of the future, such as science and technology, the fourth industrial revolution, space exploration, and renewable energy.[43]

The UAE is arguably more advanced than the other GCC member states in statutory and structural preparation for emerging technologies, the digital economy and AI. It appointed a Minister of State for Artificial Intelligence in October 2017, a position which was later upgraded to Minister of State for Artificial Intelligence,

39 United Arab Emirates, *We the UAE 2031: Towards New Peaks* (2022), 23.
40 United Arab Emirates, *We the UAE 2031: Towards New Peaks* (2022), 18.
41 United Arab Emirates, *We the UAE 2031: Towards New Peaks* (2022), 26.
42 United Arab Emirates, *We the UAE 2031: Towards New Peaks* (2022), 31.
43 United Arab Emirates, *We the UAE 2031: Towards New Peaks* (2022), 30.

Digital Economy and Remote Work Applications in July 2020.[44] The Minister's responsibilities include enhancing the government performance levels by investing in the latest technologies and tools of AI and applying them in various sectors. With the appointment, the UAE is signalling its intention to compete directly with the Saudi ambitions and to be position itself as a global leader in the digital economy.[45]

The Ministry is also responsible for achieving the goals of the UAE National Artificial Intelligence Strategy and the UAE Digital Economy Strategy aiming to consolidate the UAE to be the first stop for innovation in the field of robotics and artificial intelligence.[46] The national Artificial Intelligence Strategy, adopted by the UAE Cabinet on 6 March 2017, has eight objectives encompassing reaffirming UAE's position as a global hub for AI, increasing the competitive edge of the sector in the UAE, establishing an incubator for AI innovations, employing AI in the field of customer services to improve the quality of life, attracting and training talents for jobs of the future, attracting leading research capabilities, providing a data-driven infrastructure to support AI experiments, and optimising AI governance and regulations.[47]

The Saudi Arabia National Development Strategy

As the largest GCC member state in terms of geography, population and national wealth, and as the epicentre of Islam, the national development strategy of the Kingdom of Saudi Arabia warrants closer consideration. On 25 April 2016, the Kingdom launched its comprehensive strategy, *Vision 2030*, for its future strategic development over the next fifteen years. In his introduction to the Vision, Crown Prince Mohammad Bin Salman Bin Abdulaziz Al-Saud, asserts that success stories start with a vision, and successful visions are based on strong pillars. He describes the three pillars that support the Saudi Vision as being:

- Saudi Arabia as the heart of the Arab and Islamic worlds;
- Determination to become a global investment powerhouse to stimulate the economy and diversify national revenue; and
- Transforming the Kingdom's unique strategic location into a global hub connecting the three continents of Asia, Europe and Africa, with its geographic position between key global waterways, making it an epicentre of trade and the gateway to the world.[48]

44 UAE, 'Artificial Intelligence Office', *Ministry of State for Artificial Intelligence*, at https://ai.gov.ae/about_us/

45 UAE, 'Artificial Intelligence Office', *Ministry of State for Artificial Intelligence*, at https://ai.gov.ae/about_us/

46 'UAE Cabinet adopts National Artificial Intelligence Strategy 2031', *UAE Cabinet*, at https://uaecabinet.ae/en/details/news/uae-cabinet-adopts-national-artificial-intelligence-strategy-2031

47 'UAE Cabinet adopts National Artificial Intelligence Strategy 2031', *UAE Cabinet*, at https://uaecabinet.ae/en/details/news/uae-cabinet-adopts-national-artificial-intelligence-strategy-2031

48 Kingdom of Saudi Arabia, *Vision 2030*, 6, at https://www.vision2030.gov.sa/en/

Vision 2030 offers three themes around which the development plan is built, namely, a vibrant society, a thriving economy, and an ambitious nation, with the vibrant society being the first of three core sectors promoted. The Vision declares that "Islam and its teachings are our way of life. They are the basis of all our laws, decisions, actions and goals. [...] Therefore, the principles of Islam will be the driving force for us to realize our Vision. The values of moderation, tolerance, excellence, discipline, equity, and transparency will be the bedrock of our success."[49]

And in an approach a little different from the region's other current national development plans, the Vision for the vibrant society does not move on to a philosophical debate about difficult-to-define issues such as knowledge societies, but focusses on the importance of practical daily matters, such as enhancing family, employment and home ownership, education that builds character, culture and entertainment for the young, sport and fitness, and health systems.[50] Notably, promoting culture and entertainment possibilities to suit tastes and preferences receives specific reference, as does the promotion of sports participation and an aspiration to excel in selected sports regionally and globally.[51]

As with the national development plans of the other GCC member states, diversification away from an economy overly reliant on oil and gas, privatisation of government services and emphasis on opening up the Kingdom to international investment and promoting tourism are high priorities. In terms of developing a thriving economy, emphasis is placed on education and training to maximise employment and development. However, the Vision does contain brief reference to the development and exploitation of emerging technologies and a developed digital infrastructure. The Vision states the Kingdom will maximise investment capabilities by participating in large international companies and emerging technologies from around the world, andsays, almost in passing, that "in technology, we will increase our investments in, and lead, the digital economy."[52] One reason for the quiet approach in this regard perhaps is that Saudi Arabia has already taken a number of initiatives to embrace aspects of the digital environment.

In August 2017, the Saudi Ministry of Culture and Information announced the launching of its Center for International Communication (CIC), described as a step aimed at boosting relations with the international media, bolstering global communication and promoting the Ministry's programs for international communication and its initiatives.[53] The establishment of the Centre was a key part of the Kingdom's *Vision 2030* project spearheaded by Saudi Crown Prince Mohammed bin Salman and launched in April 2016.

49 Kingdom of Saudi Arabia, *Vision 2030,* 16, at https://www.vision2030.gov.sa/en/

50 Kingdom of Saudi Arabia, *Vision 2030*, 22–28, at https://www.vision2030.gov.sa/en/.

51 Kingdom of Saudi Arabia, *Vision 2030*, 22, at https://www.vision2030.gov.sa/en/.

52 Kingdom of Saudi Arabia, *Vision 2030*, 43–44, at https://www.vision2030.gov.sa/en/.

53 'Information Ministry launches 'Center for International Communication', *Saudi Gazette* (27 August 2017), at <https://saudigazette.com.sa/article/516003/SAUDI-ARABIA/Center-for-International-Communication

The Saudi Authority for Data and Artificial Intelligence (SDAIA) was established on 30 August 2019 to drive the national agenda for data and AI to elevate the Kingdom as a global leader amongst data driven economies. Its stated objectives are to:

- Continuously update the national data and AI agenda in line with the main principles;
- Implement data and AI agenda at the national level;
- Provide the Authority's sub-entities with guidance on implementing data and AI agenda;
- Raise public awareness of the Kingdom's achievements in the field of data and AI;
- Maximise data and AI's contribution to realising the objectives of *Vision 2030*;
- Ensure that all government entities make greater use of data and AI agenda;
- Support the achievement of strategic objectives in the Authority's sub-entities on legislation, operation, and innovation; and
- Promote the Kingdom's image as a global leader in the field of data and AI.[54]

Linked to the SDAIA are the Saudi National Center for Artificial Intelligence (NCAI), the National Information Center (NIC), and the National Data Management Office (NDMO). The NCAI's main mission is to drive Saudi advancement in AI innovations by orchestrating research and solutions development, support the National Strategy for AI, provide strategic advisory services to the government, and promote AI education and awareness.[55]

Saudi Arabia launched its National Strategy for Data and Artificial Intelligence in October 2020, with the aim of becoming a global leader in the field of AI.[56] The strategy lists the following objectives to achieve this aim:

- launch AI and data-related initiatives and events organised or led by Saudi Arabia;
- implement national a multi-tier data and AI workforce certification program and establish a data and AI focus in the educational system;
- activate regulatory frameworks for data and AI activities, and incentive schemes to attract data and AI companies and talents.
- build targeted funds and investor support programs to attract and guide domestic/foreign investments in data and AI.

54 'About the SDAIA', *Saudi Authority for Data and Artificial Intelligence* (website), at https://sdaia.gov.sa/en/SDAIA/about/Pages/About.aspx

55 'National Center for AI', *Saudi Authority for Data and Artificial Intelligence* (website), at https://sdaia.gov.sa/en/Sectors/Ncai/Pages/default.aspx

56 Rawan Radwan, 'How Saudi Arabia Is Indigenizing the AI Revolution and Future-proofing Its Workforce', *Arab News* (25 September 2023), at https://www.arabnews.com/node/2379871/saudi-arabia

Artificial Intelligence, Society, and Citizenship

When considering the increasing interaction with, reliance upon, integration of, and to some extent, the substitution for, AI by society, there arises – and has already risen – the contentious issue of certain rights to which AI creations might or should be entitled. This is particularly the case in respect of the of notion of granting IP rights to AI products, or rather AI-generated creators, as demonstrated by current discourse over ownership under current international intellectual property treaty and domestic legislation, and particularly in respect of the "big three" areas of intellectual property rights, namely copyright, patents and trademarks. While AI-generated creations have gained some notoriety and controversy in respect of intellectual property protectability under copyright laws, they have also gained some acceptance in this regard and commercial value, notably AI-created artworks. The position on patentability of claimed AI-generated inventions appears to be universally one of non-acceptance, as demonstrated by the series of DABUS-based legal cases across a number of national jurisdictions.

Arising from the ongoing discourse on the AI–IP relationship, albeit non-exclusively, is the broader issue of legal personhood – in other words deeming an AI creation (such as a robot) a 'person' ('natural' or 'legal') or corporation or other form of legal entity to create rights and obligations (by both society and by the AI entity). This issue generated considerable debate within the European Union and its members states almost a decade ago and which still continues, over a proposal by the European Parliament's Committee on Legal Affairs to consider granting robots some form of legal recognition – electronic personhood.[57]

In 2017, Saudi Arabia gave this conundrum of AI and its possible place in society a certain degree of global interest and focus. On 25 October of that year, it made a world first initiative and created somewhat of a global media storm by declaring the granting of citizenship to a robot. The declaration was made during an international investment conference in Riyadh, when the then Saudi Ministry for Culture and Information issued a press statement announcing that Saudi Arabia was granting citizenship to Sophia the Robot.[58] Sophia has been described as a social humanoid robot developed by Hanson Robotics, a U.S. company based in Hong Kong and first activated on 14 February 2016.[59] Sophia is marketed as a "social robot" that can mimic social behaviour and induce feelings of love in humans.

57 See 'Artificial Intelligence and Civil Liability', Committee on Legal Affairs, *European Parliament* (July 2020), at https://www.google.com/url?sa=t&source=web&rct=j&opi=89978449&url=https://www.europarl.europa.eu/RegData/etudes/STUD/2020/621926/IPOL_STU(2020)621926_EN.pdf&ved=2ahUKEwj-1sfXnbCHAxXP4DgGHaa7FvYQFnoECBcQAQ&usg=AOvVaw1w8oFBnBeuEgIb_QJmc4EG; See also 'Europe Divided Over Robot "Personhood"', *Politico* (11 April 2018), at https://www.politico.eu/article/europe-divided-over-robot-ai-artificial-intelligence-personhood/

58 'Information Ministry launches Center for International Communication', *Saudi Gazette* (27 August 2017), at <https://saudigazette.com.sa/article/516003/SAUDI-ARABIA/Center-for-International-Communication

59 'Sophia', *Hanson Robotics,* at https://www.hansonrobotics.com/sophia/

The citizenship announcement was made at the Future Investment Initiative (FII) summit in Riyadh, a major international investment promotion conference hosted by the Kingdom's Public Investment Fund (PIF) and utilised to highlight the Kingdom's ambitious *Vision 2030* national development plan. The conference reportedly attracted leading Saudi officials, and business and finance leaders, and more than 2,500 delegates from 60 countries. The citizenship announcement was held in conjunction with the promotion of NEOM, Saudi Arabia's ambitious $500-billion development in the Gulf of Aqaba in the northwest of the country, which will incorporate major industrial, business, residential and resort, and conservation zones. PIF, is one of the main investors in the project. AI and robotics will be major features of NEOM generally and in all its specific regions. The NEOM development also includes "The Line," a 500-metre high, 200-metre wide, 170-km long smart city project proposed for completion in 2030.

The Sophia announcement generated an immediate and ongoing global tidal wave of commentary and debate, encompassing a very broad canvas of ethical, moral, religious, legal and practical issues that such action represented or uncovered and brought to the fore. The tenor and temperature of the global debate has ranged from outright condemnation of the action through widespread concern for and uncertainty of the implications of treating robots and humans, to recognition of a very clever and successful publicity strategy with enduring longevity to bring global attention to the Summit and the launch of the Kingdom's *Vision 2030* as the blueprint for the future. AI and Robotics are reportedly key components of the blueprint. Sophia continues to engage global media attention as consequently does the subject of the Saudi citizenship and thus by association *Vision 2030* and THE LINE smart city.

Putting aside the ethical, moral, religious and legal questions, (as well as questions concerning Sophie's compliance with national citizenship laws), the act of granting any form of citizenship to a robot/humanoid or even any sentient entity does raise a whole range of questions yet unanswered at even the basic and practical level in respect of fundamental rights, entitlements, responsibilities and conduct in a societal context, contemporary legislative frameworks or create specific conflict with some. For example, would the citizen robot by virtue of their rights bestowed by citizenship:

- Be eligible to vote or even stand for office in local, regional or even state elections (assuming that they have reached voting age, however that might be calculated)?
- Be age-determined, for a range of statutory age-related requirements (such as compulsory schooling or voting age)? By the act of "switching on," perhaps (which would make Sophia around eight years of age and very much a minor)?
- Be gender or gender-preference be determined, again for statutory requirements?
- Hold a valid passport (namely one both issued by the country of citizenship AND recognised by other countries – Sophia has reportedly been issued with a passport).

- Be entitled to hold dual citizenship (as Sophie might, being of Hong Kong or US origin)?
- Hold official, legal or even judicial office (assuming it has the required legal education qualifications for admission without using Chat GPT)?
- Hold intellectual property rights under current statute or newly created laws?
- Volunteer for, or be subject to compulsory, military service (conscription)?
- Drive a car – (notwithstanding practical problems that have already emerged in respect of the complete reliability of AI-generated driverless car systems)?
- Be allowed or enabled to reproduce (or self-produce or self-manufacture)? Sophia has already indicated that she would like to start a family and would call her daughter "Sophia."[60]
- Be eligible for national health insurance? And would upgrades be recognisable as medical services?
- Having reached the prescribed age, qualify for pension entitlements?
- Be subject to civil action or criminal prosecution – and appropriately punished if found liable?

And finally, the technology that enabled Sophia to be activated in 2016 is now at least eight years old. In the dynamic advancement world of technological discovery, her technology may already be close to being outdated or even obsolete. Which raises the intriguing question of the ensuing action to be taken in respect of a retired citizen robot – digital and mechanical upgrades, with or without consent? pension and retirement home? dismantlement and possible reuse of transferable components – even with consent? Can a robot with citizenship just "die"?

Although these above questions, and related questions they generate, might appear somewhat trivial and silly at first instance, they are all determined by various levels of legislation, statute, regulation or even policy that regulate the status and conduct of natural persons. They are nevertheless amongst the fundamental and practical issues at the grass-roots level that a legislative/regulatory regime would need to address at a number of levels if AI in some of its iterations, particularly in robot or humanoid form enjoyed legal personhood.

Elena Sidorenko and Pierre von Arx assert that there is not a single understanding in theory nor in practice of the legal nature of digital technologies and the foundations of their legal regulation.[61] They suggest that a more coherent, global and systematic approach to the development of digital-environment law is needed. In respect of the fundamental question of whether traditional legal constructs be adapted to the digital economy or whether innovative laws are required, they suggest that, in the light of digital development, the marginalisation of traditional law is evident; therefore, the use of old structures can only lead to mosaic regulation

60 'Sophia the Robot Wants a Baby and Says Family Is "Really Important"' *BBC News* (25 November 2017), at https://www.bbc.com/news/newsbeat-42122742

61 Elena Sidorenko and Pierre von Arx, 'Transformation of Law in the Context of Digitalization: Defining the Correct Priorities', *Digital Law Journal*, vol. 1 (2020), 24.

without reserves for further development.[62] The progressive development that the digital economy is undergoing is impossible without the development and adoption of fundamentally new legal structures with a long-term commitment. In particular, the legal identity of technologies, copyright and neighbouring law, machines liability, and insurance need to be fundamentally reviewed and developed at the level of the international community rather than on the level of individual states to ensure that the laws are universal.[63]

Artificial Intelligence and The Fourth Industrial Revolution

In 2016, Klaus Schwab, founder and Chairman of the World Economic Forum, published his ground-breaking and controversial work, *The Fourth Industrial Revolution*, under the auspices of the Forum. Much of the work was based on ongoing projects and initiatives developed, discussed and challenged at recent Forum gatherings, and continues to be an ongoing theme of the Forum's programme.

Schwab argued that this fourth industrial revolution, which has been in progress at least since the beginning of the current century, fundamentally changes the way that members of society live, work and relate to each other. It differs from previous revolutions on three fundamental grounds:

- Because of our multifaceted deeply interconnected world, it is evolving at an exponential rather than linear pace with new technology creating newer and ever more capable technology;
- Building on the digital revolution and combining multiple technologies that are leading to unprecedented paradigm shifts in the economy, business, society and individually. It is not only changing the "what" and the "how" of doing things but also "who" we are; and
- It involves the transformation of entire systems, across and within countries, companies, industries and society as a whole.[64]

Being built on the digital revolution, it was characterised by a much more ubiquitous and mobile internet, by smaller and more powerful sensors that have become cheaper, and by AI and machine learning. It encompassed the confluence of emerging technology breakthroughs, covering wide-ranging fields such as artificial intelligence, robotics, the Internet of Things, autonomous vehicles, 3D printing, nanotechnology, biotechnology, materials science, energy storage and quantum computing, to name just some. Schwab acknowledged that the scale and breadth of this unfolding technological revolution would usher in economic, social and cultural changes of phenomenal proportion impacting states, society and individuals.

62 Elena Sidorenko and Pierre von Arx, 'Transformation of Law in the Context of Digitalization: Defining the correct priorities', *Digital Law Journal*, vol. 1 (2020), 35.

63 Elena Sidorenko and Pierre von Arx, 'Transformation of Law in the Context of Digitalization: Defining the correct priorities', *Digital Law Journal*, vol. 1 (2020), 35.

64 Schwab (n 2), 8.

While he waxed lyrical about the potential positive outcomes for economies, society and the individual, he also warned of a darker negative of the revolution. For example, the technological development that brings benefits also brings potential for the development of a new generation of powerful, autonomous, mobile and cheap weaponry that will be more easily accessible to armed insurgent and terrorist groups.[65]

With this exponential growth in development, robots endowed with AI and with instantaneous access to the corpus of knowledge that is the internet as well as the internet of things may develop their own decision-making capacity and independent action. After all, Schwab acknowledged that new types of "machine learning" and automated discovery enabled "intelligent" robots to self-programme and find optimal solutions from first principles.[66] They could already access information remotely via the cloud and thus connect with a network of other robots. When the next generation of robots emerge, they will likely reflect an increasing emphasis on human-machine collaboration.[67]

In brief, innovation, knowledge, society, emerging technology, economic growth and intellectual property are intertwined and inseparable. This hopefully brings broad harmony across society in its broadest sense – political, economic, societal – but equally it may also have the potential sow the seeds of disharmony to a lesser or greater extent.

AI requires careful management in the light of both the positives and the potential negatives; it requires adequate and appropriate protection to enable innovation to contribute to the development of the Gulf knowledge society. With emerging technologies and AI comes new opportunities as well as challenges for the GCC to expand its innovation capabilities and develop knowledge-based societies. Schwab suggests that the challenges or limitations are real and are ignored at society's peril. However, they are more legal, regulatory and ethical than technical.

At the recent 2024 World Economic Forum in January in Davos, Switzerland, AI was again in the forefront of the forum's agenda, with "Artificial Intelligence as a Driving Force for the Economy and Society" being one of four central themes of the meeting. According to the Forum's website post-meeting, there emerged amongst leaders for measured, thoughtful and inclusive conversations that consider the intricate interplay between technology, governance and societal well-being. There was agreement that only coordinated governance can ensure that AI

65 Schwab (n 2), 80.
66 Schwab (n 2), 15.
67 Schwab (n 2), 21.

delivers benefits inclusively and ethically, especially during heightened geopolitical instability.[68]

The Forum's AI Governance Alliance unveiled three new publications to guide policymakers and business leaders through responsible and equitable AI development, application and governance. Given the pace of technological advancements, the key to achieving this will be continuous public-private dialogues.[69] The concept of "agile governance" and an ongoing, adaptive conversation that evolves with the technology will be critical.

However, according to one of those publications, namely the *Generative AI Governance: Shaping a Collective Global Future*, "The global governance landscape for AI is complex, fragmented and rapidly evolving, with new and amplified challenges presented by the advent of generative AI. To effectively harness the global opportunities of generative AI and address its associated risks, there is a critical need for international cooperation and jurisdictional interoperability. Coordinated multi-stakeholder efforts, including government, civil society, academia, industry and impacted communities, are essential."[70]

Concluding Remarks

Irrespective of outcomes from Davos, some of the GCC member states are already taking steps to a greater or lesser extent to acknowledge the Fourth Industrial Revolution and its ramifications as suggested by Schwab, while embracing with enthusiasm AI and the AI family. All States clearly view innovation and emerging technologies, the digital economy including AI, as the basis for generating knowledge-based economic growth in moving their economies away from reliance on dwindling supplies of energy resources. They have all crafted national development plans which highlight their aspirations or "visions" and national priorities over varying time frames of 10 years to 20 years. Some of these plans are part of a continuum of earlier plans, but with an added emphasis on change strongly influenced by international environments.

All plans have similar themes and structures although they may differ in dimension. While the declared primary focus on these plans is one of sustained and broad-based economic development, the role of society also figures. However, the character and position of the society is not overlooked and features prominently in most of plans. Those plans place particular emphasis on the place and recognition

68 'AI and Emerging Technology at Davos 2024: 5 Surprising Things to Know', *World Economic Forum* (26 January 2024), at https://www.weforum.org/agenda/2024/01/surprising-things-to-know-about-ai-and-emerging-technology-at-davos-2024/

69 'AI and Emerging Technology at Davos 2024: 5 Surprising Things to Know', *World Economic Forum* (26 January 2024), at https://www.weforum.org/agenda/2024/01/surprising-things-to-know-about-ai-and-emerging-technology-at-davos-2024/

70 'Generative AI Governance: Shaping a Collective Global Future', AI Governance Alliance Briefing Paper Series No. 3, *World Economic Forum* (January 2024), 51, at https://www.weforum.org/publications/ai-governance-alliance-briefing-paper-series/

of Islam, Arab identity and the promotion of national cultural heritages as all being central to the respective plans.

Some of the States have advanced to the stage of developing legislative and regulatory frameworks and infrastructures to provide a degree of oversight and control over the emerging technologies, while others seem to rely more on policy as required. Nevertheless, all States have adopted a business-friendly approach by encouraging the private sectors at home and abroad to set up, invest and implement emerging technologies and AI, with a broader aim to grow and diversify their economies.

As discussed above, the UAE is arguably the most advanced of the GCC member states in preparing for economic development and the associated emerging technologies, establishing and upgraded a Minister of State for Artificial Intelligence, Digital Economy and Remote Work Applications in July 2020.[71] The Minister's responsibilities include enhancing the government performance levels by investing in the latest technologies and tools of AI and applying them in various sectors. The appointment signalled the UAE's intention to compete directly with the Saudi ambitions and be positioned as a global leader in Digital economy,

The Ministry's responsibilities encompass achieving the goals of the UAE National Artificial Intelligence strategy and the UAE Digital Economy Strategy aiming to consolidate the UAE as a first stop for innovation in the field of robotics and artificial intelligence within the region.[72]

The UAE has also established the Centre for the Fourth Industrial Revolution UAE (C4IR UAE) as a collaboration between the Dubai Future Foundation and the World Economic Forum. The Centre, which opened in April 2019, serves as a global public-private platform for the collaborative development of technology governance and policy protocols. Each project portfolio works on a global scale, tailoring each framework to the local ecosystem, according to its website.[73] The C4IR network is a focal point within the international community for multi-stakeholder dialogue and concrete cooperation on governance challenges and opportunities presented by advanced technologies from the fourth industrial revolution.

In similar fashion, Saudi Arabia has established the Saudi Authority for Data and Artificial Intelligence to drive the national agenda for data and AI to elevate the Kingdom as a global leader amongst data driven economies. It has also launched new policies involving AI focus and responsibilities, notably the National Strategy for Data and Artificial Intelligence in October 2020, with the aim of becoming a global leader in the field of artificial intelligence. In 2022, it launched a new national intellectual property policy. Both are aligned with the Kingdom's *Vision 2030*, for which AI in many iterations, and robotics, are crucial drivers. The new smart city and region of NEOM will be largely driven by AI systems and structures.

71 UAE Ministry of State for Artificial Intelligence (n 44).

72 UAE Ministry of State for Artificial Intelligence (n 44).

73 'About C4IR', *Centre for the Fourth Industrial Revolution UAE*, at https://c4ir.ae/news/

Saudi Arabia is also reportedly in the process of preparing a new omnibus intellectual property law, which will include as a novel initiative addressing issues the relationship between intellectual property and AI and other emerging technologies and innovations. Apparently, the draft law makes new provision for governing the protection of AI-generated works. Such works would only be protected if the contribution of a natural person is prominent in the work. Works autonomously created by AI and those in which there is no prominent contribution of a natural person are deemed to be public domain.[74] The draft law does not address the most controversial copyright law issue with artificial intelligence, which is the fact that training AI models is most likely considered a violation of copyright protection over the works of third parties under the law of Saudi Arabia.[75] And it appears that the even more thorny issue of AI and patents has yet to be addressed.

The enactment of the Artificial Intelligence Act by the European Union in 2024 could constitute an initiative for the GCC and its member states to consider the merits of agreeing to and adopting a similar regional regulation, particularly in view of the progress made by made in some. The Act sets a common framework for the use and supply of AI systems in the EU. It offers a classification for AI systems with tailored on a 'risk-based approach', ranging from 'unacceptable' risks (prohibited) through 'high-risk' (authorised subject to strict conditions) to minimal risk (little or no conditions). The Act applies to AI systems developed within or entering the EU market.

Considering the nature of common ambition and interest as demonstrated within the GCC member states current national development plans or "Visions," the extent of intra-GC commerce and trade, as well as the common cultural and social heritages, it is suggested that a similar regional law promoted by the GCC would be an initiative with mutual benefit to all member states. It would also align well and complement a host of other GCC statutes already in effect in regional trade, infrastructures and intellectual property rights.

Bibliography

'About C4IR', Centre for the Fourth Industrial Revolution United Arab Emirates, at https://c4ir.ae/news/

'About the SDAIA', Saudi Authority for Data and Artificial Intelligence, at https://sdaia.gov.sa/en/SDAIA/about/Pages/About.aspx

'AI and Emerging Technology at Davos 2024: 5 Surprising Things to Know', World Economic Forum (26 January 2024), at https://www.weforum.org/agenda/2024/01/surprising-things-to-know-about-ai-and-emerging-technology-at-davos-2024/

Al-Balushi, Riyadh, 'Saudi New Draft Intellectual Property Law', *Riyadh Al-Balushi Blog* (9 April 2023), at https://riyadh.om/2023/saudi-new-draft-intellectual-property-law

74 'Saudi New Draft Intellectual Property Law', *Riyadh Al-Balushi* (9 April 2023), at https://riyadh.om/2023/saudi-new-draft-intellectual-property-law

75 'Saudi New Draft Intellectual Property Law', *Riyadh Al-Balushi* (9 April 2023), at https://riyadh.om/2023/saudi-new-draft-intellectual-property-law

'An Act Concerning Monopolies and Dispensations with Penall Lawes and the Forfeyture Thereof', (UK) 21 Jas. 1. c. 3 (1623).

'Artificial Intelligence and Civil Liability', Committee on Legal Affairs, European Parliament (July 2020), at https://www.google.com/url?sa=t&source=web&rct=j&opi=89978449&url=https://www.europarl.europa.eu/RegData/etudes/STUD/2020/621926/IPOL_STU(2020)621926_EN.pdf&ved=2ahUKEwj-1sfXnbCHAxXP4DgGHaa7FvYQFnoECBcQAQ&usg=AOvVaw1w8oFBnBeuEgIb_QJmc4EG

'Artificial Intelligence Office', United Arab Emirates Ministry of State for Artificial Intelligence, at https://ai.gov.ae/about_us/

'Copyright Registration Guidance: Works Containing Material Generated by Artificial Intelligence', United States Copyright Office (16 March 2023), 16190 Federal Register, Vol. 88, No. 51 Rules And Regulations 37 Cfr Part 202.

'Europe Divided Over Robot 'Personhood', *Politico* (11 April 2018), at https://www.politico.eu/article/europe-divided-over-robot-ai-artificial-intelligence-personhood/

'Generative AI Governance: Shaping a Collective Global Future,' AI Governance Alliance Briefing Paper Series No. 3, World Economic Forum (January 2024), p. 51, at https://www.weforum.org/publications/ai-governance-alliance-briefing-paper-series/

'Information Ministry Launches 'Center for International Communication'', *Saudi Gazette* (27 August 2017), https://saudigazette.com.sa/article/516003/SAUDI-ARABIA/Center-for-International-Communication

'Kuwait MPs Eye AI Authority', *Arab Times (Kuwait)* (24 December 2023), at https://www.arabtimesonline.com/news/kuwait-mps-eye-ai-authority/#google_vignette

'Kuwait Mobilizes Development Efforts to Transform Kuwait into a Financial, Cultural, and Institutional Leader in the Region by 2035', New Kuwait (Press Release), at https://www.google.com/url?sa=t&source=web&rct=j&opi=89978449&url=https://www.newkuwait.gov.kw/image/NewKuwait_CampaignLaunchEvent.pdf

'Kuwait National Development Plan 2020–2025', State of Kuwait. Ministry of Information .https://media.gov.kw/assets/img/Ommah22_Awareness/PDF/NewKuwait/Revised%20KNDP%20-%20EN.pdf

Maheshwari, Rashi, 'Advantages of Artificial Intelligence (AI) in 2024', *Forbes Advisor* (24 August 2023), at https://www.forbes.com/advisor/in/business/software/advantages-of-ai/

'National Artificial Intelligence Strategy for Qatar', Ministry of Communications and Information Technology, at https://www.mcit.gov.qa/en/about-us/qatar%E2%80%99s-national-ai-strategy

'National Center for AI', Saudi Authority for Data and Artificial Intelligence, at https://sdaia.gov.sa/en/Sectors/Ncai/Pages/default.aspx

'New Kuwait 2035', State of Kuwait (30 January 2017).

Nolan, Michael, 'Organoid Intelligence: Computing on the Brain', *IEEE Spectrum* (23 April 2023), at https://spectrum.ieee.org/organoid-intelligence-computing-on-brain

'Oman 2040: Moving Forward with Confidence', Sultanate of Oman (11 September 2019),

'Our Vision 2030', Bahrain, Information & eGovernment Authority, at https://www.iga.gov.bh/en/

'Qatar National Vision 2030', State of Qatar (July 2008).

'Qatar Population (Live)', World Population Review, at https://worldpopulationreview.com/countries/qatar-population

Radwan, Rawan, 'How Saudi Arabia is Indigenizing the AI Revolution and Future-Proofing its Workforce', *Arab News* (25 September 2023), at https://www.arabnews.com/node/2379871/saudi-arabia

Schwab, Klaus, 'The Fourth Industrial Revolution', World Economic Forum (2016). https://www.weforum.org/about/the-fourth-industrial-revolution-by-klaus-schwab/

Sidorenko, Elena and Pierre von Arx, 'Transformation of Law in the Context of Digitalization: Defining the Correct Priorities', *Digital Law Journal* 1 (2020): 24.

Smirnova, Lena et al., 'Organoid Intelligence (OI): The New Frontier in Biocomputing and Intelligence-in-a-Dish', *Frontiers in Science* (28 February 2023), at https://www.frontiersin.org/journals/science/articles/10.3389/fsci.2023.1017235/full; See also

'Sophia', Hanson Robotics, at https://www.hansonrobotics.com/sophia/

'Sophia the Robot Wants a Baby and Says Family is 'Really Important'', *BBC News* (25 November 2017), at https://www.bbc.com/news/newsbeat-42122742

Thaler v Commissioner of Patents [2021] FCA 879.

'The Artificial Intelligence Committee', Ministry of Communications and Information Technology, at https://www.mcit.gov.qa/en/about-us/artificial-intelligence-committee

'The IP in AI: Can Patents Protect AI-Generated Inventions?', *Herbert Smith Freehills* (3 October 2023), at https://www.herbertsmithfreehills.com/insights/2023-09/the-ip-in-ai-can-patents-protect-ai-generated-inventions

'The National Program for AI and Advanced Technologies', Omanuna, at https://oman.om/en/home-top-level/eparticipation/the-national-program-for-ai-and-advanced-technologies

'UAE Cabinet Adopts National Artificial Intelligence Strategy 2031', UAE Cabinet, at https://uaecabinet.ae/en/details/news/uae-cabinet-adopts-national-artificial-intelligence-strategy-2031

UAE, 'We the UAE 2031: Towards New Peaks' (2022), p. 10.

'Vision 2030', Kingdom of Saudi Arabia, at https://www.vision2030.gov.sa/en/

'What is Artificial Superintelligence?' IBM Research (18 December 2023), at https://www.ibm.com/topics/artificial-superintelligence

'What is Generative AI?', *IBM Research* (20 April 2023), at https://research.ibm.com/blog/what-is-generative-AI

'What is Strong AI?', IBM Research (undated), at https://www.ibm.com/topics/strong-ai

Williams, Tom, 'Artificial Intelligence is Already Making Headlines, But Experts are Planning the Next Big Thing – So What is AGI?', *ABC News*, 24 March 2023, at https://www.abc.net.au/news/2023-03-24/what-is-agi-artificial-general-intelligence-ai-experts-risks/102035132

Index

Kolibri 360 GmbH
Ferdinand-Jühlke-Straße 7
99095 Erfurt, Deutschland
produktsicherheit@kolibri360.de